S0-FIY-576

ORIGIN
GROWTH AND
SUPPRESSION
OF THE PINDARIS

ORIGIN GROWTH AND SUPPRESSION OF THE PINDARIS

Dr M.P. Roy

STERLING PUBLISHERS PVT. LTD.
New Delhi: 110016, *Jullundur-3,*

Price Rs. 50.00

Origin, Growth & Suppression of the Pindaris

Printed at Tokas Printers, Munirka, New Delhi 110057.
Jacket printed at Sterling Printers, New Delhi 110016
First published in India in 1973 by S.K. Ghai, Managing Director
Sterling Publishers Pvt. Ltd., AB/9 Safdarjang Enclave,
New Delhi 110016 and 695, Model Town, Jullundur 3.

PREFACE

The reign of Aurangzeb constitutes a turning point in Indian history. The upsurge of the various nationalities like the Sikhs, the Jats, the Marathas etc., weakened the fabric of the Mughal Empire all over the country. The Marathas proved a formidable enemy, whom the Mughals failed to curb. Their power rapidly increased. With the decline of the Mughal Empire, the 'Grand Barrier' was levelled and soon Shivaji, his successors and descendants swept over and devastated with their numerous hordes the fertile parts of the North and South India.

Before 1760 the Marathas virtually established themselves as a paramount power. The Third Battle of Panipat was, however, a rude setback to the Maratha supremacy which received yet another blow from the British who not much after appeared as a powerful rival. The First Anglo-Maratha War did not settle the contest for supremacy between them, but the Second War did prove decisive. It confined the Marathas to Central India, Gujarat and Western Coast line and crippled their power and resources, resulting in the alarming growth of the predatory elements, of which the most conspicuous were the Pindaris who remained unchallenged for some time. They constituted a potential threat to every government in the country and profoundly affected the course of Indian history during the first two decades of the nineteenth century.

A humble attempt has been made to trace the history of the rise and fall of the Pindaris. Not much work has been done on the subject till now. The present work aims at filling this gap. A serious effort has been made here to examine the official and non-official sources on the subject in a careful and systematic manner. I have tried to present the evidence of these sources in as impartial and objective a manner as possible and have not allowed unacademic considerations to prejudice my study. I have also endeavoured to present a definite and comprehensive account of the Pindaris in a chronological order.

My studies are primarily based upon the original records of the East India Company preserved in the National Archives of India, Maharashtra Government Archives at Bombay, Uttar Pradesh Archives at Allahabad, West Bengal Government Archives at Calcutta, the Peshwa Daftar and the Alienation Office at Poona. I had literally to wade through a huge mass of material in my search for facts having a direct bearing on the subject. The National Library, Calcutta, Sapru House Library and the British High Commission Library at Delhi proved to be mines of information. The records at the India Office Library, London, were also consulted through their microfilm copies. The Italian Embassy very kindly supplied me with information regarding similar predatory bands which at one time blighted Italy. Dehradun Survey Records threw light on the Pindari incursions in the south and revealed as to how the Pindaris looted and stripped to the body the various British Surveyors.

For all Pindari activities after 1818, the Central India Agency Records proved very useful. The Hyderabad Residency Records were found to be a unique collection of Pindari activities in the south, particularly the exhaustive account written by Capt. Williams of 2nd Battalion, 15th Regiment of Indian Infantry on the habits of the Pindaris during their predatory excursions.

As far as the plan and arrangement of the thesis is concerned, I have scrupulously and gratefully followed the instructions of my guide, Dr V.P.S. Raghuvanshi, Reader in History, University of Rajasthan, Jaipur. As he desired this thesis to serve as a reference work, I have taken care not to omit any significant reference. I am very much obliged to him for the inspiration and guidance he gave me in the present study without which, I unhesitatingly own, I would not have been able to give it the present shape. My thanks are due to Dr P.M. Joshi, Director of Archives, Maharashtra Government, for his invaluable suggestions. I am also thankful to Messrs V.C. Joshi and S. Roy, Assistant Directors of Archives, National Archives of India, New Delhi through whose immense knowledge on the subject I have greatly profited in my present study. I am also indebted to Maharajkumar Dr Raghubir Singh of Sitamau for his kind suggestion to consult some Marathi-English Dictionaries which enabled me to trace the origin of the word 'Pindari'.

M.P. Roy
Lecturer in Political Science,
S.D. Government College,
Beawar

CONTENTS

OPINIONS

Report of Dr Phillips, London

The candidate has produced a most satisfying piece of work. He has discovered and explored a very wide range of materials in the National and State Archives, and has systematically used the published reports and writings of the period. On this subject he has set out the evidence in a coherent and convincing form, and has skilfully woven his story of the Pindaris into a general background of British and Maratha policy. He has not allowed the mass of evidence to obscure the main outlines which he wishes to present.

The candidate convincingly demonstrates the causes for the growth of the Pindaris, placing the responsibility squarely on the policies pursued deliberately by the British after 1805 and the Marathas from late eighteenth century. His account of the Pindari leadership and of their organisation and methods is full of new information, and his treatment of the problems of resettlement also adds to our knowledge. The careers of Pindari leaders, the character of their organisation, their mode of warfare, their savage atrocities and inhumanity, the abject condition of the Maratha states, the Third Maratha War etc., have been examined with a wealth of information that make this work an original contribution to knowledge...This book is a sound work embodying the results of patient and careful study of the original sources and displaying considerable historical insight and critical judgement.

Report of Dr V.P.S. Raghuvanshi, Reader in History, University of Rajasthan, Jaipur

The thesis of Shri M.P. Roy produced under my guidance is the first comprehensive study of the subject in all its aspects. He has carefully analysed the vast bulk of official evidence at the National Archives, and other places and given a systematic account of the Pindaris from their known origins to their suppression.

It is satisfactory in respect of its literary presentation and suitable for publication in its present form.

List of Abbreviations

S. No.	Particulars	Abbreviations
1.	National Archives of India, New Delhi.	N.A.I.
2.	Bombay Government Records, Bombay.	B.G.R.
3.	Bengal Government Records, Calcutta.	Bengal G.R.
4.	Uttar Pradesh Government Records, Allahabad.	U.P.G.R.
5.	Hyderabad Residency Records.	H.R.R.
6.	Central India Agency Records.	C.I.A.R.
7.	Poona Records: Alienation Office, Poona.	A.O.P.R.
8.	Microfilm Records from India Office Library, London.	M.I.O.L.L.
9.	Persian Correspondence in the National Archives of India, New Delhi.	
	(a) Translation of Persian Papers Received.	T.P.P.R.
	(b) Translation of Persian Papers issued.	T.P.P.I.
10.	Historical Records of Survey of India, Dehradun.	H.R.S.I.
11.	Poona Residency Correspondence.	P.R.C.
12.	Peshwa Residency Records.	P.R.R.
13.	Selections from Peshwa's Daftar.	S.P.D.
14.	Indian Historical Records Commission.	I.H.R.C.
15.	Annual Register.	A.R.
16.	Asiatic Annual Register.	A.A.R.
17.	Political Department.	Pol. Deptt.
18.	Parliamentary Papers.	P.P.
19.	Foreign Secret	For. Sec.
20.	Foreign Political.	For. Pol.

21.	Foreign Miscellaneous.	For. Misc.
22.	Quarter Master General.	Q.M.G.
23.	Governor-General.	G.G.
24.	Agent to the Governor-General.	A.G.G.
25.	Chief Secretary.	C.S.
26.	Commanding.	Comdg.
27.	Government.	Govt.
28.	Original Consultation.	O.C.
29.	Diary Number.	D. No.
30.	Volume Number.	Vol. No.
31.	Serial Number.	S. No.
32.	Volume.	Vol.
33.	Number.	No.
34.	Page.	P.
35.	Pages.	PP.
36.	Ibidem	Ibid.

1

Pindaris : A General Account

Etymology of the word 'Pindari'

The meaning of the word 'Pindari' is one of the impenetrable mysteries of modern Indian history. Etymologically, the word 'Pindari' is still a riddle. Different writers have interpreted it differently. It has its root in Marathi, and was originally used to connote 'plunder'. To some writers the word 'Pindari' is a compound of two words, 'Paiend' meaning 'road' and the verb 'Aroo' 'to shut up', thereby meaning those who shut the road,[1] that is, those who by their plundering activities block the road.

Others have traced it to a Hindi word *pind parna* (पिंड पर्णा) which also means 'plunder'. Both the above connotations seem to be equally appropriate because they give a clear picture of what the Pindaris were, mere plunderers and marauders.[2]

As the Pindaris were originally associated with the Marathas, it is easy to trace its meaning from the Marathi language. A close scrutiny of a few authentic Marathi-English dictionaries reveals that the word 'Pindari' 'Pindara' or 'Pendhari' is a Marathi word meaning[3] "a member of a body of plunderers,"[4]

In Yule and Burnell we find another very interesting explanation of the term 'Pindari'. "Both *pind-parna* (पिंड पर्णा) in Hindi and 'pindas' in Marathi signify 'to follow'; the latter being defined 'to stick closely to; to follow to the death; a disagreeable fellow', such phrases would apply to those 'hangers on of an army', who were always 'looking out for a prey'.[5]"

Sir John Malcolm was very inquisitive about the precise and authentic meaning of the word 'Pindari'. He held that the term 'Pindara' was derived from the dissolute habits of the people visiting the wine shops and taking an intoxicating drink called 'Pinda'.[6] In this connection he had consulted Karim Khan, the Pindari chief, who "had never heard of any other reason for this name."[7] Major Henley, Superintendent of the Pindari prisoners at Gorakhpur, confirmed the above view after enquiries from the Pindaris under his charge.[8] Prinsep has also accepted this explanation.

Yet another interpretation comes from Keene, who maintains that the word was derived from 'Pindara', signifying the foragers of an army.[9]

An analysis of the several etymologies given by different authorities suggests that they have tried to connect the meaning of the word 'Pindara' with one or the other aspect of the activities of the Pindaris. But the chief characteristic of the Pindaris was to plunder, hence the word 'Pind' may be held to signify plunder with which the Pindaris were actually connected in their practical life.

Origin of the Pindaris

The practice of employing professional robbers who would share the loot with the chief is as old as the system of employing trained personnel for the protection of one's country.[10] Kautilya, Brihaspati and Shukranitisara all mention such practices.[11] With the decadence of the Mughul rule, symptoms of which had become visible during the last days of Aurangzeb's rule, such practices of employing professional robbers continued to prevail.[12] According to a contemporary account of Manucci, privileged and recognised thieves called 'Bederia' or 'Bidari'[13] marched with the armies and were the first to invade the enemy's territory and indulge in plunder and pillage.[14] 'Bedars' were employed both by the Mughals and the Marathas. It appears that the duty of the Pindaris serving in the Maratha army in the early stages was to accompany the Bheenee Wallah or Quarter Master General of the Maratha army in their foraging parties and also to supply the Bazars attached to the army with grains and wood.[15]

The origin of the Pindaris is shrouded in obscurity. We come across a class of freebooters in Maratha armies, who were a sort of a "roving cavalry that accompanied the Peshwa's armies in the expedition rendering them much the same service as the Cossacks performed for the armies of Russia."[16] The Pindaris were generally of Rohilla or Pathan ancestry;[17] and had originally settled in the districts of Bijapur,[18] subsequently migrating to the neighbouring Muslim kingdoms.

Muslim historians have mentioned the Pindaris as having fought against Zulfiqar Khan and other generals of Aurangzeb. In his capture of Vellore, Zulfiqar Khan had to fight against the Pindaris.[19] The Pindaris formed a part of the armies of most of the Muslim kings of the Deccan. The disintegration of the Muslim kingdoms in the Deccan led to the gradual disbandment of the Pindaris. They were at that stage taken in the service of the Marathas. According to Sardesai,[20] the Maratha chiefs, Shivaji and Santaji Ghorpade were the first to take them in their employ.[21]

The Pindaris, under the able leadership of Poonapah, are first mentioned in 1689 at the siege of Bijapur.[22] These bandits overran Malwa in 1722 and again in 1730. As early as 1725 Baji Rao granted deeds to Holkar, Scindia and the Ponwar of Dhar, and authorised them to levy Chauth and Sardeshmukhi[23] in Malwa, on condition that half the money could be utilized by them for the maintenance of troops.[24] Scindia, Holkar and Ponwar welcomed this opportunity. The advent of Peshwa Balaji Baji Rao on the Maratha scene witnessed unprecedented expansion of Maratha power from Poona to Attock. This necessitated the inclusion of Pindaris as an indispensable part and parcel of the Maratha Army.[25]

It was at this time that one Nuzzar Ali Khan,[26] who was deputed to occupy Khandesh was obliged to request for more aid as he found that certain passes had been rendered impassable by the Pindaris. As early as 1753-54 the name of Dost Mohammed, one of the Pindari chiefs, is mentioned in one of the letters to Dattaji Scindia.[27]

In the initial stages, the strength of the Pindaris was regulated by the Maratha chiefs[28] and hence they did not pose any threat to the peace and tranquillity of Central India. But, as the Mughal and Maratha powers gradually declined, they assumed the shape of an organised banditti. They do not, however, figure in the history of the time, until 1761, when they participated in the ill-fated battle of Panipat, on the side of the Marathas, with whom they not only shared defeats as on this occasion, but also reaped the fruits of victory as in the action at Khurda in 1794. Even Tipu Sultan employed the Pindaris.[29] The Pindaris were so closely integrated with the Marathas that they formed one of the classes of the Maratha army which comprised (a) the Khasgi Paga; (b) the Silhedars; (c) the Ekas or Ekandas, and (d) the Pindaris.

Pindaris as Auxiliary to Marathas

The Pindaris served the great Peshwas as their partisans in their various campaigns in the North and the South. In 1794, after the victory of the Marathas against the Nizam in the battle of Khurda, a large number of Pindaris were, for the first time, permanently settled in Malwa on the banks of Narbada. Thereafter, the famous Maratha lieutenants of Peshwa made extensive use of the Pindaris in their various campaigns.[30] So long as these Maratha chiefs were powerful, and were able to command the Pindaris with competence, they continued to work as the most useful instrument in furthering their master's ambitions.[31] Bands of Pindaris were matchless in their long and swift marches and endurance. Small wonder, therefore, they were constantly employed by the Maratha armies. The system of Pindari warfare suited the Marathas immensely, who themselves had acted on the principle of guerilla warfare.[32] They gradually rose to be a colossus in consequence and power.[33] Thus, in the plenitude of the power of the Marathas, the Pindaris were attached to the Maratha armies in their invasions of Marwar, Mewar and Malwa. The exactions or contributions on behalf of the Marathas, reduction of the rebellious chiefs, maintaining legitimate authority and realising the tributes were some of their diverse duties which were faithfully executed by them.[34]

That the Pindaris were no more than mere auxiliaries is evident from the fact that during the early years of their service with the Marathas, like Malhar Rao[35] and Tukoji Holkar, they were always asked to encamp separately,[36] and were not allowed to plunder when within the Maratha territories. When they were forbidden to loot and plunder they were paid four annas a day as compensation.[37] This practice of paying compensation was dispensed with later on.

When the Peshwa, whose close followers they were for a long time, delegated the maintenance of the Maratha power in the North to his renowned generals, Scindia and Holkar, the Pindaris were also transferred to them. Grant Duff is of the opinion that it was part of a very subtle policy which prompted Baji Rao in throwing the Pindaris out of the Deccan; that he employed them in his campaigns in the North and ultimately left them to be finally settled there. Thus, it was Baji Rao's policy to "draw them out of the Maratha country."[38]

When Scindia and Holkar came to Hindustan,[39] both of them were accompanied by a party of Pindaris who had earlier served the Peshwa most gallantly and were, therefore, the favourites of these soldiers of fortune.[40] Ranoji Scindia employed the Pindari leader Shah Baz Khan, Gazee-ood-deen's second son.[41] Mahadji Scindia in his operations against Malwa also employed the Pindaris. Dost Mohammed and Wasil Mohammed were professed adherents of Daulat Rao Scindia.[42] Ahilya Bai also employed the Pindaris in her forces,[43] and some of the Pindari leaders continued to be faithful to the House of Holkar till the end.

The Pindaris, like the *Condottiere* of Italy[44], were a disposable force, having no master. They attached themselves as irregular cavalry to the Marathas.[45] Since they cost nothing,[46] they found their way into the service of any turbulent chieftain or ambitious adventurer.[47] We find different groups of Pindaris serving at the same time in different armies.[48]

As auxiliary, the main work of the Pindaris was to plunder. Before and during the campaign, the Pindaris would be let loose on the enemy's territory.[49] Given an absolutely free hand, they would "harass the enemy, plunder his convoys, carry the cattle from the vicinity of his camp and desolate the country."[50] In short, they performed all the predatory duties of a Maratha army, laying the neighbouring country waste for the enemy and thereby, rendering the enemy powerless. Thus, their primary aim was indiscriminate plunder beyond the territories of their employers.[51]

The Pindaris were marauders, pure and simple. They were all mounted on very swift and sturdy horses,[52] and their main business was to relieve the Maratha army of reconnoitering, and at the same time to cause great distraction to the main army by attacking its baggage and 'bazar' in the rear. Not infrequently, they pursued a defeated enemy and caused indiscriminate slaughter and plunder, after the regular troops, being exhausted, withdrew.

The Pindaris had to share the loot with the government[53] or the chief whom they served, paying one-fourth of the loot, for the collection of which, agents were maintained in the Pindari camps.[54] Important and valuable articles like elephants, palanquins, flags, *naubat* etc., were always reserved for the chiefs. The remainder of the loot would then be distributed on a fixed proportion, thus illustrating the adage "there is good faith even amongst the robbers." Sometimes, the Maratha commanders would seize the Pindari chiefs or surround their camps and force them to give up a great part of their booty.[55] However, the Pindaris would not forget to retaliate upon their benefactors and would redouble their efforts to gain more booty, so as to satisfy the rapaciousness of those by whom they were employed or supported.

Besides sharing the loot, the Pindaris were a source of income to the Marathas. They had to pay to the Maratha chiefs a tax, called 'Palpatti' for the permission to loot with impunity the enemy territory.[56]

They were also employed for supplying grains, forage and wood etc., to the Pindari 'Bazar', attached to the Maratha army. For this they were required to employ their own bullocks and horses.

The Marathas purchased the Pindari aid on the privilege of plunder. They showed special marks of favour and encouragement to the Pindaris which raised their status among the Marathas, but this did not effect any change whatever in their habits. The Maratha chiefs found it useful to attach a body of loose cavalry to their armies which required no pay, and yet, were always at their disposal to serve at any time. Scindia and Holkar especially derived great assistance from them in their constant expeditions, sheltered them and even assigned lands to some of them.

Contemporary British authorities have mistakenly attributed the employment of the Pindaris by the Maratha Chiefs to the sole motive of utilising their services against the British. A letter from Strachey to Moira states that the conclusion of peace with the British Government (1804-1805) and the reduced state of the Maratha cavalry encouraged such an idea.[57] However, the Pindaris were very shrewd people, who acted according to circumstances, sometimes deserting and at other times returning to obedience.[58] Thus, "they would avail themselves of every favourable opportunity which the weakness of their governments might afford them, and to appropriate to themselves the fruits of their spoil, returning to obedience, when compelled by force or any internal dissension to submit to control."[59]

The old Maratha confederacy collapsed following their defeat at the hands of the British in 1803. It divested them of their independence of action and resulted in their loss of influence and prestige over the Pindaris.[60] Thus, the rise of the Pindaris to power was inversely proportionate to the decline of the Maratha power. Over and above all this, the disastrous policy of non-intervention during the time of Sir John Shore, Sir George Barlow, Lord Minto and Lord

Cornwallis created a kind of vacuum in Rajputana and Central India which resulted in the unusual augmentation of the Pindari strength.[61]

As the glory and power of the Marathas waned, and confusion and chaos became the order of the day, the Maratha chiefs started establishing their independent authority which left the Peshwa completely bereft of power. The Pindaris also became independent of the Marathas, and instead of serving as auxiliaries in the Maratha army and helping it in its military expeditions, they started indulging in acts of plunder and loot in a most reckless manner. Their numbers soon increased in proportion to their gains.

At the end of the Second Anglo-Maratha War, numerous bands of Pindari marauders were operating about Central India for purposes of general depredations. But, their number was not large enough to attract notice. It was then thought that they would either soon be dissolved or would be incorporated with the regular Indian troops, as soon as these would be free from wars and expeditions. However, nothing of the sort ever happened. On the contrary, not only were they not liquidated or absorbed but were also tolerated and encouraged in their nefarious activities by the Marathas. The Maratha chiefs were "very lukewarm in their efforts for their suppression."[62] The soil proving very fertile,[63] the Pindaris rose, like "masses of putrefaction in animal matter out of corruption of weak and expiring states" and "this noxious growth of lawlessness and violence had quickened into a mighty power overawing states."[64]

These predatory bands, now no longer subordinate to any of the Indian chiefs, were like mercenary soldiers, ever ready to serve anybody for pecuniary gains. They undertook excursions on weak and disorganised states or on some petty principality which was not under the British protection. Since the Pindaris were the most hardened villains and were devoid of all human feelings of pity and compassion, no enterprise seemed to be too difficult for them as they had everything to gain and nothing to lose. They assumed so much importance and came to acquire such notoriety and power that they "became the dread and even of no inconsiderable degree of danger" to the people. They were dreaded like contagion.[65]

However, it may be observed that despite the licentiousness of the Pindaris, the nature of connection subsisting between the Pindaris and the Marathas, continued to be that of auxiliaries.[66] But they prospered at the expense of the Maratha governments and their finances witnessed "a constant augmentation."[67]

Maratha Attitude towards the Pindaris

Since their rise the Pindaris had been very closely associated with the Marathas. They had adopted the system of warfare of their masters. The Maratha chiefs' only aim was to prevent Pindari aggression on their own land[68] and they admirably succeeded in the beginning,[69] but later on their territories were thoroughly plundered. After Karim and Chitu's incarceration by Scindia, Namdar Khan, a Pindari chief and nephew of Karim Khan, out of sheer spite and vengeance chose Scindia's territories and devastated extensive regions. And yet, the helpless Marathas had no option but to tolerate them.

In difficulty,[70] and otherwise too, the Pindaris always sought the counsel of the Maratha rulers. Scindia, one of their patrons, advised them freely and frequently. Pindaris virtually continued to derive full encouragement and active assistance from Scindia. His dominions served as a place of refuge. He had never objected to their issuing forth from his territories and returning with their booty. It was chiefly with him that they conducted their correspondence and resident agents were maintained in each other's camps. Small wonder, therefore, that Scindia was also suspected of receiving a regular share of their plunder. At any rate, he was frequently presented with valuable articles by way of 'Nazar' by the Pindaris. Binayak Rao, the Raja of Saugar, almost always helped them, either by a free passage through his territories[71] or by supplying them provisions[72] etc. Sirjee Rao Ghatge, god-father of the Pindaris, was instrumental in making Scindia bestow lands and honours upon the Pindari chiefs. Trimbuckji, when in power, maintained a correspondence between the government of Poona and the Pindaris.[73]

Scindia Shahi and Holkar Shahi Pindaris

When the great Peshwas left the affairs of Hindustan to the care of Holkar and Scindia, the Pindaris formed two grand divisions of Scindia Shahi and Holkar Shahi, being the followers of the two chiefs by whose names they were respectively known.[74] They carried the flags of Scindia and Holkar along with their own.[75] It is worthwhile mentioning here that not all the Pindaris belonged to either of the two divisions.[76] Some of them joined the Bhonsla Raja of Nagpur, others the Peshwa of Poona and still others the Nawab of Bhopal and Amir Khan.

Though the Pindari leaders continued to retain the appellation of Scindia Shahi and Holkar Shahi Pindaris,[77] only a very small proportion of them retained connections with and actually served those chiefs. They had, for the most part, followed their own way, sometimes joining hands with the troops of the commanders of Holkar and Scindia and at other times quitting them at their pleasure.[78] However, it is to be noted that whatever their relations vis-a-vis Scindia and Holkar, they might "still effect to be their vassals and dependents."[79]

The parties under the following leaders were called Scindia Shahi : Chitu, Khwaja Buksh (son of late Sheikh Raja Mohammed), Bhona (an old Jemadar of the Shepherd class), Rajan Khan (brother of Chitu), Wasil Mohammed and Dost Mohammed. And the following were Holkar Shahi : Karim Khan, Imam Buksh, Hiru, Kadir Buksh, Khwaja Buksh and Bara Bhai.[80]

According to Jenkins in 1811, the strength of Scindia Shahi and Holkar Shahi Pindaris was as follows [81]:—

	Horses	Infantry	Guns
Scindia Shahi			
Chitu	7,925	1,000	4
Dost Mohammed	2,430	400	8
Karim Khan	3,500	5,150	15
Kadir Buksh	4,750	—	—
Holkar Shahi			
Tookkoo	2,000	800	5
Imam Buksh	2,000	1,000	2
Sahib Khan & Bahadur Khan	1,060	—	—
Kadir Buksh	2,150	800	4
Nathoo Bucherkah	750	—	—
Bapoo, son of Bhatia	150	—	—
Total of Holkar and Scindia Shahi Pindaris	26,715	9,150	38

In 1811, Jenkins estimated the revenue of the Scindia and Holkar Shahi Pindaris as under[82] —

Revenue of Scindia Shahi	Rs 6,95,000
Revenue of Holkar Shahi	1,40,000
Total revenue of both parties	8,35,000

The Pindaris belonging to the Holkar Shahi class, when compared to the Scindia Shahi Pindaris, were considerably inferior in strength, both in number and in importance.

Several Holkar Shahi Pindari chiefs had their cantonments in the neighbourhood of Chitu's possessions and they were said to have looked up to him for guidance and help even though his nominal connections were with Scindia.[83]

Grant of Land to the Pindaris

As early as 1794, Scindia assigned some lands to the Pindaris near the banks of the Narbada,[84] which they soon extended by conquests from the Grassia chiefs.[85] They came to possess huge tracts of land, extensive in areas and prosperous in revenue.

The lands thus allotted to the Pindari chiefs were sometimes partitioned by them,[86] among the *Shogdars* or

Jemadars and they in their turn distributed them to their *Shilladars*, having their own horses and sometimes to *Chelas*.[87]

Some of the stations which the Pindaris were able to establish were permanent in nature, while others were temporary. Those situated to the north of the Narbada were permanent and those to the south, temporary.

To conciliate the Pindaris, some of the Maratha princes concluded agreements with them, and assigned lands in order to get their own territories exempted from their raids. Scindia, by a similar agreement, had bestowed upon the Pindaris lands belonging to Peshwa and Holkar,[88] which were forcibly occupied by them. In this way the territories under the Pindaris increased rapidly.

Pindaris and Marathas—A Comparison

Some writers have wrongly drawn an analogy between the Pindaris and the Marathas. The analogy may hold true, to some extent, in respect of the usages, dress, food and manners etc., of the Pindaris and the Marathas of the days of Shivaji, but a careful scrutiny reveals that this similarity is superficial. There were essential differences between the two.[89] While the followers of Shivaji were inspired by higher and nobler ideals, the Pindaris were motivated by merely selfish, narrow and ulterior objectives. While the Marathas belonged to the same region and professed the same religion the Pindaris were a mere collection of people from different parts of the country with different castes and creeds. They were divided among themselves and were faithless to their masters, for they were ever ready to desert them and take up service with any military adventurer who might support them. The Marathas were a ruling class, the Pindaris were servile and subservient to them. The former were inspired by national feelings, the latter were merely a mercenary plundering lot.

Few would disagree with the view that the Marathas were extremely short-sighted in their policy towards the Pindaris. As a matter of sound policy, the Marathas should not have patronised the Pindari hordes. It is true that in the beginning, the Pindaris were devoted to their Maratha masters and helped them in their campaigns. They maintained the lines of supply and enabled the army to march to various expeditions without difficulty, by plundering the defeated enemy's camp and the neighbourhood. Little did the Marathas realise that they were encouraging their rapacity, and thereby endangering the peace and security of their people and themselves. The Pindaris also took full advantage of the growing confusion and chaos prevailing in the country in the later 18th century. At a later stage, the Pindaris did not care to obey the orders of their own masters—the Maratha Chiefs, although they continued to call themselves the vassals of Scindia and Holkar till their extermination by the British. The Marathas, as such, cannot escape the responsibility and blame of letting loose unscrupulous bands of marauders upon the people, who were subjected to untold miseries and unspeakable sufferings. The policy of the Marathas in using the Pindaris as their instrument of expansion can hardly be defended.

FOOT-NOTES

1 Lt. James Tod: *Origin, Progress and Present State of the Pindarras*, p.2, Camp Gwalior, October 1811.

Also : Sen in his *Military System of the Marathas* p. 74, in a footnote writes : "Bedadyasi hukum taka raste band karun." That is Bedars were employed by the Marathas for the purpose of shutting the road, in other words for plundering.

2 Meer Hassan Ali Khan : *History of Hyder Naik*, p. 149.

3 Lt. Col. Vans Kennedy : *A Dictionary of Maratha Language*, in two parts, pp. 74-75, Bombay, 1824.

पेंडारी A Pindari or mounted freebooter;

पुंड An insurgent ; a depredator ;

पुंडाई Insurgency ; depredation.

Also : Baba Padmanji : *A compendinm of Molesworth's Maratha-English Dictionary*, pp. 338 and 349, Bombay, 1882.

पुंडाई-वें Refractoriness ; Brigandage ;

पाटर The whole community of a village ;

पुंड Refractory, turbulent ; a freebooter.

4 Hobson Jobson, being a Glossary of Anglo-Indian Colloquial Words and Phrases, p. 538, 1886.

5 *Ibid.*

6 Maj. Gen. Sir John Malcolm : *Report on the Province of Malwah and adjoining Districts*, Part VIII. *Rise, Progress and Annihilation of the Pindaris of Malwah,* para 7, Calcutta 1822.

7 *Ibid.*

8 *Ibid.*

9 H.G. Keene : *History of India,* Vol. II, p. 24, Edinburgh, 1915.

10 "Ney was next entrusted with the command of a corps of partizans, a body capable of great exploits, but little esteemed, however, by the army, as they do not receive any regular pay and consequently live chiefly on plunder. Such a system as this is still but too frequently practised on the continent." *The Annual Biography and Obituary for the year 1817* : Vol I, p. 478, London, 1817.

Also "Khumsa or spoils of war, this amounted to one-fifth of the booty captured in war, four-fifth of this was to be distributed among the soldiers of Islam."

Ishwari Prasad : *A Short History of Muslim Rule in India,* Indian Press, Allahabad, 1939.

11 Kautilya writes : "Brave thieves and wild tribes who make no distinction between friend and foe could be employed."

Brihaspati laid down rules regarding the division of loot brought by licensed robbers: "When everything has been brought from a hostile country by freebooters, with the permission of their lord they shall give a sixth part to the king and share (the remainder) in due proportion." *Sacred Books of the East*, Vol. XXXIII. p. 241.

Shukranitisara also laid down certain rules "if thieves steal something from others' kingdom by the King's orders, they should first give one-sixth to the King and then divide the rest among themselves."

12 "Prince Shah Alam when he was within the territories of Shivaji, near Goa, had in his army seven thousand such, whose orders were to ravage the land of the Bardes." Manucci : *Storio Do Mogor,* Vol, II, p. 459, by W. Irvine, London, 1907.

13 Irvine in a footnote wrote : "these Bidari (from Bidar) sometimes compounded with the Pindaris are mentioned by Bhim Sen in his *Nuskhah-i-Dilkusha*", p. 459,

14 Manucei : *Storio Do Mogor*, Vol. II, p. 459.

15 "In the Bazars or Booths of these Bidaris is found every kind of food supply, vegetables, fruits and other products all purloined from the enemy s territory."

Manucci. *Storio Do Mogor,* Vol. II, p. 459.

[16] H.T. Prinsep : *History of the Political & Military Transactions in India during the Administration of Marquiss of Hastings* 1813-1823, Vol. I, pp. 36-37, London, 1825.

[17] For. Misc. 124 A: *Pindari and Maratha War Papers*, p. 28. Memorandum Relative to the Pindaris—prepared by Mr Jenkins, the Resident at the Court of the Rajah of Berar in the year 1812.

[18] Ibid.

[19] The earliest mention of Pindaris is in the year 1689 when the Pindaris were employed by some rebellious zamindars in the Deccan in plundering the districts of Bijapur.

Also : Hyderabad Residency Records : S. No. 198, Vol. No. 414, O.C. No. 50-51, 29 December 1814. Memorandum Respecting the Pindaris towards the end of the year 1814, p. 9.

Also : *Narrative of a Boondela Officer*, p. 539.

Also : *Origin of the Pindaris* by an Officer Allahabad, Reprint Chapter V.

[20] G.S. Sardesai : *New History of the Marathas*, Vol. III, p. 477, Bombay, 1948.

[21] Sen, however, mentions that Shivaji never employed Pindaris. S.N. Sen : *The Military System of the Marathas*, p. 74, Calcutta, 1958.

[22] "One of the first and most distinguished leader was a person named Poonapah, who ravaged the Carnatic and took Vellore early in the reign of Sahoojee."

Robert Adair McNaghten : *A Memoir of the Military Operations of the Nagpur Subsidiary Force, from its first formation in 1816 to the termination of the campaign Goands etc., in 1819*, p. 105, Calcutta, 1824.

Malcolm in a foot-note remarks, "Poonapah Pindary is mentioned as being in the latter part of the reign of Aurangzeb, an auxiliary of Maratha plunderers."

Malcolm : *Rise, Progress*...para 2.

[23] Chauth and Sardeshmukhi : the former was a tribute exacted from hostile or conquered territories, it amounted to Chauth, that is, one fourth of the estimated revenue, and the latter "a kind of revenue ownership, that is, Wattan, as they called it, which the leaders of the Maratha bands claimed as their own in the old Bahamani days."

Sardesai : *The Main Currents of Maratha History*, p. 80, Bombay, 1933.

[24] The Central India State Gazetteer Series : Indore State Gazette, Vol. II, p. 13, Calcutta, 1908.

[25] *Op. cit* : Sen : *Military System of the Marathas*, p. 74. (Sane, Patre Yadi Bagaire, pp. 55-56.)

[26] Lt. Col. Fitzclarence : *Journal of a Route Across India, through Egypt to England in the later end of the year 1817 and the beginning of 1818*, pp. 4-5, London, 1819.

27 *Peshwa's Diaries* : Vol. III, p. 178.

28 "Shive Chand, Bhim Sing, Mohan Sing, Hiraman and Bhopat Beldar represented that if permission were given to them to plunder in foreign territories and to reside without molestation in the Peshwa's camp, they would collect some Lugare and Beldar families for the purpose, and prayed that a 'KAUL' to that effect might be issued. Having taken into consideration this position, a new *DHAL* has been given and permission has been granted for your residence in the camp on condition that you should pay five rupees for each tent of the Beldar resident in the army and you should render to the state any elephant, palanquin, drum or banners that you may obtain in your raids."

Peshwa's Diaries, Vol. IX, p. 324.

Also : Another Maratha Officer, Triambak Rao Dhamdhere was allowed to keep fifty Pindaris in his camp, but he was told, "but for every Pendari tent exceeding that number, a palpatti or tent tax at the rate of three rupees per tent would have to be paid."

Peshwa's Diaries, Vol. IX, p. 325.

29 Microfilm, India Office Library, London : Home Misc. Series. Vol. No. 467, Letter from Arthur Wellesley, 29 March, 1803.

30 "When Holkar and Scindia came to Hindustan they were each accompanied by a party of Pindaris."

Peshwa Residency Records : Vol. No. 14, Daulat Rao Scindia and North Indian Affairs (1810-1818) Ed. J. N. Sarkar, Letter No. 134, An Account of the Pindaris under Scindia and Holkar p. 157, Bombay, 1951.

Also : National Archives of India : For. Sec. 1814, O. C. No. 1, 21 June, 1814, Edmonstone's Minute, 31 March, 1814, para 18. (Edmonstone was member of the Governor General's Council).

31 The Pindaris at one time were "a convenient ingredient of the system of warfare developed by the Marathas. In that system ever since the days of Shivaji and Santaji Ghorpade, there had always been a class of unpaid auxiliaries attached to each chief's fighting quota whose duty it was to step in the moment the battle ended and finish the enemy by seizing his property and camp equippage and destroying his power of recovery."

Sardesai : *New History of the Marathas*, p. 477.

32 The Pindaris formed "as it were a species of light troops employed in collecting provisions, in cutting off the supplies of the enemy, but principally in desolating the province through which they passed." N.A.I. For. Sec. 1814 : O.C. No. 1, 21 June, 1814, Edmonstone's Minute, 31 March, 1814, para 14.

Also : "The Pindaris who formed a regular appendage to the Maratha armies were not attendants on the fighting men, but looters, pure and simple; they were all mounted men and relieved the regular cavalry of some tasks like reconnoitring, causing distraction to the enemy by attacking his baggage in the rear, while soldiers were busy fighting in front, and usually the pursuit and plunder of a defeated enemy, while their own regular troops were too fatigued after the battle."

Sarkar : *Military History of India*, p. 155, Calcutta, 1960.

33 For. Misc. 124 : Tod : *Origin and Progress*, p. 2.
Also : H.R.R.S. No. 198, Vol. 414, O.C. No. 50-61, 29 Dec., 1814, *Sydenham's Memorandum*, 1814, p. 13, para 2.
(George Sydenham was Agent in Berar with HQ at Aurangabad).

34 N.A.I. For. Sec. 1814, O.C. No. 1, 21 June, 1814, Minute of Edmonstone, 31 March, 1814, paras 14 and 18.

35 Gardi Khan, whom Mulhar Rao employed in his expeditions to Hindustan commanded 30,000 men.
Malcolm : *Rise*, *Progress*, para 8.

36 It may be noted that "till the period of insanity of Jaswant Rao Holkar the Pindari chiefs, who served this family were kept in their proper situation...they were never allowed to sit down in the presence of the ruler." Malcolm : *Rise and Progress*, para 11.

37 "A trifling sum seems to have been allowed for each Pindari horseman; first by the Peshwa, and afterwards by the Maratha Chiefs to whom they were attached; but their plunder always formed the principal part of their pay." *Jenkins' Memorandum*, 1812, p. 29.
Also : Malcolm : *Rise and Progress*, para 10.

38 Peshwa Baji Rao I in his invasion of Malwa was followed by great numbers of Pindaris and in the words of Duff, "It probably was an object of that great man's policy to draw them out of the Mahratta country."
James Grant Duff : *A History of the Marathas*, Vol. II, p. 469.

39 The term *Hindustan* here means Northern India and Deccan or Dakhan meant Southern India.

40 H.R.R. : Vol. No. 14, Letter No. 134, p. 157.

41 *Infra*, p. 73.

42 Malcolm : *Rise*, *Progress*, para 18.

43 *Ibid*., para 8.

44 "A Condottiere (plural : Condottieri) was in the XIV, XV and XVI century a captain of roving bands of mercenaries who put his services, and the bands he led, at the disposal of the various petty states into which Italy was then divided. A sort of an old version of the "Foreign Legion." Of course, their allegiance to the employers were merely on strictly "business" terms. Some of the most famous Condottieri were :

Giovanni Dalle Bande Nere	(XVI Century),
Bartolomeo, Colleoni	(XV Century),
Alberico Da Barbiano	(XV Century)."

Italian Embassy Letter No. 421, 7 December 1962.

[45] Hobson Jobson, p. 539.

[46] M.I.O.L.L., H.M.S. : Vol. No. 467, Item No. 1, Copy to Secret Committee Letter of 26 June, 1803, "every time the regular Maratha force took the field, the Pindaris always formed the militia, reservist or auxiliaries. The Marathas knew that the services of the Pindaris were available at a cheaper rate than the same amount of assistance was elsewhere procurable."
Also : "The Pindaris receive no pay whatever, supporting themselves entirely by plunder."
Thomas Duer Broughton : Constable's Oriental Miscellaney of Original and Selected Publications. Letters written in a Mahratta Camp during the year 1809, p.22, London.

[47] M.I.O.L.L., H.M.S. : Vol. No. 521, Item No. 4, Rough notes on Pindaris.
Also : M.I.O.L.L., H.M.S. : Vol. No. 467, Item No. 1.
Also : Letter from Arthur Wellesley, 29 March, 1803.

[48] The Pindaris worked as "Auxiliaries or followers of regular armies of any power that will engage their predatory services."
Edmonstone's Minute, 13 December, 1816.
N.A.I. For. Sec. 1816, O.C. No. 14, 28 December, 1816.
Edmonstone's Minute, 13 December, 1816, p. 5.
For. Misc. 124 A : Secret Letter from Bengal, 16 August, 1811.

[49] The Pindaris were "the most active and useful agents in cutting off convoys of supplies etc., in attacking and plundering the surrounding villages, so as to make the country in the neighbourhood unproductive to the enemy. They also carried off the camels and bullocks of the camp from their pasture grounds and gave infinite annoyance to the army."
Busawan Lal : *Memoirs of Amir Khan*, Translation by H.T. Prinsep, p. 390, Calcutta 1832.

[50] For. Misc. 124 A : Letter from Lt. Sydenham, 18 March, 1810.
Also : Busawan Lal : *Memoirs of Amir Khan*, p. 390.

[51] For. Misc. 124A : Letter from Lt. Sydenham, 18 March, 1810.

[52] Please see page 34 for further description of horses.

[53] The Marathas "shared in their spoils and no doubt rejoiced in their (Pindari's) success."
M.I.O.L.L. H.M.S : Vol. No. 521, Item No. 9, Letter from Sir John Malcolm to Hastings, 1 April, 1817.
Also : "Rowjee Triumbuck during the course of a piece of conversation gave a very interesting news of the deep relationship between the Pindaris and the Maratha powers. He mentioned that the Indian chiefs had become so dependent upon the share of the Pindari

loot'' that debts would remain unpaid, in case of poor harvest (of plunder).

[54] For. Misc. 124A : Letter from Lt. Sydenham, 18 March, 1810.

[55] It was not uncommon for the Pindaris to rob the government, which they served, and on the other hand, the governments seldom lost an opportunity of extorting from them money under false pretences. Please see chapter 3 for the famous Nagpur case, when the Pindaris were looted by the Raja.

[56] Sen : *The Military System of the Marathas*, p. 73.

[57] N.A.I. For. Sec. 1814, O.C. No. 8-9, 28 January, 1814, Richards Strachey (Resident at Gwalior with Daulat Rao Scindia) to Moira, 8 January, 1814, para 24.

[58] H.R.R.S. No. 198, Vol. No. 414 : *Sydenham's Memorandum*, 1814, p. 12, para 1.

[59] *Ibid.*, p. 12, para 1.

Also : As the Maratha power waned, "the tie which connected the Pindaris with the armies of the Maratha chiefs has been loosened by the reduction of the resources of the latter and the consequent limitation of the field of enterprise." N.A.I. For. Sec. 1814, O.C. No. 1,21 June, 1814, Edmonstone's Minute, 31 March, 1814, para 15.

[60] The result of the war "in which the Maratha confederates engaged with the British government considerably diminished the dependence of the Pindaris upon these powers and gained an accession of strength from the introduction into their hordes of numerous adventurers in want of employment." *Sydenham's Memorandum*, 1814, p. 13, para 2.

Also : "Since the battle of Khurda, in 1794, they are represented to have increased considerably in numbers and insubordination, until the result of the Maratha War completely emancipated them from all control and rendered them what they now are."

Jenkin's Memorandum, 1812, p. 28.

[61] Finding no other means of subsistence "to the unemployed soldiery of India, particularly to the Mahomedans the life of a Pindari had many allurements."

Duff : *History of the Marathas*, Vol. II, p. 471.

"They represented the debris of the Mughal Empire, which had not been incorporated by any of the local Mahomedan or Hindu powers that sprang up out of its ruins. For a time, indeed, it seemed as if the inheritance of the Mughal might pass to these armies of banditti." *The Makers of British India*, W.H. Davenport Adams, John Hogg, London, p. 191.

[62] Prinsep was of the opinion that the "Mahratta states viewed an increase of the Pindaris with an eye to eventual service from their arms." The Pindaris were thus becoming and assuming a distinct place in the military strength of the Indian chiefs of the day. Prinsep : *Transactions* Vol. I, p. 32.

[63] It was found that "growing from amongst the dregs of the people, the dissolute and the idle and gaining strength from the inactivity and corruption of their local governments ... so many had of late attached themselves in community of interest to that rabble, that we have little doubt, a few years further indifferences to their aggression would have converted the greater part of the native soldiery of Hindustan into the same class and pursuits of life."
Summary of the Mahratta and Pindaree Campaign during 1817, 1818 and 1819 under the direction of the Marquiss of Hastings, p. 23, London 1820.

[64] John William Kaye : *The Life and Correspondence of Charles, Lord Metcalfe*, Vol. I, p. 4.

[65] In the days of Warren Hastings also similar hordes were formed by the disbanded Muslim troops of the Nawabs of Bengal but before they could assume the alarming proportions like the Pindaris, they were crushed by the British.

[66] N.A.I. For, Sec. 1814 : O.C. No. 50-51, 29 December 1814. Sydenham to Russell, (Acting Resident at Hyderabad), Aurangabad, 15 October 1814.

[67] McNaghten : *A Memoir of the N.S.F.*, p. 105.

[68] In order to have an effective control over the Pindaris, the Maratha chiefs "always took the precaution of keeping the possession of their families. After the peace of Seerjee Arjengaun, the Pindaris then with Scindia openly seized on their families (which had been usually lodged in or about Assergarh) in the face of his army ... their families, however, I believe, they have never since allowed to fall into the power of any one." *Jenkin's Memorandum :* 1812, For. Misc., Vol. 124A., p. 29.

[69] So much so that a pass was needed for their movement across the Narbada.
Selections from Peshwa's Diaries, Ed. by Vad and Parasnis, Vol. IX, p. 351.

[70] When the British made preparations for an attack upon the Pindaris, almost all the Pindari leaders met Appah Patunkar, the future son-in-law of Scindia for Maratha aid, besides repeatedly writing to Scindia himself.

[71] N.A.I. For. Pol. 1817, O.C. No. 34, 26 April 1817 : Maddock, Superintendent of Political Affairs at Banda to J. Adams, Chief Secretary to the Government, Ft. William, 12 April 1817.

[72] Please see chapter 4.

73 M.I.O.L.L. Close Resident at Gwalior to Adam : 23 November, 1816.

74 The exact meaning of the word 'Shahee' is not known but the body-guards of the King of Delhi were called Allah Shahees and Vallah Shahees, the latter of whom were musketeers. Each Shahee had distinct standards. The Scindia Shahee had the *Bhugwah* colour, the same as that used by the Marattas between red and orange, with a white snake in the middle. This Shahee had also hundred *hircarrahs* or scouts with sticks mounted with snake's head in silver. The Holkar Shahee had for its standards strips alternatively of black, white and blue; and each leader in both tribes had small lugees." Fitzclarence, *Journal of a Route Across India*, p. 6.

75 *Ibid.*
Also : *Jenkins' Memorandum*, 1812, p. 33.

76 N.A.I. For. Sec. 1814 : O.C. No. 1, 21 June, 1814 : Minute of Edmonstone, 31 March, 1814, para 14.

77 The Pindaris continued to preserve and cherish their original designations of Scindia Shahee and Holkar Shahee and hence the desire of the Pindaris for "preserving the form of their original connections with Scindia and Holkar." N.A.I. For. Sec. O.C. No. 14, 28 December, 1816 : Minute of Edmonstone, 13 December, 1816, p. 6.

78 N.A.I. For. Sec. 1812 : O.C. No. 8, 17 April 1812, Letter to Richardson, Agent to the Governor General, Bundelkhand, 17 April, 1812, p. 6.

79 N.A.I. For. Sec. 1814 : O.C. No. 1, Minute of Edmonstone, 21 June, 1814, para 22.

80 N.A.I. For. Sec. 1814 : O.C. No. 2-3, 4 Feb. 1814.
Sydenham to Russell, 8 January, 1814, enclosing substance of a letter from Mansa Ram to Meharban Singh, Superintendent of Dawk from Aurangabad to Kotah.

81 *Jenkins' Memorandum*, 1812, p. 25.

82 *Ibid.*

83 For. Misc. 124 : Tod : *Origin, Progress and Present State of the Pindaris in India*, p. 9.

84 The Maratha chiefs started granting lands to the Pindari chiefs "in lieu of the sum usually paid to them in cash; the Jagheers which they now hold from Scindia and Holkar are said to have been granted to their Chiefs."
Jenkins' Memorandum, p. 29.
Also : By the close of 1765, "another new factor was being added to the politics of Malwa. The Pindaris had begun to enter Malwa as an appendage to the Maratha forces."
Dr Raghubir Singh, *Malwa in Transition*, p. 320, Bombay, 1936.

85 Grasia is a term which is applied to the Rajput and other land holders in some parts of Gujarat and Saurashtra because they hold lands given to them as 'Gras' by the chieftains for maintenance. ग्रास

means a 'mouthful' and those who are given lands for their subsistence are called Grasias. It is also said that the term 'Grasia' has been derived from words गिरा and रश, that is, landlords : Gazetteer of Sirohi State, compiled in 1910 and published by the Scottish Mission Industries Ltd., Ajmer, p. 255. Lt. Col. Erskine has described the Grassias as follows : "Allied to Bhils, but ranking just above them in the social scale are the Grasias, the principal inhabitants of Bhakar and also numerous in the Aritpur and Pindwara Tehsils. The word is derived from the Sanskrit 'Grias' which signified mouthful and has been metaphorically applied to designate the small share of the produce of the country which these plunderers claim......they originally came from Mewar. They mixed up with the Bhils and a new tribe—a mixture of Rajputs and Bhils—was thus born."

Also : Duff : *History of the Marathas*, Vol. II. p. 469.

86 The lands held by the Pindari chiefs are "said to be partitioned out by them to the inferior *Shogdars* or *Jemadars*, and by these again, as far as they will go to *Shillahdars*, having their own horses, or *Bargeers*, sometimes *Chelas*..."

Jenkins' Memorandum, p. 29.

Land was not necessarily divided. In a private letter dated Gwalior, 29 August, 1812, Mr Strachey quotes an instance when "leaders of small bodies who derive no advantage from the *Jageers* held by the chiefs... were planning a union of force with a view to profitable expeditions."

N.A.I. For. Sec. 1812 : O.C. No. 17, 25 September 1812.
Letter from Strachey to Edmonstone, 29 August, 1812.

87 *Chelas* are persons either purchased or kidnapped when young and later adopted in the families; they are mounted on horses belonging to the *Jemadars*.

88 Baptiste concluded such treaties on behalf of Scindia. Bombay Government Records : Diary No. 290. Strachey to Moira, Scindia's Camp, 20 May and 13 June 1815.

89 The Marathas "were a nation fighting against oppression and religious persecution, hence bound by the strongest reciprocity of feeling to each other; the Pindaris are an assemblage of all tribes and religions, who united because it suited their convenience and will separate when it ceases to do so."

N.A.I. For. Sec., 1816 : O. C. No. 1, 15 June, 1816.
Governor General's Minute, 1 December 1815, para 145.

2

Pindaris: Their Organisation and Methods

The Pindaris were a curious assortment of diverse races, castes and communities. They mostly belonged to the two religious communities—Hindus and Muslims.[1] Though most of them were of the Islamic faith, they admitted people of all other religions to their fold, and called them 'Ogura' or strangers.[2] A contemporary official account describes them as "people of all castes with the Brahmins, Telees, Goulees, Tamolees etc."[3] They were never obsessed with any prejudices of caste or troubled by compunctions of conscience. They were devoid of national feeling and religious ties. The Pindari forces were composed of people who, either from disaffection or want of employment were induced to join it. On the testimony of Capt. Sydenham "*disbanded or disaffected* soldiers, rebellious subjects, or needy adventurers find a sure asylum amongst this body, (and) immediately becomes a Pindarra."[4] The needy, the vile and the profligate; the criminal flying from justice, or a villain who would not be tolerated anywhere else, was always accepted in their fold. So this community was composed of heterogenous elements of the most villainous and hardened part of the population which had no means of subsistence other than murder and robbery,[5] their chief cementing factor being the common hazard involved in their profession of loot and arson.

Abode

Practically, all the territories inhabited by the Pindaris were situated to the north of the river Narbada extending from the west of the possessions of the ruler of Saugar, along its bank, to the north of the territory of the Nawab of Bhopal. Its utmost length was a hundred miles and its breadth in some places was forty miles.[6]

Thus, the centre of this formidable association was in Malwa, the valley of the Narbada, the richest part of Central India, particularly in Nimawar and in the dense wilds between the Narbada and the Vindhya range, where the Pindaris 'deposited' their families securely while they were away on their excursions.[7]

Religious Beliefs

The Pindaris, as we have seen, were the followers of Islam and Hinduism. The intermingling of these people of different faiths gave rise to certain common practices among them. The Pindari women (Mohammadan as well as Hindu) invoked Devi in different forms and manifestations. Irrespective of his religious beliefs every Pindari worshipped one or other of the deities.[8] Some of them worshipped various 'Peers' or saints as their blessings were believed to help them in warding off danger. The 'Ramassah Peer' also known as 'Dev Dharma Raja', and 'Goga Peer' or, as the Mohammadans called him, the 'Zain Peer' were usually invoked by Pindari women when their husbands or relations went on plundering expeditions. The 'Ramassah Peer' was worshipped on Saturdays, when small clay or stone images of horses were offered for worship. The Pindaris were a deeply superstitious people.[9] They wore round their necks a talisman on which was engraved the figure of 'Ramassah Peer' on horse-back.[10] They would go out on plundering expeditions on the *Dashera* day or sometimes after the fast of '*Kanaqat*',[11] or a few days preceding or following the Dashera festival.

But, their rapacity and avarice had the better of their faith and superstitions, for the Pindaris did not deter from plundering temples and other places of devotion. The temples in Konkan, Girhar and Ramtek were attacked and looted during their various excursions.[12] A Paper of intelligence from Chitu's camp, traceable in Bombay Government Records, presents a typical picture of Chitu sitting under an awning, weighing an idol of gold.[13] But there are, on the contrary, a number of such instances when the Pindaris not only showed respect to the temples and prayed in them, but also offered gold 'mohurs' and spears to *Mahadev* in a temple near Sidee.[14] Some of them even built terraces of silver in places of Hindu worship.[15] They used to send presents to Hans Bharti, a 'Gossain,' for his 'Math.'[16] In the official papers there is no reference to Pindari vandalism against a mosque. Prisoners caught during the course of an excursion were often converted to Islam.[17]

Pindari Women

The Pindari women like their menfolk, were very sturdy. During the early stages of the rise of Pindaris, their women, like the Mongol women, if Malcolm is to be believed, used to accompany their husbands in most of their excursions. They were "usually mounted on small horses or camels, and were more dreaded by the villagers than the men, whom they exceeded in cruelty and rapacity."[18] Once the feelings of piety, sympathy, love and kindness were overcome, the degradation and fall of these women came rapidly. However, in spite of all their ferocity and nomadic nature, "they were still susceptible to the strongest domestic attachment."[19] They had a mortal fear of the safety of their husbands out on plundering expeditions, and, therefore, would put round their necks talisman for their safety. There is an instance of a Pindari woman, wife of one Ramzan Khan, the *Bumedar* or Quartermaster of a Pindari *Durra*, who was dissuaded from performing the 'Sati' with great difficulty.[20]

Weapons

The Pindaris were all generally armed with spears, about twelve to fifteen feet long, which they used with admirable dexterity. Sometimes, they had a sword and a shield or a short spear or 'barchhi' only. The Pindaris of inferior rank were very poorly armed with bows and arrows, pikes, clubs, iron crows and pointed iron bars. A few of them also served the purpose of digging the precious articles buried in the ground.[21] Firearms were sparingly used. Most of them did not carry heavy arms as they had to march for weeks together. The Pindaris generally avoided a pitched battle; a running battle was also not to their liking, and so they hardly felt the need to arm themselves with guns. A lance and a sword were the only arms they needed, which served their purpose of both defence and offence. However, conscious of the importance of matchlocks in fighting and scaring the villagers, every fifteenth man was armed with a matchlock.

Thus the arms of the Pindaris were generally primitive; but as time advanced, they began using guns more freely. By 1811, the Pindaris had started manufacturing guns,[22] and making their own ammunition.[23] For this purpose, they established a foundry for cannon at Satwas.[24] They were able to produce several pieces of brass ordnance.[25] Little wonder, therefore, that they had become so irresistible and invincible for a short period that their very name inspired terror in the hearts of the people.

The Pindaris had no knowledge of organised warfare and its science. War and military conquests needed infantry and artillery, but they had neither of them. Their main aim being plunder, they adopted a policy of hit and run, and for this sort of warfare, they were pretty well-equipped.

Horses

The Pindari organisation was essentially based on cavalry. The greatest wealth of the Pindari, like the Mongols and the Cossacks, was the horse. As long as the Pindari was seated on horse-back he felt secure. He loved and tended it most affectionately. During a fight or flight, it was his constant companion. The Pindari clung to it most tenaciously. The horse also understood the master perfectly well. In case of a fight, "the Pindari galloped round and round the most active of our troopers; and his very horse seems to partake of the master's cunning and dexterity, and to know exactly the moment for a quick and timely retreat.''[26] It carried him through thick and thin. Capt. Williams, in his '*Observations on the Habits of the Pindaries*,' very aptly sums up the Pindari attitude towards the horse : "as it is the chief source of his wealth, so it is the chief object of his regard; on it depends his safety and his fortune. Nothing argues greater intelligence, nothing carries with it greater disgrace than the loss of his horse, on which it is figuratively imagined a 'Pindara' should ever be mounted. No success can ever afterwards wipe away the reproach."[27]

The horse was generally fed on grains like '*chana*' and '*jaoree*'. The effort of the Pindari was to give him the best of every kind of grain he could procure.[28] When the horse was not mounted it was allowed to graze in the fields;[29] but if the crop had been harvested, the horse was fed on stalks or whatever was left.[30] When nothing better could be obtained, they were given ginger oil seeds.[31] The saddles of the horses were made of '*Namda*' (coarse woollen sheet) and were therefore capable of being used as beds, and in case of necessity, to put their plunder and provisions in.

The horse of the Pindari, though haggard, had intense pluck and was capable of undergoing great fatigue and exertion. It would gallop for forty to fifty miles at a stretch. Curiously enough, Capt. Williams, who was closely connected with the operations against the Pindaris, observes, from a review of nearly seven hundred captured horses, that "many of them were lame, crippled, old, or worn out, yet upon these they penetrated several hundred miles in the rear of our (British) armies, and defied both opposition and pursuit,[32] and traversed the most rugged mountains and impassable roads, which an ordinary horseman would have failed to do.

It is indeed interesting that the horse was occasionally given balls of opium to stimulate it for great exertions.[33] Some were given preparations containing opium, arsenic, blue stone and other ingredients.[34] The Pindaris never bred horses, but purchased them from the Maratha dealers.[35]

Clothes and food

The Pindaris were a very scantily dressed people. Their outfit consisted of a quilted jacket reaching the knee, with a turban on the head, which was usually tied with a handkerchief. Some of them wore a quilted cap, instead of a turban, which also was fastened round the chin, so that it did not fall down during their march. Their drawers were made of thick coarse cloth. In view of the fact that they had to undergo long marches with great rapidity and, from time to time, had to undertake fighting also, the outfit which they chose was ideally suited to them. The Maratha soldiers of the time also wore a more or less similar outfit, as the Mongols and the Cossacks did.

The Pindaris were a very hardy people, capable of bearing excessive hardships, fatigue and hunger. They could satisfy their hunger with the coarsest of the cakes of wheat or '*Jowar*' or parched peas or grains.[36] Like the Mongols they were gluttons when food was available. We are told that their abstinence was at times extraordinary. During a retreat they often fed themselves on corn plucked from the nearby fields.[37]

The Pindaris, when leaving their headquarters, provided themselves with a few '*Chapatis*' and their horses a few feeds. For future supply they depended on plunder. In case of failure to obtain food, they were exposed to temporary privations, which they endured cheerfully.[38] Strangely enough, there is no instance of Pindaris killing bullocks for food, although some of them were followers of Islam; but there are a number of cases when they killed sheep for the purpose.[39]

Preparation Before Excursion

The Pindari standards were raised annually. During the dry season, excursions were undertaken with great regularity, which often coincided with the Hindu festival of Dashera.[40] Either on the Dashera day or on the 'parva' of Diwali or on the '*Kanaqat*' they would cross the river Narbada on horseback. In case the river was not fordable, they crossed it by boats. Before setting out, they assembled at an appointed place, and chose a seasoned leader called *Lubheareah* and placed, themselves under him for that particular expedition. Sometimes, the principal Pindari chief sent his most confidential 'chelas' as leaders of the expeditions. The Lubheareah was never a hereditary endowment. He was at the head not because of his birth, but by virtue of his popularity, personal bravery, pre-eminence and military abilities.[41] In short, he was 'chosen to be the leader on account of his experience and acknowledged courage.

Irrespective of internecine feuds or enmity among them, they rendered unquestioned allegiance to a Lubheareah, once the leader was chosen by common consent. Consequently, peace, cordiality and amiability prevailed among them and the plundering expeditions undertaken in a team spirit. A settlement of mutual differences and quarrels was generally postponed to the period of respite.

At the outset, the Lubheareah would send his *vakeels* to other *Thokdars*,[42] to join him in his excursions. On their meeting him, he would let them know of his true designs. After mature deliberations and consultations among the various *Sardars*, the plan and conduct of the coming expedition was decided upon.

While in the camp, the leader maintained general discipline and extracted obedience without much difficulty. Those who disobeyed him were mounted on camels and paraded in the camp.[43] But once the Pindaris set out on an expedition, the leader could hardly enforce discipline. During an expedition, he was neither able to punish disobedience nor was he successful in commanding submission to his authority. He, nevertheless, tried to maintain his leadership as much as he could through conciliation and cajolery. The main reason of obedience among the Pindaris was the awareness that their safe return to their land of hope and security entirely depended upon him. Yet an important inducement to obedience was the hope of plunder. Once the business was over they usually relapsed into insubordination.

Before setting out on an expedition the Lubheareah galloped to some distance from his camp without declaring his intention to any one, and blew a trumpet which was a signal to everyone to leave anything that he might be engaged in and prepare to march as quickly as possible. The Lubheareah, then, with the flag in his hand led his followers. This method enforced upon them a constant state of preparedness.[44]

Their Spy System

The Pindari chiefs rarely went ahead of the Lubhur. They remained at their respective headquarters and Jagirs, so as to escape the blame for disturbances, and to keep a watch over the security of Pindari families.[45] But communication with the party was maintained by them through the *harkaras* (scouts) disguised as *fakeers* and *gossains*.[46] They were also employed to procure information from British and Indian chiefs' territories, regarding the deployment of the troops.[47] The system of obtaining information was excellent and upto-date, with the result that they could ascertain the names of wealthy inhabitants of various towns and villages in advance.[48] It appears from the accounts in the official papers that the British Government also succeeded in getting regular news about them by associating their spies with the Pindaris. They were disguised as labourers or fakeers and hence could not be suspected of espionage.

Puja to the Narbada River

Since the Pindari settlements were situated to the north of the Narbada, they had to cross it before setting out on an expedition. The water level of the river rises during the middle of June and so it presented a barrier to the Pindaris from June to October.[49] It was fordable only after October. The Pindaris then performed 'puja' to the river and set out on an excursion.[50] They seldom crossed it after May, even if the river were fordable, lest on their return they should find it uncrossable.

Pindari Conduct during Excursions

During the early stages, the Pindari expeditions did not

extend beyond their base on the Narbada. But as they gained strength and the field nearer home became impoverished, they began extending their activities further, and went to far off places.[51] The average strength of the Pindari parties out on excursions varied from one thousand to four thousand.[52] But at times their number rose to as many as ten thousand. They were all mounted but not necessarily on the best horses. Out of a thousand, the proportion of good cavalry was never more than four hundred and the rest six hundred were usually mounted on inferior horses; but even these were very hardy and capable of enduring the greatest fatigue of long marches.

Since the destination was pre-determined, the Pindaris reached there by the shortest possible route, maintaining maximum secrecy of movement. They did not resort to any plundering on their way and kept to a direct, undeviated and unfrequented course.[53] Thus, no knowledge whatever of their approach could be had by the unfortunate victims of their attack. In the beginning they moved at a leisurely pace of about ten miles a day, but gradually increased it to thirty or forty miles;[54] this pace was increased by another ten or fifteen miles in case of emergency and was maintained for days together.

No barrier could arrest the Pindaris in their march to the central point of plunder—whether it was the chain of forts, or of military posts. They even passed through the divisions of the army drawn up against them. It was typical of the Pindaris that they never used the same route again on their return. When pursued, they seldom took the predetermined route by which they had earlier decided to escape in case of an attack. It has been observed that the incursions of the Pindaris were always undertaken in the dry season and along the paths where water was easily available. They seldom used the highways.[55]

The Pindaris usually started their march about half an hour after day-break and continued marching until it was nearly mid-day. They then halted for two or three hours near the villages and again moved forward, stopping at sunset to refresh themselves.[56] At nine in the night, they changed their location and did so again at twelve, moving about two or three *koss* each time. Each of these halts was called a *tull*. They occasionally made a third change too in their positions. The perpetual change of positions confused their pursuers. The suddenness with which they appeared at a place diametrically opposite to that in which they were last seen, gave an air of magic and mystery to their movements. They always marched in long flanks and thus covered a vast area.

The Pindaris were scattered over an area of more than a koss, so that their numbers appeared incalculable. Their strength daily increased as they very frequently carried off young boys from different villages *en route*, and compelled them to take care of their cattle and property. To carry the booty and the captives, they seized every horse they came across. Not infrequently, each of them had two or three captured horses. In distant expeditions, they did not march fast and long, but kept their horses in wind and free of burden for the return march.

At night, when it was difficult to keep together on account of darkness, they continually called each other by name and from the noise that arose from these exchanges, the general direction of the march was easily maintained. If the Lubheareah changed his route, he sounded his trumpet and a word by mouth was passed from one to another. Although much confusion was caused, they were able to unite again in a short time. In case they were attacked at such a moment, they immediately dispersed and galloped away.

In spite of this apparent disorder, the Pindaris still maintained some degree of order among themselves. Each *thok* had its distinguishing *Lugee* or standard and proceeded in an orderly manner as circumstances permitted. During the march, the individuals seldom separated from the thok, and if by chance any one strayed from the main body, no notice was taken of him.

Sometimes, the Pindaris detached themselves in bodies of ten or twenty or a few hundred each. and scoured and swept the country through a circle of many miles, either in the front or in the flanks of the Lubhur. When attacked, the Pindaris resorted to the tactics of leading their adversaries into some ambush, and then tried to destroy them. But this depended upon the enemy strength. Their object was always to fight to advantage. When the thok was hard pressed, the bravest and the best-mounted volunteered to defend it.

In case the 'toll' was dispersed as a result of defeat, the Lubheareah sounded his trumpet to gather them. Stacks of straw or stubble, houses or a village were set on fire to direct the straggling parties to the rendezvous.[57] The light could be seen from a great distance and worked as a rallying point for the whole Lubhur. It sometimes happened that individuals remained separated from 'toll' for several days but such was their intuition that they soon discovered the track of their party by the remains of their fires, desolate villages or by enquiries from people on the road.

When the Lubheareah arrived at a place where he intended to halt, he would dismount and fix the flag on the ground. Those who followed immediately began to collect forage. Leaving the Lubheareah in the rear, the thok tried to keep as close together as it possibly could. No other regularity was otherwise maintained by the Pindaris. The Lubheareah was expected to guard the safety of the Lubhur. In the day time, the Pindaris unsaddled their horses, but once night approached, they re-saddled them, and even slept with the bridles in their hands. Thus on the least alarm, they sprang on the backs of the horses and were out of sight in an instant.

When resistance was offered by the people, they dismounted and deployed the best horsemen to form covering parties.[58] They were expected to be ready to face an enemy, while the plundering parties were looting and making off with their collections. The covering party kept firing from some protection upon the villagers, or (in the event of villagers having no firearms) showered large stones upon them and forced them to fly. At this moment the Pindaris charged and stormed the village. If, during the resistance by the villagers, one or two of their party were killed or seriously wounded, they gave up the attack.[59] The Pindaris were generally afraid of fire-arms and seldom ventured to attack a place which had them.[60] The wounded comrades were carried away on horseback if it was possible, otherwise they were left to the mercy of the villagers.[61]

The moment the Pindaris were able to overcome resistance in a village, they would at once divide themselves into a number of small parties for the purpose of plunder,[62] scattering themselves over the whole region, and passing with extreme rapidity from one place to another.[63] It was common to find different parties spread over wide areas and plundering in distant places.[64] Wellesley, the Acting Resident at Gwalior, in his letter to Adam, dated 10th March, 1816, wrote that it was a "part of their (Pindari) system by a variety of subsidiary invasions in different quarters to distract the attention of pursuers, with the view to covering the operation of the main object or at least of securing a prize in one instance, if they fail in another."[65] Once the booty was seized, they reassembled at the appointed place outside the village and moved off with the same secrecy and rapidity with which they had advanced. As Malcolm says, "the Pindaris when they came to a rich country had neither the means nor inclination, like the Tartars, to whom they had been compared, to settle and repose. Like swarms of locusts, acting from instinct, they destroyed and left waste whatever country they visited... the Pindaris were fed and nourished by the very miseries which they occasioned."[66]

Secrecy and surprise were, therefore, the key to their success. Little wonder, the British or Indian troops which guarded the frontiers often failed to check them. If pursued, when laden with booty, the 'tattoos' or bullocks were generally relieved of their burdens and left alone. In some cases, the plunder was even thrown away and the Pindaris escaped to the jungles and hills with the most valuable plunder on their person. When pursued, the Pindaris "march hundred miles in two days, three hundred miles in a week, or five hundred miles in a fortnight."[67]

The Pindaris were in a state of perpetual preparedness. When they halted and expected an attack by the enemy, they often distributed themselves into small parties of four each, in which one held the horses and kept watch, another cooked the food, and the remaining two slept.[68] When once the Pindaris had passed the frontier and had little fear of the enemy, they encamped at one place for six or seven days continuously, recouping their lost energy and ravaging the country around.[69]

The Pindaris would capture people during the course of their excursions and hold them for ransom. According to Malcolm, these were never 'sold' in the market.[70] But, Lord Hastings in his 'Private Journal' has stated that "not only the Pindaris would satisfy their lust but also took away all the young girls, tied three or four like calves on a horse, to be sold."[71] It is difficult to disbelieve either Malcolm or Lord Hastings, both being contemporary authorities, yet the latter view appears more credible as the Pindaris, being self-centered utilitarians, could not long engage children and young women to their advantage.

Rapidity of Movements

As has already been noticed earlier, the celerity of the Pindaris during their forward march, retreat or flight was remarkable. According to Martineau, Pindaris "marched or rather darted, meeting and dispersing like the birds of the air."[72] Pindaris were known to boast that they could baffle or elude the most vigilant and efficient of the British troops. The factor of their being more nifty was considered a point of honour in case of being overtaken or surprised. (If overtaken or surprised, the point of honour was, who would flee most swiftly.) Any information regarding their movements was available only when they were right on their destination, and the victims brought the first news of the conflagration of their houses.[73] Thus, the account of their depradation was generally the first intelligence of their approach. An eye-witness observes : "The movements of the Pindaris are so rapid that all intelligence is outstripped by them, and the country destined to be the scene of their devastation is overrun by their horse(s) before it is well known that they have quitted their cantonments."[73] Such was the quickness of their march that any interception during their invasions depended on chance only.[74]

Thus, whatever the British did to obstruct the Pindaris' return, they became ineffective due to their "extraordinary rapidity and still more extraordinary intelligence."[75] Sydenham has recorded in his Memorandum of 1814, that when pressed by force of circumstances, they could easily attain very great speed.[76]

Horrors of Pindari raids

To the Pindari, rapine was a trade and cruelty a pastime. They were the most cruel, callous and cold-hearted ruffians. For the sake of plunder they would stoop down to any level and spare no atrocity.[77] They would commit the most hideous crimes with the least compunction and perpetrate the most savage outrages upon the people. They would not spare even women and children.[78]

The moment the people learnt of the arrival of the Pindaris in their villages—alarm, terror and dismay would spread over the whole area. People used to run away, although they hardly had any time to do that, leaving behind them everything in the village and seeking refuge in hills and jungles. Such was the terror of the Pindaris that people would rather starve to death in the hills than go down and face the risk of an encounter with them.[79] In case the villagers had no time to escape, immediately on learning of the approach of the Pindaris, they would close the gates of the villages or 'ghurries' (small fortresses) and keep up constant firing from the walls, if they had any matchlocks. Otherwise, they would depend on the fuselage of stones, which, however, was not always effective. Sometimes the Pindaris would withdraw before the guns, but if the resistance offered by the villagers broke down, and most often it did, as a result of the superior strength of the Pindaris, they would pounce upon the villagers like hungry beasts of prey.

The continuous acts of murder, blood and rapine made the Pindaris the very embodiment of savagery, devoid of all feelings of pity and commiseration.[80] All accounts depict them as the most degraded specimens of humanity.[81]

As it was impossible for the Pindaris to remain at a particular place for more than a few hours, they suffered no opposition. They immediately seized all those who seemed to posses money and subjected them to the most horrid torture, until they either disclosed their hoards or died under the infliction. The Pindaris preferred inflicting torture to death, for they never liked the secret of the hidden treasure to be buried in the owners' grave.[82]

A favourite mode of torture was to put hot ashes into a 'tobra' (horse nose bag) which they tied over the mouth and nostrils of their victim, whom they then thumped over the back till he inhaled the ashes. The effect on the lungs of the sufferers was such, that few survived the operation for long. Another mode was to throw the victim on his back and place a plank or beam across his chest, which two Pindaris pressed with their whole weight.[83] Such type of wanton cruelties could better be described in the language of an Official Report laid before the Parliament.[84]

"On their arrival at a village of any consequence every man was first seized and, his arms being secured, he was thrown to the ground, and ashes or dust applied to his face. A quantity of ashes being first put loosely into a cloth, which was then placed over his head, was repeatedly beaten until the sufferer's mouth and nose became filled; and to make the pain more severe, pounded chillies, when they could be procured, were added to the ashes, which were occasionally made hot. Rice beaters or yokes taken from the plough, were converted into other instruments of torture, while one was placed under the back, a second was fastened over the chest, on either side of which a Pindarry pressed his whole weight, and while in this situation many were unmercifully beaten...two persons were burnt to death, several were forced down the wells...others, while their heads were held back by their hair, had water poured into their nostrils...

infants were torn from the arms of their mothers and thrown into wells or dashed on the ground; while there is one instance of a child having been thrown into the air, and nearly divided by a swordsman while in the act of falling..."

To continue the report :

"In the town of Nundegama, Cheeralah Ramasen, a Bramin, was seized in company with his family; he was first severely beaten, ashes were then applied to his mouth and nose until suffocation nearly ensued and although the helpless sufferer gave up his entire valuables, still did they preserve in tormenting him, when he agreed to shew where he had concealed his cooking utensils and clothes. Disappointed in their expectation of booty, to avenge themselves, the Pindaris fastened round the body of this unhappy man bundles of straw which were set on fire; the agonies in which he must have expired can be more readily conceived than expressed. The case of Noonoogaloory Matim Shetty is also shocking. This poor man was first severely pressed with rice beaters and a pot of boiling oil having been procured, Margora twigs were dipped into it and the liquid sprinkled over him, so that his body was entirely covered with blisters. In this state a load was put on his head to carry to camp; but he had not proceeded far when some persons informed him that his daughter was dead, overwhelmed by the anguish of his body and mind, he threw down his load and fell prostrate; the horseman finding him immovable, brought a large stone, and letting it fall on his head killed him."

Varied were the cruelties perpetrated by the Pindaris. They would tear off the ear just to secure an ear-ring. They would cut off the hands of children to obtain bracelets. Oil would be sprinkled on clothes, cotton tied to the fingers of innocent people, and then set on fire.[85] In order to find out hidden wealth, the Pindaris had spear points, pincers and similar pointed arms inserted in their most delicate and sensitive parts. Sometimes, the Pindaris would apply red-hot irons to the soles of their victims. Equally frightful was their treatment of the mute animals, for the cattle would be maimed so that they be of no use to their owners.[86]

The Pindaris took great pleasure in destroying and burning what they could not carry with them. Grain, cloth, hay, houses and sometimes the whole village was set on fire.[87] Often they burnt the villages for pleasure.[88]

Treatment of Women

Neither age nor sex had any consideration for the Pindaris.[89] Women too were not free from molestation. They were subjected to the most inconceivable brutality. Immediately on arrival at a village, they laid their hands upon all young women to gratify their carnal desires. Those who offered resistance were immediately put to death. Stripped of their clothes and ornaments, women were violated on the public streets.[90] There were a number of instances of "these monsters having cut off the breasts of women, immediately after having offered the most horrid violence to their persons; as if their brutal appetite would have been but imperfectly satiated, unless sealed with the blood of their victims."[91] They ravished them under the very nose of their husbands and parents,[92] and so sensual and brutal were they that occasionally they did not spare even dead women from such insults.[93] Sometimes, a single woman was forced to satisfy the lust of many Pindaris one after the other.[94] In this context it would not be improper to cite the following :—

> "Nemula Achee, an unfortunate Gentoo woman, was seized, and so numerous were those whose brutal lust she was doomed to gratify, that her body swelled to an enormous size; and although every means which humanity could suggest were employed to divert her mind from the sufferings she had experienced, still did her poignant grief weigh so heavily on her spirits, that little hopes were entertained of her long surviving her distress, and a few days put a period to her misery which took place on the report of a gun that she fancied had

been discharged in consequence of the return of her tormentors...She trembled and expired. In the case of Curnum's wife of Mootoocoor...she is represented as having been particularly handsome, and was of consequence devoted to be a victim of their lust. She, however, resisted the united efforts of nine horsemen to effect her ruin, and expired under the treatment they inflicted on her; when shocking to humanity to relate, that death did not secure her person from insult as those men perpetrated the crime which this good and virtuous woman sacrificed her life to prevent."

The outrages perpetrated by the Pindaris on women obliged people to defend their honour by equally cruel means. To prevent the violation and ravishment of their wives, sisters and daughters before their own eyes, the villagers seeing that they were no more able to resist and were likely to be soon overpowered, "applied the torch of destruction to their habitation and perished with their relations in the general conflagration."[95] The women escaped violation and murder only by a voluntary death, by setting fire to their houses and perishing in them, almost committing the old brave act of *Johar*.[96] Sometimes, even the news of an imminent attack by the Pindaris was enough to force them to the wells and tanks where they drowned themselves. Those who could not escape molestation committed suicide along with their children after the Pindaris had left.[97] Some of them would stab themselves[98] and others would tear out their tongues and die instantly.[99] Besides these tortures, the Pindaris detained all the young and beautiful girls to satisfy their lust at night; while the ugly and old ones were employed for cooking food.[100]

Their unrelenting and indiscriminate cruelty and barbarity made them the veritable scourge of god. They left the innocent and unarmed villagers in a state of complete ruin. At their very approach, peace, prosperity and happiness vanished and what was left was mere desolation, penury, want and misery.

Division of Plunder

After the Pindaris had devastated, burnt, pillaged, massacred and satisfied their orgy of blood and lust, they returned to their base in Malwa. Once they crossed the Narbada and reached home, the scene changed.

After their arrival, the question of division of plunder assumed great importance and immediate distribution of the booty stated. The first claim was always of the government which they served, but in case they operated independently, the first claim was always of the chief of the 'Durra'. Contemporary writers are of the opinion that the Chief's share was the fourth part of the entire booty, but[101] it always happened that one or two of the choicest articles would be reserved for the chief in addition to his share.[102] Although the system of apportioning the booty was uncertain, it was commonly accepted that such valuable articles as palanquins, *aftabgeers* or umbrellas, *Nakkaras* and flags were reserved for the highest authority recognised by them. The Pindaris in return, always received rewards from the chiefs. But there are instances when the Chief of the State, not being satisfied with his share, would extract additional contribution.[103] However, the Pindaris also would avenge against the state in question by further plunder.[104]

The claim of the government or the chief having been settled, one fourth of the remaining part of the plunder was paid to the leader of the expedition.[105] The payment of loans and advances received or contracted earlier was the next charge on the plunder. Loans at high rates of interest were taken from rich merchants who used to reside in the Pindari camps.[106] This characteristic feature of the Pindaris contracting loans and repaying the same, deserves attention.[107] Although in theory, the owner of the horse was supposed to be the master of the spoils, in practice one-fourth of the booty was given to him as his share.[108] But in the general scramble for booty, it was impossible to determine the exact plunder secured by a Pindari and the quantity dishonestly appropriated by him.

The remaining fourth part of this plunder was apportioned among the people who stood guard at the time of plundering and held their comrades' horses. The plunderer took one part, another he gave to the person who held his horse, and the third share known as *peer bhatta* was kept by him for his exertions in extorting the loot. What happened to the remaining one-fourth part of the booty is a mystery. In the event of an *ogura* getting a large booty, the *thokdar* would often seize the whole of it, unless, of course, he was satisfied earlier.[109] Quarrels and huckstering were a common feature at the time of the division of plunder, but these were referred to the Lubheareah for his final decision, which was seldom questioned. Sometimes, the Lubheareah entered a village himself to encourage and help his people in plundering and in case the victim was rich, he claimed a share, which was more often granted, not because of fear, but out of pesonal regard for him.[110]

The practice regarding the distribution of spoils looted by the 'chelas' was somewhat different. It was expected of the chelas to deliver all that they had plundered to the chief,[111] who would give one-fourth of the plunder as their share to them. The remaining three-fourths was retained by the *Shogdars* (or *Jemadars*) who would then give one-fourth of what they received to the head of the *Durra*. Since the Durra consisted largely of those who were neither paid by the chiefs, nor possessed lands granted to them, they would, after paying one-fourth as their share to the chief "as an acknowledgement for his permission to plunder under his flag,"[112] keep the rest to themselve. It was a custom with the Pindaris that the booty captured by the slaves, (each of the Pindari chiefs had ten to fifteen slaves), belonged to their masters.[113]

When the preliminaries of the division of plunder were over, the Pindari camps presented the scene of a fair. The Pindari women conducted the sale of their husbands' share of loot because they, like all other women, were supposed to be better bargainers.[114] Purchasers flocked from all quarters.[115] The Pindaris established regular houses of agency, sending bills to places as far away as Calcutta, Benaras and Ujjain and the plundered property like gold, siver and jewels was not only sold locally but sent to distant places as Kota and Ujjain.[116]

Sometimes, when the plunder was rich and the quantity great, the Pindaris did not bother about even the costliest silks, vessels etc. It was then common to see shawls, sarees etc., priced very low and attracting no customers.

Meanwhile, the Pindari menfolk gave themselves up to drinking, music and debauchery. They invited their friends and relatives and called on them in return. All social engagements like marriage were completed then. Thus "the life of debauchery and excess lasted till all their money was gone."[117] If the money was over before the season for new campaign came, the Pindaris contracted loans at high rates of interest from the merchants living in their camps and went on gratifying their passions till a fresh expedition was undertaken by them. The Pindaris thus lived in "an alternation of brutal exertion and sensual abandonment."[118]

A reference in passing may be made here to the minting of money by the Pindaris. A mint was established in the fort of Nimawar, on the north bank of the Narbaba, where silver was coined into rupees and gold into *mohurs*; the two Rajuns, Bheeka Kunwar and the bankers Thakur Seth and Lachman Seth superintended the mint. Silver was purchased at one hundred rupees for four seers, and gold at twelve rupees a tola.[119]

Cowardice of the Pindaris

It may be observed that valour was not a quality to be found in the Pindaris. However brave individually some of them might be, collectively they were a cowardly lot. A single British trooper with a gun in his hand was more than a match for fifty Pindaris.[120] When attacked, instead of giving a battle or taking an offensive, they immediately took to their heels,[121] for their "sole aim was escape" and to them "flight was victory."[122] It is recorded that no troops in the history of the world ever displayed such a proficiency in the art of running away.[123] However, there are some instances when the Pindaris fought, and successfully too, against regular armies.[124]

A careful study of the organisation of the Pindaris hardly suggests any originality in their operating methods. Although their tactics were not identical in all respects with the Huns, the Mongols or the Tartars, whose very name inspired terror in the East or the West during the Middle Ages;[125] yet they seem to have adopted some of their practices. As with the Mongols, mobility was a great quality with the Pindaris. Both in their plundering expeditions and return march the Pindaris mystified people more by their movements than by their fighting ability. The rapacity and greed of the Pindaris were as boundless as those of the Mongols. Their inhuman barbarities, indiscriminate massacres and systematic plunders, without any consideration of age, sex and religion, created widespread panic and horror among the people.

But the analogy between the Pindaris and the Barbaric Hordes of Central Asia and Mongolia viz., the Huns, the Mongols and the Tartars should not be pressed too far. Unlike the barbaric hordes of the Middle Ages which overran extensive areas from the Black Sea to the China Sea or from Siberia to Indus, the Pindaris remained confined to the Central region of the Indian sub-continent. Besides, the Pindari menace as compared to that of the Central Asian hordes hardly lasted for more than a few decades. The latter possessed a large and well-disciplined army, seasoned and experienced in the art of warfare. Attila the Hun had knocked at the gates of Rome. The Mongols under Chengiz Khan and Taimur had successfully attacked and overthrown mighty empires of Central and West Asia. Taimur had invaded India successfully. Before them powerful empires and kingdoms fell like nine pins. The swarming numbers of these barbaric tribes had proved themselves to be an international menace, while the Pindari hordes posed, at the worst, a national threat only.

The Pindaris, unlike them, lacked all valour and heroism. They were experts only in murder, rapine, robbery and rape, possessing little military skill and constructive ability.

Indeed, the Pindaris were a heterogenous combination of disorderly elements that usually prosper on the disintegration of great empires into petty principalities under unscrupulous adventurers. These freebooters could have been turned into disciplined armies as Chengiz Khan had turned the uncivilized and cruel Mongols into a fighting nation, but the leaders of the Pindaris did not possess even a flash of the genius of such renowned leaders. They were ordinary men, not very much superior to those whom they led. When the British government decided to restore peace and order in the territories infested by them, their organisation collapsed without offering any resistance worth the name. Such people could have hardly established kingdoms or fought a regular, well-established and disciplined army like that of the British.

FOOT NOTES

1 *Origin of the Pindaris:* By an Officer of the East India Company, Allahabad Reprint.

2 H.R.R. : S. No. 220, Vol. No. 424. 26 February, 1817; Capt. Williams: Observations on the Habits of the Pindaris during their Predatory Excursions, p. 203.
Also : Supplement to the Government of India Gazette, Thursday, March 6, 1817.

3 H.R.R. S. No. 202, Vol. No. 203: Translation of a Paper of Intelligence, from Chitu's Cantonment at Nimawar, p. 133.

4 *Sydenham's Memorandum*, 1814, p. 14, para 3.

5 Even persons considered to be outcastes in society such as Jugglers and men who showed bears, tigers and other tame animals became Pindaris.

6 Fitzclarence : *Journal of a Route Across India*, p.8.

7 Tod : *Origin, Progress and Present of the Pindaris*, Part III, p. 21, Gwalior, 9 July 1815.

8 Malcolm : *A Memoir of Central India including Malwa and Adjoining Provinces*, Vol. II, p. 146, London, 1880.

9 On the 19th September, 1817 when Karim Khan was getting ready for the coming war against the British, his cantonment at Bersia caught fire and the whole of it was burnt to the ground. Karim was much disheartened at this accident which he considered as a bad omen.

N.A.I. For. Sec. 1817 : O.C. No. 9-10, 28 October, 1817, Jenkins to Adam, Nagpur, 9 October, 1817, enclosing a Translation of a Paper of Intelligence from Karim's camp.
Also : Supplement to the Government Gazette, Thursday, 6 November, 1817.

10 Malcolm : *A Memoir of Central India*, Vol. II, p. 147, foot-note 3.

11 Among the Hindus, to propitiate the souls of their dead relatives (Pitras) Brahmins are feasted. It begins from the period of dark moon preceding Dashera. This generally corresponds to the last fortnight of September.

12 N.A.I. : For. Sec. 1815 : O.C. No. 4, 8 December, 1815 : Jenkins to Adam, Nagpur, 17 November, 1815.
Also : H.R.R. S. No. 160, Vol. No. 200, Jenkins to Minto, 27 December, 1810.

Also : M.I.O.L.L. H.M.S. Vol. No. 511, Pol. Cons. No. 28, 14 December, 1810 & Pol. Cons. No. 45, 9 February, 1811.

13 B.G.R. D. No. 427 : Pol. Deptt. 1816 : Translation of a Paper of Intelligence from Chitu's Cantonment, 2 January, 1816. Please see App. III.

14 N.A.I. For. Sec. 1812 : O.C. No. 40, 17 April, 1812. Heads of a Narrative by Priag Ram Pande, Jagirdar of Billounja, giving an account of Mirzapur raid.

15 N.A.I. For. Sec. 1814 : O. C No. 2-3, 4 February, 1814, Sydenham to Russell, Aurangabad, 8 January, 1814.
Also : Intelligence from a Pindari Camp.

16 N.A.I. For. Sec. 1814: O.C. No. 2-3, 4 February, 1814, Sydenham to Russell, Aurangabad, 8 January, 1814.
Also : N.A.I. For. Sec. 1812: O. C. No. 2-6. 1 May, 1812 : Intelligence from a Pindarry Camp, 1 May, 1812.

17 Dunna Pindara reported "Jeejoo Pindarrah was my master. Ten years have elapsed since he made me a Moosulman." Uttar Pradesh Government Records : Mirzapur Collectorate, Pre-Mutiny Records, Letters issued November, 1811 to April, 1812. Vol. No. 75, Translation of the Heads of the Deposition of Dunna Pindarrah, as taken before the Acting Magistrate on the 19th and 20th March, and 5th April, 1812, p, 136.

18 Malcolm : *A Memoir of Central India*, Vol. II, p. 147.

19 H. Murray etc : *Historical and Descriptive Account of British India*, Vol. II, p. 189, 3rd Edition, London.

20 N.A.I. For. Pol. 1817 : O.C. No 25, 1 March, 1817, Jenkins to Adams, Nagpur, 8 February, 1817.

21 "The equipment of a Mongol warrior consisted of a Javelin...... bow and arrows, and a sword."

K.S. Lal: *History of the Khaljis*, p. 148, Allahabad, 1950. Likewise the Marathas were also armed with a large spear and a sword dangling by the side and a shield on the back.

22 N.A.I. For. Pol. 1811 : O.C. No. 60, 7 June, 1811, Jenkins to Lt. Gen. Hewett, Vice President in Council, Nagpur, 13 May, 1811.

Also : N.A.I. For. Pol. 1811 : O.C. No. 41, 25 October 1811, R. Strechey to Hewett, Scindia's Camp, 5 October, 1811.

Also : Fitzclarence : Journal of a Route Across India, p. 6.

23 H.R.R. S. No. 202, Vol. No. 203 : Translation of a Paper of Intelligence from Hindia, 14 October, 1815.

24 N.A.I. For. Pol. 1811 : O.C. No. 60, 7 June 1811, Jenkins to Hewett Nagpur, 13 May, 1811. Satwas is a small village near Hindia.

25 N.A.I. For. Pol. 1811 : O.C. No. 60, 7 June, 1811 : Jenkins to Hewett, Nagpur, 13 May, 1811.

26 *Summary of the Maratta and Pindaree Campaign*, p. 105.

27 H.R.R. S. No. 220, Vol. No. 424 : Capt. William's Observations, p. 214.

28 H.R.R. S. No. 220, Vol. No. 424 : Capt. William's Observations : p. 208

29 The Pindaris feed their horses with grain from the fields. But there is the typical instance of Chitu who enjoined them "to abstain from this practice and such as disobey are mounted on camels and led through the camp, but they do not obey his orders."

N A.I. For. Pol. 1817 : O.C. No. 37, 22 March, 1817 : Jenkins to Adam, Nagpur, 23 February, 1817.

30 McNaughten : *A Memoir of the N.S.F.* p. 109.

31 For. Misc. 124 A : Parliamentary Papers : Pindari Aggressions : Report from the Commission assembled at Cumbum, para 24.

32 *Capt. William's Observations*, Note E, pp. 225-226.

33 J.H. Stocqueler : *The Oriental Interpreter and Treasury of East India Knowledge*, p. 187, London.

34 H.R.R. S. No. 207, Vol. No. 268 : Col Doveton Commanding the Hyderabad Subsidiary Force to Russell, Resident at Hyderabad, enclosing information obtained from a Pindarry taken prisoner by the Mysore Horse.

Capt. William does not agree with this view. He was of the opinion that "after a very fatiguing march, when their cattle are much tired, those who have the means, give them a small quantity (about half a tola) made into a ball with some flour and a little ginger or some other stimulant." Thus this was the only occasion when opium and other things were administered to the horse or when the horse might be ill. Note 'B', p. 223.

35 *Capt. William's Observations : p.* 208.

36 McNaughten : *A Memoir of the N.S.F.*, p. 109.

37 *Capt. William's Observations*, p. 214,

38 H.R.R. S. No. 207, Vol. No. 268, Doveton to Russell, enclosing information obtained from a Pindarry prisoner by the Mysore Horse.

39 For. Misc. 124 A : Parliamentary Papers : Pindari Aggressions : Report from the Commission assembled at Cumbum, p. 60, para 34.

40 It was the custom of the Pindaris "to get ready during the Daserah season, September-October when the rivers became fordable, for incursion into the British territory following perhaps the tradition of the Kings of ancient India to start on the conquering expeditions *digvijayon* during the season."
Indian Historical Records Commission, Proceedings of Meetings, Vol. XVI, December 1939, Calcutta. "Defence of the Frontier of Bihar and Orissa against the Maratha and Pindary Incursions", by K.P. Mitra, p. 6

41 *Capt. William's Observations :* p. 204.

42 Please see glossary.

43 N.A.I. : For. Pol. 1817 : O. C. No. 37, 22 March, 1817, Jenkins to Adam, Nagpur, 23 February, 1817.

44 *Capt. William's Observations*, p. 205.

45 N.A.I. : For. Sec. 1815 : O.C. No. 6, 23 December, 1815, G. Wellesley, Acting Resident at Gwalior, to Adam, Scindiah's Camp, 4 December, 1815.

46 *Fakeers* and *Gossains* are generally employed "as spies, and their mendicant profession and wandering life, with the respect they receive and the access they obtain into the camps and towns, render them well calculated for the profession."
For. Misc. 124 A. P.P. Jenkins' Memorandum, 1812, p. 29.

47 B G.R. : D. No. 424, Pol. Deptt. 1815 : Translation of a Paper of Intelligence from Hindia dated 14 October, 1815.

48 Parliamentary Papers respecting the Pindarry and Maratta Wars : 1824 : For. Misc. 124 A : Report from the Commission assembled at Cumbum, p. 56, para 24.

49 *Sydenham's Memorandum*, Note, p, 63.

50 H.R.R. S. No. 219, Vol. No. 270 : Translation of a Paper of Intelligence from Hindia, 13 October, 1816, enclosed in a letter from Jenkins to Adam, 22 October, 1816.

51 Prinsep : *Transactions* : Vol. I, p. 40.

52 Parliamentary Papers : Extract from Capt. Sydenham's Memorandum of the Pindarries towards the close of 1809.

53 *Origin of the Pindaris :* By an Officer, Ch. V.
Also : Duff : *History of the Marathas*, Vol. II, p. 471, London, 1878.

54 *Ibid.*

55 N.A.I. : For. Pol. 1817 : O.C. No. 18, 11 February, 1817, Lt. Stewart's Report.

56 Night and middle of the day were reserved for rest.

57 *Cumbum Report*, p. 51, para 6.

58 This body of horse was expected not to embarrass themselves with spoil, a prohibition, which was most disregarded.

59 *Capt. William's Observations :* p. 210.

60 *Ibid.*

61 *Ibid.*

62 For. Misc. 124 A : Thomas Marriot Colonel and Commissioner of Kurnool, to Secretary to the Madras Government, 8 April, 1816, p.. 40.

63 For. Misc. 124 A : Papers respecting the Maratha Wars : Secret Letter from Bengal, 25 March, 1812, p. 9.
Also : *Sydenham's Memorandum*, 1809.

64 B.G.R. D. No. 288 : Pol. Deptt. Strachey to Moira, Scindia's Camp, 30 November, 1816. Strachey states that the Pindaris carried two depredations at the same time in as distant places as Mirz apur and Surat.

65 N.A.I. For. Sec. 1816 : O.C. No. 50, 30 March, 1816,
G. Wellesley to Adam, Scindia's Camp, 10 March, 1816.

66 Malcolm : *Rise and Progress* : Part VIII, para 4.

67 *Sydenham's Memorandum*, 1814, para 4, p. 17.

68 N.A.I. For. Pol. 1817 : O. C. No. 21, 11 February, 1817.
Russell to Adam, Camp at Neemgaon, 4 January, 1817.

69 N.A.I. For. Pol. 1817 : O.C. No. 95, 22 February, 1817,
Russell to Adam, Hyderabad, 23 January, 1817.

70 It is a remarkable fact, "and one of the few creditable to the late community of the Pindaries that among the numerous prisoners of all ages and sexes whom they took, though they employed them as servants, gave them to their chiefs, and accepted ransom for them from their relations, they never sold them into bondage, nor carried on, like the Brinjaries, a traffic in slaves."
Malcolm : A Memoir of Central India, Vol. II, p. 166.

71 H.R.R. S. No. 160, Vol. 200 : Letter No. 20, Jenkins, Resident at Nagpur, to Minto, 27 December, 1810.
Also : Private Journal, Vol. II, p. 112.

72 H. Martineau : *British Rule in India*, p. 252, Bombay, 1857.

73 The first "that was heard of this body, after its crossing the Nerbudda, was its appearance on the western frontiers of the districts of Masulipattam." Prinsep : *Transactions* : Vol. I, pp. 330-331. Also : Fitzclarence : Journal : p. 11.

74 B.G.R. D. No. 280, Item No. 2, Pol. Deptt. 1812 : R. Jenkins to Francis Warden, Chief Secretary to the Government of Bombay, 11 October, 1812.

75 N.A.I. For. Sec. 1817 : O.C. No. 1, 8 March, 1817, G.G.'s Minute, 21 January, 1817, p. 25.

76 For. Misc. 124A : Secret Letter from Fort St. George, 29 April, 1816.

77 B.G.R. : D. No. 393, Pol. Deptt. 1813 : J. Williams, Asstt. Incharge at Baroda Residency in a Letter to Warden dated 3 February, 1813 claims on what appears to be a hearsay account that the "Pindaris marched 125 *Koss* in a space of two days."

78 Seton, one of the Members of the Governor General's Council, represented the Pindaris "to be pre-eminent in acts of wanton and needless cruelty", whose rapacity and appetite for plunder was never whetted.

N.A.I. For. Sec. 1817 : O.C. No. 3, 8 March, 1817, Seton's Minute 3 March, 1817, p. 12.

79 Accustomed to "continual scenes of blood and rapine and their very subsistence depending chiefly on the miseries which they occasion to their fellow creatures, the Pindaris naturally acquire the most cruel disposition and the most licentious propensities." *Sydenham's Memorandum*, 1814, pp. 14-15, para 3.

Also : N.A.I. For. Sec. 1816 : O.C. No. 11, 28 December, 1816, Seton's Minute, 8 December 1816.

80 After one of the incursions Maj. Pepper while passing through some of the hills between Narsanrowpattah and Innacondah, observed the "poor miserable inhabitants creeping from their hiding places, for the purpose of obtaining water."

N.A.I. For. Sec. 1816 : O.C. No. 40-49, 20 April, 1816, Oakes, Collector Guntoor, to the Chief Secretary to the Government of Fort St. George, 21 March, 1816.

Also : N.A.I. For. Sec. 1816 : O.C. No. 18-23, 4 May, 1816, Newhanham, Magistrate Kudappa, to Madras Secretary, Kudappa, 28 March, 1816.

81 *Sydenham's Memorandum*, p. 14, para 3.

Also : Fitzclarence : *Journal of a Route*, p. 9.

82 Malcolm in a footnote mentions a very interesting piece of conversation he had with an old Pindari on the reasons for the absence of character and compunction in them, to which he gave

a very shrewd answer. He said, "our occupation was incompatible with the fine virtues and qualities you state, and I suppose if any of our people ever had them, the first effect of such good feelings would be to make them leave our community."
Malcolm : *Rise and Progress*, para 8.

83 Stocqueler : *The Oriental Interpreter*, p. 187.

84 Prinsep : *History Transactions* : Vol. I, p. 39.

85 *Cumbum Report* : pp. 54-56, para 19.

86 Sardesai : *New History of the Marathas* : Vol. III, p. 480.

87 *Sydenham's Memorandum*, 1814, p. 15, para 3.

88 N.A I. : For. Sec. 1816 : O.C. No. 40-49, 20 April, 1816, T.A. Oakes, Collector, Guntoor to the Chief Secy. to the Govt. of Fort St. George, 21 March, 1816.

89 *Cumbum Report*, p. 51, para 6.

90 Malcolm narrated an incident in which "the chief of Kanoongoe at 70 years of age was forced to ascend a high tree and remain till he produced the prescribed fine." Foot-note to para 23. Malcolm : *Rise, Progress & Administration of Pindaris*, of Malwa.
Also : Capt. William's Observations, p. 211.

91 N.A.I., For. Sec. 1816 : O.C. No. 40-49, 20 April, 1816, Oakes to the Chief Secy,, 21 March, 1816.
Also : For. Pol. 1817 : O.C. No. 19, 17 May, 1817, J. William, First Asstt. Incharge. Baroda Residency to Warden, Baroda, 26 March, 1817.

92 N.A.I.: For. Sec. 1816 : O.C. No. 11, 28 December, 1816, Minute of Mr. Seton, 8 December, 1816.
Also : N.A.I. : For. Sec. 1817 : O.C. No. 3, 8 March, 1817, Seton's Minute, 3 March, 1817, p. 12.
Pindaris the "inhuman wretches having cut off the breasts of the chaste and virtuous females, immediately after having committed upon their persons the worst of brutal violence, as if lust could not be completely gratified, unless followed up by murder."

93 Prinsep : *History Transactions*, p. 40.

94 For. Misc. 124 A : PP : Revenue Letter to Fort St. George, 22 April 1818, p. 64, para 2.

95 For. Misc. 124 A: PP : *Cumbum Report*, para 55.

96 For. Misc. 124 A : PP. Delzell to Madras Chief Secretary, 18 March, 1816.

97 Johar : An act of self-immolation performed as a last resort by the Rajput women on seeing their men-folk defeated and dying in action. To quote an instance of that heroic resolution which excites the admiration of man, "the inhabitants of Ainavote, a village in the western division of this district : on the approach of the merciless ruffians......, resolved to sacrifice themselves and their families, rather than submit to the ravishment of their wives and daughters ; and when their noble resistance was overpowered by

the superior strength of their assailants, they applied the torch of destruction to their habitations and perished with their relations in the general conflagration."
For. Misc. 124 A : Extract from a letter from Delzell to the Madras Chief Secretary, 18 March, 1816.

98 M.I.O.L.L.: Extracts from a letter by Mr. Lord, Magistrate of Nellore to the Chief Secretary at Fort St. George,
Also : M.I.O.L.L. H.M.S. : Vol. No. 511, Pol. Cons. No. 45, 9 February, 1811.

99 N.A.I. For. Sec. 1812 : O.C. No. 40, 17 April, 1817, Heads of Narrative by Priag Ram Pande, Jagirdar of Billomja, Mirzapur.

100 For. Misc. 124 A: PP. *Cumbum Report*, p. 56, para 19.

101 N.A.I. For. Sec. 1815 : O.C. No. 70-71, 20 June, 1815, Wauchope to Adams, Bandah, 3 June, 1815.
Also : N.A.I. For. Sec. O.C. No. 72-73, 20 June 1815 : Lt. Thomas Barron Comm. at Lohargaon, to Wauchope, Lohargaon, 4 June, 1815.

102 Lt. Col. R.G. Burton : *The Maratha and the Pindari War :* compiled for the General Staff : pp. 6-7.

103 Malcolm : *A Memoir of Central India*, Vol. II, p. 147.
Also : N.A.I. For. Sec. 1816 : O.C. No. 7, 1 June, 1816, Jenkins to Adam : Enclosing Translation of an Akhbar from a Newswriter at Hindia dated 22 May, 1816.

104 Scindia "not being satisfied at having received his share would sometime extort still large sums of money from the Pindaris. This would be done by Pindaris making an additional contribution to their ability. However, the Pindaris would not sit silently, they would retaliate by attacking upon his territories."

105 Although the Pindaris "may practice good faith in their internal dealings, the engagements which are formed between them and their employers are frequently violated on both sides. It is not uncommon for the Pindaris to rob the government which they serve and on the other hand, the government seldom loses an opportunity of extorting from them money under false pretenses."
For. Misc. 124 A : Papers Pindary & Maratha Wars : Letter from Sydenham, 18 March, 1810, p. 5
Also : Sydenham's Memorandum, 1814, p. 24, para 8.

106 The actual share of the leader has not being positively ascertained, because nobody has definitely mentioned about it. However, there are indications that it amounted to one fourth.

107 Malcolm : *A Memoir of Central India*, Vol. II, p. 147.

108 Thornton : *History of the British Empire*, Vol. IV, p. 420.

109 Sydenham's Memorandum, 1814, p. 23, para 8.

110 Capt. William gave an instance when "Kalu Rounce Ka Bheeka heard of an Ogura in his Thok, having gained about 600

rupees; as he had neglected giving any part of it to him, Bheeka took the whole by force."

Capt. William's Observations: Note D, p. 225.

111 Capt. William's Observations: p. 212.

112 The *Chelas* "of course deliver all their plunder to their immediate Chief".

Jenkins' Memorandum, 1812, p. 29.

113 Jenkins' Memorandum, p. 29.

114 N.A.I. For. Sec. 1812: O.C. No. 2-6, 1 May, 1812: Translation of the Heads of the Deposition by Dunna Pindarrah.

115 Malcolm: *Memoirs of Central India*, Vol. II, p. 147.
Also: Edward Thornton: *History of the British Empire In India*, Vol. IV, p. 420, London, 1843.

116 That "merchants were sent for from Ojjein to purchase many of the valuables obtained, those of Nemawur not being sufficiently wealthy."

Thornton: p. 330.

Also: "Three Seits in consequence have come from Ujjain with bills to the amount of three lacs for the purchase of it (jewellery). One of the *Sahookars* is a *Gomashtah* of Juggut Chand Seit, another of Chunni Lal Bhugwandas of Ojjein."
H.R.R.: S. No. 207, Vol. No. 531, Wellesley to Adams, enclosing extracts of news, p. 29

117 N.A.I.: For. Sec. 1814: O.C. No. 1-4, 11 February, 1814, Translation of Intelligence concerning the Pindaris from Burhanpur enclosed in a letter from Sydenham, 15 January, 1814.

118 Malcolm: *A Memoir of Central India*,, Vol. II, p. 147.

119 Thornton: *History of British Empire in India*, Vol. IV, pp. 420-21.

120 N.A.I. For. Sec. 1816: O.C. No. 5-6, 27 January, 1816, Translation of a Paper of Intelligence from Hindia, dated 1 January, 1816.

121 N.A.I. For. Sec. 1816: O.C. No. 40-49, 20 April, 1816, Oakes to Chief Secretary, 21 March, 1816.

Also: "The Pindaries never attempted to plunder the meanest village when the distance of a single matchlock was opposed to them."

N.A.I. For. Sec. 1816: O.C. No. 1-2, 27 January, 1816, C.C. Johnstone, Comdg. Field Force, Kurnool, to the Quarter Master General of the Army, Kurnool, 17 December, 1815.

122 N.A.I. For. Sec. 1812: O.C. No. 7-8, 3 April, 1812: Whitehead, Capt. Comdg., above the Ghats, to Gough, Major of Brigades, Lohargaon, 17 March, 1812.

Also : The Pindaris "did not attempt to defend themselves as they instantly sought shelter in the thicker part of the jungles." M.I.O L.L. : Vol. No. 520, Item No. 5, Letter from Resident at Nagpur, 30 October, 1816.

123 Sydenham's Memordandum, 1809, p. 2. "They avoid fighting, for they come to plunder and not to fight."

124 Burton : The Maratha and Pindari War, p 6.

125 N.A.I. For. Sec 1812 : O.C. No. 32-33, 30 October, 1812, R. Strachey to His Exellency Lt. Gen. Sir George Nugent, Scindia's Camp, 12 October, 1812.

Also : N.A.I. For. Sec. 1812 : O.C. No. 88-89, 25 February, 1815, C.T. Metcalfe Resident at Delhi to Adam, Scindia's Camp, 2 February, 1815.

126 The people of Central India and adjoining areas, who had to suffer the horrors of the raids, in their minds must have prayed like the Christians in the Churches of Eastern Europe, who had suffered at the hands of the Mongols. They used to pray : "from the fury of the Mongols, good Lord deliver us."

3

Pindari Leaders

Pindari Ancestry

To trace the growth of the predatory system in its various stages, a study of the ancestry of the leading Pindari chiefs is necessary.

The first Pindari chief of note was Gardi Khan.[1] As early as 1633, his great grandfather Nusroo, a Muslim of Tooraye tribe, had served in the artillery of Shahji under a Beldar. By dint of sheer intelligence and hard work, Nusroo had risen to the rank of *Jemadar* of Beldars. He was succeeded by Chicknie to the same post under Shivaji. His was an uneventful career. Chicknie died as a *Jemadar* and was succeeded by his son, Gazee-oo-deen Khan. This was the time when Sahu, the Maratha *roi faineant*, transferred the reins of the administration to Peshwa Baji Rao I. Gazee-oo-deen, who was in command of a small party of horsemen, came under the control of Baji Rao I. Baji Rao soon raised Gazee-oo-deen from the rank of *Jemadar* to that of *Bargeer*, a rank in the artillery section of the Maratha Army. Pleased with his work, he gave him, as a gift, the village of Satpurah.[2]

By 1730 Baji Rao had launched his grandiose schemes of conquests. In one of the expeditions to Ujjain in 1730, undertaken by Mulhar Rao Holkar against Daya Bahadur, the Mughal Subedar in Malva, Gazee-oo-deen was killed in action. Two sons survived him—Gardi Khan and Shahbaz Khan.

At the young age of sixteen, the elder son Gardi Khan succeeded his father in the command of the horse, and rapidly rose to eminence as a leader of the Pindaris. Mulhar Rao Holkar employed him for the purpose of plundering and devastating the enemy country and cutting off his supplies. He was, thus, a pioneer who set the Pindaris on the path which they were to follow in future, as auxiliaries to the Marathas. Gardi Khan, who was courageous and enterprising, eminently succeeded in this work. In recognition of his services, Mulhar Rao Holkar honoured him with a "*Zeree*", a golden flag,[3] which was considered a rare honour. This gave the Pindaris a sort of status in the Maratha Army. Within a short period his contingent increased considerably as large numbers of freebooters joined his camp. According to an estimate, at one time the number of his followers was thirty thousand and they formed a large and distinct part of Holkar's irregular army.[4] In 1735, Gardi Khan accompanied Holkar in another expedition to the north, in which he obtained a lot of booty. Again, pleased with thy meritorious services rendered by him and his followers, Mulhar Rao gave the village of Kannouj (on the north of the Narbada river) to Gardi Khan.[5]

Despite the faithful services rendered by Gazee-oo-deen and Gardi Khan, in the various expeditions to Hindustan, the respect that they commanded was not commensurate with their strength and usefulness. In fact, the Pindaris, as we have seen, were treated almost as outcastes. Maratha chiefs considered them of a low origin and generally treated them as their scavengers in plunder. No wonder, therefore, that the Pindari leaders were rarely allowed to present themselves before the Maratha chiefs, and even if permitted, the privilege of sitting was denied to them.[6] Although titles were conferred on them and land bestowed in recognition of their services, the Maratha chiefs always doubted the propriety of such favours. Thus, the Pindaris continued to occupy a very low place in the Maratha army till the period of the insanity of Jaswant Rao Holkar.

The death of Jaswant Rao Holkar witnessed a sudden increase in the strength of Pindari hordes which coincided with dissensions among the Maratha leaders. The gradual extension of the areas of Maratha expeditions in Northern India had its effect on the relationship between the Maratha chiefs and the Pindaris. No longer were the Pindaris mere servants acting on the orders of the Marathas; they were now beginning to enjoy more liberties.

To resume the narrative of the exploits of Gardi Khan, we find that he was acquiring great popularity and his strength rose to 30,000. At the time of his death in action at Ujjain in 1735, his followers amounted to 50,000 horses.[7] This force lived exclusively on plunder. In pursuance of the instructions of their overlords they laid waste village after village. The death of Gardi Khan meant a great loss to his fraternity.

Gardi Khan was succeeded by Lal Mohammad, a weakling. Under Lal Mohammad, the disintegration of the 'durra' began. Various *Jemadars* and *Torahdars* separated themselves and set up independent durras.

Imam Buksh followed Lal Mohammad and almost led the life of a pensioner in Bhopal. He was given a village in gift by Ahilya Bai, the Holkar Rani.[8] He hardly made his mark as a leader. His place in Holkar's service as a Pindari chief was taken by Kadir Buksh, "an ignorant but brave man". He too failed to make an impression on the events of the day. Tookoo and Bahadur Khan were the other two Pindari leaders of note, who were not in the direct line of the descendants of Nusroo. At the end of the Pindari campaign in 1818, Kadir Buksh surrendered to the British, who settled him at Gorakhpur while Tookoo and Bahadur Khan were granted cultivable lands for subsistence in Malwa.

Gazee-oo-deen had two sons—Gardi Khan and Shahbaz Khan. Gardi Khan joined the Holkar, and Shahbaz the Scindia.

Shahbaz Khan was a mere stripling at the time of his father's death and remained at Meeragaon, near Poona, the place of his birth. When he came of age, he entered the service of Ranoji Scindia as a Bargeer. After remaining as a *Bargeer* for a short period, Ranoji raised him to the command of a body of horse. Shahbaz Khan accompanied him in an expedition to the north, along with Ramchandra Ganesh and Tukoji Holkar. When he was killed in action at Tonk, he was succeeded by Heeroo and Burrun, who grew in importance as Pindari leaders, in the service of Mahadji Scindia. Both accompanied him to the north and were generally employed in the affairs of Northern India and were settled near Bersia. In recognition of the services rendered by them, Mahadji Scindia bestowed on them a 'jagir' in Satwas on the Narbada. When Mahadji Scindia died, they were in command of about 5,000 Pindaris. At that stage they offered their services to Bhopal, whose Nawab Chote Khan had died, and whose affairs were being looked after by his Dewan Raja Himmat Rao. Himmat Rao knew that the Pindaris were in the service of Scindia. He was, therefore, afraid of employing the Pindaris in an attack on Nagpur, which the latter had suggested, since it would embroil him with Scindia and complicate matters. Consequently, he did not accept the offer. The Pindari chiefs then changed their plan and placed their services at the disposal of Bhonsla Raja of Nagpur for an attack on Bhopal. This offer was gladly accepted by Raghoji Bhonsla. Bhopal was ravaged with vengeance, and the once flourishing city was laid waste. Malcolm wrote that right upto the time the Pindari war ended, Bhopal had not recovered from the terrible desolation wrought on it on this occasion.[9] However, the Pindari chiefs were not allowed to enjoy the fruits of their spoils, for, when they reached Nagpur with their loot, their camp was surrounded and subjected to a thorough plunder. Not only were the Pindaris looted but their chief leader Burrun was also captured. He, subsequently, died in confinement. Heeroo escaped and took shelter with Daulat Rao Scindia in Poona but soon afterwards died at Burhanpur.[10]

During Burrun's confinement, one Doobla Jemadar took over the command of his durra. After Doobla's death, the nominal command passed over to his son Rajun, but the real authority was assumed by Doobla's adopted son, Chitu. He distinguished himself by his tireless energy and enterprise and soon became the chief Pindari leader. The end of the Pindari campaign saw the indomitable Chitu carrying on the struggle single-handed. He was ultimately killed by a tiger.

The heredity of the Pindari chiefs clearly reveals that in the beginning they served the Marathas in petty positions of Bargeers and Jemadars. But they soon proved their worth in Maratha warfare and increased their influence and strength. This added to the prestige and reputation of the hereditary leaders of the Pindari organization. In some cases, however, other leaders like Chitu, not claiming hereditary connections with the Pindari chiefs, also exacted due respect and recognition because of their services to the Pindari cause.

Pindari Leaders—Their Lives

Courageous and strong, fierce and desperate, confident and enterprising, capable of undergoing the utmost privations and fatigue, the Pindari chiefs were an extraordinary lot. Even in the most hazardous situations they remained undaunted and displayed great qualities of judgment and leadership.[11] To Capt. Williams, these people with a degree of discipline were likely to be most formidable instruments in the hands of an able and ambitious chief.[12] They enjoyed the trust and confidence of the mass of the Pindaris. But the glamour of their personality was blighted by the nefarious activities of plunder and loot which they pursued throughout their lives, making them the most contemptible, cruel and rapacious people of their times. The Pindaris had a devil-may-care attitude towards life.

With the decline of Maratha power, the Pindari chiefs began adding to their possessions by conquests or gifts. A few adventurous leaders like Karim and Amir Khan even aspired to become full-fledged rulers.

The life-sketches of the various Pindari leaders traced here, not only give us an insight into their activities, but also throw light on the growth of their organisation.

Heeroo and Burrun

Heeroo and Burrun were two of the most celebrated Pindari Chiefs. Burrun first took up service in 1797 with the Raja of Berar[13] and not long afterwards he attached himself to Scindia. They soon quitted his service and settled in Malva near Bhilsa. However, they remained loyal to the House of Scindia, since the time of Ranoji and Mahadji.

The two chiefs were inimical towards each other on account of the murder of Mohammad Hussain, Burrun's son, perpetrated by Heeroo. There are two versions about their own deaths. According to one version, both had died a natural death. The other and the commonly accepted version is that Heeroo died at Burhanpur and Burrun in his confinement at Nagpur.[14] Heeroo left two sons, Dost Mohammad and Wasil Mohammad; and Burrun, the two Rajuns, the younger and the elder.

Dost Mohammad

The next in name and consequence, after Heeroo was the eldest of his two sons, Dost Mohammad. At one time, he was a leader of great distinction among the Pindaris, while in the employ of the Raja of Nagpur. In 1804 Dost Mohammad succeeded his father in command of his Pindaris.

He was the nominal head of the Scindia Shahi Pindaris. He received the land of Bagrode from Scindia, but this did not exempt the latter's territory from plunder to which it was usually subjected. He built a fort there, which was, however, incapable of defence as it was not on a high elevation and without a ditch around it. There was another and smaller defenceless fort at Dahanode[15]. He had for long lived in Gyaraspur also. By way of a grant, he received the village of Choti Bari from the Bhonsla Raja, though the village belonged to Bhopal. His revenues were considerable. In 1811, according to Jenkins his annual revenue amounted to Rs. 1,95,000[16] which soon rose to Rs. 9,50,000[17]. This was distributed as follows[18]:—

Pergunna	Computed Revenues	Remarks
Bagrode	50,000	
Dhammode	30,000	Near Bagrode to the east.
Gunj Bassodah	1,50,000	16 miles west of Bagrode.
Aroon and Sarorah	3,00,000	Assigned by Daulat Rao Scindia.
Selwanee, Belwance and Chunowteeac	4,00,000	On the north bank of Narbada. These lands originally belonging to Bhopal were seized by Pindaris from the Raja of Berar.
Annual contribution levied from Agur	20,000	
	9,50,000	

Thus Dost Mohammad controlled extensive lands viz., Bagrode, Dhammode, Gyaraspur near Bhilsa, Ratgarh, Barrah, Sehore and Mhow in Saugar and Deoree region; Chatoor Chitrapur, Jytharee and Oodipur near Chainpur Baree and Karangarh[19].

In 1811, Dost Mohammad had 2,430 horse, 400 infantry, and 8 guns.[20] However, in 1814 he had 4,000 cavalry, 1,200 infantry and 7 guns[21]. His strength was considerably increased with the dispersion of Karim Khan's force. His durra consisted of about, 10,000 horse including 8000 matchlockmen and about 7 guns.[22] Besides, he had a considerable body of irregulars also, both in cavalry and infantry. One section of his Pindaris served Vazier Mohammad Khan of Bhopal. His strength in early 1814 was[23]:

Horse of all descriptions	16,000
Foot including two Battalions of Matchlockmen	4,000
Total	20,000
Guns, of which two were cast in 1814	6

He had one 'Bazar', one 'Jhunda', one 'Nishan' or 'Luggee', one 'Naubat' on a camel and one 'Singh' or horn. His flag was of 'Bhagwa' (saffron) colour.[24] His chief supporters and officers were his brother Wasil Khan, Jemadar Ghulam Hussain, Ramzan, Abdulla etc. It is significant that his durra contained more Muslims than any of the other Pindari forces.[25]

During the last few years of his life, he never left Bagrode. He died a peaceful death, while in camp at Churan Teeruth, near Bhilsa on 7th March, 1815[26].

Unlike other Pindari chiefs, Dost Mohammad was very much faithful to Daulat Rao Scindia, who, in turn, allowed him the privilege of retaining the booty secured in plunder. He was always ready to serve Scindia at a moment's call.[27]

Wasil Mohammad

The younger son of Heeroo, Wasil Mohammad was also a Pindari leader of note. He was a man of medium height, and of a complexion darker than that of his brother Dost Mohammad. He wore a plain turban,

On the death of Dost Mohammad in 1815, Wasil Mohammad assumed the command and leadership of the Pindaris of both the parties. Consequent upon the increase in his power, his boldness and ferocity also increased. His depredations extended far and wide.

Kadir Buksh

Kadir Buksh and his father Burrun,[28] a renowned Pindari chief, were both confined by Bhonsla. When Burrun died, the teen-aged Kadir Buksh was still in jail. However, on the eve of the Maratha War of 1803, Kadir Buksh was released on Scindia's intercession. Though short in stature, he had a fair complexion. Brave and enterprising, he lived entirely on plunder. He did not have much of land except Nalkhera near Ujjain. Holkar had granted him some land, which he neglected completely and allowed it to remain fallow. Having little to depend upon, he supplemented his resources by what he received from the Nawab of Bhopal. For some time he had no alternative but to act in collusion with the Nawab of Bhopal against Scindia. His cantonment was at Raiseen. He commanded about a thousand horse, of which fifty were of a fairly good description. Later, his strength increased. According to an estimate he had 2,150 horse, 800 infantry,[29] 4 guns, 4 elephants, one 'singh', one 'jhunda', one 'bazar' and one 'nishan' or 'lugee'. His 'Russuldars' had a 'singh' and a 'luggee' each. He was a Holkar Shahi Pindari. His supporters were:

Bahadur	300 Horse
Bomdela	200 Horse
Mulkhan	200 Horse
Bhure Khan	700 Horse
Chuttan	300 Horse
Nalena	100 Horse

Imam Buksh

Imam Buksh or Noor-ool-Moolkas, as he was also called, was the son of Lal Mohammad.[30] Imam Buksh was a hereditary Pindari. His grandfather Nathoo was in the employ of Malhar Rao Holkar. He possessed a rare distinction as his family was of "the real Pindari caste, that is from time immemorial, to have been Pindaris".[31] He had a son Gulam Kadir by name.

He received lands from Holkar, viz., Hurrangaon, Kurwande and Kantapur near Bhopal. His lands adjoined that of Karim, with whom he had matrimonial alliance. His daughter was married to Namdar Khan, a nephew of Karim. He had about 450 horses of very good and middling character. He commanded about 2,000 horse, and 1,000 infantry, with two guns[32]. He had 4 elephants, 2 jhundas, one luggee, one singh, and one bazar. His flag was yellow. His 2,000 cavalry was divided as under[33]:—

Private Pagah	100
His Russaldars who each had a Luggee were as follows :	
Junglee Rao	300
Nathoo	200
Khuda Buksh	400
Pardesees, Marathas, etc.	1,000
Total Pindaris under Imam Buksh	2,000

Imam Buksh commanded all the Pindaris who were with Holkar.[34]

Bappoo Khan

Bappoo Khan was the leader of 1,000 horse only under Imam Buksh. He was a Holkar Shahi Pindari. At Holkar's behest a few villages were given to Bappoo Khan by Imam Buksh, who had earlier usurped them from Mian Khan Pindari[35] to whom these villages were given originally by Bappoo Khan's father.

Rajun

The two Rajuns were sons of Doobla Mehar, the original patron of Chitu. The two brothers were known as Bara and Chota Rajuns.

The Bara Rajun was a man of short stature, stout and of dark complexion. He had a sword wound on his right arm, which he was unable to use. He was mostly dressed in the Maratha fashion.

Rajun was intimate with Vazir Mohammad Khan, the Nawab of Bhopal. He had a son named Ilahi Buksh.

When Chitu was captured by Daulat Rao Scindia in 1807, Rajun went over with his entire durra to Holkar, where he was received well. On Amir Khan's mediation, Holkar conferred upon him the title of Nawab Raja Mohammad Ikhtear O' Doula[36] and gave him a flag of gold cloth and an elephant.[37] He was also granted Turana and Kaitha parganas, yielding a revenue of 20,000 per annum.[38]

The younger Rajun or Chota Rajun, as he was popularly known, was a tall and fair man.

Satwas was their headquarters, where the families of the two chiefs were kept. A small force of two hundred infantry and four guns was garrisoned for protection. To meet any emergency, adequate stocks of grain were maintained. The durras of Chitu and the Rajuns were stationed at a village Bhooreah, at a short distance from Satwas. A small force of 500 Sikh infantry with guns was posted for guarding the different approaches to Satwas.[39]

Though Rajun, the elder, had no great personal influence, yet owing to his ancestry he commanded more respect than any other Pindari leader. Even Chitu, the *de facto* leader of Doobla Jemadar's durra, paid respect to Rajun, continued to treat him as his elder, and consulted him frequently. Rajun seldom went on distant expeditions and rarely treated the 'ryots' harshly. He was reputed to be humane and moderate in character.[40]

Chitu

Chitu, a *Jat* by birth, belonged to the Mewati tribe, who were well-known for their licentiousness. In his childhood he was bought during a famine by Doubla Mehar or Doobla Khan[41], a Jemadar in Burrun's durra, while on an expedition with Mahadji Scindia to Gohud,[42]

He was adopted and brought up as a 'Kunwar' or son by Doobla in the true fashion of a Pindari.[43] After Doobla's assassination at Asirgarh in 1793, on Karim's instigation,[44] his two sons, the two Rajuns, continued to be considered as the head of the durra. But for all practical purposes, Chitu, who after many vicissitudes had risen to power and influence, now commanded a very strong durra, because of his superior abilities and daring spirit.

Chitu was greatly indebted to Karim for his rise to power. However, rivalry for leadership resulted in enmity between them to such an extent that he even made an unsuccessful attempt to kill Karim and his brother Heeroo.[45] Failing in his attempt, Chitu took shelter with Raza, a minor Pindari chief.

Chitu was a man of great foresight. He realised that difficult times lay ahead for the Pindaris. He, therefore, set up his headquarters in the hills and wild regions of the Narbada and the Vindhyachal mountains. Though his cantonment was at Nimawar, he mostly lived at Satwas. Mahadeo Rao was his Diwan and Appaji Pant was his 'Fadnavis'.[46] Mangi Ram and Dhakun Seth were the bankers in his durra, advancing funds, either for the purchase of horses or for meeting their daily needs. These loans were promptly repaid after a plundering excursion.[47]

Sarje Rao Ghatge, a powerful Maratha chief and father-in-law of Daulat Rao Scindia, was very favourably disposed towards the Pindaris. In 1805, Scindia honoured Chitu with titles. He was given the title of Nawab and he assumed the pompous name of Nawab Mohammad Kamal Khan Mustakeen Jung Bahadur.[48] But he continued to be called by the common and more popular name of Chitu. However, he maintained his position, status and dignity by receiving a salute of five guns and the beating of drums on return from excursions.[49]

In spite of his allegiance to Scindia, he had made himself virtually independent of him. Even his master's territories were not exempt from his depredations. No wonder that Scindia had been forced to send expeditions against Chitu, but none was successful in bringing him to book. A competent critic has attributed this failure to the insincerity of the ruler, the weakness of those employed, the mutinies of their troops or the collision of interests which continually existed between the half-independent chiefs of Scindia.[50] Jean Baptiste, a French general of Scindia, was entrusted with the task of defeating Chitu and other Pindaris. He succeeded in concluding with them formal agreements by which it was settled that the Pindaris would refrain from plundering Scindia's territories and would furnish small contingents to serve Scindia, who would give land to them for their maintenance. After some hesitation Scindia ratified these treaties, and 'sanads' were granted to them. Chitu received the Panj Mahals—Nimar, Rajgarh, Talien, Satwas and Kil-lichpur. This was the "first occasion on which he was recognized as a chief in the exercise of legitimate rule."[51] Chitu was then at the apex of his power and position. Besides the above grants of lands, Chitu had received Singpur Bari and Chipaner from Bhonsla; and Leileepur from Vazier Mohammad Khan.[52] His revenues[53] which amounted to five lakhs and eighty seven thousand rupees were distributed as follows :

Satwas and other districts to the yearly amount of	1,00,000
Arone, Shadhowra and the Panj Mahals received from Scindia	3,00,000
Jageers usurped from Peshwa	20,000
Jageers received from the Raja of Nagpur-Kuerleara and Chi-choolee	1,67,000
Total Jagir held by Chitu and Rajuns	5,87,000

Chitu, who was a capable organiser, displayed considerable ability in administering his lands. Sir John Malcolm, who later took possession of his lands, was deeply impressed with "the indications of a regular form of government, as far as such a state of things could exist in Malwah."[54]

In April 1807, Chitu, like Karim, was arrested while in Scindia's camp and sent to Gwalior. His durra went over to Holkar and remained with Amir Khan, who allowed them to settle their families in the fort of Raiseen.[55] Almost all the Pindaris then made continual and infrequent inroads in the territories of Scindia. However, negotiations were opened soon after and by the end of 1811 Chitu was released.

Soon after his release Chitu joined hands with Karim for a brief period.

Chitu had a force consisting of about 25,000 Pindaris. He posted them all over his lands. His troops were dispersed on duty at various points. The durras of Chitu and Rajun and those of other minor Holkarshai Pindaris were stationed within a short distance of one another. The following parties of the Pindaris were encamped at Hindia, Satwas, Kuppas, Kanode and between these places and the Narbada.[56]

Under Chitu	15,000
Kadir Buksh	2,000
Bara Bhai's	3,000
Sahib Khan Jemadar	2,000
Bahadur Khan	2,000
Bhika	1,000
	25,000

In addition to the above force, he maintained 2,000 infantry, for garrisoning the forts etc., as 'Seebundees' in his districts and as guards in this camp. Mewatees were largely recruited in his durra. He had six elephants, two *palkees*, a *naubat*, two grand *bazars*, two flags, besides one hundred *hircarras* (Scouts). The flag of Chitu was of a *bhugwa* colour with a small white snake in the centre. His first standard was presented to him by the Bhonsla Raja of Nagpur.[57] The hircarra sticks too, were headed by a small snake's head, which was made of silver. Some of the petty *Jemadars* like Bhiku Lodi and Sahib Khan also had their own bazars and standards and encamped separately from Chitu's camp.

Chitu had twelve guns, some of which were placed at Satwas and Nimawar. By 1811, he had employed two or three Europeans for casting his guns.[58] Unlike other Pindari chiefs, he went out on excursions, only at the head of the whole durra or the greatest part of it. If half of it moved, Rajun commanded it; if they went in a group of three or four thousand, they were usually headed by Kallo Bakra or Sheikh Dulla etc.

Ummaid Kunwar, Junglee Kunwar, Hari Kunwar and Kalloo Kunwar were his principal officers.[59] Though blind of one eye, Ummaid Kunwar, who commanded Satwas, was an excellent officer. When Kushal Kunwar and Wasil Mohammad attacked Satwas, he very ably defended it. Junglee Kunwar was incharge of Singpur Bari; Hari Kunwar looked after Chipaner; Kalu Kunwar was household Superintendent of Chitu.

Holkar Shahi Pindaris looked upon Chitu as their friend, philosopher and guide. He, on his part, cared for their general welfare. At one time, he would help them with money; at another, he would negotiate with the Indian Rajas to obtain some grant of land for the Pindaris.

In his personal appearance, Chitu was a man of middle stature and had a fine physique. He had an oval face with moustaches and a wheatish complexion. He was bald and had a few broken teeth. He wore the short Maratha drawers, also called 'Ghurghees' and sometimes he wore the Muslim long drawers. He always wore a turban in the Pathan fashion.[60] He had a son named Mohammad Punnah, who was of nearly the same stature, complexion and appearance and wore similar dress as his father, but was lean.

Chitu was undoubtedly one of the ablest of the Pindari chiefs, as well as the most powerful of the class. He was a man of great art and prudence. By treating the two Rajuns with consideration he was able to conciliate the Pindaris who had great respect for the Rajuns. His word was honoured without any reservation while that of others could be disobeyed. He enjoyed the confidence of Scindia, with whom he had acquired great influence. According to Blacker, his character was "comparatively superior."[61]

Liberal by nature, Chitu distributed land among his followers, while other leaders never did anything of the kind.[62] Consequently, most of the leaders of small bodies, who did not derive any advantage from the Jagirs held by their chiefs, were forced to go out on plundering excursions to maintain themselves.[63]

He was an intrepid warrior. In personal bravery he was second to none. It was he who exhorted the Pindaris to carry on the struggle, when all of them wanted to give up because most of them thought that their cause was doomed. To this Chitu replied that they "had no place to go to and that they had therefore better made one (more) effort."[64] This may be animal courage, yet courage he had, courage to fight against the mighty British. Chitu had acquired such confidence in his power that even at a time when there was peace, he boasted that "to punish the English is easy." In one of his letters to Scindia he solicited his help but at the same time told him that in case his help was not forthcoming "the six durras will form six separate bodies and will ravage and destroy the country of the English."[65] It may be mere boast, but at least it shows how brave and resolute Chitu was. On one occasion he said that once provision had been made for his family, he would carry fire and sword to the environs of Calcutta and that he would distribute the Company's land amongst the Pindaris.[66] He was a man of extra-ordinary doggedness and tenacity. Once he had taken a decision, he would not flinch from it, whatever the obstacles. Having entered the fray with the English, he carried on the struggle single-handed, till the last moment.

Karim Khan

Boodun,[67] a Jemadar of Rane Khan in Mahadji Scindia's service, who fought in the battle of Panipat,[68] had a son named Karim Khan,[69] who was born near Bersia.[70] When his father was killed in action at Shahpur, Karim was still of a very tender age.[71] He was then brought up by Yar Mohammad, his uncle. He showed an aptitude for a life of adventure from the very beginning, and at the early age of fourteen, commanded nearly a thousand horse. In the battle of Khurda in 1794, he gained a larger booty "than he ever did at any other period of (his) life."[72] Thereafter he went to Malwa and took up service with Jaswant Rao Holkar and served with him for a few years. Subsequently, he joined Amir Khan, who ceded to him Kokra, in the district of Shujawalpur, of which he later became the complete master. He also served and secured the grant of some land[73] from Hyat Mohammad Khan, the Nawab of Bhopal, whom he helped in defeating the Bhonsla Raja of Nagpur. Karim got an immense booty out of this enterprise. He dates his rise from this time. He then joined Scindia, who on the recommendations of Sirjee Rao Ghatge, bestowed upon him honours and confirmed him in the possession of Shujawalpur and Bersia. Scindia raised him from the position of a Jemadar and honoured him with the title of Nawab Sarfaraz-o-Daolah.[74] An elephant for his *naubat* was also presented. Soon he built a fort at the site of a former village Jerkeerah, and named it Karimgarh. Meanwhile, Karim continued to roam about the whole of the country, looting, plundering and carrying fire and sword. At that stage, he managed to obtain possession of some of the lands of Scindia and his Jagirdars. At the end of the Maratha War in 1803-1804, Karim possessed a pretty extensive, compact and well cultivated country, fairly-governed. He seemed to have a regular system and an organised form of government. In 1805, in order to raise his position, status and respectability, Karim Khan persuaded Nawab

Gaus Mohammad of Bhopal to marry his daughter to him.[75]

When war broke out between the British and the Marathas, Karim joined hands with Amir Khan and, taking advantage of the disturbed times as well as the absence of Scindia and Holkar, seized Ashta, Sehore, Itchwar, Shujawalpur, Sarangpur and Shahajahanpur. This was in addition to the lands which he already held, viz., Satwas and Chipaner. He was then the master of eleven pergunnas[76] yielding a revenue of "more than fifteen lakhs of rupees."[77] The leadership of a big durra, and possession of vast and fertile lands did not free him from the traits of a Pindari. In his own district, Malcolm writes, "Men possessed of property were oppressed" and "all without his limits were given to the rapacity of his followers except such as chose to save themselves by the payment of annual contribution to this chief."[78]

Thus, because of loot or collection of tributes, or fine, or compensation for immunity from plunder paid by neighbouring chiefs, or revenue from his lands, Karim's treasury was always full. He was at this time at the zenith of his power. For the first time a Pindari chief appeared to be on the point of becoming the ruler of an organised State.[79] Among the Pindari chiefs "there was none whose means or influence at all approximated to those of Karim." Want of artillery was one of the obstacles in the fulfilment of his ambitious designs.

Karim entered into an alliance with Vazier Mohammad Khan of Bhopal for the express purpose of recovering Raiseen and Hoshangabad, which were then held by Nagpur. In 1806, he was in possession of at least eleven districts of Bhopal with a revenue of about five lakhs, of which Shujawalpur, Bersia, Sarangpur, Ichawar and Chipaner were the most important.[80]

Thereafter, the drama of Karim's life entered its denouement. Even though Karim was virtually independent, he continued to owe allegiance to Scinida for the sake of convenience in order to seek his protection in case of emergency.

He tried to enter Bhopal with the help of Gaus Mohammad, but Vazier Mohammad proved too shrewd and alert to be taken in, and therefore, Karim was compelled to seek fortune elsewhere. Just at that moment he received summons from Scindia to wait on him.

Daulat Rao Scindia viewed the rise of Karim Khan to power with alarm and anxiety. His meteoric rise had excited his fear and jealousy. He realised it well that it was not possible for him to destroy the power of Karim Khan by honest and open warfare[81] and hence resorted to treachery. In 1806, he extended an invitation to Karim Khan which the latter accepted much against the advice of his followers and with fear lurking at the back of his mind. Continued success had added to his vanity and increased his confidence. Karim Khan in a most noble and royal dress, no less pompous than Daulat Rao Scindia's,[82] advanced to meet Scindia with a force of 3,000 chosen horse. Scindia was encamped at Ketchegwarrah, near the fortress of Suttunbaree, belonging to a Grassia chief. For long, Karim had been contemplating the addition of Suttunbaree to his lands. Shrewd as he was, Scindia promised that the fort would be handed over to him after its reduction. Like a consummate artist, he praised Karim Khan (not without foundation) for his administrative talents and abilities. Scindia flattered his vanity to giddy heights when he told him that he would soon entrust the province of Malwa to his excellent management. To convince him of his sincerity, he declared his intention to visit his camp. Karim at once started making necessary preparations to accord a fitting welcome to his liege-lord. A *musnad* and a *chabootra* (high seat) were erected by heaping one lakh and twenty five thousand rupees,[83] covered with rich muslin cloth on which Scindia was seated when he visited his vassal. The whole money was to be given to Scindia as '*Nuzur*' (present). Scindia was all praise for Karim Khan. He shrewdly pretended that in Karim Khan he had found exactly those very remarkable qualities of a statesman and a soldier which he had for so long sought in vain. Having been flattered,

Karim prayed that a number of districts be assigned to him in return for four and a half lakhs of rupees, to which Daulat Rao Scindia readily agreed. Besides, he also offered to transfer Islamnagar, Ganj Bassonda and Bhilsa for which Karim had requested some time ago.

Scindia employed another stratagem to allay his suspicions. Immediately after his arrival, Karim appealed to his 'lord' to conquer Suttunbaree for him. Scindia promptly agreed and with one great effort brought the fortress under his control. To throw Karim off his guard, he ordered *Sunnuds* to be prepared to be given to Karim and an investiture was arranged. Karim Khan with a few followers went to receive the *Sunnuds* and the keys of the fortress. When everything seemed all right, Daulat Rao Scindia on some pretext withdrew and that was a signal for attack. Armed men from behind the tent walls rushed in and Karim Khan, the vainglorious Pindari leader, and some of his followers, were bound up. A gun was immediately fired, when the army, kept in readiness for the purpose, rushed upon the rest of the Pindaris, who escaped towards Bhopal and Raghogarh.[84] Though the loss of lives was insignificant, Scindia's army obtained a huge plunder.[85] Hearing the news of her son's arrest, Karim's mother and other members of her family ran for their lives to the jungles of Baglee with whatever they could carry and ultimately took shelter in the territories of Zalim Singh, the Raja of Kota. She and her son Shahamat Khan were allowed to settle in the village of Belandi, in the pargana of Chipabarod. All facilities were provided to her, including free supply of firewood. Karim was shut up in the fort of Gwalior to spend his time in a solitary dungeon. He was thus "tumbled from the height of prosperity to the gloom of a prison."[86]

The Pindari followers of Karim who had escaped, now directed their attention to Scindia's territories. Kushal Kunwar, Namdar Khan, Karim's nephew, and Shahmut Khan his son, motivated by red-hot anger and desire to avenge themselves inflicted as much injury on Scindia as they possibly could.

In 1811, when Karim had been in prison for four years, negotiations were started with Scindia for his release. On learning of the latter's intention to free Karim and Chitu, Mr. Strachey, then resident at Delhi, represented to Scindia that the release of Karim and Chitu was unwarranted, unjust and impolitic in his own interests. The Raja of Nagpur was also alarmed and tried in vain to dissuade Scindia from his intentions. Scindia's avarice overcame his prudence and this "pest was let loose on society."[87] Karim was set free on payment of six lakhs of rupees,[88] in November 1811. But he had to leave his brother Heeroo at Gwalior as a hostage for his future good conduct.[89] Daulat Rao Scindia also tried to amend his past conduct by honouring Karim and giving him presents. A *Khilut* with elephants, horses, palanquins and all the insignia of a chief of first rank were given to him so that he could forget the severities and indignities practised on him during his captivity. But the wound inflicted upon him was too deep to be healed so easily. Shortly after his release, his old adherents and new recruits too gathered around his flag. His army then amounted to 25,000 cavalry and some infantry. His depredations extended far and wide. He was soon in possession of lands more extensive than those which he had possessed before his capture. Scindia was the first to feel the impact of his avaricious policy and bore the full brunt of Karim's hostility. But Karim was able to enjoy his liberty for a few months only. Soon he was in captivity in Holkar's court. During his confinement, Karim was very slightly guarded,[90] often going for hunting without an escort. Consideration was also given to the question of his release; whereupon, the British[91] and the Scindia[92] repeatedly wrote to Holkar strongly protesting against the proposed move. Holkar's attention was particularly drawn to the injury Karim was likely to cause to Holkar himself, as Scindia had earlier suffered. However, Karim Khan soon managed to escape from Holkar's camp and joined his durra at Bersia. On a representation made by the British at the escape of Karim, Holkar disowned all responsibility and passed the same on to a mutinous section of his army. However, Metcalfe maintained that Karim escaped with the connivance of some of Holkar's officers.[93] This was the period when the British were entering Malwa to exterminate the Pindaris. Karim at that time made, in vain, repeated overtures to the British for entering British service[94] in return for grant of some lands and property.

A letter attributed to Daulat Rao Scindia, the authenticity of which is very doubtful, instigated Karim to join hands with the Marathas in a bid to overthrow the British. Karim joined Wasil Mohammad and the two were to join Scindia at Gwalior. Karim then received a message from Scindia disowning the Pindaris and ordering them to keep away from him. This enraged the Pindaris who plundered Scindia's territories, but soon Karim had to flee for life.

Karim was one of the most active and enterprising of the Pindari leaders, and was distinguished for his cunning. Even in his defeat he commanded great respect and honour amongst the Pindaris who voluntarily joined him in his reduced state.[95] He was a man of considerable ability. But he had a great weakness for women and whenever he saw a handsome woman, he carried her off forcibly.[96]

As early as 1811, Karim Khan collected a fairly strong body of Pindaris. He had two battalions of Infantry, well-disciplined and commanded by a European named Ball,[97] fourteen guns of different calibre and six to eight thousand cavalry very well mounted. When at the height of his power, he had 10,000 horse and 1,000 infantry.

Karim, as a result of grant and conquest was able to amass huge lands from Scindia, Bhopal and Nagpur. He held the 'Punj Mahals' consisting of Ashta, Sehore, Doraha, Devipur, Sarungpur, Sohagpur, Kushalpur and Bahadurgarh.[98]

His cavalry was distributed as follows:-[99]

Name of the Leader	*Horses*
Kushal Kunwar	350
Imam Buksh	315
Namdar Khan	275
Deedar Buksh	203
Khuda Buksh	164
Tookkoo	159
Buksh Khan	155
Ramzani	134
Nathoo Jemadar	132
Dharma Jemadar	86
Bheeka Kunwar	12
Holkar Kunwar	10
Bhurna Kunwar	5
Good Horse	2,000
Looters and Followers	2,000
Total Force	4,000

Amir Khan

Amir Khan is one of the most striking Indian personalities of the early 19th century. He cannot be regarded as a Pindari chief, but he was one of the patrons of the Pindaris and his association with them was very intimate.

Unlike the Pindari chiefs, Amir Khan came of a very respectable family. Nawab Ameerood-doula-Mohammad-Amir Khan was, by birth, an Afghan of the Rohilla Tribe.[100] His father Mohammad Hyat Khan was a priest,[101] who owned some land in Sambhael, Rohilkhand.

According to Busawan Lal, a contemporary of Amir Khan, "a star of the constellation of glory, and a sun in the heaven of renown,[102] Amir Khan "came forth like a constellation in the zodiac of honour."[103] He was born at Farrukhabad in the Hijri year 1182, (16 May 1768 to 6 May 1769).[104] While still in his teens, he left home against his father's wishes, joined Ghulam Kadir Khan's army, but soon returned home. At the age of twenty, he again left home and by turns served Najaf Kuli Khan, Raja Bagh Singh of Khetri, Bijai Singh of Jodhpur, Ismail Beg Khan, Gaekwad of Baroda, a Pandit of Nasik, Naro Shankar Pandit, Bala Rao, Raja Jai Singh, Durjan Sal and finally Jaswant Rao Holkar.[105] For a very brief period he served Mahadji Scindia, under the leadership of Muzzuffar Khan, in whose cavalry he received his military initiation. After Mahadji's death, Amir Khan's services were transferred to Daulat Rao Scindia[106] but soon he resigned this service too. The Nizam was also his employer for a very short period.[107] During all these services Amir Khan and his followers were employed as Seebundees or local militia with an average pay of fifteen rupees a month. During these services, he employed Pindaris freely to assist him in his jobs.[108] He also served Gaus Mohammad of Bhopal, as *Killedar* of Fatehgarh fort.[109]

Amir Khan distinguished himself in one of the actions under Lachman Rao, Jagirdar of Mahipatpur against Raja Jai Singh and Durjan Sal, the Grassia chiefs, in honour of which his command was raised to five hundred men. He was presented with a '*Palkee*' and he became a *Palkee Nusheen.*[110]

Amir Khan's service with Jaswant Rao Holkar laid the "foundation of a firm and lasting friendship" and proved to be the turning point of his career.[111] "He rose to the possession of that power and influence which rendered him formidable as a predatory chief",[112] and an eminent disturber of peace. Most cordial relations prevailed between them. The desperate fortunes of Jaswant Rao Holkar in 1798 brought Amir Khan in close contact with the Holkar a connection which ultimately proved disastrous to the family; for the time being, however, it proved beneficial to them both.

Amir Khan was as much devoted to plunder as any other Pindari[113] chief but he was different from them in some respects. He was more systematic and consistent in his actions. There was a stag, when he moved about with all the paraphernalia of a regular army, aiming, unlike the Pindaris, at political influence.

Amir Khan began his relations with Jaswant Rao Holkar on the basis of equality and "as companion in arms."[114] But soon the relation became that of a dependent chief. It may be said to the credit of Jaswant Rao Holkar that he treated him as an honoured guest and brother.[115] He assigned to him the pargana of Sironje.[116] Henceforth, he was almost identified with Holkar's government.[117] With the insanity of Holkar in 1808, he became master[118] of the House of Holkar and appointed his brother-in-law, Gaffoor Khan, as his representative to control affairs at Holkar's court. So great was his hold over the Holkar's court that ministers were made and unmade at his command. Sometimes, he would put Holkar's minister Balram Seth to confinement, and at other times he would not only release, but restore him to power. Dhurma Koor and Subaram Chowdhry were put to death through his active connivance.[119] He even went to the extent of prohibiting the Holkar's ministers from carrying on correspondence with the British government on behalf of Holkar without his prior approval.[120]

Amir Khan was a notorious freebooter and a mercenary, employed and discharged at pleasure (only his connection with Holkar was lasting. He was a man of great ambition and of sanguinary nature), and so great was his delight in bloodshed that Tod considered him as "one of the most atrocious villains that India ever produced."[121] He was an upstart but by sheer dint of bravery, bloodshed and rapine he rose so high that he became the master of almost the whole of Central India and Rajputana.

He was a man of enterprising character and considerable military talents, who distinguished himself during the wars with Jaswant Rao Holkar by his activity and energy. Unlike the Pindaris, his ambition was not limited to robbery or plunder of a village; he had aggressive political designs, for which purpose, he maintained a large and well-organised army, which became a terror to the Rajput states. He was assisted by Pindari leaders Imam Buksh, Kadir Buksh, and Ramzan Khan and their Pindari followers, numbering ten to twelve thousand, who were often in attendance on him.[122] He ultimately made himself so important that his co-operation was sought by various persons. He even received offers from the British for going over to them in return for money and land. When Amir Khan was in Bundelkhand, Lord Lake approached him and was even ready to elevate him to the position of the ruler of a state, carrying a revenue of eighteen lakhs of rupees, provided he accepted British protection.[123] This offer, the shrewd and cunning Amir rejected with contempt. But later on, with the change of circumstances, Amir Khan was obliged to seek British protection and friendship. In one of his letters seeking the hand of friendship, he wrote to Seton, Resident at Delhi :—

> To serve in the house of a friend
> (is) better than to rule in that of another,
> My friend, set your heart at case.
> In me you have a friend who wishes
> to give you pleasure, and (not) to annoy."[124]

On another occasion, through his agent Shiv Narain, he made an overture to the British for confirmation of land in Jaipur, Jodhpur and Mewar, besides Seronj and Koonch, in the name of his son Vazier Mohammad Khan. He, on his part, proposed to leave for Haj to Mecca and Madina.[125]

He not only received letters seeking his friendship from the British, but in the course of the Second Maratha War while he was at Ajmer with Holkar, both of them received an offer of friendship from Maharaja Ranjit Singh of Lahore. Being in need of a secure and comfortable abode both of them decided to go over to the Punjab. On the way, they unnecessarily interfered with the family affairs of Patiala and then marched to Amritsar, where Amir Khan assured Jaswant Rao Holkar that he could get help from Shah Shuja, the King of Kabul.[126] But nothing came out of the whole affair and both returned to the scene of their old exploits.

Amir Khan had little compunction in achieving his ends. We have much evidence testifying to his unscrupulous and mean character.[127]

With the death of Mohammad Shah Khan, another adventurer in Central India, Amir Khan received a fresh accession of strength, for all the troops of the former were incorporated in his. The troops of Amir Khan "have been estimated the best, as to infantry and artillery of any in India."[128]

For all his power and authority, Amir Khan depended upon his army, an armed rabble of free companies as they were, over whom he retained a limited measure of authority. Very often he was a prisoner of his mutinous troops, who, on non-payment of their salaries, as these were seldom paid regularly, would almost threaten him to death.[129] They were in a constant state of mutiny and kept their chief under restraint.[130] The army of Amir Khan subsisted entirely upon plunder and loot, for which internecine wars in Rajputana provided ample prospects.

The period of 1816-1817 was the highest water-mark of his power. He was riding roughshod over the whole of Hindustan. None escaped his fury. He was deciding the fate of kings, removing them from his path by murder or otherwise at his sweet will. It was at this period that Amir's son Vazeer-ood-Daula was to be affianced to a daughter of Bappoo Scindia[131] and the nuptials were to be performed at Ajmer.

Amir Khan was a very shrewd observer. He had realised the need of the troubled times and participated in the events most actively. He was a very ambitious man and therefore undertook projects of most ambitious nature. At one stage, so confident had he become and so flushed with power, that he was said to have "even aspired to the throne of Delhi and to have received from his officers the homage paid to the Mughals."[132]

Namdar Khan

Namdar Khan was the son of Habeboolah Khan or Heeroo and was the nephew of Karim Khan. He was of a short stature, had a fair complexion and was mostly dressed in short drawers and a plain turban.

Being enterprising by nature, Namdar Khan, after Karim's incarceration, made Scindia's kingdom the main theatre of operations and laid waste the whole region. His followers joined Durjan Sal's party,[133] and the combined force of the two leaders plundered and devastated Scindia's territories. They were so bold that they carried their depredations right into the Maratha camp.

With Karim's defeat near Manohar Thana by Chitu, Namdar Khan and other Pindaris fled to Bhopal where they temporarily settled and gave all possible assistance to the Nawab. While in Bhopal, he sent his followers to the villages belonging to the Nawab, where each horseman received a daily allowance of one rupee and four annas, in addition to provisions. Over and above all this, they extorted a sum of fifty rupees from each village for exemption from loot and plunder.[134]

It is indeed interesting that in 1815 he had sought British protection. In a most entreating letter he appealed to them : "I might please God if permitted to pass my life under the shadow of the protection of the British government."[135] The appeal remained unheeded. Ultimately he surrendered to the British.

Kauder Buksh

Kauder Buksh was the son of Munnoo Khan, a Jemadar of Beldars.[136] Munnoo Khan commanded five hundred cavalry. He was imprisoned by Doobla Khan in 1793, who later poisoned Munnoo Khan.[137] Munnoo Khan was a leader of enterprising nature.

Kauder Buksh was tall, well-built, of fair complexion and moderate temperament. His dress consisted of Maratha drawers and turban in the 'penchwah' fashion. [138]

He was the chief of Holkar Shahi Pindaris. He received land from Holkar, but that was soon confiscated. However, he remained faithful to the Holkar House throughout his life. His revenues amounted to Rs. 20,000 per annum.

His cavalry consisted of about 4,000 Pindaris including two hundred infantry, three guns, two elephants, one flag and one 'bazar'. His flag was white. His cantonment was at Kantapur, though, at one time, he had shifted it to Lohurdah near Satwas.[139] His chief supporter was Bahadur Khan. Long before the start of Pindari operations, Kauder Buksh was trying to seek British protection. Chitu resented this. He drew the attention of Amir Khan and wrote, "Kauder Buksh, not retracing his steps from the paths of infamy, continued his intimacy with the English and meditated the plunder of the camp and followers of your slave." Chitu was able to inflict punishment on him. The end of the Pindari war saw his surrender to the British.

Khwaja Buksh

Khwaja Buksh was the son of Reza Khan, who commanded three hundred Pindaris. He was a Scindia Shahi Pindari, attached to his 'Khasge' troops.[140] For some time, he remained close to the person of Daulat Rao Scindia who allotted him lands in 'jagir', 'Koorwye and 'Bhowrasa' on the banks of Betwa. His revenue was Rs. 25,000 annually. He commanded a force of about three hundred cavalry.

Sahib Khan and Bahadur Khan

The two brothers, Sahib Khan and Bahadur Khan, were the sons of Briam,[141] who was the first to become a Pindari in the family. They were stationed at Kunnode, where Tookoo, another minor Pindari chief also lived.[142]Kunnode was a joint grant to the two brothers by Holkar, in addition to a share in Nimawar.

Sahib Khan's son Lal Khan who was married to Chitu's daughter, was murdered after the marriage by a woman 'Fakeer'. [143]

Rosan Beg, a chief of Holkar's force, once captured the two brothers and confined them to the care of Tulsi Bai, Holkar's mother, who, however, released them on payment of three lakhs of rupees.

The two brothers, Sahib Khan in particular, were often used as messengers for the government they served.

In 1811, their strength was 1,060 horse. But gradually it rose to about 5,000 cavalry.[144] They had two guns, a *bazar*, one *naubat* mounted on a camel, two elephants and one palanquin. Their cantonment was at Ekhehra. Their flag had alternate strips of white and black on blue cloth.[145] Ghassita Danglia, who was married to Sahib Khan's sister was his principal officer.[146]

Kushal Kunwar and Moti Kunwar

The two sons of Karim[147] occupied a place Ashtadoosh near Bagrode. They subsisted on plunder alone, as they had no lands allotted to them by any prince. Their force was negligible. Kushal Kunwar was thin, short in stature, and of a fair complexion.

Fazil Khan and Bheekhan Khan

Both of them belonged to Karim's party. However, they soon joined Jaggoo Bappoo with their followers numbering about two hundred. They were Scindia Shahi Pindaris though some of their followers were Holkar Shahi.

Deedar Buksh

Deedar Buksh was the eldest son of Burrun. He survived Kadir Buksh, a Scindia Shahi Pindari of note, who served Jaggoo Bappoo in his attack on Bhopal in 1812. While the seige was on, he was murdered by a Sikh. Being the son of Burrun, Deedar Buksh was held in high esteem by the Pindaris and was looked upon as a chief of rank.

Tookoo Khan and Gulab Khan

The two brothers, Tookoo Khan and Gulab Khan were the sons of Gurdee Khan,[148] who was killed by a Pindari *Jemadar* on account of personal enmity. Holkar thereupon, bestowed the command upon Tookoo Khan, and Gulab Khan, who received elephants and standards. The two 'parganas' of Kunnode and Kathegaon were given in Jagir. They were stationed at Kunnode near Satwas. They held lands from Scindia also.[149]

Tookoo held the rank of Jemadar. He commanded 2000 horse, 800 infantry and five guns.[150] He also had one

Singh, one *Bazar*; two *Jhundas*, one *Naubat*, one camel, and one *Dunka*. His force was distributed as follows:—

Private Pagah	500
His Russuldars	
each having a Nishan and a Singh, were as under:	
Burrun	400
Baun Buksh	300
Remzan Jemadar	400
Kuber	100
Tookoo, son of Thybee	300
	2,000

His flag was alternately stripped white and red. His principal officers were his cousins; Kalla, Heeroo, Nathoo, Bunchan, Suleman-ka-Khoda Buksh, Kale-ka-Kunwar, Remzan Jemadar, Kuber etc.

At the end of the Pindari War, both the brothers surrendered to the British, who rehabilitated them as farmers.

Sheikh Dulla

Sheikh Dulla was one of the most enterprising, adventurous and brave Pindari leaders. Though he commanded a very small number of followers, his exploits were really romantic. His boldness in attacking Nagpur with a few hundred followers only, is an instance of his enterprising nature. His annual incursions in Berar were really most adventurous. He continued to evade arrest, in spite of the several defeats he sustained at the hands of the British.[151]

Buksoo

Hussain Buksh or Buksoo, as he was popularly called, was one of the most romantic adventurers among the Pindaris. He was reckoned as a man of great courage, sagacity and skill. He was a tall, handsome young man, fair-complexioned and had an athletic frame.

Though he was brave and enterprising he was extremely cautious. He never took risks. If possible, he would rather adopt other means than take a risk. His prudence and cunning were manifest in several extra-ordinary retreats. A born Pindari, he was on the horse-back since his early childhood and had developed into an excellent rider and could undergo every kind of hardship and fatigue. He was neither elevated by success nor depressed by defeat; this courage and presence of mind never failed him and he always set an example of perseverance and fortitude to his followers. He was very genial. On account of his bravery, cool-headedness and amiability, Buksoo won popularity among the Pindaris.

During the heyday of Pindari menace, India was confronted with a perilous situation. The anarchical conditions of the time produced a galaxy of bold and intrepid adventurers. By sheer merit and ability most of them rose to eminence, and some like Chitu, Karim and Amir displayed extraordinary tact and skill in organising their newly-carved territories. Even the contemporary British officials, Malcolm and Stewart, were amazed at the varied qualities of the Pindari leaders. Surprisingly enough, the Pindari chiefs were all upstarts, a product of disturbed times, who were instrumental in establishing a reign of terror in Central India and Rajputana, which for the time being benumbed all the Indian chiefs, as well as the British. How the British handled the Pindaris through diplomacy and war, will be unfolded in the following pages.

FOOT-NOTES

1 Some writers have traced the Pindari ancestry to another line. They write: "One of their first and most distinguished leaders was a person named Ponapah, who ravaged the Carnatic and took Vellore early in the reign of Sahojee. This chief is said to have been succeeded by Chingody and Hool Sewar who commanded fifteen thousand horsemen at the battle of Panipat, and under whom the Pindari system would seem to have assumed a more regular form."

Origin of the Pindaris, by an Officer of the East India Company Chap. V.

2 Tod : *Origin, Progresss and Present State of the Pindaris*, p. 2.

3 *Ibid.*
Also : Malcolm : *Rise and Progress*, para 7.

4 Malcolm : *Rise and Progress*, para 8.

5 Fitzclarence : *Journal of a Route*, p. 5.

6 Malcolm : *Rise and Progress*; para 10.
Also : Thornton : *The History of the British Empire in India*, p. 406.

7 Tod : *Origin Progress and Present State of the Pindaris*, p. 3.

8 Malcolm : *Rise and Progress*, para 8.

9 *Ibid.*, para 12.

10 *Ibid.*

11 "I doubt not the Pindaris are, like most other men, individually courageous, and indeed we saw many instances of this independent spirit in the cours e of our operations against them."
McNaughten : *Memoir of N.S.F.*, p. 117.

12 Capt. William's Observations, p. 215.

13 *Sydenham's Memoir*, 1814, p. 26, para 11.

14 Tod : *Origin Progress and Present State of Pindaris*, p. 3.

15 N.A.I. For. Sec, 1814 : O.C. No. 9, 11 February, 1814, Wauchope to Adams, Camp Kootee, 23 January, 1814.

16 For. Misc. 124 A : Jenkins' Memorandum, 1812, p. 25.

17 N.A.I. For. Sec, 1814 : O.C, No, 9, 11 February, 1814, Wauchope to Adams, Camp Kootee, 23 January, 1814,

18 *Ibid.*

19 For. Misc. 124 A : Jenkins' Memorandum, 1812, General Statement of the Jagheers held by the Pindaris at the end of 1811, p. 32.

20 *Ibid* ., p. 25.

21 For. Misc. 124 A : Statement of the amount of Pindaris according to an account received from Hindia, 20, April 1814 enclosed in the letter from Capt. Sydenham to Henery Russell, Resident at Hyderabad, Aurangabad, 24 April, 1814.

22 H.R.R. S. No. 195, Vol. No. 413 : Sydenham's statement of Pindaris received from Hindia on 20 April, 1814, enclosed in the letter from Capt. Sydenham to Henery Russell, Aurangabad, 24 April, 1814.

23 N.A.I. For. Sec. 1814 : O.C. No. 9, 11 February, 1814, Wauchope to Adams, 23 January, 1814.

24 N.A.I. For. Sec. 1814 : O.C. No. 2, 21 January, 1814, Memorandum relating to the Pindarries, 21 January, 1814.

[25] For. Misc. 124 A : Pindary and Maratha War Papers : Letter from Lt. Sydenham, accompanying his Memorandum of 1809, 18 March, 1810, p. 5.

[26] N.A.I. For. Sec. 1815 : O.C. No. 55-56, 7 March, 1815, para 5.

[27] "When Dost Mohommed was a child, his father gave him into the lap of Mahadji Scindia......... Daulat Rao Scindia has such favour and regard for Dost Mohommed that were he even to plunder his own country he would scarcely say anthing to him." N.A.I. For. Sec. 1812 : O.C. No. 2-6, 1 May, 1812 : p. 22. Translation of the Heads of Deposition of Dunna Pindarrah.

[28] Tod had mentioned Kadir Buksh to be son of Ramzan Khan, who commanded 500 horse. Ramzan was captured by the Nagpur Raja and while in confinement he died there.
Tod : *Origin Progress and Present State of Pindaris* p. 10.

[29] P.R.R. Vol. No. 14 : Letter No. 134 : An Account of Pindarries under Scindia and Holkar, p. 155, mentions this figure to be 4,000 cavalry of Kadir Buksh : while Jenkins in his Memorandum submitted in 1812, calculated the number of his horse to be 4,750.

[30] *Ibid.*, "Imam Buksh is the son of Gunee Khan, a chief of five hundred horse, who was killed at the battle of Poona." (October, 1802).

[31] For. Misc. 124 A : *Jenkins' Memorandum*, p, 32.

[32] For. Misc. 124 A: *Jenkins' Memorandum*, 1812, p. 25.

[33] M.I.O.L.L. H.M.S : Vol. No. 506 A. Item No. 2.

[34] P.R.R. Vol. No. 14 : Letter No. 134, An Account of the Pindarries under Scindia and Holkar, p. 155.

[35] *Ibid.*

[36] *Sydenham's Memorandum*, 1814, p. 35, para 17.

[37] M.I.O.L.L., H.M.S. Vol. 506 A, Item No. 2.
Also : *Jenkins' Memorandum*, p. 30.

[38] *Sydenham's Memorandum*, 1814, p. 35, para 17.

[39] *Jenkins' Memorandum*, p. 30.

[40] N.A.I. For. Sec. 1818 : O. C. No. 391, 24 July, 1814, Brig. Gen. Sir John Malcolm to Adam, Camp at Tapah, 11 April, 1818.

[41] Tod mentioned the name as Dowlut Khan in Heeroo's service, p. 9.

[42] *Jenkins' Memorandum* : p. 30.

[43] Wilson :*The History of the British India*, p. 132.

[44] *Sydenham's Memorandum*, 1814, para 11.

[45] *Jenkins' Memorandum*, 1812, p. 30. It may please be noted that this Heeroo, brother of Karim, is in no way connected with the Pindari leaders Heeroo and Burrun.

46 B.G.R. Political Department D. No. 427 : M. Kennedy to Guy Lenox Chief of Surat, 28 December, 1815.

47 For. Misc. 124 A : *Sydenham's Memorandum*, 1814 : p. 36, para 19.

48 N.A.I. For. Sec. 1814 : O.C. No. 18-10, 25 February, 1814, Sydenham to Russell, 31 January, 1814.
Also : Jenkins mentions the title as *Nabob Kumaul Mahommed Moostoo Kurreem Jungh* in his Memorandum, p. 30.

49 N.A.I. For. Sec. 1814 : O.C. No. 18-19, 25 February, 1814, Sydenham to Russell, 31 January, 1814.

50 Malcolm : *Rise and Progress*, para 16.

51 Malcolm : *Rise and Progress*, para 16.

52 P.R.R. Vol. Letter No. 134 : An account of the Pindarries under Scindia and Holkar, p. 155.

53 According to Sydenham's Memorandum of 1814, Chitu's revenues amounted to between "three to five lakhs of rupees".
Sydenham's Memorandum, 1814, para 12, pp. 29-30.

54 Lt. Col. Valentine Blacker : *Memoir of the Operations of the British Army in India During the Mahratta War of 1817, 1818 and 1819*, p. 105, London 1821.

55 *Sydenham's Memorandum*, 1814, p. 27, para 11.

56 N.A.I. For. Sec. 1814 : O.C. No. 18-19 : 25 February, 1814, Sydenham to Russell, 31 January, 1814.

57 Jenkins' Memorandum, 1812, p. 30.

58 Sydenham's Memorandum, 1814, p. 32, para 15.

59 They were all '*chelas*' or adopted sons of Chitu.

60 Jenkins' Memorandum, 1812, p. 30.

61 Blacker : *Memoir of the Operations of the British Army in India*, p. 105.

62 A.O. P.R. Translation of a paper of Intelligence from Chitu's Camp at Malthawun, dated 31 December 1813 :
"Next day he held a 'durbar' and partitioned out the Pergunnahs of Sutwas, Gopaulpore, Seepaner and Nemawar to his matchlockmen."

63 N.A.I. For. Sec. 1812 : O.C. No. 17, 25 September 1812 : Private letter from Strachey to Edmonstone, Chief Sec. at Fort William, Camp Gwalior, 29 August, 1812.

64 N.A.I. For. Sec. 1817 : O.C. No. 37 : Jenkins to Adam, enclosing a paper of Intelligence from Scindia.

65 N.A.I. For. Sec. 1816 : O.C. No. 1-8, 28 Dec., 1816 : Close to Adam, Gwalior, November 20, 1816 enclosing letter No. 3 from Chitu to Daulat Rao Scindia.

66 N.A.I. For. Sec. 1817 : O.C. No. 1-3, 23 January, 1817, Close to Adam, 23 January, 1817. Also letter No. 2 from Chitu to Meer Khan :

"to the environs of Calcutta the tumult shall be spread...that out of these Jagheers will be produced to the extent of my sweet wishes."

67 For. Misc. 124 A : Sydenham's Memorandum, 1814 : p. 36, para 21. Also P.R.R. Vol. No. 14, Letter No. 134, p. 110 ;
Also : Tod : *Origin Progress and Present State of Pindaris*, p. 4.

68 P.R.R. Daulat Rao Scindia and North Indian Affairs, Vol. No. 14, Letter No. 134, An Account of the Pindarries under Scindia and Holkar, p. 10
Also : According to Malcolm Karim was son of Mohammad Dawud a Commander of a body of plunderers under Raghoba. Malcolm's account of the parentage of Karim Khan seems to be more correct as he got it testified by the Pindari leader himself. Malcolm : *Rise and Progress*, para 20.

69 Jenkins in his Memorandum mentioned that "Karim Khan is the son of Sher Khan." p. 30. Rustam Khan a Pindara, had three sons, Sher Khan, Surmust Khan and Shamsher Khan. Sher Khan had two sons, Karim Khan and Heeroo ; Surmust Khan and Shamsher Khan had Sundut Khan and Hussain Khan respectively as their sons. Hussain Khan was a common Pindari horseman in the '*durra*' of Dost Mohammad.

70 Malcolm : *Rise and Progress*, para 20.

71 While Malcolm mentioned the age of Karim Khan as eight years, Tod gave the age as 5 years when Karim's father died. Malcolm seems to be correct.

72 Malcolm : Rise and Progress ; para 21 ;
Also : Wilson : *History of British India*, p. 132.

73 The Nawab of Bhopal gave him the *pergana* of Bhonnrassah, Khurkeerah, Hurringaon and Wuljamool.

74 *Sydenham's memorandum*, p. 32, para 21.

75 For. Misc. 124 : Origin Progress and Present State of Pindaris. Tod's Report on Bhopal, from Gwalior on 15 September, 1814.
Also : Malcolm : Rise and Progress, para 23, mentioned that he "married a lady of that branch of the family of Bhopal which is settled at Ratgurh". Tod seems to be more correct as he wrote an account of Bhopal from Gwalior in 1814 and was nearer to the event.

76 Sydenhams Memorandum, 1814, pp. 38-39, para 21 Karim received land from the Scindia, Holkar, Bhopal and Kota yielding revenue of several lakhs of rupees.

77 Malcolm : Rise and Progress, para 23.
Also : Duff *A History of the Maratha*, Vol. III, p. 326.

78 Malcolm : *Rise and Progress*, para 23.

79 In 1805 Karim had attained "a degree of power which only required consolidation to have become the foundation of a substantial

state." Wilson : *History of British Empire* p. 132.

80 C.I. State Gazetteer Series : Bhopal State Gazetteer, Vol. III, pp. 21-22, Calcutta, 1908.

81 Such was the reduced position, status and power of the House of Scindia that he needed stratagem in the battlefield to defeat an enemy.

82 Karim "proceeded with a degree of ostentatious splendour scarcely inferior to that of the chief to whom he professed allegiance."
Thornton : *The History of the British Empire in India*, Vol. IV, p. 409.

83 Tod mentioned the figure to be one lakh only.
Tod : *Origin Progress and Present State of Pindaris*, p. 5.

84 English Records of Maratha History : P.R.C. : Vol. II, Daulat Rao Scindia's Affairs, 1804-1809 : Letter No. 207, G. Mercer, Resident to Daulat Rao Scindia to Sir George Barlow, Governor General (1805), Camp near Sackenbaree, 24 November 1806, p. 293.

85 Tod gave a very interesting account of the scene that followed the attack upon the Pindaris : "the scene on this occasion which presented itself was novel ; here a Maratha driving a buffalo with his spear, on which was perched some unfortunate child...there a footman groaning under a load of pots and pans...... A third displaying at his lance's point the coloured turban now gaily streaming as a banner, which by the bridle led, followed a courser lately bestridden by some bold marauder, and, last scene of all, the elephants, ruths, *palkuees* and other emblems of state of the now fallen Kurreem."
Tod : *Origin, Progress & Present State of Pindaris*, p. 6.

86 *Ibid.*

87 *Ibid.*

88 The Parliamentary Papers Regarding the Pindary and Maratha Wars mention the figure to be ten lakhs. To quote "Cheetoo and Karim whom he had held in confinement during many years, but whom his pecuniary distress have at length induced to liberate on their agreeing to pay a ransom of ten lacs of rupees under the security of Zalim Singh of Kota."
Extracts Secret Letters form Bengal : 16 August, 1811, p. 1.

89 N.A.I. For. Pol. 1812 : O.C. No. 27, 17 January 1812 : Strachey to Minto, Scindia's Camp at Gwalior, 30th December, 1811.

90 N.A.I. For. Sec. 1814 : O.C. No. 17-19, 4 March, 1814, R. Strachey to His Excellency the Earl of Moira, Scindia's camp, 12 February, 1814.

91 N.A.I. For. Pol. 1812 : O.C. No. 39, 4 September, 1812, C.T. Metcalfe, Resident at Delhi to Holkar, 3 July, 1812.
Also : Political letter from Bengal 15 October, 1812. p. 14.

Also : N.A.I. For. Sec. 1814 : O.C. No. 17-19, 4 March, 1814, Strachey to Moira, 12 February, 1814.

92 N.A.I. For. Pol. 1812 : O.C. No. 15, 21 February, 1812, Strachey to Edmonstone, Gwalior, 7 February, 1812.
Also : B.G.R. D. No. 408, P.D. 1814 : R. Strachey to Moira, Scindia's camp, 12 February, 1814.

93 N.A.I. For. Pol. 1817 : O.C. No. 12, 17 October, 1817, Metcalfe to Adam, Delhi 28 September, 1817. Holkar's reply to British representation was "that a mutiny broke out in the infantry to whose charge he had been committed and that he had effected his escape God knows how."

94 N.A.I. For. Sec. 1814 : O.C No. 99-100, 6 December, 1814 Metcalfe to Adam, 16 November, 1814.
Also : N.A.I. For. Pol. 1814 : O.C. No. 45, 25 April, 1814.
R. Strachey to George Swinton, Persian Secretary to His Excellency the Governor General.
Also : N.A.I. For. Pol. 1815 : O.C. No. 47, 25 April, 1814, Arzee received from Karim Khan Pindara Record, 12 November 1814.

95 B.G.R. Pol. Deptt. 1818 : D. No. 447 : Malcolm to Adam, Camd Ujjain, 22 March, 1818.

96 N.A.I. For. Sec 1812 : O.C. No. 2-6, 1 May, 1812, Intelligence from a Pindary camp and deposition of Dunna Pindara.

97 N.A.I. For. Pol. 1811 : O.C. No. 45, 21, December, 1811, Jenkins to Russell, Nagpur, 30 November, 1811.

98 M.I.O.L.L. H.M.S. Vol. No. 110, Item No. 281.

99 For. Misc. 124 A : Origin and Progress, Sydenham's Memorandum of 1814, p. 42.

100 Asiatic Annual Register : 1810-11, Vol. X I, p. 34. London, 1812.
Also : Busawan Lal : *Memoir of Amir Khan*, p. 1

101 Malcolm : *Memoir of Central India*, Vol. I p. 263.

102 "Some doubt has hitherto been entertained whether the name of this chief was properly Meer Khan or Amir Khan. This book seems to settle this question. His seal bears the Persian sentence- (Khoda Khood Meer Khan Saman ust Ahab-i-Tawakkul Ra) God himself is the steward for the good of all that relies firmly on him. The play of words may have led to the notion that the chief's name was Meer Khan."
Busawan Lal : *Memoir of Amir Khan*, p. 1.

103 *Ibid.*

194 *Ibid.*
Also : A.A.R., 1810-11, Vol. XII, p. 34.

105 Busawan Lal : *Memoir of Amir Khan*, p. 49.

106 A.A.R : 1810-1811 : Vol XII, p. 35.

107 B.G.R. D. No. 143, 1803 : Sec. Pol. Deptt. J.A. Kirpatrick, Resident Hyderabad to A. Wellesley, Hyderabad, 30 May, 1803.

108 Busawan Lal : *Memoir of Amir Khan*, Book First : Chap. IV p. 36

[109] Central India State Gazetteer Series: Bhopal State Gazetteer, Vol. III, p. 18.

[100] Busawan Lal : *Memoir of Amir Khan*, p. 31.

[111] Busawan Lal : *Memoir of Amir Khan*, p. 97

[112] Auber : *Rise and Progress*, Vol. II, p. 454.

[113] Amir Khan was "in connection, in habit, and in principle, essentially a Pindari."

P.R.R. Poona Affairs : (1816-1818), Edited by G.S. Sardesaei, Bombay, 1958, Letter No. 135, Marquiss of Hastings to the Court of Directors, Gorakhpur, 19 May, 1818, p. 381.

[114] C.U. Aitchison : *A Collection of Treaties, Engagements and Sanads Relating to India and the Neighbouring Countries*, Vol. III, containing the Treaties Relating to the States in Rajputana, Calcutta, 1892, p. 209.

[115] B.G.R. D. No. 267 : Sec. Pol. 1810 : A. Seton, Seton, Resident at Delhi to C. Lushington, Acting Secretary to Government Ft. William, Delhi 28 May, 1810.

[116] Busawan Lal : *Memoir of Amir Khan*, p. 102.

[117] B.G.R. D. No. 266 : Sec. & Pol. 1810 : Edmonstone to Seton Fort William, 29 May, 1810.

[118] Busawan Lal : *Memoir of Amir Khan*, p. 365.

[119] M.I.O.L.L. H.M.S : Vol. No. 511, Bengal Political Consultations No. 131.

[120] M.I.O.L.L. H.M.S. Vol. No. 511, Bengal Political Consultations No. 30, 29 October, 1810.

Also : "He appears, however, to consider Holkar's presence or orders, as no longer necessary to give a sanction to his measures." N.A.I. For. Pol. 1810 : O.C. No. 42, 30 June, 1810, Seton to Edmonstone, Delhi, 5 June, 1810.

[121] "Amir Khan though originally a mere soldier of fortune, is now a powerful military chief."

N.A.I. For. Sec. 1816 : O.C. No. 3, 20 April, 1816, Seton's Minute : 17 April, 1816.

[122] Busawan Lal : *Memoirs of Amir Khan*, pp. 32, 147 and 236.

[123] Busawan Lal : Memoirs of Amir Khan p. 242.

[124] N.A.I. For. Sec. 1810 : O.C. No. 1-5, 15 May, 1810, Seton to Edmonstone, Delhi, 25 April, 1810.

[125] C.I.A.R. File No. 5 : Amir Khan (Jaora) Commander-in-Chief Holkar's Army, Letter from Shiv Narain, Agent and Newswriter, Received 26 June, 1815.

[126] During the month of May, 1810, Amir Khan's *Vakil* in the court of Maharaja Ranjit Singh, presented an application of request from his master to Shooja-ul-Mulk and "procured from His Majesty a *Khelat* and the formal investiture, the Soubahdaree of Sind for Meer Khan" that "Meer Khan received the Khelat with the usual

formalities and had ordered all his guns in camp to be fired in honour of the occasion."
N.A.I. For. Pol. 1810 : O.C. No. 131, 29 May, 1810, Letter from Sydenham Resident, Hyderabad, 4 May, 1810.

127 While interfering in Jaipur-Jodhpur wars, he told Jaswant Rao Holkar, "My last advice to you is that you join Raja Man Singh, leaving me to take the side of Raja Jugut Singh in this war. We should by that means turn the conflict to our own purposes, spinning it out at our pleasure, till the resources of both were exhausted and till both were in our power."
Busawan Lal : *Memoirs of Amir Khan*, p. 309.
The murder of Sewai Singh, a Jodhpur Sardar, under the most calculated and shameful circumstances also justified this estimate of Amir Khan.

128 N. A. I. For. Sec. 1816: O. C. No. 1, 15 June, 1816, Governor General's Minute, 1 December 1815, para 26.

129 The soldiers used to become mutinous and they "pelted him with stones, from a terrace above, to such an extent that the bruises were a hundred times worse than swords."
Busawan Lal : *Memoirs of Amir Khan*, p. 319. At another stage they almost strangled him with his own turban.

130 One of the Sardars of Amir Khan waited upon Metcalfe, alongwith a letter signed by eight other Sardars, proposing to place themselves under the British, impressing upon Metcalfe that none of the Sardars have confidence in Amir Khan and that there was a general determination among them not to serve him. Metcalfe refused to entertain their appeal. N. A. I. For. Sec. 1811: O. C. No. 1, 26 December, 1811. Metcalfe to Edmonstone, Delhi, 9 December, 1811.

131 N. A. I. For. Sec. 1814: O. C. No. 6-7, 17 June, 1814. Wauchope to Jenkins, 31 May, 1814.
Also: N. A. I. For. Pol. 1811: O. C. No. 55, 26 July, 1811, Metcalfe to Edmonstone, Delhi, 6 February, 1811.

132 M.I.O.L.L.H.M.S. : Vol. No, 511, Item No. 13, Memoradum on the Political State of India.

133 The Grassiah chief of Bahadurgarh and Scindia's inveterate enemy.

134 N. A. I. For. Sec. 1817: O. C. No. 3-4, 4 February, 1817, Close to Adam, Gwalior, 10 January, 1817, and the Akhbars of Chitu and the Pindaris : 30th December, 1816.

135 N. A. I. For. Sec. 1815: O. C. No. 31-33, 14 March, 1815, Strachey to Adam, Camp Malpura, 21 February, 1815.

136 *Sydenham's Memorandum*, 1814, p. 53, para 35.

137 P. R. R. Daulat Rao Scindia and North Indian Affairs. 1810-1818, *An account of Pindaris under Scindia and Holkar*, Vol. No. 14 Letter No 134, p. 155.

Tod also agrees with this account in his *Origin Progress and Present State of Pindaris* on p. 11; However, Jenkins in his Memorandum mentions that Munnoo Khan was killed in action between Scindia & Holkar's Pindaris p. 32.

138 A fashion of wearing turban, in which the turbans are tightly twisted.

139 *Jenkins' Memorandum*, 1812, Papers Pindaris Wars, p. 32. Also: *Sydenham's Memorandum*, 1814, p. 53, para 35.

140 Private Treasury Troops.

141 For. Misc. 124 A: Tod: *Origin & Progress*, Tod mentions "Sahi Khan and Bahadur Khan are sons of Himmat Khan, a chief of 600 killed at the battle of Assye." p. 11.

142 Infra p. 118.

143 *Sydenham's Memorandum:* p. 54, para 37, 1814.

144 For. Misc. 124 A : Tod, Origin Progress and Present State of Pindaris, p. 11.

145 Jenkins in his Memorandum mentions the flag of the two to be black in colour, p. 33.

146 *Sydenham's Memorandum*, 1814, p. 54, para 37.

147 With the same famous Pindari leader.

148 Jenkins in his Memorandum mentions the two as the sons of Gazee ood-deen, a Pindari leader of note, who won distinction by his conspicuous bravery in the battle of Indore against Scindia. For. Misc, 124 A : Pindari War Papers p. 32.

149 In a letter to Adam, Wauchope mentions that the revenues of Tookkoo and Gulab Khan amounted to eighteen lakhs per annum N. A. I. For. Sec. 1814, O. C. No. 9, 11 February, 1814, Wauchope to Adam, 23 January, 1814.

150 *Jenkins'* Memorandum, 1812, Pindary & Maratha Wars, p.25.

151 Letters to Europe, 1820, Military Department, Secret and Special Branch, p. 192.

4

Pindaris in Central India

Central India in Cauldron

It is a truism, that in the history of every country there comes a period when people, impelled either by want or depravity, subsist upon such means as need little exertion or effort. Indian history witnessed such a period in Central India with the dismemberment of the mighty Mughal Empire. The death of Aurangzeb in 1707 amidst his Deccan Campaign, led to the growth of centrifugal forces and ushered a period of great anarchy.

Central India, of all the Mughal provinces, may be said to have enjoyed peace, comparatively speaking, from 1770-1800. This prolonged peace and consequent prosperity may be attributed to Ahilya Bai, (1767-1795), the renowned queen of Indore, who was one of the most pious, just and able rulers of India. During her reign, the Holkar dominions in Central India enjoyed unbroken peace. Tukoji Holkar (1795-1797), who succeeded Ahilya Bai, left no stone unturned to preserve the tradition of his predecessor. The untimely death of Tukoji Holkar in 1797, removed the keystone of the arch of prosperity, and the entire structure collapsed. Central India was plunged into anarchy. Jaswant

Rao Holkar's succession led to turmoil, blood-shed and devastation. The period that now commenced was a time of trouble and tribulation.

The Indian princes were all busy in achieving their own personal ambitions, and in the process, had become so weak and spineless that they had no strength left either to put an end to this state of affairs or to prevent feudal wars. Theirs was a divided house. Internecine wars were the order of the day. With the result that the Indian states became mere shadows of their former selves.

Central India, indeed, presented a very sorry spectacle of a hunting ground of merciless and wanton bands of marauders, desperadoes, freebooters and bandits. It was a perpetual scene of war. Over and above, there was no army worth the name to give protection to the people. And if at all it existed, it was busy spreading misery around and was an instrument of tyranny rather than relief. Some idea of the anarchic conditions, then prevailing in Central India, can be had from the fact that Jaswant Rao Holkar was able to collect a body of 70,000 men, who joined him with the motive of plunder when troubles regarding the succession at Poona started in 1798-99.

The downfall of the Mughal Empire and the consequent decay that set in, enabled the Subedars, created by the Mughals, to assume independence. The newly rising Marathas took advantage of the confusion thus created, and attacked these provinces. The first region which felt the brunt of the Maratha invasion was Malwa. But instead of assuming direct responsibility for its proper administration, the Marathas were content with levying *chauth*. Malwa soon became the haven of adventurers.

The great evil that grew in Central India in such great measure was not a sudden growth, but was a gradual development as a result of unchecked personal ambition of Indian rulers. Each was fighting the other, by constant inroads into neighbouring dominions. The various tributaries, seeing their masters in distress and disgrace, were in constant rebellion against them. The armies of their overlords were almost always in a mutinous mood, and therefore, were in a perpetual state of insubordination. It was thus natural that predatory organisations multiplied and flourished. This was more so in Central India, as observed by Sir Alfred Lyall, as this region was the stronghold of Maratha power. But with its defeat at the hands of the British, the Maratha states lost their former vitality and effectiveness.[1]

Causes of the Growth of the Pindaris

The causes of the growth of the Pindari menace in Central India and elsewhere deserve a careful study.

The hope held by the British statesmen that the Pindari elements would, in course of time, settle down as peaceful citizens was completely belied. This did not happen because of the indifferent and tolerant attitude of the Indian chiefs.

The crushing defeat of the Marathas resulted in the destruction of a large part of their army and hence the chiefs could not maintain the remaining numbers and were forced to disband them. The disbanded soldiers were left with no profession other than that of agriculture, towards which they felt apathetic.[2] Thus, left with no choice, they joined the marauding numbers of the Pindaris.[3]

Both the Rajas of Nagpur and Indore had considerably reduced the strength of their armies in 1805.[4] Scindia deliberately refused to maintain a large army as a matter of policy. He thus destroyed all chances of martial races taking up the military services under him. The states which had entered into an alliance with the British and relied on the British Subsidiary Forces, hardly needed large armies. As far as the petty zamindars and independent chieftains are concerned, except for a few bodyguards, they could barely afford to maintain regular forces.

With the gradual establishment of British authority over large parts of the country, small-scale wars, which had been a perpetual feature in the country, ceased all of a sudden.[5] This led to the disbandment of old military establishments. Thus the discontented and dismissed soldiers from the Indian states gladly joined the Pindari ranks and swelled their numbers.[6]

The destruction of the power of Tipu Sultan, the extinction of the political independence of the Nizam and the Peshwa further increased the number of the Pindaris.[7] The demobilised soldiery of Tipu Sultan "collecting together,... invited everyone without employ to their side; and breaking off in small bodies under adventurous leaders" they joined numerous bands of freebooters. The Peshwa had confiscated the whole of the land held by the ordinary *jagirdars*, which resulted in a lot of unemployment and displacement leading to great disaffection among the military class of people. This also added to the number of Pindaris.[8] The Pathan and Muslim troops no more found a rallying centre to which they could show their loyalty. Thus, discharged soldiers from Hyderabad, Kurnool, Poona, Indore, Gwalior and Nagpur were let loose, ready to be recruited by the Pindari hordes.[9]

To all these causes may be added another and a very interesting one, which helped considerably in increasing the Pindari numbers. The Pindaris on their march to any place of attack were usually joined by volunteers, for the sake of loot, particularly from Indian armies.[10] Besides, the very people who had earlier been plundered joined the main party. Seeing no future security for the property which they might again possess, they were driven by want and despair to join the Pindaris, and in their turn attempted to regain their losses by plundering their neighbours. In a foot-note Fitzclarence, in his book, *Journal of a Route Across India*, quoting Dow gave an interesting illustration of similar practice which prevailed during the Mughal times: "when Ghusero, son of Jehan Ghuir, rebelled and burnt the suburb of Delhi in 1606, many, to retrieve their affairs, joined him to make reprisals on the world for the loss which they had sustained."[11] Thus, if the original strength of the party when it started on an excursion was five hundred men, it was but natural that with the joining of volunteers and others,[12] on its arrival at the grand scene of action, it increased to as many thousands.[13] Thus the "Pindaris were fed and nourished by the very miseries which they occasioned for as their predatory invasions extended, property became insecure, and those who were ruined by their depredations were afterwards compelled to take resort to a life of violence as the only means left them of subsistence. They joined the stream they could not withstand and endeavoured to redeem their own losses by the plunder of others."[14] These chaotic conditions in Central India were practically the same as those which prevailed in Europe of the Middle Ages.[15]

It may be observed that if the British had taken immediate steps when the Pindaris had just started posing a threat to their territories, the great Pindari menace would have been nipped in the bud. But the British at first pursued a policy of isolation and self-complacency, which resulted in the enormous growth of the predatory elements.

Early Incursions Before 1806

With the death of eminent Maratha leaders like Nana Phadnavis, Mahadji Scindia and Tukoji Holkar, the cohesion of Maratha states disappeared for ever. Internal dissensions and conflicts connected with the succession at Poona and the Scindia-Holkar rivalry for the control of the Peshwa government, emboldened the Pindari chiefs to assume independence. They now began their incursions without fear or favour. In these incursions, which were a regular annual feature, the Pindaris hardly spared any one. An account of these depredations given here is mainly based on the original records and diaries of the officers of the East India Company which are full of reports of the raids of the Pindaris. In these raids the Pindaris perpetrated the most horrible cruelties and literally laid waste vast tracts of fertile land.

As early as 1783, the Pindaris entered the Company's Bombay Presidency districts. Taken by surprise, twenty-five of them were, however, killed by the English forces.[16]

In 1795, at the instance of Nana Phadnavis, the Pindaris destroyed the forage of the Nizam and the Mughals.[17] The Pathans and the Pindaris in the name of the Holkar and the Scindia plundered the people in the Peshwa territories. Their leader Shahmat Khan nominally subordinate to Holkar, laid waste the Nagpur Raja's domains in 1798.[19]

In 1800, the Pindaris repeated their incursion on the Nagpur territories. They were earlier in the service of Jaswant Rao Holkar.[20] A year later, the Pindaris from Scindia's territories, numbering about 7,000, suddenly descended on the Narbada and attacked and plundered the town of Onkareshwar.[21]

The year 1803 witnessed certain regions of Central Provinces, Nimar, Hoshangabad etc., suffering terribly at the hands of the Pindaris. This happened immediately after the great famine in the same year. Subsequently acute distress prevailed among the people who finally resigned themselves to fate. During the period 1803-1818 there was not a single village which was not visited more than once by the Pindaris.[22]

In 1804, the Pindaris entered the districts east of Ujjain and instead of the usual mode of warfare, viz., hit and run, carried their plundering activities in a most leisurely manner.[23]

The British agent at the Court of Baroda in 1805, while on his way to Ujjain, was attacked and looted. The Pindaris also laid waste the territories of the Peshwa. They sacked a large town Sangamner about 60 miles from Nasik.[24] Another party of the Pindaris, 5,000 strong, entered Berar and plundered the whole region.[25]

In the beginning of 1805, Amir Khan, with his Pindaris, invaded the Doab and Rohilkhand regions. But his attack on Moradabad was repulsed by the Magistrate and Collector Messrs. Wright and William Lycester,[26] and one Crawford pushed back another incursion on Pathargarh.[27]

About 6,000 Pindaris headed by Chitu invaded the Nizam's territories. They attacked Amrawati and plundered villages on the way. Here they met with some resistance and suffered casualties. Berar always offered a very great prize to the freebooters.[28] Lt. Col. Doveton reported that two more parties, besides the one which appeared near Amrawati, entered the Nizam's dominion. This party of Pindaris belonged to Chitu. It spread and dispersed itself over so extensive an area, that it became almost impossible to pursue them.[29]

Pindari Attack On Nagpur

The internal dissensions and military weakness of the Bhonsla, exposed his state to constant Pindari inroads. The Nagpur army was utterly incapable of defending the State. Year after year Pindari depredations continued.

Pindaris, belonging to Jaswant Rao Holkar, committed serious depredations in the territories of Raghoji Bhonsla in the year 1800.[30]

In 1806, after plundering the Nizam's territories in Berar, the Pindaris infiltrated into the Bhonsla Raja's dominion. They plundered the town of Sohagpur and burnt the religious city of Ramtek.[31] The Pindaris then advanced towards Nagpur. Hearing about the incursion the Raja worked day and night arranging the defence and deployment of the troops. The soldiers in the first instance refused to march, unless they received their arrears of pay. Meanwhile, six to eight thousand Pindaris advanced via Sohagpur to Sewney and Chapra. On this movement of Nagpur troops, about 2,000 Pindaris got into their rear and plundered their *Bazar* and baggage. They let themselves loose on Ramtek, from where they separated into small parties and plundered Rundurden, Goondyong, Tuckanry and a number of other villages on the river Wardha. They also succeeded in killing and dispersing a party of Nagpur soldiers out for reconnoitring.[32] They were successful in creating utter confusion in Nagpur. The Raja requested the British Government for aid to repulse the Pindaris, and offered to pay two lakh rupees in return for help. The offer was rejected because of the policy of non-intervention. As a result of the great confusion then prevailing in Nagpur, the Raja determined to send his family and valuables to Chunda, a fortress, for safety.[33] He began to conscript troops to fight the Pindaris.

In 1807, the Pindaris repeated their attack on the Nagpur territory. During a skirmish, one of Chitu's adopted sons and Ramzan Khan, a Pindari leader, were killed at Singpur by Jaggan Nath Chowdhry. The Raja's troops fought bravely. Saddeek Ali Khan and Jaggan Nath Chowdhry commanded Bhonsla's troops at Chowragarh.[34] However, the Raja's party, in the end was the loser. It lost several horses, elephants and camels. The Pindaris committed great barbarities upon the people. They reached within ten miles of the city of Nagpur.[35]

In January 1809, a Pindari attack on Nagpur was successfully repulsed with a loss of two hundred horses to the Pindaris.[36]

In June 1809, Amir Khan decided to attack Nagpur. The Pindaris rallied themselves under his banner. His standing army at that time swelled to more than 40,000 besides 24,000 Pindaris.[31] The Pindaris were the followers of Karim and Chitu, who were then under detention of Scindia. Amir Khan extracted forced contributions from Saugar, Gur Kota and other places on the way.[38]

Lord Minto, when he learnt of the proposed attack on Nagpur, in spite of the policy of non-intervention, decided to give gratuitous relief to the Nagpur Raja.[39] Though the Raja had no claim upon the Company's protection, Lord Minto decided to intervene. He feared the establishment of Amir Khan's influence in Nagpur, a territory adjacent to the Nizam, another Muslim kingdom. He believed that "an enterprising and ambitious Musalman chief, at the head of a numerous army, irresistible by any power except that of the Company, should he be permitted to establish his authority on the ruins of the Raja's dominions, over territories contiguous to those of our ally, the Nizam, likewise a Mahomedan, with whom community of religion, combined with local powers and resources, might lead to the formation of projects for the subversion of the British alliance; of such a question there can be but one solution," —expulsion of Amir Khan from Nagpur.[40] The Secret Department at Fort William also agreed with this view of Lord Minto.[41]

When Amir Khan moved his army towards Nagpur, Lord Minto ordered two British forces into the field under

Barry Close with orders to throw the invader out. Amir Khan rapidly retired before the British advance.[42] The British forces surrounded Amir's possessions. His capital Seronj was occupied and when Amir Khan's designs were on the point of being completely foiled, Lord Minto issued orders for their withdrawal, for fear of the displeasure of the Home Authorities. The British withdrawal enabled the two Sardars of Amir Khan, Mannoo Mian and Saif Mian to reoccupy Seronj on March 23, 1810.[43] Lord Minto seems to have committed the greatest mistake of his career in dealing with Amir Khan. He had been rightly criticised for the withdrawal of the British army at a time when the annihilation of Amir Khan's power was almost in sight. But Lord Minto, in reply to his critics, defended his action by maintaining that direct British rule over Nagpur would have immensely increased their political responsibility and saddled them with enormous expenditure for its defence.[44]

In the winter of 1810, the Pindaris invaded Nagpur territories, going right upto the walls of the Residency.[45] They invaded Girhar, a place held in veneration by both the Hindus and the Muslims and more so by the Pindaris. All possible cruelties were perpetrated by them and the most savage outrages were committed on women, hundreds of whom killed themselves by drowning and setting fire to their person.[46] At the same time, a large number of them were carried away by the Pindaris. There was scarcely a village in the vicinity of Nagpur for miles around, which had not been visited and destroyed by them.

The two Pindari chiefs, Karim Khan and Chitu were released in November, 1811. After their release, the forces of Karim and Chitu joined hands and their estimated number amounted to nearly 60, 000. Chitu shared the feelings of Karim Khan and other Pindari chiefs that they should all unite and fight against the common enemy, the British and their ally, the Bhonsla Raja of Nagpur. This grave threat to the peace and tranquillity of India caused great fear and alarm all over the country. However, soon it was allayed by Scindia in his usual astute manner.

Karim wanted to avenge his humiliation at Daulat Rao Scindia's hands by committing the greatest excesses on his territory and of others. Though Karim and Chitu had joined hands, their differenees continued because Chitu had received lands and money from the Bhonsla. He, therefore, suggested regions other than Nagpur, although Karim was desirous of first attacking the latter, which he considered as the goose that laid the golden egg. This led to an open rift. Scindia took advantage of the same and approached Chitu, who after some persuasion by him and the Raja of Nagpur, agreed to join against Karim. Chitu withdrew from the coalition. The combined forces of Chitu and Scindia defeated Karim in the battle of Omutwarrah.[47] When Karim's own *Jemadars and Toredars* saw the battle going against their leader they deserted him and joined Chitu.[48] Karim fled with a small party of followers to Manohar Thana and later to Shergarh in Kota and took shelter there. Though his family continued to remain there, Karim soon left and went over to Amir Khan, who received him with great cordiality and generous hospitality.

After the Dashera of 1811, which was celebrated by a concourse of about 25,000 cavalry, the Pindaris repeated their almost regular annual raid on Nagpur. A party of 5,000 strong reached Nagpur, close to the heights of the British Residency. A minor skirmish took place between Amrat Rao Bukshy and the Pindaris. Bukshy held his ground and ultimately forced them to withdraw. He then moved to another part of the town, where Ganpat Rao Subedar kept the Pindaris at bay by continual cannonade.[49] Despite the best efforts of the Nagpur Generals, the Pindaris ultimately entered a quarter of the town Mangalwari, set fire to it, and plundered the people. They were successful in carrying away three elephants, which belonged to the Raja, who made an unsuccessful attempt to rescue them.[50] But soon the Pindaris withdrew from Nagpur territories in the south-easterly direction. It is significant that the Pindaris in their incursion into Nagpur did not suffer any loss whatsoever.

One body of the Pindaris, taking advantage of the absence of the Raja of Nagpur who had proceeded to attack

Bhopal, entered into the Nagpur territories and devastated large areas.[52] A part of this body plundered a village Kahpah, twenty miles north of Nagpur.[53] This time the Pindaris suffered some loss at the hands of Nagpur troops stationed at Jabalpur and Saugar.[54] The Pindaris then turned towards Gaya and Patna,[55] but on getting a report of the movement of the Allahabad troops, they were frightened and decided to return. On their way back, they passed through South Behar and Sarguja.[56] In this region, which had not previously witnessed Pindari incursions, the Pindaris levied heavy contributions on the people.

Another party of 3,000 Pindaris of Dost Mohammad's durra under Ramzan Khan and Gulab Kunwar, proceeded towards Jabalpur.[57] They plundered the town on the night of November 2, and ravaged all the villages near the town. They also plundered a valuable convoy of merchandise which belonged to the merchants of Mirzapur.[58] After plundering Jabalpur and the neighbouring area the Pindaris returned to Bagrode.

The end of 1813 saw Dost Mohammad attacking and plundering the Nagpur territory, while another body made its appearance near Mirzapur.[59] The Pindaris went and returned by the same route, viz., that of Burhanpur.

Another body of Pindaris, in 1814, numbering about 5,000 attacked Nagpur but was opposed by the Bhonsla troops under Salib Raj Pandit and Baji Khan.[60]

After the Dashera of 1815, the Pindaris attacked the south. Of the two parties that left the Pindari haunts, the one belonging to Wasil Mohammad marched towards the Nagpur territory. After plundering many villages in the immediate neighbourhood of Nagpur, they took the south-easterly direction and extended their depredations up to Chattisgarh.[61] It plundered the religious centre of Ramtek again, where Hindu pilgrims were looted and one section went as far as the town of Chapra, seventy miles beyond Ramtek.[62] In vain, the Nagpur forces tried to stop their advances. The Pindaris broke into a number of parties and escaped towards the Nizam's territories without sustaining any loss.

Yet another party of the Pindaris attacked the Nagpur territory and plundered the Chattisgarh, Umred, and villages near about Nagpur and Chanda.[63]

One body of Pindaris plundered Ramtek for the third time and advanced within twenty miles of Nagpur.[64]

The towns of Chattisgarh and Chapra were thoroughly plundered. The ravages and excesses of the Pindaris were considered to be a revenge for the Nagpur Raja's connections with the British.[65]

Pindari Incursions in Bhopal

Towards the close of the 18th century Bhopal witnessed the plundering bands of Pindaris riding rough-shod through its territories. Great misery prevailed in Bhopal and the surrounding areas. It suffered most from the Pindaris of Namdar Khan who once reached within two miles of the city of Bhopal. The Nawab in order to save his skin, encouraged the Pindaris to settle in his territory. The Pindaris from time to time gave all possible help to the Nawab, yet Bhopal territories continued to suffer at their hands.

In 1810, the Pindaris began to raid some of the districts of the Bhopal ruler.[66] About 12,000 Pindaris left Bagrode, under Dost Mohammad and proceeded towards Bhopal.[67] But, owing to a dispute between Dost Mohammad and Ramzan Khan, another Pindari leader, Dost Mohammad returned to Bagrode, his headquarters, while Ramzan continued his march and carried his depredations to Saugar.[68] Dost Mohammad promised to protect Bhopal from Pindari incursions and other enemies in lieu of which he was granted some lands in Jagir by Vazir Mohammad Khan of Bhopal.

In 1816, one party of Pindaris attacked the Bhopal region and perpetrated great cruelties. The helpless Nawab Vazir Mohammad Khan of Bhopal himself reported to the British that great misery prevailed in the state owing to Pindari incursions.[69]

Meanwhile, Karim's durra under his nephew Namdar Khan assisted Vazir Mohammad Khan of Bhopal and Durjan Sal of Kichi in their hostilities against Scindia in which action he acquitted himself creditably.

In June 1817, Pindaris from Karim Khan's durra spelt great havoc in Bhopal. In October they invaded the Bhopal territories for the second time during the year. They plundered villages and carried off cattle. However, they returned to Gyaraspur very soon.

Pindari Incursions in Gwalior

As already mentioned earlier, though the Pindaris were auxiliaries to the Marathas, and considered Scindia as their patron and well-wisher, they did not spare his territories.

One body of Pindaris, believed to be the followers of Karim, led by Durjan Sal, a rebel Sardar of Scindia, plundered villages within twenty miles of Gwalior[70]. One party of this body attacked Chimmuck where a small post of Gwalior Army was stationed for purpose of forage. The Pindaris very boldly attacked and not only succeeded in plundering the village but also defeated this body and returned with five hundred horses and some cattle captured.[71]

Another body of Pindaris ran into about two hundred cavalry of Daulat Rao Scindia near Gur Kota, and a fight ensued which resulted in a clean defeat of Scindia's forces. Several of his soldiers were killed and wounded. Eighty horses were taken by the Pindaris. The remainder escaped to the nearby fortresses.

By 1812, the Pindaris came into more prominence. Supported and aided by Amir Khan and the loose predatory bands, the Pindaris swept through Central India from end to end, passing through Malwa and Bundelkhand as and when they liked. The unchecked license given to the Pindaris enabled them to increase their numbers enormously. More than 50,000 Pindaris and other free-booters were now loose in Central India.[72]

In March, 1813, one of Scindia's officers Lal Khan was deputed to attack Appa Kunde Rao, a rebellious chief, but Lal Khan instead fell upon Dost Mohammad and mauled him badly. Dost Mohammad, leaving twenty-five dead, fled to Pithari, from where he shifted to Rahat-garh.[73]

The *Killedar* of Asirgarh, Yashwant Rao Lad, almost threw off the nominal allegiance to Scindia and employed Pindaris for the express purpose of plunder and loot. He and his Pindaris committed all sorts of atrocities.[74]

Two bodies of Pindaris set out in February and March, 1813. One crossed the Narbada for the south to attack Daulat Rao Scindia's possessions while the second went towards Nagpur and plundered the people on the way.

One party of Pindaris, two thousand in number, though originally intended to go on a distant expedition to Jabalpur, soon changed its course and confined itself to ravaging territories around Gwalior.

In November, 1813, the Pindaris of Chitu's durra laid waste the Scindia's possession south of Narbada. Dost Mohammad did not lag behind. He burnt and sacked more than thirty villages.[75]

On 24th January, 1814, eight thousand of Dost Mohammad's Pindaris ravaged and destroyed Ratgarh and the country surrounding it, belonging to Appa Kunde Rao.[76] However, soon the Maratha forces were able to inflict a severe defeat upon the Pindaris, a few of whom were killed, fifty taken prisoner and three hundred horses captured. The Pindaris then fled to Bhilsa.[76]

Alarmed by the continued increase of power of the Pindaris and their repeated incursions in his territories, Scindia decided to adopt another stratagem for their capture. Baptiste was ordered to lead an expedition against them. But he had another plan up his sleeve. He knew that the Pindaris were not united, and if one party were attacked, the other would take alarm and then it would be difficult to capture them separately. He, therefore, brought over Chitu and Dost Mohammad to his views by promising them *Jagirs* etc., and then negotiated for the same with Kushal Kunwar and other Pindari chiefs of Karim's party. However, nothing came out of this design of Baptiste.[78]

Pindaris' Incursions in Saugar

Nearer home, Saugar was a great point of attraction to the Pindaris. The Pindaris had their haunts almost on the border of Saugar territories. It was, therefore, repeatedly attacked and plundered.

In 1813, instead of going to Jabalpur, as was originally decided, the Pindaris attacked and ravaged the country near about Saugar. The town itself received their attention. They carried away a great number of women.[79]

In 1814, 2,500 Pindaris under Ramzan Khan, Wasil Mohammad and Subhan Kunwar plundered the Saugar villages[80] as reported by T. Boroughs, Commanding Lohargaon, to Wauchope, Superintendent, Political Affairs, Bundelkhand.

In June 1815, the Pindaris again attacked Saugar where they committed ravage and barbarities which surpassed all their former acts. About sixty villages were plundered and burnt. About four hundred men, women and children were massacred in cold blood and about hundred men and women carried off as prisoners.[81] A great deal of property in gold, silver and cash was also taken away. The cruelties perpetrated were of the most wanton nature, particularly their treatment of the women, which excited the utmost dread and horror of the Pindaris.[82]

Two separate bodies of Pindaris from the durra of Muzhar Buksh and Wasil Mohammad invaded Saugar territories. Four thousand Pindaris of Muzhar Buksh left Bhilsa on the 13th May, 1816 and plundered the Saugar region. They committed great atrocities in the villages near Saugar but soon returned to Gyaraspur due to rains.[83]

When the British started making preparations for an all-out attack on the Pindaris, they in their alarm did not venture to go out for distant excursions. One of the parties of Pindaris which reached the bank of Narbada to reconnoitre the area and attack Saugar, was surprised by Major Clarke and Lt. Bulkley on the 25th of April, 1817. About two hundred Pindaris were killed and wounded. The British loss was only one private killed. Bulkley also inflicted a loss of about hundred killed and wounded including the son-in-law of Sheikh Dulloo.[84]

Yet another party went towards the Saugar territory, where they were allowed a free passage by the Saugar Raja, Benaik Rao.[85] They were furnished with supplies too,[86] and what was more, business men of the town were sent to the Pindari camp to help them to meet their supply position.[87] Benaik Rao, when questioned about his conduct, maintained that he was compelled to adopt this attitude because of the absence of his troops which had been despatched to Belelle to guard against the Nawab of Bhopal and the possible Pindari attack on his frontier in that direction.[88] The Pindaris on their arrival at Saugar sent agents to negotiate a free passage. The Raja knew that he was not capable of defending his territories and in case he refused to give permission, the whole Saugar territory would be over-run by the Pindaris. Benaik Rao maintained that the Pindari durras numbering nearly 50,000 were living right on the Saugar frontier and they constantly used the Saugar region for passage and yet commit depredations. Had he demurred, the Pindaris would have committed yet greater horrors. Had the British power and military might been ready to help him, he could have been bold enough to refuse a passage.[89] Adam accepted this explanation and exonerated Benaik Rao of all the blame for helping the Pindaris.[90]

In May, 1817 Saugar again fell a prey to the devastation of the Pindari freebooters who were scattered practically all over the region. The Saugar Raja was absolutely apathetic to the scene of devastation. Not only did he not make efforts to stop this, but when approached by the Pindaris to pay his contribution for exemption from Pindari raids, Benaik Rao replied that he had no money to pay, and that the Pindaris in lieu of payment were free to raid and plunder a few villages if that would satisfy them.[91]

In October, 1817, the Pindaris once again invaded Saugar, plundered the villages and carried off cattle and women.[92]

The British were worried on account of the frequent Pindari raids, which reached their peak in the first decade of the 19th century. Wide and extensive regions were laid waste. No more could the people live in peace. The Pindaris soon constituted themselves into a grave threat to the British Dominion in India, as they made repeated inroads in British territories. The British prestige was rapidly declining, to the extent that the people began emigrating to areas where they could at least enjoy security of life.

FOOT-NOTES

1 Lyall mentions the figure of disbanded soldiers as half a million, while Marshman puts the figure as 1,00,000.

2 The frame "of Indian polity continually brings forward a great proportion of individuals who can hardly find subsistence in the present state of things, but as soldiers. A military life is their preferable hereditary destination."
N. A. I. For. Sec. 1816 : O. C. No. 1 15 June, 1816 : Governor-General's Minute, 1 December, 1815, para 23.

3 B. G. R. D. No. 403, Pol. Deptt. 1813 : Richard Strachey to Adam, Scindia's Camp, Gwalior, 19 November, 1813.

4 In 1805 Holkar temporarily left the Deccan for Punjab, when numerous bodies of his soldiers were turned loose. Having no other means of subsistence, they joined the Pindaris in large numbers. Another circumstance also occurred which helped in swelling the

ranks of the Pindaris when Holkar's army turned mutinous and consequently discharged, went over to Scindia and offered their services, which were naturally refused. Whereupon finding no other source of employment, those soldiers joined the ranks of Pindaris. N. A .I. For. Sec.1817: O. C. No. 1, 28 January, 1817. Close to Hastings, Gwalior, 7 January, 1817.
Also : On the British reduction of Hathras, a large body of disbanded and unemployed soldiers of Hathras joined the Pindaris and followed them in their Deccan campaign.

5 The increase of Pindari numbers "is the natural consequence of their extended territorial establishments and especially of the momentous changes in the state of India, produced by the operation of our subsidiary alliance and the result of the Marhatta War. Deprived of their accustomed sources of subsistence, they have augmented the bands of predatory troops..."
N. A. I. For. Sec. 1814: O. C. No. 1, 21 June, 1814:
Minute of Edmonstone, 31 March, 1844, para 17.

6 Hastings himself admitted "those who cannot be received by us or by regular states necessarily resort to the Pindaris."
N. A. I. For. Sec. 1816: O. C. No. 1, 15 June, 1816:
Governor-General's Minute, 1 December, 1815.

7 M. I. O .L. L. H. M. S. Vol. No. 521, Item No. 9.

8 N. A. I. For. Pol. 1817: O. C. No. 11 February, 1817, Elphinstone to Moira, Poona, 8 January, 1817.

9 N. A. I. For. Sec. 1816: O. C. No. 1, 20 April, 1816 :
Governor-General's Minute, 13 April, 1816, para 12.

10 In "both French and English versions of the Russian campaign, the Cossacks are called clouds and swarms, and represented as flights of locusts, as well from their countless number as from their devastations; yet their aggregate amount did not exceed forty thousand with all the divisions of the Russian army."
Blacker, p. 19.

11 Fitzclarence : *Journal of a Route Across India*, p. 11.

12 The very "people who were plundered frequently followed the party in the hope of receiving what they had lost, or making up for it, on the Pindary system; and in this way the Lubhur was gradually increased, as a river is swelled in its course by the accession of inferior streams."
Op. cit., McNaghten : *A Memoir of the Nagpur Subsidiary Force*, p. 116.

Also : Thus the "Bhilala chief of Bakhatgarh and Selani on the Nerbudda, whose lands had been devastated by the Pindaris put themselves at the head of their retainers, and being joined by numbers in similar cases, became even more dreaded plunderers in Nimar than the worst of the Pindaris."

Central Provinces District Gazetteers : Nimar District. Vol.4. p. 38.

13 The "party of Pindaris which lately ravaged Ganjam, consisted of 1,500 horse when they passed the Nerbudda; but their numbers had increased to 5,000 when they entered the Company's territory," *Origin of the Pindaris* : By an Officer, Allahabad Reprint, Foot-note, Chap, VII.

14 Malcolm : *Rise and Progress*, para 4.

15 The state of "society in Central India was similar to that of Europe in the early part of the Middle Ages, when robbers, and outlaws, free companions and banditti, were objects of less horror than the more powerful and equally rapacious barons." Wilson : *History of the British India*, p. 212.

16 B. G. R. D. No. 28, Item No. 22 : Col. Morgan, Chief of Surat, to Bombay Council, 11 February, 1783.

17 Duff : *History of the Marathas,* Vol. II, p. 283.

18 Selections from Satara Rajas and Peshwa's Diaries : Vol. V, Baji Rao II : Rao Bahadur Ganesh Chimnaji Vad.

19 P. R. C. : Vol. V, Nagpur Affairs, 1781-1820, O. C. No. 27, Colebrook, Resident at Nagpur to Earl of Mornington, Nagpur, 17 October 1799.

20 P. R. C. : Vol. V, Nagpur Affairs, 1781-1820, O. C. No. 34, Colebrook to the Governor-General, 23 April, 1800, p. 50, para 4.

21 S. P. D: Vol. 1 to 46 : Peep into Maratha History : Letter No. 32, Shrimantji Rajeshwari Dada to Peshwa, 26 August, 1801.

22 The whole villages were "*be-ehirav*—without a light or village fire." Central Provinces Gazetteers : Hoshangabad District, Vol. A, pp. 32-34.

23 B. G. R. : D. No. 161, Item No. 3, Col. Murray to Maj. Gen. Nicol, Camp at Ujjain, 5 October, 1804.

24 B. G. R: D. No. 165 Item No. 6: Intelligence from Baroda, 1 March, 1805.

25 N. A. I. For. Sec. 1806 : O. C. No. 86-90, 10 April, 1806, Col. W. Wallace to M. S. Elphinstone, Resident at Nagpur, Camp at Akola, 26 November, 1805.

26 Bengal Government Records: Judicial Department: Letters from the Court of Directors to the Governor General in Bengal, 17 December, 1806.

27 H. R. S. I. : Bengal Secret Consultation, 1805, p. 86.

28 H. R. R. S. No. 122, Vol. No. 171, Col. Close, Resident at Poona, to Lt. Col. Wallace, 22 October, 1805.

29 N. A. I. For. Sec. 1806 : O. C. No. 86-90, 10 April, 1806, Wallace to Elphinstone, Akola, 26 November, 1805.

30 P. R. C.: Vol. V: Nagpur Affairs: 1781-1820. O. C. No. 34, H. T. Colebrook, Resident at Nagpur, to the Earl of Mornington, Governor-General, Nagpur, 23 April, 1800.

31 N.A.I. For. Sec. 1806: O. C. No. 54-55, 13 March, 1806, Letter No. 10, Elphinstone to Sir George Barlow, Governor-General, Nagpur, 4 February, 1806.

32 *Ibid.*

33 N. A. I. For. Sec. 1806: O. C. No. 47, 27 March, 1806, Elphinstone to Barlow, Nagpur, 12 February, 1806.
Also: B. G. R. Pol. Deptt. 1806, D. No. 178, Item No. 4
Col Wallace to Baroda Resident, Maj. A Walker, 24 Feb. 1806.

34 N. A. I. For. Pol. 1807: O. C. No. 70A, 30 April, 1807: Jenkins, Acting Resident at Nagpur, 9 April 1807.

35 M. I. O. L. L.: H. M. S. Vol. No. 520 Item No. 5, Bengal Secret Cons. 1807.

36 N. A. I. For. Pol. 1809: O. C. No. 10, 11 February, 1809, Sydenham to Edmonstone, Hyderabad, 13 January, 1809.

37 Marshman : *History of India*, p. 296.

38 N.A.I. For. Sec. 1809 : O.C. No. 6, 8 July, 1809, Letter No. 11, Jenkins, Acting Resident, Nagpur to Lord Minto, Nagpur, 12 June, 1809.

39 Duff : *History of the Marathas*, p. 325, Vol. III.

40 Lord Minto in India, By his great-niece—the Countess of Minto, p. 192, London, 1880.

41 N.A.I. For. Sec. 1810 : O.C. No. 19, 2 May, 1810 : From Secret Department to Maj. Gen. Leger, Comdg. the forces, Fort William, 28 April, 1810.

42 Military Department : O.C. Nos. 38 and 56, 17 April, 1810 : J. Gordon to Lt. Col. Ball, Adjutant General, Camp in Tearee, 4 April, 1810.

Also : Lt. Col. G. Martindale, Commanding Bundelkhand to Lt. Col. Ball, Adjutant General, 1 April, 1810.

43 N.A.I. For. Sec. 1810 : O.C. No. 19, 2 May, 1810 : From Secret Department to Maj. Gen. Leger, Comdg. the forces, Fort William, 28 April, 1810.

44 H.R.R. S. No. 160, Vol. No. 200 : Letter No. 20, Jenkins to Minto, 27 December, 1810.
Also : Parliamentary Papers, Extract Secret Letter from Bengal, 16 August, 1811.

45 H.R.R. S. No. 160, Vol. No. 200, Letter No. 20, Jenkins to Minto, 27 December, 1810, para 5.

Also : Parliamentary Papers, Extract Secret Letter from Bengal 16 August, 1811.

46 H.R.R. S. No. 160, Vol. No. 200, Letter No. 20, Jenkins to Minto, 27 December, 1810, para 5.

47 Thus was "dissolved by the folly of the two chiefs one of the most alarming confederacies not only to Scindia but to every established government."
Tod : *Origin Progress and Present State of Pindaris*, p. 8

48 Subsequent to his defeat "some of his adherents were dispersed. Some joined Cheetoo, some proceeded to Doast Mohemmed near Rahtgur, and others fled towards Bhopal."
N.A.I. For. Pol. O.C. No. 24, 8 February, 1812 :
Strachey to Minto, Gwalior, 19 January, 1812.

49 N.A.I. For. Pol. 1811 : O.C. No. 9, 13 December, 1811, Jenkins to Lt. Col. Hewett, Vice-President, Governor General's Council, Nagpur, 18 November, 1811.

50 P.R.R. Vol.V (Nagpur Affairs, 1781-1840) Letter No. 194, Jenkins to Hewett, Nagpur, 18 November, 1811.

51 In the action at Nagpur, described above, Amrat Rao Bukshy in one of the actions suffered a light wound from a matchlock of a Pindari.
P.R.R: Vol. V, Nagpur Affairs, Letter No. 194, Jenkins to Hewett, 18 November, 1811.

52 N.A.I. For. Nol. 1812 : O.C. No. 17, 10 April, 1812 :
Russell to Edmonstone, Hydrabad, 20 March, 1812.

53 A.O. Poona Records : Jenkins, Resident Nagpur to M. Elphinstone Resident, Poona, Nagpur, 6 November, 1812.

54 U.P.A. : Mirzapur Collectorate, p. 132. Wm. Lock, Acting Magistrate of Mirzapur to Capt. Roughsedge, Comdg. Rampur Bn. at Sonapura Mirzapur, 12 April, 1812

55 N.A.I. For. Pol. 1812 : O.C. No. 16, 10 April, 1812 : Jenkins to Minto, Nagpur, 20 March, 1812.

56 Sarguja was a dependency of Nagpur.

57 N.A.I. For. Sec. 1813 : O.C. No. 26-27, 19 November, 1813 : Wauchope to Adams, Banda, 4 November, 1813.

58 N.A.I. For. Sec. 1813 : O.C. No. 16-17, 26 November, 1813 : Wauchope to Brooks, A.G.G. Benaras, Banda, 11 November, 1813.

59 N.A.I. For. Sec. 1813 : O.C. No. 46-47, 10 December, 1813, Extracts of a letter dated the 20th November, 1813 addressed to Maj. Gen. Ward by Mr. Rettery, Judge and Magistrate, Mirzapur.

60 N.A.I. For. Sec. 1814 : O.C. No. 13, 11 March, 1814 :
Wauchope to Adam, Karauli, 24 February, 1814.

61 N.A.I. For. Sec. 1816 : O.C. No. 8-45, 26 September, 1816,
Jenkins to Adam, Nagpur, 14 February, 1816.

62 N.A.I. For. Sec. 1815 : O.C. No. 4, 8 December. 1815.

Jenkins to Adam, Nagpur, 17 November, 1815.

63 N.A.I. For. Sec. 1816 : O.C. No. 53, 2 March, 1816 : Jenkins to Adam, Nagpur, 3 February, 1816.

64 B.G.R. D. No. 432 : Pol. Deptt. 1816, Jenkins to Warden, Nagpur, 5 December, 1816.

65 N.A.I. For. Pol. 1817 : O.C. No. 85, 22 February, 1817 : Jenkins to Adam Nagpur, 21 January, 1817.

66 P.R.R. : Poona Affairs (1805-1810) Vol. VII, Edited by G.S. Sardesai, Bombay 1940 : Letter No. 342, Russell to Governor-General, Poona 12 June, 1810.

67 N.A.I. For. Sec. 1812 : O.C. No. 46-48, 13 November, 1812, Capt. J. Whitehead, Captain Commanding at Lohargaon to Wauchope. Lohargaon, 28 October, 1812.

68 N.A.I. For. Sec. 1812 : O.C. No. 42-45, 25 November, 1812, Wauchope to Edmonstone, Chief Secretary, Banda, 1 November, 1812.

69 N.A.I. For. Sec. 1816 : O.C. No. 10-15. 9 November, 1816 : Translation of a letter from Nazar Mohammad Khan of Bhopal to the Superintendent of Political Affairs in Bundelkhand, dated 17 Ruzub, Hijri, 1230.

70 N.A.I. For. Sec. 1812 : O.C. No. 1-2, 17 April, 1812 : Strachey, Resident at Gwalior to Edmonstone, 29 March, 1812.
Also O.C. No. 32-39, 17 April, 1812, R. Strachey to J. Richardson, A.G.G. Bundelkhand.

71 N.A.I. For. Sec. 1812 : O.C. No. 32-39, Strachey to Richardson, 29 March, 1812.

72 Imperial Gazetteer of India, Central India, p. 24. Cal. 1908.

73 N.A.I. For. Pol. 1813 : O.C. No. 36, 5 March, 1813 : Strachey to Minto, Scindia's camp at Bhind, 18 February, 1813.

74 Central Provinces District Gazetteers. Nimar District, Vol. A., p. 39

75 B.G.R. D. No. 403, Pol. Deptt, 183, R. Strachey to Moira, Scindia's camp, Gwalior, 15 November, 1813.

76 N.A.I. For. Sec. 1814 : O.C. No. 10, 15 April, 1814, Wauchope to Adam, Bundelkhand, 2 April, 1814.

77 N.A.I. For. Sec. 1814 : O,C. No. 16-17, 27 May, 1814 : Wauchope to Adam, Banda, 14 May, 1814.
Also : Popham to Wauchope, Lohargaon, 12 May, 1814,

78 N.A.I. For. Sec. 1814 : N.C. No. 112-123, 6 December, 1814, Copy of letter No. 32 from S. Strachey to Moira, Scindia's camp, 21 November. 1814.

79 N.A.I. For. Sec. 1814 : O.C, No. 25-26, 22 October, 1813 Wauchope to Adam. 8 October, 1813.
Also : Extracts from a Paper of Intelligence, 28 Sept. 1813.

80 I.H.R.C. Vol. XVI Calcutta December, 1939: Defence of the frontier of Bihar and Orissa against the Pindari and Maratha incursions p. 6. K.P. Mitra.

81 N.A.I, For. Sec. 1815: O.C. No. 70-71, 20 June, 1815: Wauchope to Adam, Banda, 9 June, 1815.

92 N.A.I. For. Sec. 1815: O.C. No. 72-73, 20 June, 1815: Thomas Barron, Comdg. at Lohargaon to Wauchope, Lohargaon, 4 June, 1815.

83 N.A.I, For. Sec. 1816: O.C. No. 14, 13 July, 1816: Wauchope to Adam, Banda, 25 June, 1816.

84 Supplement to the Government of India Gazette: Thursday, May 22, 1817

85 N.A.I. For. Pol, 1817: O.C. No. 59, 17 May, 1817: Adam to Maddock, Acting Superintendent of Political Affairs in Bundelkhand, Fort William, 17 May, 1817.

86 N.A.I. For. Pol. 1817: O.C. No. 59, 17 May, 1817: Adam to Maddock, Fort William, 17 May, 1817.

87 N.A.I. For. Pol. 1817: O.C. No. 57-58, 17 May, 1817: Maddock to Adam, Banda, 30 April, 1817, enclosing a deposition of Bhow Pindari on 27 April, 1817.

88 N.A.I. For. Pol. 1817: O.C. No. 57-58, 17 May, 1817: Madnock to Adam, Banda, 30 April, 1917, Translation of a letter from Benaik Rao, received on 22 April, 1817.

89 N.A.I. For. Pol. 1817: O.C. No. 57-58, 17 May, 1817: Maddock to Adam, Banda, 30 April, 1817, Enclosing Translation of a letter from Benaik Rao to the Acting Supdt. received 22 April, 1817.

90 N.A.I, For. Pol. 1817: O.C. No. 59, 17 May, 1817: Adam to Maddock, Fort William, 17 May, 1817.

91 N.A.I. For. Pol. 1817: O.C. No. 61, 17 May, 1817: Maddock to Adam, Banda, 4 May, 1817.

92 N.A.I. For. Sec. 1817: O.C. No. 35, 24 October, 1817: Wauchope to Adam at Kanpur, 3 October, 1817.

5

Pindari Incursions in Rajputana and British and Allied Territories

The decline of the Mughal power and its withdrawal from the Rajput scene opened new vistas for the Marathas. This was because conditions in Rajputana were no less chaotic than in Central India. The end of the 18th century saw several independent Rajput principalities reduced to abject helplessness due to the ravages of the Marathas. The condition of various states like Jaipur, Jodhpur, Udaipur etc., was deplorable. The Rajputs were themselves responsible for creating such a situation. They invited the Marathas and had to bear the consequences. In a struggle for the throne of Jaipur, there was a contest between the supporters of Ishwari Singh and Madho Singh, the two claimants to the throne. The Maharana of Udaipur, whose daughter was married to Raja Jai Singh, supported the claim of Madho Singh to the throne. In order to strengthen the claim, the Maharana invited Malhar Rao Holkar to his aid on promise of eighty lakhs of rupees for putting Madho Singh on the Jaipur throne. As surety, he made over the district of Rampura to Holkar. Once the system was established, it became almost a ritual with the Rajput Rajas to invite the Maratha aid on the smallest pretext. The Marathas took the fullest advantage and strengthened their hold on Rajputana, and ultimately became almost the rulers.

An excuse for interfering in the internal affairs of the Rajput states was never wanting. Being extremely weak to face the attacks of the Marathas, the Rajputs engaged them against one another, on payment.[1] The promises of payment were seldom fulfilled and hence the Rajput princes were again subjected to all sorts of humiliations and this generally resulted in fresh exactions, fresh promises, which too remained unfulfilled. Thus the ground for constant interference by outsiders in Rajput states continued. "There appeared to be no prospect of shaking off the vampires that had fastened themselves on the princes of Rajputana, as long as a drop of blood continued to circulate in the veins of their victims."[2]

The Rajputs had lost all their glory, valour and heroism. Their armies were mere shadows of their former selves. They were incapable of resisting the Marathas, the Pathans and the Pindaris, to which they all fell an easy prey. This led to their moral degradation, economic ruin and political oblivion. Rajputana appeared to be bleeding at every pore.

All this time predatory bands, whether of the Marathas or the Pathans under Amir Khan, were roving about like the "flight of locusts leaving famine and desolation in their track."

They had an ineffective control in their own states. The subordinate feudatory chiefs had assumed almost complete independence. They obeyed their masters only when it suited them. They often joined hands with the enemy against their own masters. Revenue and *Nazar* were often withheld; their obligations to their masters, including the sending of military quotas, had long ago been given up. Each prince was preying upon the other and consequently their revenues touched the rock-bottom mark. There was no administration worth the name. The feudal masters and their liege-lords were incapable of controlling this state of affairs.

The indifference of the British government towards Rajputana added to the confusion, and plunged it into complete darkness and a vacuum was created, of which the fullest possible advantage was taken by the predatory bands then roaming about there. In spite of such conditions, the Rajput Rajas were still indulging in the luxuries of wine and women.[3] They were now mere relics of their past glory.

The condition of Mewar was the worst. Nothing remained of its former glory. Of its political existence, the Indian chiefs were hardly aware. It had been finished once and for all. There was no agriculture as its fertile valleys were all laid waste; there was no revenue, the state and its people were reduced to the last stage of penury. "Steeped in the dregs of poverty, insulted and harassed by the cool, crafty and unfeeling... rapacious Pathan" and the Marathas, the House of Mewar was sunk to the lowest depths of misery.

Jaipur too suffered untold agonies at the hands of the Marathas and the Pathans, whose incursions fully undermined its resources and hence its peace and prosperity.

Pindari Incursions in Rajputana

Rajputana was reduced to a wretched state because of the selfish policy pursued by each of the chiefs and also because of the Maratha oppression for about half a century.

The Pindari incursions in Rajputana started in 1806, when Udaipur was visited by the Pindaris of Amir Khan and the armies of Holkar and Scindia.

Amir Khan and the Rajput States

Amir Khan, by interfering in the local affairs of Rajputana, became the virtual lord of the region. He stuck himself so deep in this region that as long as there was a possibility of his getting any money, he remained there and continued to exact the greatest tributes from them. So great was his hold over Rajputana that the *Thakurs* of Jaipur implored Raja Jagat Singh that "the Ameer has now taken possession of Joudhpoor and of all the principal places in Mewar to the prejudice of your proper authority: the Musulmans will shortly be the rulers of the territory of this principality."[4] He and his army of about 30,000 men were living at free quarters in Rajputana.

Amir Khan and Jodhpur

Amir Khan had been meddling in the Rajput affairs with greater vigour for quite some time. By his constant pillage and plunder, he had reduced Jodhpur to the lowest ebb of poverty.

In April 1808, by an act of most perfidious cruelty he murdered Thakur Sawai Singh of Jodhpur. Thakur Sawai Singh, a determined enemy of Raja Man Singh of Jodhpur and the partisan of Dhonkal Singh, posthumous son, legitimate heir and claimant to the throne of Jodhpur, continued to defy the Jodhpur forces. The Raja approached Amir Khan to assist him in apprehending the rebel Sardar. Amir Khan, accordingly, laid siege to the fort of Nagaur, where Sawai Singh was defending himself, but it was so well defended that Amir Khan despaired of success. He, therefore, decided to resort to stratagem. He sent word to Sawai Singh that they should meet and settle affairs. The unsuspecting Sawai Singh agreed for a meeting with Amir Khan, who gave him the most solemn assurances for personal safety. At one stage Sawai Singh refused to leave the fort, out of fear, whereupon, at the shrine of a *peer* near the fort wall of Nagaur, Amir Khan went with hardly any escort, to impress upon Sawai Singh, and took an oath of friendship and personal security. When Sawai Singh went with nine hundred of his principal followers, Amir in base violation of his word, had the tent fallen, surrounded and fired upon. Sawai Singh and his principal followers were killed on the spot and his head was sent to Raja Man Singh. Out of the seven hundred Rajput followers, who were outside the camp, hardly two hundred were able to escape. The rest were butchered. After this he took possession of the fort easily.[5]

Dewan Induraj and the head priest Deo Nath, who exercised great influence over the Raja, made efforts to wean away this influence of Amir Khan and his Pathans. Amir Khan was asked to leave the state immediately. Though he did not refuse to go, he asked for an immediate settlement of all outstanding claims against the state. During the course of negotiations, hot words were exchanged leading to the murder of the Dewan and the priest in October 1815. In spite of these shocking murders, Amir Khan and his followers left Jodhpur without the least harm. Busawan Lal, Amir Khan's biographer maintains that the assassination was perpetrated at the instigation of the *Rani* of Man Singh and his son Chattar Singh.[6] Man Singh after this event feigned insanity and left the state to his son Chattar Singh.[7]

Amir Khan and Udaipur

By 1810, Amir Khan had become the arbiter of the destiny of Udaipur, the premier state of Rajputana. Seton in his letter to N. B. Edmonstone, expressed the fear that Amir Khan would soon take possession of Udaipur.[8] Metcalfe also expressed concern to Lord Minto regarding Amir Khan establishing his sway over Udaipur and Indore. Amir Khan had gone to the extent of establishing a brigade at Jodhpur and Udaipur. Jamshed Khan was the Brigade Commander in Udaipur. Amir Khan, and Jamshed Khan, his agent, treated the Rana with the greatest indignity and terrorised him into abject submission. The rule and the power of the Rana was limited to the four walls of the city fort. Such was the enormous influence and control he wielded on the Rana that he became the cause of the cold-blooded murder of Krishna Kumari, 'the flower of Rajasthan', and daughter of Maharana Bhim Singh of Udaipur. The hand of

Krishna Kumari was sought in marriage by Raja Jagat Singh of Jaipur and Raja Man Singh of Jodhpur. They both engaged, in turn, the services of Amir Khan "one of the most notorious villains India ever produced,"[9] to help them in the fulfilment of their desire to wed Krishna Kumari. Amir Khan, after indulging in the war for the hand of Krishna Kumari, suggested to the Maharana that he should marry her to Raja Man Singh of Jodhpur, and if that was not possible, to establish peace in Rajputana, he should put Krishna Kumari to death. The meek and cowardly Maharana, seeing no way out, decided that Krishna Kumari must die. The task was given to Daulat Singh, to "save the honour of Udaipur" but he refused out-right and cursed those who even thought in those terms. Jawan Das, a brother of the Maharana, was next approached to perpetrate the deed. He went with a dagger to stab her, but was so struck with her innocence and beauty that the dagger fell from his hand and he returned without committing the carnal sin. Then the task was entrusted to the women in the harem. The mother implored and threatened and tried her best to save her daughter, but in vain. Krishna Kumari consoled her mother thus : "Why afflict yourself, my mother, at this shortening of the sorrows of life ? I fear not to die ! Am I not your daughter ?" Twice was poison administered by sister Chand Bai, but with no effect. For the third time again, she drank poison—more powerful than the previous ones. "Having drunk that, she slept a sleep from which she never awoke."[10] Before she took the last cup, she exclaimed : "This is the marriage to which I was foredoomed."[11]

In February, 1815, Jamshed Khan, committed great barbarities in the Udaipur territories. He put to death one of the nobles of Udaipur, Sardar Singh. Within seven days, his eldest son, Amar Singh, who wanted to avenge his father's death, was poisoned.[12] Even after two months of committing the murders, Jamshed Khan was still in Udaipur with 11,000 horses, infantry and thirteen guns and was encamped just twenty-four miles from the city.[13]

In April, 1815, about 9,000 Pindaris under Chitu encamped at Neemuch, from where they moved towards Chittore, looting and plundering villages on the way. They stopped at Chittor for some time, committing ravages all around it. In October, 1815, Amir Khan levied contributions in Bikaner also.

An idea of their might and undaunted spirit can be had from the way they plundered 'the outer areas of the forts of Kumulmere' (in Udaipur Region), an impregnable fort of the time, undeterred by the fearful and doughty Arabs whose garrison was stationed there for its defence.

Zalim Singh Jhala and the Pindaris

The Pindaris were first seen in the Kota state as early as 1780 and soon posed a grave threat to the peace of the southern regions of Kota. The menace assumed such proportions that the peasantry left their hearths and homes and began to settle elsewhere. This alarmed Zalim Singh, who immediately issued an assurance of protection to the peasants and requested them to return. The peasants refused to do so, unless concessicns and exemptions were granted to them. In some cases Zalim Singh remitted revenue for one year, while in others, he exempted people from all taxes for four to seven years, according to the severity of loss sustained at the hands of the Pindaris. The descendants of those killed in action against the Pindaris, were also exempted from all taxes that were due from them.

In order to free the southern regions of Kota from the repeated Pindari raids, he authorised the Pargana Officers to enlist Seebundi troops for the protection of these regions. They were paid one and a half anna a day. The area, thus covered for defence purposes, consisted of the Parganas of Suket, Chechat, Urmal, Shahabad, Ramgarh, Rampura, Ghatoli and Manohar Thana. In spite of these efforts, the Pindari devastation continued at regular intervals. On 4th February, 1814, they made an incursion into the territory of Kota and plundered the town of Baran, taking away a huge booty.[14] In November, 1814, they ravaged another part of Kota territory.[15]

Thus Zalim Singh realised that the policy of defence had proved unavailing against the Pindaris and, therefore he decided to resort to appeasement. With this aim, he successfully enlisted the support of the Gujars, Bhils and, Minas, organised them into defensive bands and placed them under one regular officer of Kota army. They were all very lightly equipped and mounted and were ordered to adopt the same tactics as those of the Pindaris.[16]

Zalim Singh took a policy decision and issued a call to the Pindaris to settle in the area allotted to them in Kota state. He invited certain Pindaris with influence and command to settle in the border *parganas* of southern and eastern Kota. They were given all facilities. Land was granted and loans given for purchase of cattle and seeds. They were more pampered than the ordinary peasants. Land was given in the *parganas* of Urmal, Suket, Mangrol, Baran, Manohar Thana etc. The Pindaris were settled in nearly forty-three villages in the border areas. Their duty was to repel the Pindari raids.

Karim's wives and sons were extended all possible respect and consideration by the Kota Raja when he was in confinement in the Scindia's 'gaol' for which he was extremely grateful. Again it was Zalim Singh, who paid the release money for Karim and Chitu. For the second time, when Karim was placed in detention, at Holkar's court, Zalim Singh again looked after his family, including his immediate followers. They were given a place to live between Gagron and Jhalarapatan and the place became famous as 'Pindaron-Ki-Chowki.' In 1815, when Col. Tod visited it, he noticed that it was a pretty prosperous place and there was an *Idgaha* constructed there, seeing which he remarked, "villains who, while they robbed and murdered even defenceless women, prayed five times a day."[17]

Zalim Singh and Amir Khan knew each other well for a long time. He had great admiration for Amir Khan's dash, bravery, and pluck. He, therefore, maintained cordial relations with him. In the marriage of Gordhan Das, Zalim Singh's son, in 1801, Amir Khan was honoured with dresses. The marriage of Ajab Kumari Bai, daughter of Zalim Singh, was attended by Amir Khan and other Pindari leaders.

In 1805, when he was leading a wandering life, Amir Khan's family was sheltered by him in Shergarh.[18] While there, one of Amir Khan's wives made Maharao Ummed Singh of Kota her *Rakhiband-Bhai.* Zalim Singh also received such *Rakhi.* In 1810, while Amir Khan's family was still at Shergarh, one of his wives gave birth to a son there. Amir Khan's brother-in-law Gaffoor Khan often visited Shergarh and received warm reception from Zalim Singh. Amir Khan repaid his debt. Once, when the Pindaris were causing great havoc, on a request from Zalim Singh, he inflicted severe losses on them and routed them out of the Kota territories.[19]

It may be noted that Bilendi and Shergarh became a sort of Pindari haven. Pindaris from all places assembled there. Because of such tolerant, sympathetic and helpful attitude of Zalim Singh the Kota territories did not suffer so much from the Pindari ravages as other places in India had. Zalim Singh's was the lonely example of such tolerant attitude and hence Kota was the only place in Central India and Rajputana, which enjoyed a wholesome peace.

When the Pindaris were defeated and dispersed, on special instructions from Metcalfe, Zalim Singh seized the lands granted to the Pindaris by him and turned them out of his territories.

Amir Khan and Jaipur

The dawn of the 19th century saw the resources of Jaipur declining. During the first half of the 19th century, it was continually subjected to external aggression and internal strife. Jaipur had sunk to the lowest level of degradation. All the glamour of the Imperial State had vanished. The non-intervention policy left Jaipur high and dry. Cornwallis had directed Lake to "abandon the alliance at present subsisting with the *Rajahs* of Jyenagar, Burtpore and

Machery and with the *Rana* of Gohund."[20] This conduct of the British has been rightly condemned as contrary to all norms of diplomacy.

The removal of British protection left Jaipur an easy prey to the Marathas, the Pindaris and the Pathans. A period of great agony ensued. Amir Khan took the fullest advantage of the internecine wars between Jaipur and Jodhpur on the question of Dhonkal Singh, a pretender to the throne of Jodhpur. He started the ravage of Jaipur which did not stop for years to come. Though defeated by Shiv Lal, Amir Khan destroyed and plundered the whole of Jaipur territory. Daulat Rao Scindia too sent his forces under Bappooji Scindia who reduced the state to abject misery. His return was purchased by the Raja of Jaipur. Shekhawati, a feudatory of Jaipur was attacked and plundered.

The middle of 1808 saw the complete destruction and exhaustion of the state. Things had hardly settled, when Krishna Kumari set afoot fresh internecine wars. The beginning of 1811 again witnessed Amir Khan and his hordes carrying death and devastation in Jaipur. Shekhawati too suffered immensely.

The troubles of Jaipur were hardly over, when Amir Khan again invaded Jaipur and most ruthlessly put the people to death and laid waste the countryside. Appeasement alone saw his withdrawal.

The advent of Lord Hastings did not see any improvement in the situation. Jaipur continued to attract the Pathan freebooters. Amir Khan was again seen laying siege to Jaipur. However, he soon retired in July, 1816. Thus Jaipur was utterly exhausted and ruined.

Pindari Incursions in British and Allied Territories

Pindaris had their eyes on the neighbouring provinces, which under the British rule were comparatively more stable, secure and prosperous.[21] They extended their activities to these areas. With the fruits of their depredations, they were able to maintain large hordes without the necessity of collecting territorial revenues.[22]

Pindari Incursion in Mirzapur District

In 1812, about 3,000 Pindaris[23] who belonged to Dost Mohammad, under Ramzan's leadership left Bhilsa, for excursion in the Eastern regions. They crossed Narbada at Chainpur Bari. They left 1,000 Pindaris at Bhilsa under Dost Mohammad, who "does not go anywhere in person to plunder but remains at Bhilsa to protect the families of the Pindaris."[24] This body penetrated through the region of Bundelkhand and Rewa. They had an understanding with Raja Jai Singh Dev of Rewa.[25] He not only allowed them a free passage, but also fed them. Passing through Rewa, the Pindaris ultimately reached the districts of Mirzapur and Benaras through the Bogela Ghat.[26] There was great consternation all over the region. The Pindaris succeeded in reaching within four miles of the city of Mirzapur.[27] After a halt and consultation, because of the presence of two British Battalions at Mirzapur,[28] thinking discretion to be the better part of valour, they returned. They went in the direction of Bijaigarh after crossing the river Soane. The attack on the British territories of Mirzapur district was greatly successful both in regard to the booty seized and the little hindrance encountered by them.[29] Even though the British forces were stationed in the region, they were unable to defend the area owing to their small number. Showing their inability to defend the people, Capt. Roughesedge wrote in a letter dated March 23, 1812 that "the inhabitants of most of the large villages have fled to the jungles, in which it is right not to interrupt them for there is little prospect of the forces at my disposal being enabled to give them any efficient protection."[30] The Pindaris turned towards Gaya.[31] They were stopped at Hariharpur Ghat by Bijai Singh Dewan, a Jagirdar of that region, who forced them to change the direction after a short fight in which the Pindaris lost a few of their comrades and twenty horses. The Pindaris then went to Narbada through Sohagpur and Jabbalpur.

The Pindari excursion to the east through Bundelkhand and Rewa to Mirzapur was a great success. Col. Martindele reported that Daulat Rao Scindia was the instigator of the inroad of the Pindaris into the Mirzapur district,[32]

Pindari Incursion in Gujarat and Surat

The wealth of Surat attracted the Pindaris, who repeatedly attacked this region. They carried away large booty from there. In 1808-9, they ravaged the Gujarat territories, which suffered for the second time in 1812 also. One party of Pindaris under Chitu, about four to five thousand in number, went towards the Gujarat region. They plundered Surat, entering Gujarat through Mewar and spread themselves almost all over the region. Chitu had orders from Peshwa to lay waste the English territories.

In 1812, when Jaswant Rao Holkar advanced to Poona, the Pindaris entered into the Gaekwad's territories and caused great havoc,[33] in view of which Capt. Carnac was ordered by the Bombay Council to depute agents to watch their activities.[34]

Another party of Pindaris 14,000 in number, under Chitu's leadership advanced towards the Western Ghats and plundered town after town. Moha, Soopa, Kalayanwari,[35] Navsari and Attavesy[36] suffered immensely. It was believed that thousands of people took refuge in the town of Surat.[37]

Pindari Incursions in the South

The continued impunity, increase in number, and boldness of action resulted in the unabated menace of the Pindaris. They soon extended their depredations to the far off places. The prosperous South was a continuous attraction to the Pindaris. They decided to try their fortune in the South.

Incursion in 1815

The Dashera of 1815 was celebrated with all the pomp and show by the Pindaris of Chitu's durra at Nimawar.[38] After long preparations, on the 14th of October, 1815, a body of 8,000 Pindaris advanced towards the South. They consisted of the parties attached to Kadir Buksh, Tookkoo Jemadar, Sahib Khan and Chitu.[39] Mohammad Rajun, the younger brother of Chitu also went to Deccan. Soon after their departure, the Pindaris broke into two parties. One party advanced towards the Nizam's territories. This party went upto the Ajanta Ghats, crossed the Godavary and spread terror everywhere.[40] More than eighteen villages were plundered.[41] They carried off huge amount of stores and grains.[42] Guntukal was plundered; the mint being inside the fort, however, remained safe.[43] The advance of the party was, however, checked by Major Fraser of Nizams's reformed Infantry. Major Fraser with three hundred infantry and a hundred horse sprang a complete surprise upon the Pindaris. They ran away and hence their loss was comparatively small. This set-back was of no avail for it neither checked their incursion nor deterred them from further depredations. They continued their march, right through the Nizam's dominion from north to the south, and reached the banks of the Krishna, where they waited for the river to recede.

The second party, which went through the Nagpur territory also continued its march through the Nizam's dominion, carrying death and devastation along its route. It also reached the Krishna, where the two parties met. The Pindaris returned because the river was not fordable, which was something unusual for the time[44] (on November 20, 1816). But they caused great destruction in Hyderabad and the British territory along the river Krishna.[45] For the time being Kurnool and Gulbarga escaped punishment.[46] On the way Pindaris ravaged Masulipattam. Moving along the bank of Godavary and Wardha the Pindaris returned to Nimawar.

The excursion of the Pindaris was a great success both because of the little loss they suffered and the great wealth they brought with them. They committed the most extensive destruction throughout the territories they visited. The Deccan was swarming with Pindaris.

The booty collected by them[48] in their plundering excursion "was greater than that of any previous expedition, in so much the merchants were sent for from Oojein to purchase many of the valuables obtained, those of Neemawar not being sufficiently wealthy."[48] Chitu was the greatest gainer. His share of plunder was brought on four elephants.[49]

The Pindaris claimed that "they never in their lives before obtained so rich a *lubhur*. The countries they visited, they say, had been so little disturbed that each headman of a district had to the amount of 500 pagodas, 500 gold mohuis, 16 gold '*Karas*' (or rings for the wrist or ankles), pearls, silk clothes etc., so that the report is that they have brought two crores of rupees worth of plunder."[50] The loot was so abundant that the Pindaris despised the common articles, which heretofore, they had valued most.[51] It may be observed that the Marathas as well as the disaffected sons of the Nizam were suspected to have encouraged the Pindari chiefs to undertake this expedition.[52]

The eruption was so sudden and so rapid that every place they visited found itself unprepared to repel the Pindari attack.[53] Before any force could move against the Pindaris, they would have long ago quitted the Company's territories with all impunity.

First Incursion of 1816

Feeling highly pleased with the masterly way in which they conducted the expedition, the Pindaris organised a second expedition, immediately following the first. Pindaris from all sides joined the party.[54] On Wednesday, February 6, 1816, at about ten o'clock in the morning, Chitu's party set out.[55] The Pindaris placed under Junglee Kunwar, Bheeka Kunwar, Hari Kunwar and Ummaid Kunwar crossed the Baglateer Ghat. Karim Khan's durra numbering about six thousand under Kushal Kunwar and Buksh Khan also accompanied them. Grasia Kunwar of Dost Mohammad's durra with two thousand Pindaris, Imam Buksh and Kadir Buksh with four thousand Pindaris and five hundred each from Segonewala and Bhoongaonwala Grasia chiefs,[56] all confederated.[57] In all about 23,000 men set out from Malwa. They had orders to plunder the English and the Nizam's territories.[58] At the same time, they were not explicitly ordered to refrain from looting the territories belonging to Scindia, Holkar and the Peshwa.[59] The horsemen, under the leadership of Rajun the younger, included the villagers of Satwas and other rabble that usually accompanied the Pindaris. However, he had to return from Nagpur on account of illness.[60] On February 17, 1816, another *Lubhur* of five thousand Pindaris from Chitu's durra, well-equipped and well-armed left for the Deccan with the intention of going towards Chinapattam (Madras).[61] At Masulipattam, they found the river Krishna full and, therefore, they returned.[62] Kadir Buksh commanded the Lubhur.[63] The areas lying between the Godavary and the Krishna were most exposed to the Pindari incursion.[64]

So rapid was their movement and such the secrecy, that the first that was heard of the Pindaris was their appearance in Masulipattam on March 10, 1816. On the 11th, they marched thirty miles and plundered seventy-two villages and committed the greatest cruelties. On the 12th, fifty-four villages were destroyed. They marched to Guntur town, part of which was thoroughly plundered, including the houses of the British civilian officers like the Magistrate etc.[65] Due to the presence of a few soldiers and civilians the treasury and the collectorate were saved from being looted. They ravaged the country in all directions and over a wider expanse of territory, and perpetrated the greatest barbarities upon the people.[66]

The Pindaris crossed the river Krishna near Beswara and proceeded towards Guntoor division. The Guntoor Circar, one of the prosperous of the Company's possessions in the South, was devastated in a most savage manner. They committed the most cruel outrages and carried off a prodigious booty.[67] So great was the devastation in Guntoor and Kurnool that the people in those regions evinced a desire to emigrate in the expectation of enjoying peace and security of life at other places.[68] Cuddappa also suffered severely. The Pindaris remained in the Madras Presidency for twelve days, and for twelve days there was an orgy of rapine and ruin.

The village of Guntoor was attacked by several bodies of Pindaris, numbering two thousand.[69] Besides Kurnool, Guntoor and Cuddappa; Amravati, Mangalghery, Cumbum, Murkapooran, Turlapaddoo, and about a hundred other villages in that area were plundered and burnt, and women tortured and insulted.[70] The continued success increased the natural ferocity of the Pindaris. Devastation, violation, and death were the horrid concomitants of their march.

The Pindaris adopted and pursued the same tactics as they had adopted earlier, moving simultaneously to different places far apart from each other and moving very rapidly. This time they covered a larger area than they had done ever before.

Besides the huge plunder which they took away, two Europeans were also taken prisoners.[71] Dehradun Survey Records mention a number of instances when several students, James Macdonald, Grimshaw, Borthwick, Cauxton, Lambton and Walker, and some officers of the military institution were stripped to the skin, beaten and wounded.[72]

The plundering parties returned after an absence of about three months. They took away four elephants, sixty camels and innumerable horses. On their way back, at Dewal Ghat near Ajanta, they were attacked by the Mysore Horse under Col. Doveton. About three hundred of the Pindaris, left behind to fight a rear-guard action, were never heard of afterwards, presumably they were killed in fighting.[73] In another place, near the Krishna river, the Pindaris on seeing the English army on the opposite bank, ran away. At that time, they did not sustain any loss whatsoever. However, the Pindaris did suffer in their Deccan campaign. In almost all the villages, five to ten horses were usually left behind, killed or wounded. Still the Pindaris were able to carry off booty worth about one crore. Buksh Khan, who brought the elephants, was honoured by Chitu, who presented him with a 'shawl', a turban and one thousand rupees.

Madras 4th Indian Cavalry from Hyderabad was detailed to check this body. However, before they reached Krishna, the Pindaris had already crossed the river and escaped. It may be observed that although the British forces happened to be present in Kurnool for the settlement of a disputed succession and they were detached against the Pindaris in all directions, the Pindaris escaped with no serious loss to themselves. They baffled the English armies with no point of attack. On their return they moved along the north bank of the Krishna, passed through Hyderabad and Peshwa's territories, laying them waste, and reached safely the Narbada region in detached bodies.

Another party of the Pindaris which had moved towards Ganjam received severe injuries at the hands of Lt. Borthwick. The remainder of this party, for the second time, fell in the line of Capt. Caulfield, who inflicted heavy loss on the Pindaris. But for the ravines and *nullas* through which the Pindaris were pursued, the whole party would have been annihilated. Yet another body of Pindaris suffered at the hands of Major MacDowell, who took them completely by surprise. Most of them fled, leaving all their plunder and horses. Thus, nearly the whole body of Pindaris recrossed the Narbada before the 17th May and again with huge plunder. They committed destruction, pillage, murder and rape with the usual ferocity during the course of their free ride in the south. An idea of this can be had from the fact that the Pindaris stayed in the Company's territory for just eleven days and yet during this short period, more than three hundred and thiry-nine villages were plundered and set on fire; one hundred and eighty-two people were put to death in a most brutal manner; innumerable women raped; hundreds of them committed suicide by drowning or burning themselves. Five hundred and five people were severely wounded and three thousand six hundred and three were subjected to torture.[74]

One body of the Pindaris entered the Deccan via Dewal Ghat and through the Ajanta passes.[75] They ravaged the Masulipattam area. Peddar and Rajmundry were also attacked. Between Rajmundry and Ellora, village after village was deserted, people taking shelter in the hills and Sunderbans of the Godavary.[76] The stationing of the Nagpur Subsidiary Force at Nagpur produced a discouraging effect upon the Pindaris. Col. Walker's active pursuit of the Pindaris right across the territories of Scindia compelled them to re-cross the Narbada. Although Col. Walker pursued them for about thirty-five miles, he did not succeed in overtaking them.[77] However, he was able to kill about fifteen Pindaris.

Second Incursion of 1816

One durra of Pindaris, five or six thousand in number, left Wasil Mohammad's camp[78] on November 5, 1816 under the charge of Ramzan Lubhereah, Madina Lodh and other chiefs.[79] They crossed the Narbada at Chauragarh and took the road to Jabbalpur, which was in the greatest alarm. They were all excellently mounted and were a daring and courageous lot. Before the whole Battalion and the guns could be mustered against the Pindaris, they were able to force Major Wisset of the Right Brigade, who was deputed to intercept them, to withdraw.[80] On arrival of the guns, however, the Pindaris retreated.

Major Fair, commanding the Right Brigade of Infantry with camp at Gourwarrah, went out to attack the Pindaris, but he was unable to find them. On the same evening (November 13, 1816) he found the villages all round him in conflagration. That was a positive proof of their presence. So Major Fair went towards Simeria, where he found a large body of Pindaris dismounted and busy preparing and eating their meals. Immediately after the arrival of the British, contrary to their mode of warfare, the Pindaris put up a fight and continued to defy the British; but on the arrival of the guns, they fled. They plundered and set on fire almost all the villages that came their way. Capt. Mackay, commanding a detachment from Major Fair's Brigade, also had an engagement with this party the next day; but it was unable to inflict any material loss on them.[81] The durra under Ramzan went as far as Ganjam, which district they entered on the night of December 18, and wrought havoc among the people.[82] Soon after leaving Ganjam, on account of a quarrel with Ramzan, Madina Lodh separated from the main body of the Pindaris, and took a direct route to Bhilsa, where he reached safely with his two thousand followers.[83]

Ramzan, with the main body of the Pindaris, continued his march by way of Chattisgarh, Sohagpur and Chanda, where Capt. Caulfield inflicted severe losses on them. The remnant of this body received further punishment at the hands of Major Clarke. The leader of the party, Ramzan himself, was killed in action.[84] It could not be rightly ascertained whether he was killed in the fight with the British or by some people who attacked the party before it reached Chanda.[85] Another leader of repute, Gulam Kadir, son of Imam Buksh, was also killed. It was reported that all the Pindaris except fifteen hundred were killed.[86] When the remaining Pindaris reached their haunts great distress prevailed in their camp.[87]

The success which attended the Pindari excursion in the Deccan, encouraged them to undertake yet another expedition to the south.

Third Incursion of 1816

In December, 1816 the Pindaris, composed entirely of men from Wasil Mohammad's durra made a second appearance in the south.[88] As was typical of the Pindaris, nothing was heard of them between their crossing the Narbada and their arrival in the Northern Circars. They made a sudden appearance, as if by magic, in the town of Kimedy and the neighbouring villages, which they thoroughly plundered and burnt.[89] However, the Pindaris received a check by the accidental presence of the British troops, which had been despatched to put down the refractory chiefs and an insurrection in Orissa. But for this force, the whole region would have been laid waste.

Lt. Tweedle, who was defending the frontier with a Company of Madras Infantry, had to withdraw before the Pindari advance. This greatly emboldened them. They attacked a part of this army on the night of December 19, 1816. Major Oliver, realising the precariousness of the situation, decided to take the Pindaris unawares, and in this task he achieved a signal success, despite the handicap of small numbers and want of cavalry. Seeing their designs foiled, they took the route to Ganjam which they plundered on the 25th of December. So horror-stricken were the people and such was the universal alarm that the people fled to the jungles and hills, leaving everything behind. The Pindaris, after a thorough plunder of a part of Ganjam town, soon retired.

Lt. Borthwick immediately decided on a pursuit. On the 27th December he fell in with about one thousand Pindaris but Borthwick was not satisfied with this minor encounter. He decided to continue his pursuit. Blind with confidence which success bred in them, the Pindaris did not go far and encamped nearby. Lt. Borthwick took only fifty men and after a circuitous route fell upon the enemy. He killed about twenty men and fifty horses. Although he was not able to inflict a severe loss, after this action no Pindari was heard of in this region. The Pindaris in their discomfiture decided to give up the idea of attacking Cuttack.

The town of Puri and the temple of Jagannath were not free from the danger. The Pindaris, learning of the presence of the British troops stationed there, left the province and went towards Cuttack, thence, along the Narbada, back to their haunts. Their retreat was not free from action against them. Lt. Borthwick, at the head of 2nd Bengal Infantry, pursued the Pindaris very closely, killing the stragglers who fell in his hands and keeping the main body in continuous flight.[90] When the Pindaris reached near Sohagpur, they were surprised by Col. Adam's detachment under Capt. Caulfiled, who had heard of the retreating Pindaris. On the night of January 24. 1817, he was able to kill about four hundred of them. The number of horses captured was also the same. When the remainder tried to escape by a pass in the north, they were again pounced upon by Major Clarke on January 26, who killed about one hundred and fifty of them. The Pindaris suffered heavily.[91]

One party of the Pindaris penetrated into Mysore territory and destroyed and burnt several villages in the neighbour hood of Chitaldroog.[92]

Another body of the Pindaris from Chitu's durra, which proceeded by the Burhanpur road towards Jalna and Aurangabad, was met by Major Lushington,[91] wth the 4th Madras Cavalry. He was returning from the Peshwa's territories to Jalna. On December 25, 1816 he learnt at Pipalwadi of the Pindaris, entry into Peshwa's territory by the Wakli Ghat and their plunder of the south-east of Poona.

Perhaps the Pindaris were plundering at their leisure in fancied security, altogether oblivious of the presence of the British troops in the neighbourhood. Major Lushington, at once, started to meet them and on the night of 25th at one in the morning, after a forced march of about fifty miles, he reached Sogaon on the morning of the 26th December, where be learnt that the Pindaris had already left the place. Major Lushington immediately decided to pursue the enemy in as light a manner as he could. He left all the sick, and heavy baggage and after only half an hour of rest, started with about three hundred and fifty men. After covering a distance of twenty miles, at Kaim, he found that the Pindaris had left after a night's halt and plundering in the neighbouring villages. After forty-five minutes of rest at this village, he resumed his pursuit to Kawa, where, at last, he found them busy cooking their afternoon meal. Though the Pindaris were three thousand strong, they instantly ran away. They were pursued for about ten miles, when due to excessive fatigue and continuous movement, the pursuit was given up. Still the British force killed seven to eight hundred Pindaris,[94] and captured about a thousand horse. The only casualty that the British suffered was of Capt. Drake, who was speared by the Pindaris.[95]

Major Lushington was not so fortunate as to overtake the Pindaris with the main body of his regiment.[96] However, the manner in which they were pursued compelled them to retreat without doing much damage, as they might otherwise have done.

Thus, the checks which the Pindaris received at the hands of Major Lushington and MacDowell completely paralysed them and they fled back to the Narbada in great confusion. The Pindaris found the fords and passes well-guarded by the British forces and, therefore, a good number of them perished at their hands; only a few of them reached their headquarters safely.

Baffled in their designs, the Pindaris took the southward direction and passed within twenty miles of Nagpur, plundering the villages on their way. They crossed the river Wardha into the Nizam's territory before Col.

Doveton, who was stationed in the south, could do anything to stop them.

This body of the Pindaris, at the lowest estimate, amounted to about six thousand. They went as far as Nirmal on the Godavary, and on December 21, 1816 they were at Bider.[97] So far, the Pindaris had marched in the most leisurely manner, without tiring their horses, plundering the area to the right and left of their track. For some time, they stationed themselves at Bider and sent parties all round, plundering the region.[98] While at Bider, the Pindaris had taken no decision regarding their penetrating further into the Campany's districts. This afforded time for a light force to move from Hyderabad under Major MacDowell. On the morning of January, 15, 1817 he contacted the Pindaris about thirty miles west of Bider.[99]Large numbers of Pindaris were killed and wounded and they made a most precipitous flight. They lost about a thousand horse. They had to abandon nearly all the horses and plunder. Their dispersal was so complete that after this action they thought of nothing but personal safety and retreat.

A small party of Pindaris struck off towards the west near Poona and passed along the north of the city at a distance of about three miles, when they were challenged by a party of Peshwa's Brigade stationed at his Powder Magazine. Shrewd as the Pindaris were, they gave the excuse that they were part of Peshwa's cavalry and belonged to Trimbuckji Danglia. They were, thus, allowed to pass unmolested. Having got about 14 miles from Poona, they started their plunder and loot.[100]

Dissatisfied with the manner in which, for want of energy, the Pindaris had suffered humiliation and defeat at the hands of the British army, one of the leaders of the party, Sheikh Dullo, a brave and able man of uncommon skill, separated from the main body. With about three to five hundred Pindaris,[101] he rapidly passed through the Peshwa's territory and entered into the Konkan. After thoroughly plundering the area, the party returned without much loss as compared to the other parties. The extreme rapidity and inspiring leadership of Sheikh Dulloo saved this body from the fate which overtook others.

On his return to the banks of the Narbada, Sheikh Dulloo found the fords leading to Chitu's durra occupied by the British forces. He was attacked and fired upon, but he, along with the main body, swam across the river on May 21, 1817 sustaining some loss. The less adventurous and poorly mounted Pindaris, who were left behind, took shelter in the hills and jungles where they were killed and wounded by the hill tribes and wild animals. Those of the Pindaris, who succeeded in getting across, immediately plundered each other and the strong seized the property of the weak.[101] Sheikh Dulloo joined his durra with only one hundred and ten men, but brought a very rich and select booty of gold and pearls.

The interception of the Pindaris and the severe punishment inflicted upon them during their excursions to the south, made almost ineffectual impression upon the Pindaris. Soon after, Chitu sent two fresh plundering parties to the south. This was because the loss sustained by the Pindaris in one season or in one excursion, even were it great, did not have the effect of deterring the Pindaris from undertaking further excursions.

Incursion of 1817

In January, 1817, the Pindaris made another incursion into the British territories.[103] They committed horrible ravages upon the people. One party went to the Poona territories, where it overran the whole region. Kalyan, Bhiwandi and Salsettee towns were thoroughly plundered.[104] The Konkan region including the Swarndurg also suffered at their hands.[105] British infantry proved unequal to the task of protecting it from their ravages.[106]

One party of the Pindaris attacked the town of Kalol and villages near Godhra, killed a number of people and ravished women sheltered in a temple.[107]

On April 17, 1817 Lt. Dacre and a small escort were killed by the Pindaris, who were, later on, pursued by Maj. Smith and routed at Pathari in Khandesh.[108]

Another party of the Pindaris went towards the Gujarat region, but was opposed by the Bhils, who killed a number of them. As the road was impassable on account of the jungles and the resistance by the Bhils, of whom thousands had collected, the Pindaris had to return.[109]

In October, 1817 Kauder Buksh was detached by Chitu, with a party of about three hundred horses, towards Konkan. It returned through Mysore, after ravaging the country.[110]

During the years 1815-1817 the Pindaris repeatedy attacked the south, and went to far off places perpetrating unbelievable cruelties upon the people. The expeditions of 1816-1817 were the boldest which the Pindaris had so far undertaken.

Incursion into Peshwa's Dominions

The Pindaris were under the employ of the Peshwas right from their infancy. The Peshwas, no more in the heyday of their power now, were repeatedly attacked by the Pindaris and by their frequent incursions in the Peshwa's territories had laid them waste.

A party of Pindaris belonging to Karim and Chitu numbering 5,000 sneaked into the Peshwa's domains, after having plundered Burhanpur, Adilabad and Ajanta regions. In the western Ghats, after crossing Kesarbari Ghat, the Pindaris divided themselves into a number of parties and carried fire and sword throughout the region. The main body pushed as far as Sanganer, a town of Vinchur Jagirdar, a subordinate feudatory of the Peshwa. The Peshwa sent Bapuji Gokhley to drive out the Pindaris,[111] who returned via Nasik.[112]

Yet another party of the Pindaris crossed the Narbada on Sunday, the 18th of October, 1812, entered into the Peshwa's territory and laid waste a number of villages. They were reported to be at different places at the same time, viz., Khapah, Burhanpur, Matchengaon, Wardha and Hingun Ghat, fifty miles south of Nagpur.[112] This clearly shows that the Pindaris had, thus, spread right through the territories of the Peshwa and the Nizam.

In 1813, two bodies of Pindaris crossed the Narbada, one of which, numbering two or three thousand, went to the Peshwa's territories. It reached within forty miles of Poona, and ravaged the whole region. From Poona, they went towards the Nizam's dominion, and again crossing the Godavary they entered into the Peshwa's territories.

In December, 1815, having received a beating at the hands of Lts. Burton and Sutherland in the Nizam's territories, the Pindaris escaped towards Poona, which was greatly agitated and reached within fourteen miles of Poona.[114] They spread themselves in all directions and committed the most daring acts of cruelties and violence.[115] Another body of Pindaris, after crossing the Godavary plundered a great deal of the Peshwa territories including Pandharpur and the villages round the city.

Pindari Incursion in Nizam's Territories

The Pindaris were greatly fascinated by the Nizam's dominion. The rich commercial towns like Amrawati offered great scope for plunder. In spite of the hazard of the Hyderabad Subsidiary Force, the Pindaris continued to plunder the Nizam's domains year after year. Berar was a hunting ground for the Pindaris.

In 1806, the Pindaris attacked the Nizam's territories in a body of 5,000. They entered Berar to the north-east of Ellichpur.[116] They attempted an attack upon Amrawati also but were repulsed by the Nizam's troops. Another body entered Berar via Gawilgarh range of hills, thirty miles east of Ellichpur and attacked the opulent city of Amrawati,[117] but was repulsed by the British troops stationed there, who inflicted considerable loss on the Pindaris. The orders to the British army were "to drive them beyond the frontiers." [118]

One party of Pindaris attacked the western parts of Berar. Raja Govind Buksh, one of the senior officers of the Nizam, took quick steps to check the Pindari advance. His promptitude prevented a very serious penetration by the Pindaris;[119] yet they were able to cause havoc.[120]

In December 1807, the Pindaris entered Berar province for the second time, but retreated most precipitately owing to the warm reception they received at the hands of the troops of Nawab Salabat Khan of Hyderabad.[121]

Another body of Pindaris entered Berar and plundered right upto Ellichpur, where they received a general check to their progress by the troops of Salabat Khan of Ellichpur, in December, 1810.

In 1813, two parties of Pindaris crossed the Narbada, one of which, after crossing into the Nizam's territory, passed within twelve miles of Aurangabad and Ellora. On the way, they plundered two officers of the Company's forces. The Pindaris killed or wounded the greater part of the followers.[122] They were commanded by Roshan Beg and Ramdan who had 7,000 to 8,000 Pindaris. They plundered the districts of Berar.[123]

In another encounter, the Nizam's Cavalry attacked a party of two hundred and fifty Pindaris, who after a short struggle, ran away. But another party of the same body plundered villages fifteen miles away from Amrawati on January 31, 1814.[124]

About 9,000 Pindaris set out for Hindia in three bodies. One party of 2,500 under Sheikh Dulloo, the terror of Berar, after committing the greatest ravages there, went towards Khandesh. Sheikh Dulloo was twice beaten off in surprise raids. He lost about fifty horses.[125]

A party of two hundred Pindaris plundered a merchant party of forty-four bullocks laden with opium and spices valued at Rs. 50,000. Silk and indigo worth about Rs. 5,000 were also plundered. This party had started from Amrawati. The villages were completely sacked and burnt; grain fields were destroyed; people killed and wounded; women taken away.[126]

Berar did not get any respite from these plundering hordes. The winter of 1815 again saw them in action. One party of Pindaris entered Berar in three divisions of two thousand each and plundered several villages in the district of Mulkapur. It was during this excursion that Capt. Blake, commanding the 2nd Battalion, inflicted a loss of about sixty killed.[127] In one of the villages, Maker,[128] they violated sixty women, twelve of whom died during the ravishment.[129] 4,000 Pindaris of Wasil Mohammad and two thousand of Karim commanded by Ramzan and Namdar Khan respectively invaded Berar territories and committed great depredations.[130] Ramzan took away a huge plunder.

Pindari Incursion in Bundelkhand

As mentioned earlier, during the Pindari incursion into the district of Mirzapur, Bundelkhand region also received their attention. It too suffered at their hands.

In March, 1810 a party of about 12,000 Pindaris attacked the Mahiyar and Bundelkhand regions. They plundered a number of villages on the way and burnt them, and the same tale of woe was repeated by the people.[131] The plunder of Mahiyar over, they immediately set out towards the Rewa territories, where after a night's journey, they appeared the next morning to once again indulge in their depredations.[132]

The Pindaris on their way to Rewa laid waste the territories of Raja Doorjan Singh of Mahiyar, while they did not touch a single village or person of Rewa.[133] This was due to an understanding between the Rewa Raja and the Pindari chief Karim Khan[134] by which the Pindaris were not only allowed a free passage in consideration of Rs. 10,000/- but also provided five horsemen who guided them through the Rewa territories.[135] Mr. Richardson, Agent to the Governor General at Banda, was of the opinion that Daulat Rao Scindia was the instigator of the Pindari inroads in the British territories of Mirzapur and other places.[136] In January, 1814 one body of Pindaris under Ramzan Khan proceeded to the Bundelkhand area. On January 13, 1814 they committed the most cruel outrages and put to death by torture about one hundred people.[137]

One of the bands of the Pindaris which belonged to Wasil Mohammad's durra ventured to ravage territories between Bundelkhand and Saugar, but were surprised by Capt. Ridge from his post at Lohargaon. The Pindaris were routed and driven back.[138] Capt. Ridge, giving an account of the affair with the Pindaris, reported that the moment he sighted the Pindaris, he gave them a pursuit, whereupon they broke into three parties and each took a different direction. However, he inflicted punishment upon them. It was during this pursuit that Capt. Howarth died of exhaustion.[139]

From the above account of the Pindari incursions, several conclusions can be drawn. Right from the beginning, the Pindaris did not meet any opposition from either the Indian chiefs or the British government; consequently they became impudent and bold. The territories of the Company, which the Pindaris had so far scrupulously avoided, did not escape their depredations because of the policy of non-intervention which freed them from the fear of the British reprisals. Thus, within almost two decades, the Pindaris had acquired an influence and strength that appeared a development full of threat to the future security of the British power in India.

It may safely be concluded that the indifferent attitude of the Marathas and the apathy of the British were responsible for the rise, progress and the growth of the Pindaris.

FOOT-NOTES

1 Maharana of Udaipur sustained a very serious defeat at the hands of Scindia in 1717, invited Holkar to his aid in return for sixty-four lakhs of rupees. In 1762, Holkar took possession of Rampore and was able to extract fifty-one lakhs of rupees and went away. Scindia thereupon besieged Udaipur, but after prolonged negotiations withdrew ; the price of withdrawal was sixty three and a half lakhs of rupees, out of which thirty-three lakhs were paid in cash and jewels and land was mortgaged for the remainder......... Jawad, Neemuch etc. Holkar followed and succeeded in getting Neembhaera.

2 Wilson : *History of India*, p. 123.

3 The case in point was the Jaipur Raja, who was so infatuated by a Muslim dancing girl, Ruskapoor, that he gave up everything except the highest noble to pay respects to her, a mere dancing girl as she

was. The *ranis* too were expected to respect and honour her. On this question feelings were strained in the House of Jaipur.

4 Busawan Lal : *Memoirs of Amir Khan*. p. 360.

5 N.A.I. For. Pol. 1808 : O.C. No. 43-44 : Archibald Seton to N.B. Edmonstone. Delhi, 8 April, 1808.

6 Busawan Lal : *Memoirs of Amir Khan*, p. 437.

7 Malcolm : *Memoirs of Central India*, Vol. I, pp. 278-279.

8 N.A.I. For. Pol. 1810 : O.C. No. 77, 6 August, 1810 : Seton to Edmonstone, Delhi, 8 July, 1810.

9 Tod : *Annals and Antiquities of Rajasthan*, Vol. I, p. 538

10 Tod : *Annals and Antiquities of Rajasthan*, pp. 538-41.

11 Malcolm : *Memoirs of Central India* Vol. I, p. 275.

12 N.A.I. For. Sec. 1815 : O.C. No. 25-26, 21 March, 1815, Carnac to Warden, Baroda, 12 February, 1815.

13 N.A.I. For. Sec. 1815 : O.C. No. 3-4, 23 May, 1815, Carnac to Warden, Baroda, 12 April, 1815.

14 N.A.I. For. Sec. 1814 : O.C. No. 17-19, 4 March, 1814, Strachey to His Excellency the Earl of Moira, Scindia's camp, 12 February, 1814.

15 N.A.I. For. Sec. 1814 : O.C. No. 110-111, 6 December, 1813, R. Strachey to Adam, Scindia's Camp, Gwalior, 20 November, 1814.

16 Kota State Archives : 1845-1864 : Basta No. 3 to 121.

17 Tod : *Annals and Antiquities of Rajasthan*, Vol. II, p. 1607.

18 Kota State Archives : 1863, Basta No. 73, Bhander 1.

19 Busawan Lal : *Memoirs of Amir Khan*, p. 271.

20 C. Ross : *Correspondence of Lord Cornwallis*, Vol. III, p 548, Cornwallis to Lake, 19 September, 1805.

21 N.A.I. For. Sec. 1816 : O.C. No. 3-8, 27 July, 1816 : Memorandum accompanying the letter from Sydenham to Russell, Aurangabad, 1 April, 1816, para 1.

22 The many "rich districts the Pindaris now possess furnish them with the means of subsistence almost independent of their predatory acquirements and the strong holds they contain situated in a country were calculated by nature for defence, are points of rendezvous for their deposit, security, and mutual counsel for combined aggressions."

Tod : *Origin and Progress*, p. 12.

23 N.A.I. For Sec. 1812 : O.C. No. 7-8, 3 April, 1812 : Capt. Thomas Whitehead to Capt. Gough, Lohargaon, 17 March, 1812 : This letter mentions the Pindari strength to be 12,000.

24 U.P.A. : Mirzapur Collectorate : Pre-Mutiny Records : Letters issued November 1811 to April, 1812 : Vol. No. 75, Translation of a deposition, 20 March and 5 April, 1812, p. 136,

25 N.A.I. For. Sec. 1812 : O.C. No. 3-5, 26 March, 1812 : Whitehead, Capt. Comdg. above the Ghats, Lohargaon to Capt. Gough, Major of Brigade Head Quarters in Bundelkhand, para 4-5. Also : O.C. No. 7-8, 3 April. 1812 : Translation of a letter from Richardson, Agent to the Governor-General to the Raja of Rewa. 18 March, 1812.

26 It was reported by the Assistant Incharge of Nagpur Residency that Chitu in his conversation with the Rajuns remarked that he had received orders from the Peshwa to lay waste the country of the Mughals and the English (By the term Mughals, it was probably meant to be the territory of the Nizam). A.O. Records from the Peshwa Daftar, Poona : Asstt : Incharge Nagpur Residency to Elphinstone at Poona, Nagpur. 1 November, 1812.

27 U.P.A. : Mirzapur Collectorate : Pre-Mutiny Records : Letters issued November 1811 to April, 1812 : Vol. No. 75, Translation of deposition of Dunna Pindarah as taken before the Acting Magistrate on 19th and 20th March, and 5th April, 1812.

28 Maj. Gen. Wood Comdg. at Benaras reported that there were about 2,054 British forces at Mirzapur, while 1,600 were irregulars of Amrit Rao and that of the Raja of Benaras. Translation of a letter from Richardson, Agent to the Governor-General to the Raja of Rewa, 18 March, 1812.

29 N.A.I. For. Sec. 1812 : O.C. No. 6-7, 26 March, 1812 : Brooke, A.G.G. Benaras to N.B. Edmonstone, Benaras, 20 March, 1812.

30 N.A.I. For. Sec. 1812 : O.C. No. 17-20, 3 April, 1812 : Report from Capt. G. Roughesedge, Comdg. Ramgurh Battalion to Capt. Smith, Comdg. Detachment at Gaya.

31 I.H.R.C. Proceeding Vol. XVI December 1939 : Defence of the frontier of Bihar and Orissa against Maratha and Pindary incursion, 1800-1819.
K.P. Mitra.

32 N.A.I. For. Sec. 1812 : O.C. No. 6-7 17 April, 1812 : J. Richardson, A.G.G. Banda, to N.B. Edmonstone, 3 April, 1812.

33 B.G.R. D. No. 280, Item No. 2, Baroda Resident to Bombay Council, 26 November, 1812.

34 B.G.R. : D. No. 280, Item No. 2. Minute of 20 October, 1802.

35 B.G.R. : D. No. 393, Translation of a letter from Merwanjee Dorabjee to Dungee Rustamji, 31 January, 1813, Received 3 February, 1813.

36 B.G.R. : D. No. 393, William Roome, Major Comdg. at Surat to the Adjutant General of the Army at Bombay, Surat, 31 January, 1813.
Also ; N.A.I. For. Sec. 1813 ; O.C. No. 7-9, 5 March, 1813 ;

Warden to G. Dowdeswell, Chief Secretary, to the Supreme Government, Fort William, 5 February, 1813.

37 H.R.R. S. No. 169, Vol. No. 44, H. Russell to Adam, Hyderabad, 23 October 1813.

38 Meanwhile "the Dussera of 1815 had been celebrated at Cheetoo's cantonment of Nemawar by a greater concourse of Pindarees than had ever before been assembled at one time."
Prinsep : *Transactions* : Vol. I. p. 328

39 N.A.I. For. Sec. 1816 : O.C. No. 22-23, 13 January, 1816 :
Translation of a Substance of a deposition by Salabut Pindarra on 20 December, 1815.

40 B.G.R. : D. No. 293, P.D. 1815 : Elphinstone to Moira, Poona, 10 December, 1815.

41 N.A.I. For. Sec. 1816 : O.C. No. 14-18, 13 January, 1816 :
J.A. Oakes, Collector Timrecottah to the President and members of the Board of Revenue, Fort St. George, Madras.

42 N.A.I. For. Sec. 1816 : O.C. No. 18-23, 4 May, 1816 :
Head of Intelligence, Received by Col. Walker, 4 March, 1816.

43 N.A.I. For. Sec. 1816 : O.C. No. 1-3, 13 January, 1816 :
Woodhouse, Major Comdg. Detachment, Kampti, to the Major of Brigades, Ceded Districts, 26 November, 1815.

44 N.A.I. For. Sec. 1816 : O.C. No. 1-3, 13 January, 1816 : P. Bruce, Magistrate Bellary to Col. Webber, Comdg. Ceded Districts, Bellary, 30 November 1815. The Pindaris "failed in several attempts to cross the Krishna at Gudwale, Pungtoor, and Moree Konde Ghats."

45 N.A.I. For. Sec. 1816 : O.C. No. 1-3, 13 January, 1816 :
Chaplin, Collector Yeratummaray Cheroo, to P. Bruce, Magistrate, Zillah Court of Bellary, 26 November, 1815.

46 N.A.I. For. Sec. 1816 : O.C. No. 4-9, 13 January, 1816, Collector Charles R. Ross to the Chief Sec. to the Govt. of Fort St. George, Ooyalwara, 6 December, 1815.

47 The Pindaris "brought with them all sorts of goods plundered, as silks, cotton stuffs etc., to a vast amount. Great quantities of all sorts of plundered stuffs and vessels have been brought in. Shawls worth 500 rupees are selling for 50; and for women's sarees worth 200 rupees, purchasers cannot be found at 20. Gold and silver ornaments are also extra-ordinarily cheap."
H.R.R. S. No. 206, Vol. No. 531, Substance of the news of Chitu's durra, dated 7th and received on 16th Jan. 1816.

48 Three "Seits in consequence have come from Ujjain with bills to the amount of three lacs for the purchase of it (jewellery). One of the *Shahookars* is a *Gomashtah* of Juggut Chand Seit, another of Chunni Lal Bhagwandas of Ujjein." H.R.R. S. No. 206, Vol. No. 531, Substance of the news of Chitu's durra dated 7th and received on 16 Jan. 1816.

49 Of the highly valuable plunder that Chitu got, one of the items was an idol of gold weighing five seers.
N.A.I. For. Sec. 1816 : O.C. No. 5-6, 27 January, 1816 :
Translation of a Paper of Intelligence from Chitu's camp, 2 January 1816.
Also : Rajun, his younger brother also returned with all sorts of goods plundered, as silk, gold, silvcr etc. A large amount of spices brought, which were shared by every one. H.R.R. S. No. 206, Vol. 531, Substance of a news of Chitu's Durra, dated the 7th received on 16th January, 1816. (Intelligence sent by G. Wellesley, Acting Resident, Scindia's camp, Gwalior).

50 B.G.R. : D. No. 427, Political Department, 1816 :
Translation of a Paper of Intelligence from Hindia. 30 Decemher, 1816.

51 B.G.R. D. No. 428 : Political Department, 1816 : Wellesley to Adam Scindia's camp, 1 February, 1816.

52 N.A.I. For. Sec. 1816 : O.C. No. 4-9, 13 January, 1816 :
Collector Ross to the Chief Secretary to the Government of Fort St. George, Ooyalwara 6 December, 1815.

53 N.A.I. For. Sec. 1816 : O.C No. 10-13, 13 January, 1816 :
Russell to W. Chaplin, Collector at Bellary, Hyderabad, 5 December, 1815.

54 N.A.I. For. Sec. 1816 : O.C. No. 9, 9 March, 1816 : Jenkins to Adam, Ramtek, 13 February, 1816. "8,000 Pindaris belonging to Chitu, 1,000 to Wasil Mohemmed and 1,000 to Namdar Khan. Almost all the durras furnished their quotas."
Also : N.A.I. For. Sec. 1816 : O.C. No. 10-11, 9 March, 1816 :
Translation of a Paper of Intelligence from Chitu's camp at Nimawar, 10 February, 1816.

55 N.A.I. For. Sec. 1816 : O.C. No. 54, 2 March, 1816 : Extract of Intelligence from Hindia, 9 February, enclosed in a letter from Jenkins to Adam, Kamptee near Nagpur, 14 February, 1816.

56 Places in Scindia's territory south of Narbada near Hindia, mostly inhabited by Gassari.

57 B.G.R. D. No. 428 : Pol. Deptt. 1816 : Jenkins to Adam, Kamptee near Nagpur, 14 February, 1816.

58 N.A.I. Fo. Sec. 1816 : O.C. No. 8-45, 26 September, 1816 :
H. Russell to G. Strachey, Secretary to Fort St. George, 19 February, 1816.

59 N.A.I. For. Sec. 1816 : O.C. No. 10-11, 9 March, 1816 :
Translation of a Paper of Intelligence from Chitu's cantonment at Nimawar, 10 February, 1816.
Some of the British Officers including Prinsep were of the opinion that a regular conspiracy was going on against the British. Towards that object Balaji Kunjar, lately one of the Peshwa's ministers, went

from court to court with the express purpose of inciting the Maratha Rajas to rise against the British. He also visited Chitu.

60 H.R.R. : S. No. 206, Vol. No. 531, G. Wellesley, Acting Secretary, to Adam, Gwalior, 16 March, 1816.

61 B.G.R. : D. No. 428, Pol. Deptt. 1816 : Wellesley, Acting Secretary at Gwalior to Adam, Scindia's camp, 10 March, 1816.

62 N.A.I. For. Sec. 1816 : O.C. No. 16, 23 March, 1816 :
Substance of news from Chitu's camp received, on 2 March, 1816.

63 N.A.I. For. Sec. 1816 : O.C. No. 10-11, 9 March, 1816 :
Translation of a Paper of Intelligence from Chitu's camp, 10 February, 1816.

64 H.R.R. S. No. 211 : Vol. No. 238, Minute of Commander-in-Chief.

65 N.A.I. For. Sec. 1816 : O.C. No. 8-45, 26 September, 1816 :
Delzell Asstt. Magistrate Guntoor's house was completely sacked.

66 The Pindari "spoilations in this neighbourhood are marked with the most savage barbarities...despoilation of their property and the barbarous cruelty of their invaders, exhibited a picture of the most consummate misery."
For. Misc. 124 A : Maratha & Pindary War Papers : Letter from the Magistrate Guntoor, J.A. Delzell to the Madras Secretary, dated the 15th March, 1816, p. 36.

67 J.E. Edcodeca, BDI Ssonade, Missionary Bishop, The A.R. on a view of the History, Politics & Literature for the year 1816, Chap. XVII, p. 170, London 1817.

68 N.A.I. For. Sec. 1816 : O.C. No. 27-39, 20 April, 1816, Delzell to the Secretary to the Government of Fort St. George, Guntoor, 16 March, 1816.

69 N.A.I. For. Sec. 1816 : O.C. No. 27-39, 20 April, 1816 :
Delzell to Officer Commanding, the Field Force at Kurnool, Guntoor, 16 March, 1816.

70 The Pindaris "committed the greatest excesses murdering many of the inhabitants and wounding others, and violating their women even in public streets."
N.A.I. For. Sec. 1816 : O.C. No. 40-49, 20 April, 1816 :
T.A. Oakes, Collector Guntoor to Chief Secretary to the Government of St. George, Guntoor, 21 March, 1816.
Also : N.A.I. For. Sec. 1816 : O.C. No. 27-39, Translation of a letter from Ougole, Guntoor, 20 March, 1816.

71 N.A.I. For. Sec. 1816 : O.C. No. 32, 25 May, 1816 :
Letter No. 4, Close to Moira, Gwalior, 9 May, 1816, para 7.

72 H.R.S.I. Vol. II, pp. 409-411.

73 N.A.I. For. Sec. 1816 : O.C. No. 7, 1 June, 1816 : Jenkins to Adam, enclosed translation of an Akhbar from a news-writer at Hindia, dated 22 May, 1816.

74 Supra pp. 54-55.

75 B.G.R. D. No. 432: Pol. Deptt. 1816: Lt. Col. Colin Milnes, Comdg. Detachment to Elphinstone, camp near Yawla, 19 December, 1816.

76 N.A.I. For. Sec. 1816: O.C. No. 50-55, 20 April, 1816: J. Long, Magistrate, Rajmundry to the Chief Secretary to the government of Fort St. George, 23 March, 1816.

77 M.I.O.L.L. H.M.S.: 520: Item No. 5, Letter from Resident at Nagpur, 30 October, 1816.

78 Wasil Mohammad did not go out for excursion, nor did he allow parties to issue forth from his durra for a long time. "This forbearance" of Wasil Mohammad was "ascribed to the influence of Baptiste."
N.A.I. For. Sec. 1816: O.C. No, 68, 20 April, 1816: Wauchope to Adam, Banda, 2 April, 1816.

79 N.A.I. For. Pol. 1816: O.C. No. 29, 30 November, 1816: Wauchope to Adam, Banda, 16 November 1816.

80 N.A.I. For. Pol. 1816: O.C. No. 25, 17 December, 1816: Major A. Fair, Comdg. the Right Brigade to Col. Walker, Camp Gourwarrah, 13 November, 1816.

81 M.I.O.L.L.: H.M.S, Vol. No. 520, Item No. 5, Memo No. 360.

82 *Ibid.*

83 N.A.I. For. Pol. 1817: O.C. No. 38, 1 March, 1817: Wauchope to Adam.

84 "Ramzan son of Bajee Narsia and Shikar Khan Jemadar were killed in the attack that was made upon them. Ramzan's wife was desirous to burn herself but was persuaded by Wasil Mohammad and his mother Bala Bai." N.A.I. For. Pol. 1817: O.C. No. 38, 1 March 1817: Wauchope to Adam.

85 N.A.I. For. Pol. 1817: O.C. No. 38, 1 March, 1817: Wauchope to Adam.

86 N.A.I. For. Pol. 1817: O.C. No. 25, 1 March, 1817: Jenkins to Adam, Nagpur, 8 February, 1817.

87 On the return of the Pindaris "nothing but lamentations and sounds of woe are to be heard in the durrah. They swore that "they never will issue forth to plunder, but will cultivate the field for subsistence." N.A.I.: For. Pol. 1817: O.C. No. 14, 8 March, 1817: Akhbar of Shahmat Khan.
Also: Substance of a paper of Intelligence of Muzhur Buksh's durra.

88 N.A.I. For. Pol. 1817: O.C. No. 45, 11 January, 1817: Russell to Adam, Hyderabad, 21 December, 1816.

89 N.A.I. For. Pol. 1817: O.C. No. 69-71, 28 December 1816: James Nicol, Acting Adjutant General of the army, Presidency of the Fort William, to J. Adam, Acting Chief Secretary, Fort William, 28 December, 1816.

90 Supplement to the Government of India Gazette : Thursday, 30 January, 1817.

91 N.A.I. For. Pol. 1817 : O.C. No. 38, 1 March, 1817 : Wauchope to Adams.

92 Supplement to the Government of India Gazette, Thursday, 30 January, 1817.

93 Major General Sir Thomas Law Lushington, G.C.B., a former Director of the East India Company.

94 N.A.I. For. Pol. 1817 : O.C. No. 11, 21 January, 1817 : Major Lushington, Comdg. Light Regiment and Cavalry to Elphinstone, camp near Kame : 27 December, 1816.
Also : The annual Register, 1817, Chap. XV.

95 N.A.I. For. Pol. 1817 : O.C. No. 11, 21 January, 1817 : Lushington to Elphinstone, camp at Kame, 27 December, 1816 :

96 N.A.I. For. Sec. O.C. No. 27, 15 April, 1816 : Russell to Adam, Hyderabad, 28 March, 1816.

97 N.A.I. For. Pol. 1817 : O.C. No. 45, 11 January, 1817 : Russell to Adam, Hyderabad, 21 December, 1816 :
Also : O.C. No. 46, 11 January, 1817, Russell to Adam, Hyderabad, 23 December, 1816.

98 N.A.I. For. Pol. 1817 : O.C. No. 7, 21 January, 1817 : Russell to MacDowell, Comdg. a Detachment, Hyderabad, 31 December, 1816.

99 N.A.I. For. Pol. 1817 : O.C. No. 15-17, 4 February, 1817 : MacDowell to Russell, camp at Goonjootee, 15 January, 1817.

100 N.A.I. For. Pol. 1817 : O.C. No. 27, 18 January, 1816 : Elphinstone to Adam, Poona, 26 December, 1816.

101 Supplement to the Government of India Gazette : Thursday, June 19, 1817, gives the figure to be eight hundred Pindaris, who went with Sheikh Dulloo.

102 N.A.I. For. Pol. 1817 : O.C. No. 39, 19 April, 1817 : Jenkins to Adam, Nagpur, 26 March, 1817 : Enclosing Intelligence from Chitu's camp, 19 March, 1817, para 14.

103 The prisoners taken in this excursion reported that they had specifically been asked by Daulat Rao Scindia to plunder British territories.

N.A.I. For. Sec. 1817 : O.C. No. 1, 18 January, 1817 : Adam to Close, Fort William, 14 January, 1817.

104 B.G.R : D.No. 434, Pol. Deptt. 1817 : Balington, Judge and Magistrate, Thana to Warden, Thana 28 December, 1816.

105 B.G.R. : D. No. 435 : Pol. Deptt. 1817 : J.T. Sparrow, Resident, Fort Victoria, to Henderson, Bombay Council, 24 February, 1817.

106 N.A.I. For. Sec. 1817 : O.C. No. 1-3, 11 February, 1817 : Close to Adam, Gwalior, 23 January, 1817, para 3.

107 N.A.I. For. Pol. 1817 : O.C. No. 19, 17 May, 1817 :

J. William, First Assistant Incharge, Baroda Residency to F. Warden, Baroda, 26 March, 1817.

108 James Burgers, *Chronology of Modern India* 1494-1894, p. 305, Edinburgh, 1913.

109 B.G.R. D. No. 437 : Pol. Deptt. 1817 : Extract from an Akhbar received by Daulat Rao Scindia.

110 C.I.A.F. No. 281 : Bhopal Book No. B2 : Issues to Government from 31-8-1818 to 17-12-1818 : Copy of a letter No. 281, dated 27 September 1818 from Capt. W. Henley in-charge of Political Duties at Bhopal to Adam.

111 Selections from Satara Rajas and the Peshwa's Diaries : Vol. V. Baji Rao II, by Rao Bahadur Chimnaji Vad.

112 N.A.I. For. Pol. 1810 : O.C. No. 25, 14 December, 1810 :
H. Russell, Acting Resident Poona, to Lord Minto, Poona, 17 November, 1810.
Also : P.R.R. (Poona Affairs 1781-1820) Vol. VII, Letter No. 361, Russell to Governor-General, Poona, 17 Nov., 1810.

113 A.O. : P.R. : Jenkins to Elphinstone, Nagpur, 31 October, 1812.

114 N.A.I. For. Sec. 1815 : O.C. No. 89-91, 10 January, 1815 :
Elphinstone to Adam, Poona, 15 December, 1814.

115 N.A.I. Por. Sec. 1815 : O.C. No. 89-91, 10 January, 1815, Capt. D. Campbell, Commanding, Siroor to Elphinstone, 15 December, 1814.

116 B.G.R. D. No. 175, Item No. 8, Lt. Col. Wallace to Major Walker at Bombay, Camp near Akola, 27 November, 1806.

117 N.A.I. For. Sec. 1806 : O.C. No. 91-92 10 April, 1806: Lt Col. Wallace to Col. Close, Camp near Akola, 29 November, 1805.

118 N.A.I. For. Sec. 1806: O. C. No. 34-35, 10 April, 1806: Lt. Col. Wallace to Col. Close, Resident at Poona, 18 November, 1805.

119 N.A.I. For. Pol. 1807: O.C. No. 122, 25 February, 1807 : Private letter without date from Capt. Sydenham to N. B. Edmonstone.

120 N. A. I. For. Pol. 1807 : O. C. No. 42 A : 12 February, 1807 : Chief Secretary Fort William to G. E. Mercer, Resident with Scindia.

121 H.R.R. S. No. 128: Vol. No. 407 : Doveton to Sydenham, Resident at Hyderabad, 10 December, 1807.

122 H.R.R.S. No. 413 : Statement of the Pindaris according to an account received from Hindia on April 20, 1814.

123 B.G.R. D; No. 392, Deposition of a Pair of Cossids : 2 January, 1813.

124 N.A I. For. Sec. 1814 : O.C. No. 15-16; 4 March, 1814 : Sydenham to H. Russell, Aurangabad, 7 February, 1814.

125 N.A.I. For. Sec. 1814 : O.C. No. 23-25, 18 March, 1814 : Translation of an Akhbar enclosed in a letter from Resident at Nagpur, 20 February, 1814.

[126] H.R.R. S. No. 195, Vol, No. 413 : Statement of Pindaris from Hindia in April, 1814, by Sydenham: Aurangabad, 28 April, 1814.

[127] N.A.I. For. Sec. 1815 : O.C. No. 35-38, 25 November, 1815 : Sydenham to Russell, Aurangabad, 28 October, 1815.

[128] 'Maker' is a small village in the Berar District.

[129] N.A.I. For. Sec. 1815 : O.C. No. 40-41, 25 November, 1815 : Col. Doveton to Russell, Camp at Akola, 30 October, 1815.

[130] N.A.I. For. Sec. 1816 : O.C. No. 27, 3 February, 1816 : Wauchope to Adam, Banda, 23 January, 1816.

[131] N.A.I, For. Sec. 1810 : O.C. No. 9-10, 26 March, 1810 : Capt. Whitehead, Lohargaon to Capt. Gough, 18 March, 1812.

[132] N.A.I. For. Sec. 1810 : O.C. No. 9-10, 26 March, 1810 : Translation of a Letter From Raja Doorjan Singh, Chief of Mahiyar to Capt. Whitehead.

[133] N.A.I. For. Sec. 1812 : Martindale, Commanding in Bundel Khand to Lt. Col. Pagh, Adjutant General, Fort William, Calcutta.

[134] The Rewa Raja and"the Chief Karim Khan had an interview on the banks of Gogra....A vakeel had reached Rewa from Karim Khan twelve days before the marauders entered that district in order to obtain the Raja's permission for guides and a free passage throughe his country, this...has been granted."
N.A.I. For. Sec. 1112 : O.C. No, 3-5, 26 March, 1812 : Whitehead to Gough, Keitah.

[135] N.A.I. For. Sec. 1812 O.C. No. 7-8, 3 April, 1812 : Translation of a letter from Jag Mohan Singh of Semerah, dependent on Rewa to Hindoo Singh, his Mukhtar at Banda, 10 March, 1812.

[136] N.A.I. For. Sec. 1812 : O.C. No. 6-7 17 April, 1812 : J. Richardson A.G.G. Banda to N.B Edmonstone, Banda 3 April, 1812.

[137] N.A.I. For. Sec. 1814 : O.C. No. 9, 4 February, 1814 : Wauchope to Adam, Camp at Koty, near Rewah, 19 January, 1814.

[138] N.A.I. For. Pol. 1817 : O.C. No. 40, 26 April, 1817 : Adam to Maddock, Fort William 26 April, 1817.

[139] Supplement to Government of India Gazettee : Saturday, April 26, 1817.

6

British Policy Towards the Pindaris

Policy of Non-Intervention

The British Parliament passed the Pitts' India Act for the better management of the affairs of the East India Company in 1784. Of all the clauses, the most striking was the one which prohibited all aggressive wars in India. Article 34 of this Act said :

> "And whereas to pursue schemes of conquest and extension of dominion in India, are measures repugnant to the wish, the honour and policy of this nation... That it shall not be lawful for the Governor General and the Council without the express command of the Court of Directors, or the Secret Committee, in any case (except where hostilities have actually been commenced or preparations actually made for the commencement of hostilities against the British nation in India, or against some of the princes or states whose territories the Company shall be engaged by any subsisting treaty to defend or guarantee) either to declare war or commence hostilities, or enter into any treaty for making war, against any of the country princes or states

in India, or any treaty for guaranteeing the possessions of any country, princes or states"...

Lord Cornwallis

Lord Cornwallis who took charge as the Governor General was instructed by the Court of Directors to follow the policy of non-intervention as envisaged in the Pitts' India Act. He reached India with a firm resolve to follow the dictates of the Court. However, on arrival here, he found that the rising power of Tipu was a great menace to the British Empire. He, therefore, sought the friendship of the Nizam and the Marathas and concluded the famous Triple Alliance in 1790.[1] In the Third Anglo-Mysore War Tipu was defeated with the help of the Nizam and the Marathas. According to the Treaty of Sirirangpattam concluded in March, 1792 Tipu had to surrender nearly half of his dominion, large portions of which were given to the Nizam and the Marathas.

Sir John Shore

Sir John Shore who succeeded Lord Cornwallis in 1793 as officiating Governor-General was wedded to the policy of strict non-intervention. In spite of the entreaties of the Nizam for help against the Marathas, Shore, sincerely anxious to carry out the policy of the Directors, decided "that the Company was not required to intervene."[2] The Nizam was humiliated at Khurda by the Marathas in March, 1794. Sir John Shore, a strict devotee of non-intervention, "lamented the increased power of the Marathas, but he did nothing and contemplated nothing. He lamented the prostration of the Nizam but only took credit for having foretold it."[3]

It cannot be denied that conditions in India did not really warrant such a cautious attitude on the part of the British Government. However, the condition of India, particularly Central India, was during this period most anarchic. Major Palmer observed that "the most miserable neglect and disorder" prevailed, and "a large army (i.e. of Scindia) is employed in seeking its own subsistence by exacting unjust contributions from the defenceless Rajas of Hindustan."[4]

Shore had observed that amongst the Rajputs there was not one who could stop the Maratha tide. Meanwhile, the Marathas too had lost their glory, and were getting emaciated due to internal dissensions and distractions.

Thus the period between the departure of Warren Hastings from India, and the arrival on the grand scene of action of Marquess of Wellesley, (1798-1806) was a period of comparative peace and tranquillity, but for the Third Mysore War. This period can, on the whole, be termed as one of non-intervention as far as the British Government is concerned. The British most scrupulously avoided wars or intervention in Indian affairs, at times, at the cost of their honour,word and peril, just to keep to the letter of Pitts' India Act of 1784. But this temporising and short-sighted policy by the British had ultimately to be abandoned.

Lord Wellesley

As early as 1804, Lord Wellesley warned the Home Authorities that "we run a great risk from the freebooters system. It is not known to the Governor-General and you can have no idea of the extent to which it has gone and it increases daily."[5]

Lord Wellesley, therefore, had a scheme of his own to curb the growing power of the Pindaris. His idea was to guarantee protection to all the Indian States under the famous Subsidiary Alliance policy. However, the scheme did not meet the approval of the Home Authorities.[6] Castlereagh, President of the Board of Control, had approved of the measures against Mysore and permitted steps to be taken in combating the growing French influence in the courts of Hyderabad and Mysore. Yet he did not see an urgent need for measures against the Pindaris because the immediate danger from Tipu and the growing French influence had been liquidated.

On the Maratha scene, Jaswant Rao Holkar was the rising star. He had recently inflicted a severe defeat on the combined forces of the Peshwa and the Scindia, almost within sight of Poona, which made Peshwa fly for life. Peshwa took shelter with the British and concluded the famous Treaty of Bassein on December 31, 1802. Lord Castlereagh, besides treating it as "inexpedient and dangerous" thought that it "tended to involve us in the endless and complicated distractions of the Maratha Empire." Circumstances soon proved that Castlereagh was right and the British were in no time at war with Scindia and the Bhonsla.

The advent of Wellesley saw the war against the Scindia and Bhonsla terminate most successfully. The French influence, whatever remained of it, disappeared completely. Scindia's control over the Mughal Emperor and all the prestige associated with it, was now transferred to the British. All was going well. But the events took a serious turn with the beginning of the war with Jaswant Rao Holkar, which proved disastrous for the British influence in general and Wellesley's in particular. Col. Monson had to make a disastrous and disorderly retreat to Agra from Mukund-dwara pass in Rajputana. Dissatisfaction was brewing among the *Jats*; and Lake's repeated failure before the fort of Bharatpur added another failure in the otherwise triumphant career of Wellesley. He received a severe jolt for these reverses. The debts of the British Government in the recent wars had increased from seventeen million to thirty million. Daulat Rao Scindia, too, was smarting under great dissatisfaction. So long as the British arms met with success, the Court did not raise any objection, though it was mindful of the increasing war expenditure. But the moment defeats followed one another, the Directors felt that the time had come for the recall of the man, whose forward policy had resulted in great advances being made by the British, and which the Court of Directors could not comprehend. The Directors also realised that if Wellesley was left unchecked in his ambitious schemes of conquest, he might put the British Government in India in jeopardy, and therefore, it was thought expedient that they return to the non-intervention policy, which had been so successfully pursued during Cornwallis' and Shore's time, and thereby the affairs of Indian States were "left without the pale of our relations."[7] Lord Wellesley left India in 1805.

Second Term of Cornwallis

Under the aforesaid circumstances the Court was obliged to depute Lord Cornwallis again to India. Cornwallis, an old man of 67 years, landed at Calcutta on July 30, 1805, "with strict injunctions to make no further acquisitions of territory and to abstain from assuming new responsibilities in relation to native states."[8] He was to revert to the policy of non-intervention by abandoning Wellesley's system of Subsidiary Alliances "as far as was consistent with the treaties already concluded" and thus follow a policy of quiescence. Therefore, immediately after his arrival, he issued instructions to Lake to abandon all aggressive designs.[9]

The policy which Lord Cornwallis adopted was not only that of conciliation but of retraction. He was of the view that such measures of conciliation, as he was soon to follow, favoured the British interests in India. His idea was to carry on the political affairs in India on the safe principle of limited liability unless British interests were involved and to adopt an "attitude of a placid spectator unconcerned with the quarrels or misfortunes" of Indian Rajas.[10] Thus by following this policy of masterly inactivity which left the whole of Central India and Rajputana to take care of itself against the Maratha intruders and Pindari freebooters, Cornwallis hoped to maintain peace in India. He agreed in toto with the principles laid down by the Court and observed on the same : "This resolution of abandoning all connections with the petty states and generally with the territories to the westward of Jumna" is founded upon "my knowledge of the entire conformity of those grand principles to the provisions of the legislature and to the orders of the Hon'ble the Court of Directors.[11]" Thus the British Government was determined to avoid interfering in the internal affairs and dissensions of the various Indian Rajas.[12] Cornwallis thought of the various treaties concluded with them as nothing less than "a network of embarrassing ties and compromising guarantees."[13]

He even hoped that by restoring the conquests made in the Maratha War, Indian chiefs would be reconciled to the presence of the British in India. To achieve this aim

Cornwallis made a clear analysis of the situation and in order to follow the policy of non-intervention effectively, he contemplated the following five principles :

"Firstly, to restore to Jaswant Rao Holkar all the territories of the Holkar family including those of which he had been deprived during the recent war.

"Secondly, to conciliate Daulat Rao Scindia by the restoration of Gohud and the fortress of Gwalior.

"Thirdly, to abandon the defensive alliance with the Rajput and Jat states, by which Lord Wellesley had sought to create a barrier between British territories and the Mahratta powers.

"Fourthly, to compensate these native states for the loss of British protection by distributing amongst them all the territories which the British Government had acquired to the westward of Jumna.

"Fifthly, to withdraw, if practicable, the Emperor Shah Alam to some town near Calcutta and to leave Delhi in the possession of Daulat Rao Scindia, with liberty to restore the Mahratta power in Hindostan."[14] Cornwallis, however, did not live to carry out his intentions. He died at Gazipur in October, 1805 within three months of his arrival in India and left the task of retraction and pacification to Sir George Barlow.

Sir George Barlow

Sir George Barlow, a Senior Member of the Bengal Council, succeeded Cornwallis as the Officiating Governor-General. The policy which had been inaugurated by Cornwallis was most faithfully carried on by Barlow. He made no attempt whatsoever to stop the Gurkha infringements or the increasing inferno of disorder and anarchy in Central India. He was content to "maintain the *cordon sanitaire* around the plague spot."[15] Such was his policy that, all that had been conquered from Jaswant Rao Holkar was restored to him. The famous treaty of Surji Anjungaon was confirmed. Barlow refrained from every kind of relationship with the Indian states, with whom the British were at war in the time of Wellesley. The Rajput and the Jat states with whom defensive alliances had earlier been concluded, were also left in the lurch. Bharatpur and Alwar were the only exceptions. The repeated entreaties of Jaipur went unheeded. Though, during the period of the Second Maratha War, the Raja of Jaipur helped the British forces against Jaswant Rao Holkar, it was not forthcoming as promptly as the British would have liked. Seizing the opportunity, Barlow, not prepared for the continuance of an alliance with Jaipur on the ground of inexpediency, dissolved the same.[16]

The policy which Sir George Barlow pursued was one of "disgrace without compensation, treaties without security and peace without tranquillity.[17]" It left the Maratha independent and free to follow the policy of aggression. So long as the Marathas respected the British territories, it did not matter to him what the Marathas and other free-booters did. He discarded Wellesley's dictum whereby independent and protected states were to serve the purpose of barrier between the Maratha states and the British provinces. Surprisingly enough, Barlow was also of the view that the mutual war between Scindia and Holkar and their aggressions in Rajputana strengthened the British Government. He was further of the opinion that "their mutual jealousy and distrust, the nature of their respective interests and the internal causes of dissension which exist among them" would weaken them and leave the British free to pursue the policy of non-intervention.

The Maratha rulers, Scindia and Holkar, took the fullest possible advantage of this policy and committed aggressions, unhampered and undaunted by consequences. Meanwhile, the Pindari freebooters had become extremely bold and in 1806 committed aggression on the British ally, the Nizam. The British remonstrances to Scindia resulted in no improvement of the situation. The only extenuating circumstance was the capture by Scindia of Karim Khan and Chitu, but there was no respite from their horrors. Their durras continued their depredations with unabated vigour.

Lord Minto

Lord Minto who succeeded Barlow was also directed to continue the policy of non-intervention in India. He was supposed to keep away from all complications and maintain absolute neutrality. But very soon he discovered that it was not such smooth sailing in India, there being present more than one disturbing element and the Pindaris constituting the most important one.

On the first invasion of the British territories by the Pindaris, he reported that people in Central India were suffering cruelly at their hands.[18] He wrote to the Court of Directors entreating them to consider whether "it was expedient to observe a strict neutrality amidst these scenes of disorder and outrages, or to listen to the voice of suffering humanity and interfere for the protection of the weak and defenceless states who implored our assistance against the ravages of the Pindaris and the Pathans."[19] There was no encouraging response from the Home Authorities. He wrote another letter to the Court pointing out that "the augmented numbers, the improved organisation and the increasing audacity of the Pindarees, rendered the adoption of an extensive system of measures for their suppression, a matter of pressing importance."[20] He made it very clear to the Home Authorities that so long as the British left the Pindaris free to act, there would be no peace and that the expectation of the British security by diminishing its political ascendency on the continent of India would be fruitless.

When Jenkins drew the attention of Lord Minto to the condition of anarchy in Central India, particularly due to the ravages of Amir Khan, Minto expressed his inability to act. At the same time he added "the Government will not consider its interference to be admissible excepting only under circumstances of the most unquestionable exigency as connected with the tranquillity of the British Dominions or those of its allies."[21] This policy of non-intervention and indifference in Indian affairs pursued by Barlow and Minto was indeed not likely to be appreciated by those whom it was intended to placate. Moreover, within the short period from the departure of Lord Wellesley in 1805 to the departure of Minto in 1813, the policy of non-intervention "had already brought forth an abundance of evil fruits."[22] These were;

Firstly, Scindia and Holkar, not caring for the anarchic conditions prevailing in their own states, were committing aggression on the Rajput states and creating similar confusion there as well.

Secondly, Bhopal was repeatedly threatened by Bhonsla and the Scindia. Nagpur in turn was menaced by Amir Khan.

Thirdly, a general dissatisfaction against the British prevailed amongst the Indian states, and conspiracies were being hatched against them.

Fourthly, Peshwa Baji Rao, though he had concluded an alliance with the British, was secretly making efforts to get out of it.

Fifthly, internal anarchy and disorder were increasing in Malwa and Rajputana. The rebellious and mutinous troops of Scindia and Holkar were making confusion worse confounded by going about and levying their own contributions in lieu of the salaries which were never regularly paid. Scindia and Holkar were in severe financial straits, Scindia being worse. He had no regular source of income whatsoever; "the only source of revenue to which Scindia would look, independently of the payments which he and his officers received from the British Government under the Treaty of November 1805, was the forced contribution which he levied from the Rajput states."[23] The system of *Dhurna* had also reached new heights and even Daulat Rao Scindia was not spared. It was apparently reduced to a regular system. British withdrawal of the protection to Nagpur resulted in the Pindaris threatening the capital right upto the British Residency. Poona, too, suffered at the Pindari hands.

However, Minto was not sitting silent. He continued to inform and hammer into the minds of the Court of Directors the increasing danger of this system. Besides, he was taking active measures for the defence not only of the British territories, but also of the allies—the Nizam, the Bhonsla, and the Peshwa. With this end in view he maintained a close watch on the activities of the Pindaris and their leaders. Military posts were established at several places to check the Pindari inroads.[24]

Such was the policy of peace, neutrality and non-intervention which produced evil results both for the Indian states and the British Gevernment.

Sir John Malcolm, a vigorous opponent of non-intervention, maintains that had this policy, which followed the departure of Wellesley and "which came like a mildew to blight the fruits of our great successes," not been followed and had Wellesley been given a free hand, he would have succeeded in establishing peace in India and perhaps the Pindari menace would not have assumed such huge proportions.

Treaty of Surji-Arjungaon and its Failure

The above resume of the political and military situation in India after the departure of Wellesley till the arrival of Hastings shows that the year 1805 was a critical year in the history of the British rule in India. It was also the year of Trafalgar, which once and for all proved Britain to be the queen of the seas, which compelled Napoleon to attempt an over-land attack upon the British possessions in the East, particularly on India. This resulted in the British establishing contacts with Persia, Ranjit Singh and the North-West Frontier areas. Lord Minto, to counteract the possibility of an over-land attack on India, gave all his attention to external affairs much at the cost of internal issues and continued to adhere to the policy of non-intervention. This policy, however, led to more trouble later, and in the very heart of the country patches of disturbance and disease were left to heal themselves.

The peace which culminated in the settlement of 1805 was far from satisfactory, particularly the treaties with Scindia and Holkar.[26] The weak and feeble states of Rajputana including Udaipur, Jodhpur and Jaipur, presented as on a silver platter to Scindia's and Holkar's rapaciousness, ultimately weakened them so much as to make them an easy prey to the Pindaris and to Amir Khan's Pathans. No wonder, very soon the predators were roaming freely over the length and breadth of the country. The defects of the treaty soon became apparent and "it could no longer be disguised that the settlement of 1805 was, after all, but an incomplete arrangement, which must ere long be entirely remodelled."[27]

Unsuccessful Application of the Policy of Defence

Since non-intervention was the basic policy, the British only adopted measures of defence and these too were just local efforts. No concerted defence policy or measures were adopted to check the Pindari menace. Once the evil of Pindari attack was over like the monsoon, they would again relapse into complacency.[28] A few detachments here and there in the forts or stations spread over the whole expanse of the Deccan and Central India were the only measures adopted to check the growing evil of the Pindaris. But these measures were mere palliatives and temporary expedients and consequently there was no peace whatsoever.[29] No such system of defence, no amount of soldiers and no distribution of troops could protect the country against the Pindari depredations.[30] In spite of the best efforts made by the army, the zeal and perseverance of British officers, nothing could stop the annual raids. Besides, it was impossible to protect the whole British and allied frontiers extending to thousands of miles and that too when the "regular troops unfitted them for competing with the unincumbered, rapid and desultory movements of the Pindari horse."[31] and thereby proving the futility of the precautionary measures.

Under the circumstances, the use of the infantry was absolutely out of question. The infantry was no match to the Pindari cavalry which flew like birds in the air.[32] To say nothing of the infantry, even the British cavalry, was no match to the Pindari horse.[33] Seton, a member of the Governor-General's Council, therefore, felt that "unless the power of the Pindaris be crushed altogether, the evil may rather be said to be transferred than annihilated, since the same men, though expelled from one part of the country, may collect and stand up in some other quarter to be the perpetual annoyance of every regular government."[34] Major Lushington inflicted a very severe punishment on the Pindaris, but without much consequence. The loss sustained by the Pindaris in one season (even if it were great) would not prevent the repetition of outrages in the next.[35] The Pindari hordes, beaten once or twice were only humbled rather than crushed. The defeat or destruction of any particular chief would result in the ruin of an individual without removing the evil of the Pindari menace.

It was also difficult to organise a permanent system of defence against such an enemy. It would need a standing army to be kept in a state of constant preparedness and yet it was not certain that the Pindaris would be checked.[36] Russell, reporting Col. Doveton's efforts in the beginning of Lord Hastings' reign, observed that nothing was omitted by him in his movements against the Pindaris which judgement and decision could suggest. Their escape from a pursuit so well-planned and so promptly executed only afforded an additional proof of the impossibility of acting against them with any certain effect. "Their skill in concerting their enterprise and their boldness in executing them; their capability in enduring fatigue, the great rapidity of their movements the accurate knowledge they appear to have of the country and the facility and correctness with which they invariably procure intelligence, must always secure them against any measure directed merely to the defence of the territories which are the object of their eruption."[37]

Moreover, the defence measures had to be repeated annually.[38] But if action were to be taken against the Pindaris by waging a regular war with the intention of finishing them off once and for all—then "the business would be thus finished by one effort which would not cost half as much as the defensive provisions of a single season."[39] The maintenance of a standing army, and consequently almost ever-preparedness resulted in a lot of expenditure. It was a perpetual drain on the resources of the Company, whose financial position was already not very sound.[40]

Edmonstone also admitted the impracticability of the defence measures and pleaded that all possible efforts should be made to strike at the root of that intolerable evil viz. the Pindaris.

In the most emphatic language, Seton also favoured abandoning defensive measures which had proved "futile and unavailng,[41] and pleaded the inevitability of resorting to the offensive. So strongly was he convinced of the Pindari menace that he wrote in his minute that "unless we seek the Pindaris, they will again seek us."[42]

Lord Hastings was also opposed to the defensive policy. He wrote, "My own professional opinion has been unequivocally given and it has been confirmed by the recorded declarations of the Officers Commanding the Hyderabad and Poona Subsidiary Divisions, that a chain of defensive stations is nugatory against a force composed like that of the Pindaris."[43]

In support of his argument, Hastings went on to quote Col. Walker's report in which he emphasized the inadequacy of the defence measures which could be gauged from the fact that the chain of forts were situated at a distance of ninety miles from each other, through which it was very easy for the Pindaris to sneak in and out. Hastings further wrote, "There is no occasion for describing the facility with which a body of cavalry so lightly equipped as the Pindaris can penetrate through such a space before any information can reach the post on either side, or readily they may return by another similar opening after having performed their work of devastation."[44]

Estimate of Pindari Strength

From time to time, estimates have been given by various authorities regarding the number of Pindaris in the first and second decades of the nineteenth century. Jenkins believed that in 1804 there were not less than 13,000 Pindaris.[45] But Malcolm, who was in Scindia's camp in 1804, estimated that the Pindaris with Scindia alone, amounted to 10,000, out of which, he observed, at least six thousand were cavalry. In 1809, their strength according to Sydenham, was 20,000,[46] but Jenkins estimated the same as 24,550.[47] In the beginning of 1812 their number was estimated to be 25,000. Out of this number six to seven thousand were effective cavalry, while three to four thousand were of a middling character, and the rest were mere 'tattoos.' But in August, 1812 Jenkins gave their strength as 34,000. The total number of irregular horse subsisting entirely on plunder was estimated by Fitzclarence and the Governor-General as 40,000 and 80,000 respectively.[88] On the basis of official accounts, Hamilton has calculated the strength of the Pindari chiefs in 1814-1815 to be as follows[49] :—

Under Chitu's command of which 5,000 were good	10,000	
Besides the Holkar Shahi Pindaris above	5,000	
Karim Khan's band	4,000	
Dost Mohammad's	4,000	
Under independent leaders of inferior note	6,000	
	29,000	Horse

In fact, it may be observed that the strength of the Pindaris was always liable to be exaggerated. "The disposition of the mind, especially when under alarm, to magnify objects indefinitely, contributes not a little to swell the numbers of an irregular body in idea and report. Squadrons and battalions, from their distinct and compact formation, are to be contemplated separately, like individuals; while the same number of troops, particularly horse, scattered over a plain may appear almost innumerable. On this account, hyperbolical expressions are continually applied to considerable bodies of irregular horse, and never to regular corps."[50]

The actual number of the Pindaris cannot be estimated as they were never seen together.[51] They usually marched in small parties and this was one of the main reason of their being exaggerated. Their strength was visualised according to the slaughter, arson and rapine they committed. The Pindaris, in order to overawe the Indian chiefs and the British Government, always endeavoured to let their power and number appear formidable. They directed their emissaries to spread false and exaggerated accounts of their successes and in case of failure, to contradict and belittle them.[52] Under these circumstances it was difficult, nay impossible, to form a correct estimate of their real number, which varied, if not from day to day, at least from time to time.[53] However, it cannot be doubted that in case of emergency, they were capable of putting as many as 60,000 horsemen in the field.

There was a controversy between Lord Hastings and Edmonstone, a senior Member of the Council, on the growth of the Pindari menace. Edmonstone was of the opinion that the Pindaris had not increased in proportion to the passage of time. He further maintained that the very nature and composition of the Pindaris precluded them from increasing their numbers. The object of the Pindari leaders was plunder and not warfare, and therefore, unlimited increase in number would diminish the individual share of the loot, which was not in the interest of the Pindaris. But Lord Hastings was of an absolutely different view. He believed that the increase in their number added to their vanity, status, and security.

Edmonstone cut across Hastings' reasoning by very forceful arguments. He was of the view that the increase in their numbers was the natural result of their extended territorial aggrandisement. He believed that the imposition of the Subsidiary Alliance on the Indian States and the end of the Maratha Wars had deprived the people of their accustomed sources of subsistence. Between starvation and predatory life, they chose the latter and swelled the Pindari bands. But Edmonstone maintained that the increase had not been progressive. He believed that their actual number had been considerably over-rated. In support of his argument, he quoted Jenkins' authoritative Memorandum. Jenkins, in a statement prepared in September, 1809, put their number at 24,550. But in a subsequent Memorandum prepared in August, 1812, their number was estimated to be 34,000. Mr. Strachey, who held a different opinion on the issue, commented in a private letter to Edmonstone, "Were I to hazard a conjecture (regarding) their numerical strength, I should reckon on a deduction of at least one-third of the aggregate." The one-third of 34,000 would put the figure to be nearly 11,600. Hence the increase was not unusual. The controversy between the two was not conclusive. Each was unable to convince the other regarding the correct estimate of the real strength of the Pindaris.

In 1814, Sydenham computed the Pindari strength to be 20,000; while in 1804, the Pindaris numbered 13,000 only. Thus it may be observed that during the period of 1804 to 1814, the Pindaris increased by about 7,000 only, which, looking to the circumstances, seems to be not much of an increase. Thus Edmonstone seems to be more correct in his estimate of Pindari numbers.

Seriousness of Pindari Threat

Since ages past, all history of mankind has proved that marauders and military adventurers were responsible for creating conditions of anarchy, ruin and chaos, conditions which obtained in India during the middle ages; and continued till much after the British had established their power. According to Dow, India was torn to pieces. All laws, divine and temporal, were trampled under foot by the various warring elements.

Position of Pindaris at the Arrival of Lord Hastings

As Pindari operations began to extend to the territories adjacent to the British possessions or to the possessions of their dependent princes, the British Government could not remain indifferent to them. It was feared that they constituted a grave threat to the peace of the country as a whole. In course of time, it was feared that they might constitute themselves "as a distinct political interest." This was not merely a conjecture. At one stage the Pindari chiefs possessed rich districts, owned formidable strongholds and pursued an independent career, and this naturally alarmed the British Government.

We find that the Prince Regent of Portugal, also, on receipt of a memorial from the people of Goa, complained of the Pindari menace to the British.[54] The British too, as alluded above, were alarmed at their increasing depredations. So serious was the menace that at the time of concluding the Subsidiary Treaty of May 27, 1816 with the state of Nagpur, the Pindaris were distinctly mentioned by name and the Raja was not only guaranteed security against the various Indian chiefs, but also against the Pindaris.[55]

With a large number of separate groups of the Pindaris operating over an extensive area, the problem could not be solved with the extirpation of a group or two. They were formidable depredators, who worked on the principle that they had "everything to hope from success and whose condition, defeat did not render more desperate."[56] Besides the prevailing anarchy and chaos contributed very largely to their growth and power and proved conducive to their free indulgence in acts of plunder and loot. The wide range over which they operated can similarly be gauged from a Minute of Lord Hastings relating to the Pindari menace which reads thus: "No part of our extended frontier from Loodianah to Cuttack is safe from incursions."[57]

The British territories in India remained, on the whole, free from the ravages of the Pindaris until 1811, partly because the wealth of the parts ruled by the Indian chiefs still engaged the attention of the plunderers and also because the judicious disposition of the British troops and the treaty with Rewa discouraged them. But this did not continue for long. Soon, the Pindaris ventured to cross the British frontiers and those of their allies. Such importance had they assumed and such notoriety had they earned that during one such invasion of Madras territories in 1816, civil and military officers readily abandoned their posts of duty and joined in the general fight. When Hastings learned of this, he was constrained to remark that in the event of an invasion by a European army "the consternation could not have been great."[58] The danger rapidly spread right up to the gates of Fort St. George and the Madras Government was so awe-struck that instead of taking action against the invaders, it sought the advice of the Governor-General, who out of sheer disgust wrote back, "Why, I believe, if the Government House at Madras was on fire, (the Governor, would ask whether he should extinguish it or not."[59] Again such was the fear of the Pindaris that while they were still two hundred miles away from Madras, all classes of people rushed into the fort for safety, and utmost alarm prevailed. That was history repeating itself. It was reminiscent of the old days of Hyder Ali knocking at the gates of Madras. It was during these days of nervous tension that "an idle rumour reached Madras of the arrival of the Pindaris at the Mount; all was uproar, flight and despair to the walls of Madras. This alarm originated in a few *dhobies* and grass-cutters of the artillery having mounted their *tattoos* and, in mock imitation of the Pindaris, galloping about and playing with long bamboos in their hands in the vicinity of the Mount. The effect was such, however, that many of the civil servants and inhabitants on the Mount Road packed up and moved to the fort for protection. Troops and messengers, etc., were seen galloping towards the Government House, and thence to the different public authorities. Such was the alarm in the Government House that on the afternoon of that day, an old officer, anxious to offer some advice to the Governor rode smartly up to the Government Gardens, and on reaching the entrance, observed the younger son of the Governor running with all possible speed into the House. The child having got to a place of security ventured to look back and then discovered in the old officer a face which he had seen before, when turning back again, he exclaimed, 'Upon my word, Sir, I was so frightened, I took you for a Pindari."[60] All this goes to show the general apprehension of the Pindaris among the people at that time. They had become so formidable that the British were forced to believe that the Pindaris "if properly united, under an able commander, would prove the utmost dangerous enemy that would arise to disturb the peace and prosperity of India."[61]

Thus the Pindaris gradually assumed that boldness, that strength and that importance, which is normally a feature of a regular army, and therefore, no civilised government could remain blind to the horrors and enormities perpetrated by the Pindari hordes.

Hastings' Attitude to the Pindari Problem

In a very short time Hastings, after he had thoroughlysurveyed the whole situation, adopted a clear attitude towards the Pindari problem. He communicated the same to the Court of Directors in a more emphatic language than that of Lord Minto. He drew their attention to the increasing danger of the Pindaris. He made it quite clear to the Court that unless the Government "became the head of a league embracing every power in India, and was placed in a position to direct its entire strength against the disturbers of the public peace,"[62] the British existence in India would continue to be in danger.[63] He resolved to rid India completely of the Pindari menace, to conclude alliances with the Rajput Rajas and to establish a general control over all the Indian chiefs.[64]

There is little doubt that the British were prompted to exterminate the Pindaris by humanitarian considerations. The sufferings of the people demanded that the freebooters be totally annihilated. But an important consideration behind the drive against them was the removal of Maratha supremacy over the Rajputs. In fact, Lord Hastings aimed at reducing the political pretensions of the Marathas from all over Hindustan and uniting all the Rajputs under the British.

Hastings had at this time, a team of very efficient civil and military staff to assist him—Elphinstone in Poona, Munro in Madras, Malcolm in Central India, and Metcalfe, Tod and Ochterlony were civil officers in Rajputana while Hislop, Malcolm, Adam, Doveton and Marshall etc., were military generals. A chain of brilliant Residents in Indian courts supplied the smallest bit of information to the British Government and kept it abreast. The Minutest detail did not pass unnoticed. The letters written by these Residents to Hastings are a specimen of their rare brilliance and political acumen. Thus, Hastings received the most sound advice from them, which enabled him to take prompt decisions. With their help he realised that if peace, prosperity and plenty were to be achieved in the strife-ridden India, it could be done only after the predatory system was erased and the unnatural state of anarchy and disorder was ended. He, therefore, entreated the Home Authorities for action. He tried to impress upon them that the Pindaris, if suffered to continue further, would become a political threat of great magnitude. He wrote, "I have urged strenuously the wisdom of suppressing those free-booters and extirpating them from their retreats, while they were yet in a condition which allowed of our doing so with moderate effort."[65] But he held out a warning that, "if these free-booters were not crushed before they attained the degree of strength to which their confederacy was rapidly tending, they would attract Scindia and Holkar into the vortex of their interests and we should become involved in an extensive war."[66]

Hastings was of the definite opinion—an opinion in which he was thoroughly convinced—that the expulsion of the Pindaris alone would not help in the establishment of peace in India, but the more important task was the prevention of its revival. With this end in view he started negotiations with almost all the Indian chiefs in Central India, Rajputana and the Deccan, who were directly or indirectly connected with the Pindaris. He went to the extent of making friends even with those who had openly given their support to the Pindaris or connived at them. The only condition was their promise to give up the earlier mode of life and lend whole-hearted support in their suppression. With the Pindaris, who were rightly considered to be the greatest pest that ever affected any country,[67] he was not going to have any truck whatever. Hence he believed it to be his supreme duty as the representative of a paramount power to finish the Pindari menace for ever.[68] It is instructive to note here the reactions of some of his colleagues in the Executive Council when Lord Hastings proposed a bold plan against the Pindaris.

Attitude of His Colleagues

Hastings was convinced that it was impossible to deal with the Pindari pest in any other manner, except by direct extermination. But he was thwarted in his endeavour to take any action against the Pindaris by the systematic opposition of two of his Councillors, Edmonstone and Dowdeswell.[69] The basis of the disagreement was their exaggerated dread of the power and participation of Scindia in the war that would follow.[70]

As far as the real issue of the Pindari menace is concerned there was not much of divergence of opinion among his colleagues.[71] But they dreaded the consequences of a general war that their suppression would eventually entail. They were, thus, divided on the means to achieve their objective of dealing with the Pindaris. But the objections of his councillors did not deter him.

As early as 1814, Lord Hastings had drawn the attention of the Council to "the expense now annually incurred for the movement of the troops, a precaution against those free-booters is of itself an evil that loudly calls for remedy."[72] Hastings and Seton both maintained that it was a criminal waste of the Company's already depleted resources. Besides, as had been amply proved, mere defence measures were of no avail against an enemy as elusive as the Pindaris were.[73] Even Edmonstone was in agreement with this view. In his Memorandum drawn up early in 1812 he admitted that a defensive system "indeed, is but a palliative and in its operation, a temporary expedient.[74] He, however, maintained that operations against them could not be undertaken because "an enterprise against the Pindaris might probably without any previous design on our part lead unavoidably to the persecution of military and political operations and arrangements of a very extensive and complicated nature."[75] He further maintained that if the British ever committed the mistake of undertaking operations against the Pindaris the consequences would be disastrous, in so far as it would result in enormous expense and the complete departure from the declared and "prescribed principles of our policy which the engagements would involve."[76] He also argued that the action against the Pindaris might help in dispersing them 'but they could not be rendered extinct'. He, therefore, was of the opinion, in sharp contrast to that of Hastings and Seton, that any action against the Pindaris would result in "involving hazards, difficulties, embarrassments and arrangements of such magnitude and complexity as to render the systematic pursuit of it an object of doubtful expediency."[77]

Thus Edmonstone was not in favour of large-scale military operations that would lead to major reshuffle in political and diplomatic relations. He thought that the Pindaris were not a direct concern of the British Government,

However, Metcalfe, though not a member of the Council, trained in the school of Wellesley, exercised great influence over Hastings, himself an advocate of forward policy. Hastings agreed in toto, with the views held by Metcalfe.

Plans to Exterminate the Pindaris

During the period when acute differences of opinion prevailed, a number of plans to combat the Pindari menace were prepared by various authorities. The aim of all those plans was to liquidate the Pindaris in such a manner that the British would not be involved in a full-scale war against the Marathas in general and Scindia in particular.

Sydenham's Plan

Sydenham was of the opinion that though the Pindaris continued to assume a menacing proportion, no step was taken to check that menace. The Marathas looked upon them with indulgence. He felt that the burden of preventing the growth of Pindaris rested entirely on the British shoulders. He, therefore, suggested a course which would not involve the British Government in a regular war with Indian chiefs and at the same time put all the responsibility on them for the conduct of the Pindaris.[78] He, proposed a six point plan[79]:—

(a) "That the leaders of the durra or their nearest relations shall constantly reside at the Courts, to whose authority they were subservient.

(b) "That the families and property of the Pindaris shall be kept in forts belonging to the government they serve, and that their leaders shall not be allowed to occupy forts, as Cheetoo does, much less build them, as Karim and Dost Mohemmed have done.

(c) "That the numbers of each durra shall be fixed according to the pleasure of the government to which it is attached, and not be subject to increase.

(d) "That the Pindarra leaders shall not be suffered to cast or keep cannon or to maintain establishments of infantry beyond what is absolutely necessary for their personal protection and for purposes of revenue.

(e) "That they shall not be allowed to keep boats on the Nerbudda or to cross that river in boats, belonging to Scindia or the Rajah of Berar, which on that account should always be kept on its southern bank.

(f) "That under the foregoing stipulations the Pindaris be permitted to hold *jageers* to be situated to the Nerbudda, and be considered as auxiliaries to the government which employ them, such government being held responsible for any act of aggression committed by the Pindaris upon the territories of the British Government or its allies."

Commander-in-Chief's Plan

Nugent, the British Commander-in-Chief, a military man as he was, was naturally inclined to more effective and drastic measures. He suggested that Martial law principles be applied to the arrested Pindari leaders. This, he thought, would deter them in sending their durras to the British provinces afterwards.[80]

Russell's Plan

Russell's plan was nothing but to secure British possessions in the south and, for this, he presented a novel scheme. This was to divide the British troops into light detachments. Each was to carry over the pursuit to the next fresh detachment, which would continue the pursuit, thereby tiring and ultimately annihilating them. He maintained that at least one thing was bound to result—the Pindaris would not have time to loot and plunder.[81]

Seton's Plan

Seton wanted the Pindaris to be regarded and treated as robbers and murderers. His belief was that the dispersion of the Pindaris from their haunts could be attempted in three ways :—

(a) By keeping on the defensive.

(b) By advancing and pushing on towards the Narbada one or two strong but light armed detachments, the approach of which would alarm the Pindaris and probably deter them from attempting, during that period, the invasion of the British territories. He recommended the postponement of large-scale operations against them until the next season by which time it could be hoped that the reaction of Home Authorities to this venture would also become clear.

(c) The third and unquestionably the most efficient mode was to assemble a force sufficient to attack the Pindaris in their own positions and if practicable to dislodge and disperse them.[82] Seton also suggested that all those Indian chiefs who suffered or were likely to suffer by the Pindari menace be asked to co-operate with the British in their extirpation.

General Plan for the Reduction of the Pindaris

As the Indian Chiefs were not making efforts for the suppression of the Pindaris, it had become incumbent on the British to work for their extirpation. A general plan was, therefore, prepared according to which Hyderabad Subsidiary Force was posted at Ellichpur and a light detachment at Hoshangabad. The Poona Subsidiary Force was to take up position near Ahmednagar and another detachment was to be stationed on the frontier of Karauli in Rajputana.

Daulat Rao Scindia was to be asked to help the British in the execution of the plan. The whole plan was to be explained to him and he was to be promised that the land seized by the Pindaris would be restored to him.

Holkar's co-operation was also to be sought for the passage of the British troops. Rajputs were also to be made interested. Vazir Mohammad Khan of Bhopal was to be guaranteed protection against the Pindari invasion.

The Pindari chiefs, if they surrendered, were to be given some subsistence. Chitu was to be conciliated by a grant of land.

Home Authorities Plan

The Home Authorities had a plan of their own. Like Edmonstone and Dowdeswell, they also had a mortal fear of being embroiled in an extensive war against the Marathas. That was the secret of the unwillingness of the Court of Directors in sanctioning operations against the Pindaris and risking a general war. In a letter dated September, 5 1816, the Court maintained its previous stand as enunciated in their letter of 29th September 1815, by which no action was to be taken against the Pindaris. The Court went on to suggest ; "If instead of declaring a general war against all predatory associations, you avail yourselves of the advantage to be derived from the discordant elements of which they are composed, and of the dissensions which prevail among their leaders, it appears to us not unreasonable to expect that any project for uniting all the freebooters against you under the banner of Maratha chiefs may be defeated, but that you may from time to time obtain a partial co-operation from one or other of those chiefs according to the league in which the peculiar interests of each may be affected by any incursion of the Pindaris, and that you may even derive from some of the Pindari leaders themselves occasional aid against such of their associates as they appear to regard as rivals.[83]"

Hastings was indignant at the Court's suggestion and rejected it outright on the ground of its being impracticable. He put the blame on himself and his Government for not keeping the Court of Directors fully informed of the atrocious character of the Pindaris, otherwise they would not have suggested such a perfidious plan. Lord Moira expressed very strong reaction to their proposals in an able minute. He wrote, "When the Hon'ble Committee suggests the expedient of engaging one portion of Pindaris to destroy some other branch of the opposition, I am roused to the fear that we have been culpably deficient in pointing to the authorities at Home the brutal and atrocious qualities of those wretches....that nothing would have been more repugnant to the feeling of the Hon'ble Company than the notion that the Government should be soiled by a procedure which was to leave the colour of confidence or of common course with any of those gangs."[84] Therefore, he rightly rejected the proposal 'for it was Machiavellian.' He further argued that the employment of Pindaris by the British would mean the latter compromising their honour, besides giving quarter to those rapacious people who would still be free to continue their exploitation of the British allies.

Seton agreed with the Governor-General completely. He recorded "Had the Hon'ble Committee been fully aware of the detestable conduct of these monsters in human form, it would never have contemplated so unnatural a co-operation."[85] In his opinion a Pindari, by his character and habits, was "altogether unfit to co-operate with the British soldier."[86]

Thus various plans were mooted by military officers, political agents and the Home Authorities but nothing came out of these as the Governor-General was convinced that interim or half-hearted measures against the predatory bands were of no avail. However, these plans helped Hastings to draw out his final plan for the extirpation of the Pindaris.

While the Councillors were still debating the issue, shocking news was received about the outrages perpetrated by the Pindaris in the South. Alarmed and shocked by the diabolical deeds of the Pindaris,[87] even die-hards as Edmonstone and Dowdeswell, the two dissenting members were also converted to the opinion of the Governor-General. Hastings said, "The ravages of the Pindaris in the Ganjam District, with the consequent danger to Cuttack, and the extent of depredations committed by these atrocious *banditti* in the territories of our ally the Nizam, have at length induced my colleagues"[88] to agree to a war against the Pindaris. Edmonstone and Dowdeswell were prompt enough to write a letter to Hastings, "we have no hesitation in declaring our unqualified opinion .... in the furtherance of the measures and arrangements which your Lordship may deem necessary or conducive to the success of the plans which you have resolved to pursue and we have no doubt, ... to promote them by the zealous co-operation,"[89] with the proviso that they were to refrain from all offensive operations.

Seton who was all along realising the gravity of the situation, now not only agreed with what his colleagues said, but strengthened the Governor-General's hands in a strong minute : "this is a crisis not to be foreseen by the Hon'ble Court and therefore not to be held as standing within their interdict." While showing his understanding of the situations he declared in the most emphatic terms "I must cordially concur in opinion with the Governor-General and Edmonstone, as to the absolute necessity of resorting to more active measures against the Pindaris than have hitherto been adopted."[90]

Finally, the Council passed a unanimous resolution on December 21, 1816 that "the extirpation of the Pindaris must be undertaken, notwithstanding the orders of the Courts of Directors against adopting any measures against the predatory associations which might embroil us with Scindia."[91]

Hastings was very happy at the changed attitude of his colleagues. This was a very important moment in his career. It was not merely the triumph of his policy but the assertion of the force of humanity and civilization over counsels of despair. However, in a minute of December, 1816 he lamented the delay in getting that concurrence. He declared that this concurrence "would have been of infinite importance six weeks earlier."[92] Action meant preparations, but preparations would have taken time, and by that time the hot season would have begun. Hastings did not think it proper to expose his troops to the hot winds, when they had already been debilitated by cholera.[93]

Attitude of the Home Authorities toward the Pindari Problem

The Home Authorities were convinced of the wisdom of the policy which they had enunciated in 1805 and they repeatedly expressed their desire for the continuance of that policy.[94] They were still gripped by the fear of the British involvement in a general war which, they feared, would be an inevitable corollary to the Pindari extirpation. They, therefore, again sent instructions to the Governor-General that "we are unwilling to incur the risk of a general war, for the uncertain purpose of extirpating the Pindaris. Extended political and military combination we cannot at the present moment sanction or approve."[95] The letter from the Secret Committee enjoined upon the Governor-General not to do anything which might embroil the Company in a war with Scindia or the Marathas in general. They also prohibited the Company from making any material changes in the political relations.

The Home Authorities were not fully informed of the affairs and were, therefore, greatly over-rating the danger of a Maratha war or an involvement with Scindia. They feared the financial consequences also, besides the parliamentary criticism against any territorial extensions. Hence, they were reluctant to take any step which would disturb peace, little conscious of the fact that a storm could burst forth with all its fury at any moment.

They continued to press that nothing was to be done without their concurrence. Consequently, they instructed that "the question of undertaking measures and operations for suppressing the predatory powers of Hindustan" be given up and that they should abstain from the actual adoption of any measures directed to that object until you should have received our commands, confining yourselves in the interval to a system merely defensive."[96]

Lord Hastings wrote a very comprehensive Minute in December, 1815 drawing the attention of the Home Authorities to the danger of the increasing strength of the Pindaris. In this Minute, he proposed a complete reversal of the policy so far pursued. This implied a revision of British relations with the Indian states including the Marathas. But his colleagues appended dissenting notes.

Meanwhile, in England, far-reaching changes took place in the Board of Control, which had an indirect effect on the course of policy in India. George Canning, took the place of the Earl of Buckinghamshire who died in 1816, as the President of the Board of Control in June, 1816. Meantime, the general peace which now prevailed on the Continent, after the recent defeat of Emperor Napoleon Bonaparte, set them free to devote all their energies to the Indian question. He was called upon to take decision on the various proposals sent by Lord Hastings, and particularly on the recent but forceful Minute of December, 1815. New as he was to the task, he was not willing to take grave decisions affecting fundamental and sweeping changes in the policy of the Board. Besides, the dissenting notes of the councillors also made him defer any decision. He, therefore, refused permission for action against the Pindaris that would involve the risk of a general war.

Lord Hastings had also written to the Home Authorities seeking permission for the formation of a confederacy of Indian chiefs in order to fight the Pindaris. But they were emphatic about their disapproval. They wrote, "we cannot concur with his Lordship. We are apprehensive, such a confederacy would prove rather a source of weakness than of strength, that it might hazard the dissolution of our existing alliances without substituting anything substantial in their place."[97]

The Executive Council could not, however, keep idle as the situation in India had become serious. Even Edmonstone was now of the opinion that the letter of September 29, 1815 from the Secret Committee gave a qualified approval so long as the Company's action against the Pindaris did not result in a general war.[98] But this did not encourage Hastings.

He genuinely lamented the attitude of the Home Authorities and in a persuasive language implored them to reconsider their stand. He drew a vivid picture of the horrors which the Pindaris had been perpetrating all over the country and tried to appeal to the conscience of the Members.

"We in this Presidency have not gazed at a horizon glowing with the flames of our ravaged villages. We have not thrilled at the screams of violated matrons or shuddered at the details of their self-immolations in consequence of their pollution. We have not sickened at the sight of insulted humanity in the spectacle of all the younger females tied three or four on a horse and carried off to be sold for slaves. We have not seen the miserable father of a family whose wretched hands had massacred his wife and children to save them from worse than death. We have not marked his eye of despair fixed in anguish on heaven when he began to doubt the quality of his frantic decision, while his agonizing soul made its appeal to its creator and tried to shake off the weight of blood by transferring it to those who stood pledged for the safety of their subjects and discharged the sacred obligations with indifference."[99]

Such a heart-rending picture drawn by the Governor-General did have some effect on the authorities at Home but still they were not prepared to sanction large-scale operations.

While the Board of Control and the Court of Directors were adamant, events were fast getting out of control in India.[100] Successive incursions by the Pindaris carried devastation and murder to the South. This acted as a last straw on the camel's back. A qualified sanction of action against the Pindaris was given by the Home Authorities.[101]

The spring of 1817 witnessed what may be called the beginning of the end of this curse. Another resolution was passed, which for the first time, authorised the Governor-General to take action. The resolution of June 4, 1817 said: "Under the circumstances of aggression which have occurred within the last year, we entirely approve of the resolution of December, 21 1816...... and we leave to your judgement and discretion, not only the defence of the territories under your charge against the aggression of the Pindaris, but the punishment of the aggressors and the adoption of such measures as may tend to the ultimate suppression of their power."[102]

Meanwhile, Moira's hopes were further raised by a change in the tone of letters from the Home Government under Canning's leadership. On receipt of the news from India about Pindari depredations and horrors in the South, the Secret Committee immediately directed the Government of India to undertake active measures for the suppression of the Pindaris. Their language was very encouraging and reassuring, for they permitted not only repelling the attackers but also "pursuing and chastising the invaders." Another letter followed which extended further assurance, "you should feel yourselves entirely unshackled in the pursuit of that course of proceeding, which, if not prevented by orders from Home, you had resolved to pursue."[103] It was also stated that if Scindia or any other Maratha chief should take part in the Pindari war, such a chief would be treated as an enemy.

Canning now gave his unqualified sanction to the suppression of the Pindaris. The despatch stated :

"We think it, however, due to your Lordship not to lose an instant in conveying to you an explicit assurance of our approbation of any measure you may have authorized or undertaken, not only for repelling invasion but for pursuing and chastising the invaders. We can no longer abstain for a vigorous exertion of military power in vindication of the British name and in defence of subjects, who look to us for protection......Any connection of Scindia or Holkar with the Pindaris against us or our allies, known, though not avowed, would place them in a state of direct hostility to us."[104]

Hastings was now absolutely free to undertake operations against the Pindaris. Within a short period he was ready for action.

FOOT-NOTES

1 The alliance stipulated that in case of an attack by Tipu Sultan either upon the British or the Nizam' the Peshwa of Poona was to assist either of the contracting parties with all military power.

2 Ramsay Muir : *The Making of British India,* 1756-1858, p: 200, London 1923.

3 J. Talboys Wheeler : *Summary of Affairs of the Mahratta States,* 1627-1856, p. 70, Calcutta, 1878.

4 *Op. Cit.* Wheeler : Summary of Affairs, p. 71.

5 *Op. Cit.* Maratha and Pindari War : For the General Staff, p. 4.

6 Lord Castlereagh's letter, 4th March, 1804. *Op. Cit.* Wheeler, p. 131.

7 Prinsep : *History of Political and Military Transactions* : Vol. I, p. 7.

8 Muir : *The Making of the British India*, p. 247.

9 Ross, C : Correspondence of Charles First Marquis Cornwallis Vol. III, p. 533. Cornwallis to Lake, 30 July, 1805.

10 Sir Alred Lyall : *The Rise and Expansion of the British Dominion in India*, p. 285, London 1907.

11 Mill : *History of British India*, Vol. VI, p. 658.

12 N.A,I. For. Sec. 1806 : O.C. No. 4, 10 April, 1806 : Capt. Sherrock to Edmonstone, Jaipur, 9 March, 1806.

13 Lyall : *Rise and Expansion*, p. 286,

14 Wheeler : *Summary of Affairs*, p. 133.

15 Price : *A History of India*, p. 491.

16 N.A.I. For. Sec. 1805 : O.C. No. 2, 7 November, 1805 : Barlow to Lake, 20 October, 1805.

17 Imperial Gazetteer of India—Central India, p.23, Calcutta, 1908.

18 M.I.O.L.L. : H.M.S, Vol. 516 A, p. 1, Letter from Bengal Government to the Secret Committee, 16 August, 1811.

19 Lord Minto to the Court of Directors : *Op. Cit*, John Clarke Marshman : *History of India from the earliest period to the present time*, p. 306.

20 Marshman : *History of India*, p. 306.

21 N.A.I. For. Sec. 1809 : O.C. No. 7, 8 July, 1809 : Chief Secretary to Jenkins, Acting Resident. Nagpur, 8 July, 1809.

22 Wheeler :*Summary of affairs*, p. 171.

23 Wheeler : *Summary of Affairs*, p. 172.

24 M.I.O.L.L. : H.M.S: Vol. 516 A, p. 13.

25 The French Republic "had entered upon its career of conquest' and was bent upon recovering the position in India which the Bourbon monarchy had lost ; and Bonaparte was in Egypt. Thus non-intervention and abstention from 'schemes of conquest' had brought about a situation of extreme danger."
Muir : *The Making of the British India*, pp. 200-201.

26 It was expected that the "treaties with Holkar and Scindia concluded in the end of 1805 and beginning of 1806 seemed to have placed the peace of India as a basis of security and stability not liable to be shaken by any future efforts of those powers" but as the future events proved it, it was not so. N.A.I. For. Sec, 1816 : O.C No. 1, G.G's Minute, 1 December. 1815, para 42.

27 Prinsep : *History*, Vol. I, p. 31.

23 Burton : *Maratha and Pindari War*, p. 7.

29 N.A.I. For. Sec. 1816 : O.C. No. 1, 15 June, 1816 : G.G's Minute, 1 December, 1815, para 6. Hastings admitted that "peace cannot be maintained on our present principles of political management," Also : N.A.I. For. Sec. 1812 : O.C. No, 28-29, 16 Oct., 1812, Resident at Daulat Rao Scindia's Court to Minto, 12 September, 1812, paras 12 to 15.

30 N.A.I. For. Sec. 1816 : O.C. No. 1, 20 April, 1816 :
Governor-General's Minute, 13 April, 1816.

31 Wilson : *History of British India*, p. 137.

32 For. Misc. 124 A : Letter from Thomas Marriot, Col. and Commissioner, Kurnool, to Secretary to the Madras Government, 8 April, 1916.

33 Sydenham was of opinion that "even the cavalry regularly equipped is scarcely capable of overtaking" the Pindaris. For. Misc. 124 A : Pindary and Maratha Wars : Sydenham's Memorandum, 1800, p. 2.

34 N.A.I. For. Sec. 1814 : O.C. No. 10, 21 June, 1814 :
Seton's Minute, 21 June, 1814.

35 N.A.I For. Sec. 1817 : O.C. No. 1, 8 March, 1817 :
Governor-General's Minute, 21 January, 1817, paras 25-26.

36 At one stage the British employed more than 30,000 soldiers against the Pindaris, a number adequate for a regular war on the greatest scale and involving an immense expenditure, yet the Pindaris had penetrated through a strong line of defence.

37 N.A.I. For. Sec, 1816 : O.C. No. 23-26, 11 May, 1816 :
Russell to Adam, Hyderabad, 17 April, 1816.

38 One of the worst features of "the evil is that the defensive measures adopted in the present season, must be repeated annually."
N.A.I. For. Sec. 1816 : O.C. No. 12, 28 December, 1816.
Dowdeswell's Minute, 10 December, 1816.
Also : Defensive arrangements "will of course be renewed on the return of the season in which the country will be again exposed to the danger of predatory excursions and must be annually resorted to."

For. Misc. 124 A : Secert Letter from Bengal, 30 June, 1813.

39 N.A.I. For. Sec. 1816 : O.C. No. 9, 28 December, 1816. Governor-General's Minute, 6 December, 1816, para 6.

40 "We have been compelled to adopt" at a considerable charge "and not perhaps without a sacrifice of credit."
N.A.I. For. Sec. 1814 : O.C. No. 1, 21 June, 1814 :
Edmonstone's Minute, 21 June 1814, para 5.
Also : "The expense now annually incurred for the movement of troops...... loudly calls for remedy."

N.A.I. For. Sec. 1814 : O.C. No. 11, 21 June, 1814 :
Governor General's Minute, 20 May, 1814.
Also : N.A.I. For. Sec. 1817 : O.C. No. 1, 8 March, 1817 :
Governor-General's Minute, 21 January, 1817, p. 28.

41 N.A.I. For. Sec. 1816 : O.C. No. 11, 28 December, 1816 :
Seton's Minute, 8 December, 1816, P. 4.

42 N.A.I. For. Sec. 1816 : O.C. No. 15, 28 December, 1816 :
Seton's Minute, 14 December, 1816, p. 3.

43 N.A.I. For. Sec. 1816 : O.C. No. 9, 28 December, 1816 : Governor-General's Minute, 6 December, 1816, para 9.

44 N.A.I. For. Sec. 1816 : O.C. No. 9, 28 December, 1816 : Governor-General's Minute, 6 December, 1816, para 9.

45 For. Misc. 124 A : Jenkins' Memorandum, 1812, p. 27.

46 For. Misc. 124A : Letter from Sydenham accompanying his Memorandum of 1809, dated 18 March, 1810.

47 For. Misc. 124 A : Jenkins' Memorandum, 1812, p. 26.

48 N.A.I. For. Sec. 1816 : O.C. No. 1, 15 June, 1816 : Governor-General's Minute, 1 December, 1815, para 63.
Also : Fitzclarence : *Journal of a Route*, p. 7.

49 Walter Hamilton : *Geographical, Statistical and Historical Description of Hindostan*, 2 Vols. London, 1820.

50 Blacker : *Memoirs :* p. 19.

51 For. Misc. 114 A : Jenkins' Memorandum, 1812, p. 26.

52 Blacker : *Memoirs*, p. 13.

53 The number of Pindaris "may be said to increase in the same ratio as the means of subsistence diminish; hunger goads them on to the work of destruction and they rejoice in anticipation of the spoils of wealthy country."
Allahabad Reprint, Chap. V.

54 M.I.O.L.L. : H.M.S : Drafts of Secret Letters to India, 1814-1820 : Letter from the Vice-President-in-Council, 16 November, 1811.

55 Fitzclarence : *Journal of a Route*, p. 3.

56 Malcolm : *Origin...*
Also : Kaye : *Life Metcalf*, p. 428.
No "enterprise seemed to be too vast for the ambition of men who carried for the most part, all that they possessed on the bows of their saddle, who had everything to gain by the disorganisation they created."

57 N.A.I. For. Sec. 1816 : O.C. No. 1, 15 June, 1816 : Governor-General's Minute, 1 December, 1815, para 214.

58 *Summary of the Mahratta and Pindaree Campaign*, p. 28.

59 *Ibid*, p. 29.

60 *Summary of the Mahratta and Pindaree Campaign*, pp. 29-31.

61 *Origin of the Pindaris* : By an Officer of the East India Company : Allahabad Reprint, Chap. V.

62 *Op. Cit.* Marshman : *History of India*, p. 318

63 Hastings believed "that without complete extinction of the predatory system, our power in India could never be deemed safe."
N.A.I. For. Sec. 1817 : O.C. No. 1, 28 October, 1817, Lord Hastings to Edmonstone, Vice-President-in-Council, Cawnpore, 10 October, 1817, para 3.
Further Hastings said "without a complete reform of the actual condition of Central India, involving the extinction of the predatory system, our power in India could never be deemed safe from

foreign attack or internal commotion, and that the only hope of our being able to receive the finances of the Hon'ble Company from the pressure of establishments disproportionate to its means, was to be found in the removal of that danger which created the necessity for maintaining them."

64 N.A.I. For. Sec. 1815 : O.C. No. 1, 21 March, 1815 : Governor-General's Minute, 9 February, 1815 : Also : Hastings' Private Journal, p. 6.

65 M.I.O.L.L. : H.M.S., G.G.'s Minute, 13 April, 1816, para 4.

66 The Pindaris threatened Scindia that if he were not to "make a common cause with them, his territories must undergo ravage as well as those of other powers." N.A.I. For. Sec. 1816 : O.K. No. 13, 28 December, 1816 : Governor-General's Minute, 12 December, 1816.

67 N.A.I. : For. Sec. 1817 : O.C. No. 1, 28 October, 1817 : Hastings to Edmonstone, 10 October, 1817, para 7.

68 Hastings believed "that to protect ourselves and our allies from specific inroads and to punish the agg ressors, is all which is either demanded by duty or dictated by prudence." N.A.I. For. Sec. 1817 : O.C. No. 1, 8 March, 1817 : G.G.'s Minute, 21 January, 1817, para 22.

69 Marshman : *History of India*, p. 318.

70 N.A.I. For. Sec. 1814 : O.C. No. 5, 21 June, 1814 : Edmonstone's Minute, 29 April, 1814, paras 82 and 165.

71 N.A.I. For. Sec. 1814 : O.C. No. 10, 21 June, 1814 : Seton's Minute, 21 June. 1814.

72 N.A.I. For. Sec. 1814 : O.C. No. 11, 20 May, 1814 : Governor-General's Minute, 20 May, 1814.

73 N.A.I. For. Sec. 1816 : O.C. No. 3, 20 April, 1816 : Seton's Minute, 17 April, 1816.

74 N.A.I. For. Sec. 1817 : O.C. No. 1, 7 November, 1817 : Edmonstone's Minute, 29 October, 1817 : para 2.

75 *Ibid*, para 7.

76 N.A.I. For. Sec. 1817 : O.C. No. 1, 7 November, 1817 : Edmonstone's Minute, 29 October, 1817.

77 *Ibid.*

78 N.A.I. For. Sec. 1814 : O.C. No. 50-51, 29 December, 1814 : G. Sydenham, Agent in Berar, to C. Russell, Aurangabad, 15 October, 1814.

79 *Ibid.*

80 N.A.I. For. Sec. 1814 : O.C. No. 16, 26 December, 1812 : G.H. Fagan, Adjutant General, to Adam, HQ Camp Soonah, 6 December, 1812.

81 Elphinstone also suggested a similar arrangement that "a number of light cavalry were required not to fight them but to hunt them out of the country."

P.R.C. (Poona Affairs 1811-1815) Pt. I, Vol. 12, Letter No. 27, Elphinstone to Vice-President, 9 August, 1811.

82 N.A.I. For. Sec. 1816 : O.C. No. 11, 28 December, 1816 : Seton's Minute, 8 December, 1816, para 14.

83 M.I.O.L.L. : Drafts of Secret Letters to India : 1814-1820 : Letter No. 118, Whitehall to Governor-General-in-Council at Fort William in Bengal, 5 September, 1816, East India House, London, 6 September, 1816.

84 N.A.I. For. Sec. 1817 : O.C. No. 1, 8 March, 1817 : Hastings' Minute, 21 January, 1817, pp. 39-40.

85 N.A.I. For. Sec. 1817 : O.C. No- 3, Seton's Minute, 3, December, 1817, p. 11.

86 N.A.I. For. Sec. 1817 : O.C. No. 3, Seton's Minute, 3, December, 1817, p. 12.

87 M.I.O.L.L. : Drafts of Secret Letter to India, Letter No. 119, Sncret Committee to the Governor-General, 26 September, 1816, para *2*.

88 Hastings' Private Journal, p. 270.

89 N.A.I. For. Sec. 1817 : O.C. No. 2, 28 October, 1817 : Edmonstone and Dowdeswell to Moira, Fort William 28 October, 1817.

90 M.I.O.L.L. : Seton's Minute, 14 December, 1816.

91 Private Journal, p. 270.
Also ; "Our unanimous opinion that the adoption of vigorous measures for the early suppression of the Pindaris was become an indispensable obligation of our public duty."
For. Misc. 124 A : Secret Letter from Bengal, from Edmonstone, Seton and Dowdeswell, 21 December, 1816, p. 45, para 3.

92 Private Journal, p. 270.

93 *Ibid*

94 The system "that was consolidated at the close of the last Mahratta war should be maintained with as little change as could be avoided."
M.I.O.L.L. : Letter from Secret Committee to the Governor-General-in-Council at Fort William, 29 September, 1815.

95 *Ibib.*

96 M.I.O.L.L. : Letter from Whitehall to the Governor-General, 29 September, 1815.

97 M.I.O.L.L. Letter from Secret Committee to the Governor-General, 29 September, 1815.

98 N.A.I. For. Sec. 1817 : O.C. No. 2, 8 March, 1817 : Edmonstone's Minu te, 26 February, 1817, paras 9-10.

99 M.I.O.L.L. Governor-General's Minute, 24 April, 1816.

100 M.I.O.L.L. Drafts of Letters : Letter No. 118 : From Secret Council to the Governor-General-in-Council at Fort William in Bengal 5 September, 1816. The Home Authorities wrote : "You are already aware of our decision against undertaking extensive operations, with the view of remodelling our political relations and extending our influence or control. We retain our doubts as to the desirableness of such a change, and our decided conviction that new hazards ought not to be incurred in endeavouring to accomplish it, and to avoid in every case, in which our honour or our safety is not immediately involved, measures of war or expense. We feel it necessary therefore to repeat our injunction against the formation of new alliances without our previous sanction."

101 The Home Authorities sanctioned action only "when actual war upon the British territories might be commenced by any body of marauders and where the lives and property of British subjects might call for efficient protection."
M.I.O.L.L. Letter No. 119, Secret Committee to the Governor-General, 29 September, 1816, para 5.

102 For. Misc. 124 A : Secret Letter from Bengal, 4 June, 1817. p. 46.

103 M.I.O.L.L : Letter No. 121, Letter from Secret Committee to the Governor-General, 4th June, 1817.

104 *Ibid.*

7

Diplomacy of Lord Hastings

Lord Hastings

Lord Hastings, Earl of Moira, took charge of the Indian administration on October 4, 1813. Hastings made it a condition precedent to his going to India that "he should be appointed Commander-in-Chief as well."[1] Before his appointment in India he had earned distinction as a statesman and soldier. He brought with him "a large fund of experience, a clear and sound judgement, and great decision of character, together with the equivocal honour of being the personal friend of the Prince Regent."[2] He was a versatile personality called upon to guide the destinies of the British Government at a very critical period.

As a Member of Parliament, he had been a bitter critic of Lord Wellesley's forward policy and particularly his ambition of establishing British sway in India.[3] He condemned in strong terms Wellesley's war with Tipu Sultan, in the House of Lords.[4] He, then, declared that "a scheme of conquest for the extension of territory was not only held generally as an improvident act, but particularly so in India." On this occasion, he condemned the whole theory of force on which, he claimed, the Government was based in India,[5]

He condemned in a forthright manner the wars of aggression.[6] But soon after his arrival in India, he had to reverse his opinion. In no time was he convinced that "it was by preponderence of power that those mines of wealth had been acquired for the Company's treasury and by preponderance of power alone would they be retained."[7] He, now, had no doubt that the diseased state of India needed drastic treatment. He declared "our object in India ought to be to render the British Government paramount in effect, if not decidedly so.....and to oblige the other states to perform the two great feudatory duties of supporting our rule with all their forces and submitting their mutual differences to our arbitration."[8] Thus, there was a complete transformation in Hastings' opinion and soon he advocated the same policy which he had so vehemently denounced earlier.

Thus Lord Hastings as the Governor-General of India was absolutely different from Hastings, the Member of Parliament, the former following the very path of the great statesman, whom he had so strongly condemned but a few years ago.

State of India on the Eve of Hastings' Arrival

About this period the whole region of Central India and Rajputana was a political Alsatia full of brigands and roving banditti. The turbulent hordes of Amir Khan, Scindia, Holkar and the Pindaris like the 'free companies' of Europe were roaming about the country spreading ruin and devastation. Lord Hastings soon realised the dangerous proportions to which the Pindaris had been allowed to grow. Besides, he also realised that the British Government could not continue the old policy of non-intervention for long. By his early training and fondness for military life, he was thrilled at the prospect of dealing a death blow to this growing nuisance.

At the time when Lord Hastings arrived, Indian States could be easily divided into three classes.[9] The first were those with whom the British Government had no Subsidiary Alliance and which were, in the heart of their hearts, inimical to them. These were the majority of Maratha States that were smarting under the humiliation of defeat and were only apparently professing freindship towards the British. In the second category could be included military powers subsisting on plunder and devastation. These had regular armies and were hostile to the British. These included most of the Pindari chiefs. The third class consisted of those that were independent but were bound to the British Government by Subsidiary or friendly alliances. In this class may also be included states like Jhansi, Dholpur, Orcha, Tehree, Panna, Rewa etc., and the states in Rajputana, who were friendly to the British but with whom no alliances had yet been concluded. They had been looking to the British for protection, but this was denied to them owing to the non-intervention policy of the British Government.

According to Metcalfe, the third category of states needed full British protection, while the first and the second required to be dealt with severely.[10]

In the above scheme it is difficult to omit leaders like Amir Khan, the notorious Pathan adventurer. In the strict sense of the word he had no state when Hastings reached India. But he was as powerful as any Indian chief and was nearly on the point of establishing himself as the head of an extensive area.[11]

Most of the important states were connected with the British by Subsidiary Alliance. namely,the Peshwa, the Nizam, the Gaekwad, Mysore, Travancore and Oudh. Though some of the states in the first flush of enthusiasm or by the force of circumstances had entered into treaty alliances with the British, some of them like the Peshwa and, to some extent, the Nizam "could not like a system which crippled them politically, restricted their freedom and lowered their prestige."[12]

There were others, like the Scindia, Holkar and the Bhonsla who virtually dictated the political and military conditions of the day. The British treaties with these states were "mere instruments of amity; their intercourse was completely unrestrained, and no control, except in relation to the allies of the British Government, was to be exercised over them."[13]

According to Moira, the disaffected Maratha states and the predatory elements were a constant source of trouble and danger to the British interests in India.[14] There was all round distrust, disorder and disorganisation in those states and yet they were able to maintain their independence. This was made possible by the non-intervention policy of the British.

Daulat Rao Scindia

Daulat Rao Scindia was the most powerful of Maratha chiefs. His resources and revenues were great and his military the best, part of which was trained and commanded by French Officers like De Boigne, Perron and Jean Baptiste, etc. Yet this very army was disorganised and was often mutinous.[15] Since he had no money to pay them, he closed his eyes to the army raising its own money. The natural consequence was indiscipline, often leading to the assumption of independent attitude by many of his commanders like Bappooji Scindia, Jaggoo Bapu, Ambaji Pant, and Jaswant Rao Bhao,[16] each of whom commanded about eight to ten thousand men.

Though Scindia was the most powerful of the Indian chiefs, he could never organise any attempt against the rising British power because of bad blood between him and Holkar. He had a mortal fear of British superiority, and therefore, in spite of his secret enemity, he did not openly displease them.[17]

Jaswant Rao Holkar

Jaswant Rao Holkar, once the arbiter of the destiny of India, was like Hyder and Tipu, the bitterest enemy of the British. His insanity in 1811 removed him from the field. A young boy was, placed on the throne under the Regency of Tulsi Bai, his mother. They were all under the thumb of the former friend of Jaswant Rao Holkar, Amir Khan and his lieutenant Gaffur Khan. Holkar, a mere boy and a tool in their hands, did not matter in Indian affairs.

Baji Rao Peshwa

Baji Rao Peshwa, whose illustrious forefathers were once the king-makers of Delhi, was the most frustrated and desperate of the lot of Indian Rajas. He felt that he had brought great humiliation upon himself and the House of Peshwa, by the Treaty of Bassein and the consequent reduction of his own power and prestige. He was, therefore, husbanding his resources and was waiting for the first opportunity to shake off the British control.

Raghoji Bhonsla

Raghoji Bhonsla, the Raja of Nagpur, was the weakest of the whole lot. He, like Scindia and Baji Rao, was also nursing a secret hatred against the British. A shrewd observer as he was, he had realised that for political and strategical reasons, the British must necessarily protect him in case of foreign invasion. Hence, he continued to evade an alliance with the British. Later, when Appa Sahib became the Raja of Nagpur, he joined the schemes of Scindia, encouraged the Pindaris, employed them and went so far as to receive the agents of the Pindari chief Chitu, upon whom he conferred dresses of honour.[18] Bhonsla like the Peshwa waited for an opportunity to rise against the British and throw off the mask of friendship.

The Rajput States

Rajputana, as we have noted before, had suffered much at the hands of the Marathas and Pindaris, and now presented a scene of chaos and anarchy. The British had, till now, kept them beyond the pale of their protection, but they could not be ignored in any scheme of the pacification of Central India. At this time, there was a genuine fear of their being overrun by Amir Khan and others if the British Government continued its indifference towards them.

Bhopal

The minor states like those of Bhopal in Central India, sandwiched between hostile Maratha states, were in a similar predicament. These could not be left over to their own fate.

Conspiracy Against the British

Lord Hastings did not take a complacent view of the prospects of the British Government in India. The Maratha states, not yet reconciled to the British hegemony, were secretly making efforts to overthrow them. The dependent states were also far from happy at their relations with the British; while the independent states of the Gurkhas and the Sikhs were not dependable. Hastings, therefore, suspected a deep under-current of discontent in the Indian states and feared a conspiracy against the British.

A secret conspiracy was being hatched by the Pindaris, the Peshwa, and other Maratha chiefs to invade the British territories. Hastings referred to the correspondence between those princes and thought that their aim was to overthrow the British. He wrote "I had traced many indications of active communications between states, which had for many years had no political intercourse....a wide conspiracy was forming for the expulsion of the British from India."[19] But the successful termination of the Gurkha war produced the desired effect of discouraging such hostile schemes against the British. It was a great damper for Scindia, who, henceforth, dared not look to the Gurkhas for any support. The direct result was that Prithvi Ram Pratap, the vakeel from the Gurkha court was left uncared for.

Hastings was rightly taking an alarmist view of the Indian situation. Scindia and Holkar were in communication to hatch conspiracies. They both acknowledged the supremacy of Peshwa Baji Rao, who sent twenty lakhs of rupees to Scindia to be in readiness to move to his assistance. The Pindaris were also in constant correspondence with Scindia. Thus Hastings was correct in saying "I see around me the elements of a war."[20]

For some time, some of the Maratha chiefs and particularly the Peshwa exhibited symptoms of extreme dissatsifaction.[21] The attitude of Holkar's army and that of Amir Khan was also suspicious. Rumours were rife that Gurkha armies were assembling on the British frontier. Besides, they were conspiring with Scindia for the overthrow of the British.

In 1816, the Gurkha Government wrote to Hindu Rao Ghatge entreating him to march to Pilibhit or Kashipur, and if that was not possible, to send 30,000 Pindari Cavalry with Amir Khan.[22] Thus a very tense atmosphere prevailed in 1816, when negotiations were in progress with Scindia for the passage of the British troops against the Pindaris. It was at this time that startling news of a conspiracy by the Gurkhas and the Marathas was received by the British.

In October 1817, two messengers were arrested at Kanpur in very suspicious circumstances. They were on their way to Kathmandu, Nepal's capital. Two concealed letters were recovered from them, which were addressed to the King of Nepal by the Nepalese agent in Scindia's Court and by Scindia himself and his ministers.[23] These letters were written in some code language "in a style of mystery and ambiguity."[24] It was ascertained from them that some sort of a combined move was planned against the British. Subsequent enquiries confirmed the purport of the letter. Besides the two letters, a wax impression of Scindia's great seal was also found in their possession.[25] According to Wheeler "these seals were to be attached to such drafts of supposed letters from Scindia as the Court of Kathmandoo might think it politic to forge for transmission to China in order to obtain resources from the Emperor"[26] against the British.

The letters were found concealed ingeniously, between the pages of a religious Sanskrit book, which were glued together.[27] The glued papers also contained empty covers, bearing the impression in ink, of Scindia's smaller seal used on important occasions. It may be observed here that Scindia was never in correspondence with the Nepalese prior to this discovery.

The closed letters were immediately sent to Capt. Close, Resident at the Scindia's Court. He was instructed to deliver them to Daulat Rao Scindia but not to mention anything else, unless Scindia himself initiated the talks. The letters were accordingly presented to Scindia in the open Court.[28] Scindia kept silent and made no attempt to explain matters. "He sunk under the confusion of the unexpected detection.

There was no denial, no attempt at explanation, no endeavour to extenuate the quality of the Secret Correspondence."[29] However, the discovery of the letters did not go without effect for Scindia's progress of negotiations was rapid.[30] It resulted in Scindia agreeing to the passage of British troops through his territories. The Gurkha conspiracy and Scindia's leading part therein "indeed afforded evidence, the most unquestionable, of his being engaged in designs adverse to our interests."[31]

Possibility of Maratha Hostility

Hastings, thus, realised that he was not only to extirpate the Pindaris but also to fight the Maratha coalition, secretly formed by them. He confirmed the fact from Trimbuckji Danglia after the latter's arrest and he unfolded that from early in 1814 the Peshwa had been busy "in organising a general confederacy of the native powers, for the purpose of driving the British out of India." Danglia further revealed that the British were only by three or four months too quick upon them" (the Pindaris) or the latter would have taken the initiative against the former.[32] Thus it was clear that a very serious crisis of great magnitude was in the offing, the importance of which can be realised by the fact that had the conspiracy succeeded, it would have definitety checkmated the progress of the British, if not thrown them out of India.

There were some who were of the view that there was no possibility of an open coalition or hostility of the Marathas towards the British because the cementing factor in Maratha politics, Baji Rao Peshwa's influence, was waning after the Treaty of Bassein. The Maratha states were mutually jealous of one another, for "all community of sentiment between the several Maratha Governments had expired."[33] Even if such an idea were to brew in their minds, their obvious "inferiority of strength would prevent each of them from meditating hostility" against the British.[34]

Of all the Maratha chiefs, Scindia was the most important, but Hastings believed that he would not fight against the British, at least on the ground of finances.[35] Besides, Hastings expressed the confidence that "Scindia would subscribe with the best grace he could to our wishes."[36] The Governor-General also believed that for such uncertain men like the Pindaris the Marathas would not stake their kingdoms; and that even if the Marathas broke in open revolt they would easily be dealt with individually for they were incapable of joining hands. Hastings was absolutely right in his estimate of the Maratha politics.

Overtures from the Indian States

Even though there were sparks of fire in the ashes, ready to start devastating conflagration, there were a large number of states in Rajputana and Central India which were very keen to seek the protection of the British. Hence, repeated overtures were made by these states for an alliance with the British.[37] But "in conformity to the provisions of the last treaty with Scindia, we have uniformly resisted the repeated and most earnest solicitations of the states of Jeynagar, Jodhpur, Odaypoor, Kota and Boondee, for the protection of our power against the lawlessness, violence, depredation and exactions of the Maratha governments and Amir Khan."[38]

In view of the worst beating which Udaipur received at Amir Khan's hands, the Maharana sought British protection, drawing attention to the distressed and desperate situation in which he was placed. The British realised the severe and galling conditions prevailing in the Udaipur state and its sad plight of having to pay tributes to every Maratha or Pathan chief, failing which the painful alternative was to have his country laid waste by the plunderer.[39] To the request made for British protection, Seton informed Harsukh Lal, the Udaipur Agent at Delhi, that British protection to his state could not be extended because of their policy of non-intervention. The Rana continued to send letters to Hastings full of professions of friendship and requests for British protection, but with no result.[40]

The Jodhpur Raja also requested for British protection, which Metcalfe refused. He replied that as long as "the present treaties with Scindia and Holkar should exist, the good faith of the British Government would render a defensive alliance with Joudhpoor impracticable,"[41] In like manner requests for British protection were made by the Rajas of Jaisalmere, Kota, Bundi, Karauli, Bikaner and Banswara, but they were all turned down.

How deep was the desire to go under the British protection can be gauged from the pathetic appeal made by the Rajput Rajas. They said that "some power in India had always existed to which peaceable states submitted and in return obtained its protection against the invasions of upstart chiefs and the armies of lawless banditti; that the British Government now occupying the place of that protecting power was the natural guardian of weak states, which were continually exposed to the cruelties and oppression of robbers and plunderers owing to the refusal of the British Government to protect them."[42] When Lord Hastings became the Governor-General of India, he reversed the policy of non-intervention and non-alignment to interference and active alliance and the result was the extension of the British protection to the Indian states.

Hastings' Diplomatic Arrangements

Hastings had drawn up a comprehensive plan for the extirpation of the Pindaris and was determined to carry out the famous principle of waging war in enemy's home. Besides, he wanted to redraw the political map of India and define the 'boundaries of each principality' and thereby eliminate the constant source of internecine wars. Contrary to orders from Home and opposition from his Councillors, he decided on the bold step of giving up the policy of non-intervention and conclude alliances with the Indian chiefs, which decision he communicated to his Councillors.

A shrewd statesman and diplomat as he was, he decided that before he took the field, it was necessary that he must have all the states in his bag. He warned the states that those which did not join the British in this task would be treated as enemies and that "in the operations against the Pindaris no one could be suffered to be neutral."[43] He wanted the fullest possible co-operation of the Indian chiefs in the great task of the extirpation of the Pindaris. He wrote: "It was my anxious desire to effect the reduction of the Pindaris, not only without involving myself with the regular powers, but with their direct concurrence."[44]

He knew that the territories of the Indian chiefs were mixed up in inextricable confusion, and in such a position, even one state hostile to the British would create a very serious situation for them. He, therefore, decided to tackle the question of relationship with the Indian states on a war footing. The task of roping the Indian states in this general plan of extermination of the Pindaris was assigned to two very brilliant and able officers of the Company—Metcalfe and Malcolm. Metcalfe with his Residency in Delhi was to deal with the states in the North and Malcolm with those in the South. The aim of Hastings in concluding alliance with the Indian states was the creation of barriers against the Pindaris and also to check the growth and extension of the two great powers of Central India, viz. Holkar and Scindia.

Metcalfe admirably succeeded in having alliances with the Rajput Rajas. Malcolm visited the three principal capitals of the Southern powers—Poona, Nagpur and Hyderabad. But he failed to have the Peshwa and the Bhonsla agree to an alliance. Hyderabad was already an ally of the British. Besides co-ordinating British strategy, Malcolm instructed all the Residents and Military Officers in the South to stand in readiness for the coming struggle against the Pindaris.

Rajput States

When the question of Pindari extirpation was contemplated by Hastings he had the Rajput Rajas in mind.[45] He wanted them to act as a barrier against the revival of the predatory system.[46] He, therefore, deputed Metcalfe to conduct negotiations with them for concluding with each of those states "a separate treaty......for combining them all in a general league, under our paramount authority."[47] Metcalfe immediately addressed all the chiefs of Rajputana through a circular letter, inviting them all to send their representatives to the Delhi Residency for the purpose of negotiating treaties with the British Government. In fact, Metcalfe had already hinted at such a proposal as early as 1811.[48]

The general basis of the treaties with them was to be the complete control of political measures and external relations by the British Government and non-interference in their internal affairs. Another condition was that "any tributes demandable under a fixed agreement with a Maratha or Pathan chief should be paid directly to the British treasury, leaving us to account for it to the party to whom it might be due."[49] It may be noted that no Subsidiary troops were to be maintained in the capitals of the new allies in Rajputana.[50]

The two governments of Kota and Bundi, situated as they were on the direct route of a possible retreat of the Pindaris, were immediately contacted. Capt. Tod was deputed to these areas because the "local knowledge will enable him (to give) the most useful direction to efforts of the Governments of Kotah and Bundi."

The news that the British had given up the old policy of non-intervention was received with exultation by the Indian chiefs, and applications poured in from all quarters for its alliance and protection. The first to depute agents at the Delhi Residency of Metcalfe was the Jaipur Raja;[51] but the first to conclude alliance with the British was Zalim Singh of Kota. The Nawab of Bhopal, whose application for friendship and alliance had earlier been rejected by Sir George Barlow, then made a fresh application through the British Resident at Nagpur. The application was received at a time when military operations against the Pindaris were about to begin and therefore he was asked to wait. But pending the consideration of this application, agreement was concluded with Bhopal, stipulating only military aid. However, a regular treaty was signed with Bhopal after the war. The Rajas of Bundi, Karauli, Banswara, Dungarpur and Partapgarh were also accepted as allies. A number of small chiefs of Malwa and Bundelkhand also entered into treaty relations with the British.

Thus, within a short period of about four months "Mr. Metcalfe, the Resident at Delhi, to whom the management of these negotiations were committed, concluded the treaties of alliance with all these princes upon the principle of subordinate co-operation and acknowledged supremacy."[52]

Alliance with Scindia

While the overall policy of seeking assistance and concluding alliances with the Indian states was being decided, the Treaty with Scindia, by which the British had been prohibited to have any relations with the Rajput Rajas, was a stumbling block. Hastings knew that the measure was "of all others, the most repugnant to the inclination of Scindia."[53] Yet that obstacle had to be removed to lay the foundation of Treaty alliances with other states. Lord Hastings knew that Scindia would not like to incur the wrath of the British for objects that did not directly concern him. Hastings had been confirmed in this opinion by Scindia's tame submission to the British demand for ending the hostilities against Bhopal.

A hint was given to Scindia that the British troops were on the march for annihilating the Pindaris, and he should cooperate with them. But Scindia's procrastination delayed matters to the extent that time for action against the Pindaris was imminent but he had not yet signed the treaty. Hastings, therefore, decided to take firm and positive steps regarding Scindia's attitude, for he had information in his possession that Scindia was secretly pledging his help to the Pindaris and the Peshwa.[54] Pindari *vakeels* were living in his court.[55] They had a free hand in the recruitment of Mewatees and purchasing of horses in his territory.[56]

Hastings' aim, in concluding a treaty arrangement with Scindia, was two-fold.[57] Firstly, to get his active co-operation against the Pindaris and secondly, to get the abrogation of the eighth article of the Treaty of 1805 which prohibited the British Government to have relations with the Rajput States.[58] The central pillar of Hastings' foreign policy was of alliance with the Rajput states, which would bring peace, prosperity and security to India.

Politically and geographically, Scindia's kingdom was strategically placed in the context of action for the Pindaris. Therefore it was all the more necessary to bring Scindia over to the British side. The partisans of the Pindaris in Scindia's court were not prepared to let the initiative pass from their hands and, therefore, they apprised Scindia of the danger he would run if the Pindaris were exterminated. He was reminded that their ruin would deprive him of the army and that too unpaid.

Scindia realised the futility of a trial of strength with British, whose arms were lately successful against Nepal and the Hathras. Assye was still fresh in his memory. He wanted to preserve good understanding with the British Government because he knew that "he stands alone without any of those expectations of resistance to our (British) power or hopes of assistance to himself on which he probably before depended for the continuance of our (British) forbearing and moderate policy."[59] He promised his co-operation to the British. Hastings was not satisfied with this alone. He wanted a clear and forthright answer from him. Word was sent to him regarding British determination to "consider the treaties existing between us as virtually dissolved,"[60] and that the British Government was no longer bound by the eighth article of the Treaty of 1805.[61] To back up his words with action and also to thwart any possibility of Scindia joining hands with Amir Khan and other Pindaris, the Governor-General soon left Kanpur and took the field in person.[62] Later events proved that his manoeuvring was brilliant.

Gwalior, though strategically situated in the centre of the richest part of his dominions, was exposed to British attack. It was separated from the British dominion by the Jumna river only. Twenty miles from Gwalior is a ridge of wooded hills between Kali Sind and Chambal, along whose banks run only two routes to and from Gwalior. Realising the strategic importance of this terrain, Hastings occupied Kali Sind route and placed Donkins' Division on the Chambal route.[63] Scindia was told that "as I had learned the approach of the Pindarries, I had thought it an attention due to my ally to place myself between him and a set of lawless plunderers."[64] Scindia found himself in a very delicate situation. He was left with two alternatives—either to accept the treaty terms offered to him or fight an open war against the British. The second alternative would involve his leaving Gwalior and the sacrifice of his fine artillery. The British occupied vantage points.[65] This compelled Scindia to accede to the British terms for a treaty. Meanwhile, Hastings issued orders to Hislop to be in readiness. In case of failure of negotiations, and on a word from Capt. Close, he was to adopt the utmost, prompt and vigorous measures for the reduction and occupation of Scindia's possessions South of Narbada.[66] He was not only to take military steps, but also to send an ultimatum to Scindia demanding further concessions of absolute cessation of his claims against the Rajputs and the cession of Ajmer to the British Government in perpetuity.[67] The Treaty of Gwalior was finally signed in 1817. Thus the march of Hastings accelerated the early acceptance of the terms offered, which were not very strict. Scindia was to supply a force of 5,000 horse, officered by the Britishers and paid by them too. But then, Scindia was to forego for three years the tribute which he used to receive from the British.

In order to undo the mischief of Scindia's troops collaborating with the Pindaris,[68] Scindia was obliged to agree to the stationing of his forces at certain stations, from where they were not to move without the consent of the British officers who were stationed there for the purpose of watching the strict observance of the treaty terms. The following places were assigned by the British for stationing Scindia's forces :-[69]

1st at Gwalior,
2nd with Baptiste near Bahadurgarh,
3rd in Mewar, and
4th in Ajmer.

Hastings passed immediate orders for the posting of a British Officer with Scindia's forces in Ajmer under Bappoo Scindia. Another British officer Major Bunce, was posted with Baptiste's forces.[70] He was also asked not to increase his armed strength during the period of operations against the Pindaris. This was specifically done to prevent the defeated, disarmed and disbanded Pindaris from joining Scindia's forces and escaping punishment.

Scindia was to deliver provisionally, the two strong fortresses of Hindia and Asirgarh.[71] Restriction was imposed on Scindia that he would not leave his capital so long as the war continued. Later, when the war ended in 1818, Scindia ceded the province of Ajmer to the British "a measure which completed the exclusion of Mahratta influence from Rajpootana.[72]

Scindia's defection and open accession to the British cause created great alarm among the Pindaris who withdrew from their former haunts. It was a fatal blow to them. Thus "the public accession of Scindia was an object of the greatest importance,"[73] because "Scindia is incapacitated from affording to the Pindarries, either openly or indirectly, that aid which it was apprehended he would contribute."[74]

Holkar

The British had, long ago, decided to give the same treatment to Holkar as to Scindia. The death of Jaswant Rao Holkar in 1811 removed an inveterate enemy of the British. But his successor, the young Holkar and the Regent Mother Tulsi Bai were also not able to reconcile themselves to British hegemony. The beginning of the Pindari operations by Hastings created a very favourable situation, in which the Holkar Government could fish.

Negotiations were soon opened with Holkar, to whom many of the Pindaris looked up as their protector. The imbecility of the Holkar Government delayed matters, resulting in protests and fruitless negotiations, whereupon Holkar was informed that "neutrality in such a conjuncture of affairs, when it can only serve the purpose of the opposite party, must be regarded by the British Government and its allies, as a demonstration of a resolution to support the Pindaris."[75] Treaty terms were offered to the Holkar Government, but they were rejected. The mutinous army of Holkar, impatient for a showdown, took the field. Tulsi Bai gave orders to her forces to march and she declared herself in agreement with the Peshwa with whose fate she associated hers. [76] Almost simultaneously, the battle drums were sounded by the army of Peshwa. The military chiefs of Holkar decided to march towards the Deccan to join hands with the Peshwa. But their way was blocked by the British forces under Sir Thomas Hislop and Sir John Malcolm.

Tulsi Bai now changed her opinion. This *volte face* on Tulsi Bai's part resulted in a sudden revolution on December 17, 1817. The Maharaja, Dewan Ganpat Rao, and Tulsi Bai were placed in confinement by Roshan Beg, Roshan Khan, Ram Deen and Gafoor Khan.[77] Finally Tulsi Bai was murdered. Holkar's army now itching for an immediate action attacked the Mysore Horse and seemed to be ready for a showdown with the British. Malcolm was forced to take action. He observed: "I could no longer delay in giving my decided opinion to His Excellency Sir Thomas Hislop that the army of Holkar should be immediately attacked."[78]

The Holkar Army was very advantageously posted on the left bank of the Seepra, opposite Mahidpur. The left flank of their army was protected by a curve of the river and the right by a difficult ravine. The only ford open to guns was very well-guarded. Undeterred by the nature of the terrain, the British Forces very boldly attacked Holkar's army. The battle of Mahidpur took place on December 21, 1817. Holkar's army put up a very stiff resistance. Action lasted from noon till about three in the afternoon when the Holkar troops began to withdraw. The British captured 70 guns, while several pieces were thrown in the river,[79] the defeated army ran towards Rampura. A brilliant and decisive victory was gained by them.[80] A treaty of peace and alliance was concluded with Maharaj Malhar Rao Holkar on January 6, 1818 at Mundsore,[81] Augean stables of Holkar's court were cleaned.

Treaty with Amir Khan

When efforts were made to conclude alliance with the Rajput Rajas, it was thought fit to separate Amir Khan from the Rajput affairs. His influence had reached alarming proportions. He undermined the resources of Jaipur, Jodhpur and Udaipur and, like worms, was eating into their vitals and had completely impoverished them. There was a fear in the Governor-General's mind that Amir Khan might, in course of time, become the master of Rajputana.

The British Government was negotiating with Amir Khan for some time,[82] Donkin at that stage thought it better to buy off Amir Khan than fight with him, but he soon had to change his opinion. He recorded "Mir Khan, I thought then worth buying .... but I consider him now after our signal success in the light of commodity the demand for which has gone by and by no means worth purchasing at any price."[83]

Though Amir Khan was desirous of seeking British protection, he was not very keen.[84] He adopted the policy of wait and watch. He was awaiting the result of the negotiations with Scindia and, therefore, delayed the conclusion of a treaty. It was also known that Amir Khan was in negotiation with Peshwa Baji Rao, who invited him to South.[85] He played for time and kept the Poona envoys in good humour, till things emerged clear from Delhi.

Sir David Ochterlony, to whom the settlement of all disputes with Amir Khan had been delegated by Metcalfe, moved with British Troops near Amir Khan's forces.[86] He had two motives for this action; first to overawe Amir Khan to finalise his treaty with the British and thereby prevent the disgruntled and refractory troops of Amir Khan from joining hands with the Pindaris. The second was "to influence the dilatory policy of the Court of Jyepore,"[87] with which negotiations were still going on. All these efforts were made to keep Amir Khan away from his possible confederacy with the Pindaris. Hastings drew the attention of Metcalfe to the importance of detaching Amir Khan. He wrote that it was essential "to secure his aid in a grand co-operation of predatory powers."[88]

Metcalfe immediately drafted certain proposals guaranteeing the land which Amir Khan held in perpetuity to him and his heirs. He was to disband his army and give his artillery to the British for money. He was to relinquish his predatory life, withdraw his forces from Rajputana and to restore all lands and forts to the British, who in turn were to transfer them to the rightful owners. He was also asked to fix his residence at a place within the territory assigned to him and was not to leave that place without British permission. Metcalfe also informed him that in case Amir Khan refused to comply with the terms offered,[89] war would immediately be declared against him and in that case "we shall guarantee to him (Holkar) whole of his hereditary territory, instead of confirming Amir Khan in that part."[90]

In the course of negotiations Amir Khan made a demand for the grant of land in his native place, Rohilkhand.[91] But the Governor-General was averse to any grant of land beyond that which had been promised to him as per the draft treaty. "The grant of an estate in Rohilcund is nearly impracticable and extremely undesirable."[92] On the other hand caution and prudence required that territory to be granted should be so situated that it would have no connection with Rohilkhand. On the refusal to give him land in Rohilkhand, Amir Khan proposed that land be granted to his sons in the form of Jagir. This too was refused but he was assured that "in case of his continued loyalty" and "in the way of an exchange for a part of his present possessions" land could be granted to him in future.[93]

After prolonged negotiations with Amir Khan, through his agent Saeed Khan of Afzalghur treaty was finalised on November 2, 1817[94] by which it was stipulated that all Pathan free-booters would be disbanded[95] and territories wrested from Rajputs by them would be restored to their owners. Land given to him by Holkar would be granted in perpetuity. Amir Khan was given one month to ratify the treaty.

When Saeed Khan appended his signatures to the treaty, grave doubts were expressed by all, about Amir Khan's sincerity. The situation became all the more doubtful because of the Peshwa and Nagpur affairs.[96] But strangely enough, almost all senior British officers had faith in him.[97] Even Metcalfe who doubted him earlier was constrained to observe: "I do not as yet see sufficient reasons to doubt the disposition of that chief to fulfil the engagement."[98] Amir Khan delayed ratification.[99] Donkin believed "I do not think that delay on the part of Mir Khan implies treachery as a matter of course, although it would facilitate his practising it, were he so disposed."[100] The British continued negotiations, as their interest demanded that negotiations should not break down, till Scindia agreed to their terms, lest a hostile Amir Khan may encourage him to go out openly in the field.[101]

It was, then, decided that should the period for ratification expire without something constructive coming up, Amir Khan should be regarded as an enemy.[102] Accordingly, instructions were issued to Metcalfe allowing him power to order both Maj. Gen. Sir David Ochterlony and Maj. Gen. Donkin to take field, not only in the case of Amir Khan not ratifying the Treaty, but even if he was not disposed to fulfil the stipulations after ratification of the Treaty.[103] But this situation did not arise because Amir Khan finally accepted the treaty on December 19, 1817.[104] Lord Hastings attached great importance to this treaty because "Amir Khan, the nucleus round which all plundering bands in the country would otherwise aggregate, dismiss his army, without cost to the government and become a feudatory of the British state; and recognizing as the special duty of that relation the suppression of every predatory association existing or that may hereafter be attempted."[105] Meanwhile, to relieve Amir Khan from the burden of maintaining his forces, the Governor-General issued immediate orders to Sir David Ochterlony through Metcalfe, to entertain a body of infantry and cavalry at the pay then prevailing in the British Army.[106]

Hastings was all along very happy at the conclusion of the alliance. He treated Amir Khan with consideration. His request for loan was immediately accepted. A Jagir to his son was also assured.[107] By one stroke of the pen, Amir Khan was detached from the predatory cause and a possibly expensive, long, dreary war avoided.

The War with Peshwa

At the time when treaties had been concluded with Scindia and Amir Khan and Pindaris were extremely alarmed, Peshwa and Bhonsla broke out hostilities against the British. Thus "two separate dramas of a subordinate, though eventful, character were acted on other stages."[108]

Though the Peshwa had been forced to conclude a treaty with the British, he was not happy with what had happened and, therefore, was waiting for an opportunity to overthrow the British yoke which pressed him heavily. The opportunity, a very tempting one too, came with the opening of the Pindari campaign. Under the guise of preparing and collecting the forces for the Pindari War, which acted as a sort of a thick veil over his activities, the Peshwa recruited fresh forces[109] and secretly prepared for a showdown with the British. He earnestly endeavoured to excite other Indian chiefs to give all possible support to the Pindaris.[110] When approached by the British to co-operate with them in their war against the Pindaris, the Peshwa not only readily consented, but professed all his co-operation in such an enterprise. Ostensibly, he seemed to be making preparations for exterminating the Pindaris.

Meanwhile, Elphinstone was not sitting idle. He kept the Government informed of all that had been taking place at Poona. He had faith in the Poona Subsidiary Force's fidelity to the British. However, to be on the safer, side he put Gen. Smith on the alert and asked him to be in readiness to move to the succour of the British, should an occasion arise.

Meanwhile, hectic activities were going on at Poona. Confidential messages were sent to the Maratha chiefs by the Peshwa entreating them to rise simultaneously. He also made secret overtures and successfully persuaded a few soldiers of the Poona Subsidiary Force to desert the British. Money was distributed among them. A few deserted and an impression was given to the Peshwa that the moment hostilities break out the rest would all rise against the British.

Thinking that he was ready to fight against the British, the Peshwa suddenly broke out in hostility. Hislop was then on march towards the Narbada. He decided to go to the help of the Poona Residency,[111] as the exigencies of the situation demanded.

Hastings heard of the revolt at Poona on November 14. He feared that the campaign might be disturbed and weakened by the withdrawal of the British forces under Hislop. His reading proved correct. Hislop had already made a move towards Poona directing Malcolm to proceed with a small force to attack Chitu. But Hislop had hardly gone far, when he received orders from Hastings to adhere to his original plan.[112] He immediately retraced his steps.[113] Hastings thought Brig. Gen. Smith's forces to be sufficient to tackle the situation at Poona.[114] The Peshwa attacked the British Residency at Kirkee on November 5, 1817. The Residency was burnt to ashes. Elphinstone was just able to escape. Ultimately they defeated the Peshwa inflicting heavy losses. Baji Rao fled. General Smith occupied Poona on November 17. Gen. Smith pursued Baji Rao and defeated him in two successive wars at Koregaon and Ashte in January and February, 1818 respectively. Peshwa surrendered to the British and was pensioned off to Bithur at eight lakhs of rupees a year. Peshwaship, the symbol of Maratha unity, was abolished.

War with the Bhonsla Raja of Nagpur

The Nagpur Raja, who also felt humiliated by the treaty with the British, had a burning desire to overthrow the latter. For some time past the conduct of the Raja had become suspicious to them.[115] Though an ally, they had no faith in him and, even before the outbreak of hostility, instructions had been issued to Brig. Gen. Hardyman to be in readiness to advance on Nagpur in case of an emergency.[116] Adam, the Chief Secretary to the Government, instructed Jenkins to ask Brig. Hardyman to march to Tilwari Ghats on the Narbada and to keep ready to advance at a moment's notice. However, in the event of his receiving news of an action of hostility by the Nagpur Raja, he was to act on his own.[117] On the basis of events, the Governor-General felt that "an additional British Force should be established in the Rajah's territories with the least practicable delay."[118]

Following the footsteps of the Peshwa, Appa Sahib, the Bhonsla Raja, on the night of November 26, 1817 attacked the British Residency.[119] The British troops at Nagpur were on some height. Though outnumbered, they put up a stiff resistance. Their only fear was of the ammunition and supplies running short. In the end the Nagpur Forces were defeated, but not till they had inflicted severe losses in killed and wounded.[120] The fight took place on the heights of Sitabaldi. Two separate battles, in fact, had taken place. One at Sitabaldi and the other at Nagpur on December 16, 1817 which sealed the fate of Appa Sahib, who ran away.

Offers of Help

While these dramas were being enacted, an appeal was made to the Indian chiefs, to help the British to put an end to the accursed system of Pindari freebooters. In order to do so it was necessary to pool all resources because of the very nature and constitution of the Pindari hordes. They were pointed out "as the proper objects of a secure retributive justice and render their destruction a species of moral obligation."[121]

A number of letters were addressed to various Rajas[122] requesting them to help the British and to send a body of cavalry or infantry under trustworthy leaders to act in concert with the British army under Major General Brown or Sir David Ochterlony.[123] The British also asked the petty states to exert themselves to the best of their ability in destroying those Pindaris who might attempt to cross into their territory[124] through the various passes. The aim of this move was "the maintenance and extension of public tranquility on the ruins of that nefarious system of predatory association to which they were so long the devoted victims."[125] Working upon the fears and hopes of the Indian chiefs, Malcolm made them aware of the fact that not only their hopes and interests but their very existence was at stake. The British were motivated by one more reason and that was to establish a barrier against the extension and revival of the predatory system.[126] Adam drafted a letter of instructions to Metcalfe in which he laid down the policy to be pursued.[127] Metcalfe was instructed to approach the petty states in the vicinity of Delhi as well as others for the purpose of asking them to put their forces at the disposal of the British, to be utilized as auxiliaries under British officers.[128]

The political relations of these states were to be entirely under the British control, in return for which they were guaranteed territorial integrity. They were allowed complete freedom in the exercise of internal administration. The states were requested to give free admission to the British troops into their territories while they were pursuing the Pindaris. The Indian chiefs readily accepted the British proposal.[129]

Zalim Singh of Kota, because of his great capabilities and friendship to the British, was considered an "efficient instrument for upholding and promoting the system which it is proposed to substitute for that which has so long desolated the central provinces of India."[130] Hastings wrote personal letters to the Rajas of Kota and Bundi for interposing and destroying the Pindaris.[131]

Tod was deputed to concert measures with the Rajas of Rajputana, particularly Kota and Bundi, for the purpose ef deploying their forces to intercept the Pindaris in the event of their retreating through their territories and also to guard the principal fords of the Chambal.[132]

Begum Samru of Sardhana[133] and Fyz Mohammad Khan of Dadri[134] were requested to send their forces, which were to be ultilised only as guards on passes or as escorts along with their regular detachments.[135]

Maj. Bunce was sent to Jean Baptiste's camp "to watch his proceedings and those of his officers commanding separate detachments and prevent their giving aid or countenance or even maintaining communications with the Pindaris or other freebooters and generally to see that stipulations of the treaty as regards Scindia's officers are punctually executed."[136]

The Bhils of Mewar were organised in the general system of war against the Pindaris. In the event of any groups of Pindaris taking the direction of Bhil habitats, their Chiefs were requested to ensure their destruction and for that a large sum of money was distributed among them.[137] In the wars of 1804, the co-operation of the Bhils was found to be of considerable advantage to the British.[138] Their habits, resources, hardihood, and fierce and fighting nature were of immense help. Besides, the strategic position of their land was such that they could easily check the flight of the Pindaris to Gujarat.[139] Hence, the Governor-General attached great importance to conciliating the Bhils.[140]

Hislop, in agreement with the views of the Governor-General, immediately adopted measures which were conducive to the general success of the operations against the Pindaris. He impressed upon the Resident, at Hyderabad, Poona and Nagpur "the expediency of their endeavouring to conciliate the Bheels and Ghounds in the hilly tracts with the view of inducing them as well to give information of those freebooters as to impede their passage, through their fortresses and to destroy them, should they fall into their hands."[141] Thus, with this end in view, immediate engagements with the chiefs of Barrah, Sunawara, Saunt, Dungarpur and Banswara were concluded to help the British.[142]

A circular letter also made an appeal to the chiefs of Bundelkhand,[143] rousing their sense of danger, and requesting them to keep vigilance particularly when the Pindaris after defeat might try to escape through their territories. They were requested to take all possible measures for blocking the passage and also to pursue and destroy the flying Pindaris.

The appeal made by the British Government had a very encouraging response from the Indian chiefs. They and their people had been suffering the greatest misery at the hands of the Pindaris. They were, therefore, prepared to make any sacrifice for the extirpation of the Pindari menace. Hence, when the appeal went round, they all came forward and gave their most unqualified and whole-hearted support to the British.

The Gaekwad of Baroda, even before the appeal was issued, had declared that in the event of the British Government being involved in any contest, the whole resources of the state would be placed at the disposal of the British.[144]

As a result of the appeal, the Nawab of Bhopal gave his active support. The Thakurs of Sewun, Phoongarh, Rampura, and the Rani of Chouragarh declared their readiness to co-operate.[145] The chiefs of Ali Mohan and Bersia subscribed to the engagement for the suppression of the Pindari menace.[146] Begum Samru of Sardhana sent two Battalions of Najeebs and eight guns to serve the Reserve Division of Sir David Ochterlony[147] to Gurgaon on 20th September, 1817.[148] Fyz Mohammad Khan of Dadri gave one thousand well disciplined Telingas, with four guns and a small party of cavalry.[149] His uncle, Fyz Tullah Khan also joined Sir David Ochterlony with four hundred horse.[150]

Ummed Buksh Khan took the field in person with a Battalion of Najeebs, two guns, one galloper gun, twenty camel-swivels and cavalry.[151] Maharao Raja Bane Singh of Alway gave five hundred horse and five hundred foot with two guns and two swivels to be placed under Ummed Buksh Khan, an Alwar General.[152] The Bharatpur Raja promised all possible aid, which [153] was subsequently sent to Agra in the form of 1,200 horses. Raja Kirat Singh of Dholpur agreed to send 300 horse 700 foot to be placed under Maj.Gen. Donkin and also to place at the disposal of the British "whatever supplies his country produces". The Patiala Raja sent three hundred and fifty horses and the chiefs of Jind and Khaital gave hundred horses each.[154] The Rewa Raja furnished a body of horse, which joined Hardyman at Mirzapur. The Nagpur Raja promised aid to the extent of 3,000 horses and 200 foot, to be placed under the British command, but he delayed the despatch of the same.[155]

The Mysore Raja also expressed his sincere desire to help the British in their hour of crisis. He promised to do his best. Accordingly he supplied a full contingent of Mysore Silledar Horse.[156] Nawab Shamsher Bahadur of Banda offered to protect the Banda boundary against any incursion by the Pindaris.[157] Raja Zalim Singh of Kota supplied 500 cavalry and 4 guns which he placed at the disposal of Col. Tod for use against the Pindaris.[158] Even Maharaja Ranjit Singh expressed joy and satisfaction at the British determination to "inflict punishment on the accursed tribes of Pindaris." [159]

The diplomacy of Lord Hastings created a most favourable situation for the British. He was able to rope in almost all the Maratha and Rajput states in the British orbit. There was all round jubilation at the prospect of deliverance from the Pindari yoke. The response from the Indian Rajas was most encouraging. They gave their mite in men, money and material. Many of them came forward of their own accord and contributed beyond their capacity.

FOOT-NOTES

1 Mohan Sinha Mehta : *Lord Hastings and the Indian States*, 1813-1823, p. 2, Bombay, 1930.

2 Marshman : *History of India*, p. 310.

3 Hastings "had also been a severe critic of Lord Wellesley's ambitious policy, and came out resolved to make no new conquests." Muir : *The Making of British India*, p. 249.

4 On 11th April, 1791.

5 That Government "was founded on injustice and had originally been established by force."
Hansard : 31 : *George III*, pp. 145-147.

6 The War "which now subsided was a serious calamity whether favourable or adverse, it was no less the subject of deprecation and regret."
Hansard : 31 : George III, pp. 145-147.

7 Lord Hastings *op. cit.* Lt. Col. C.E. Luard.

8 Lord Hastings *op. cit.* W.H. Davenport Adams : *The Makers of British India*, p. 187.

9 Keene : *History of India*, Vol. II, pp. 25-26.
Keene and Prinsep had both tried to categorise the states as above.

10 Metcalfe in his famous 'Note' to the Governor-General expressed the view that the "first class might be utilised, if not conciliated, while for the second extermination was the appropriate remedy." *Ibid.*

11 *Ibid.*

12 Mehta : *Lord Hastings and the Indian States*, p. 4.

13 Duff : *A History of the Marathas*, Vol. III, p. 317.

14 *Ibid.*
Governor-General's Minute; 1 December, 1815.

15 "the clamours and mutinies of discontented armies" was a regular feature.
N.A.I. For. Sec. 1816 O.C. No. 1, 15, June, 1816 :
Governor-General's Minute; 1, December, 1815, para 52.

16 The armies "of Scindia and Holkar are broken into different bodies under separate chiefs acting almost independently seeming to pay little regard to the authority" of Scindia and Holkar. N.A.I. For. Sec. 1816 : O.C. No. 1, 15 June, 1816 : G.G's, Minute, 1 December, 1815, para 49.

17 Scindia was evidently aware of the danger of provoking the resentment of the British Government and in all probability he never had any intention of exposing himself to a defeat at British hands.

18 *Central Province District Gazetteers*, Nagpur District, Vol. A,p. 43, Edited by R.V. Russell, Bombay, 1908.

19 *Parliamentary Papers :* Operations in India with their results from the 30th April 1814 to 1st January, 1823. The Marquis of Hastings' Summary of Operations in India, p. 95.

20 Hastings' contention was proved by the expression of surprise by Umer Singh Thapa and Runjore Singh, the two Gurkha Generals who surrendered, were surprised at not finding the Marathas in the field against the British. *Hastings' Summary of Operations*, p. 96.

21 Blacker : *Memoirs*, p. 12.
Also : G.R. Gleig, *The History of the British Empire in India*, Vol. III, p. 324, London, 1835.

22 Hindu Rao Ghatge was requested that somebody must "move with the army of the Pindaris and with the Nuwab Mir Khan Buhadoor, ...You must consider me as in every respect united with you...or if there should be any delay in your coming, send the Pindaris and Mir Khan only with 30,000 horse and do you preserve, appearances with them." N.A.I. For. Sec. 1816 : O.C, No. 10-14 7 Sept. 1816, Translation of a Persian Letter from the Gurkha Government to Hindu Rao Ghatge, 26 May, 1816.

23 N.A.I. For, Sec. 1818 : O.C. No. 7, 26 June, 1818 :
Hastings to Metcalfe, Gorakhpur, 1 June, 1818, para 2.

24 *Ibid.*

25 M.I.O.L.L. Hastings' Letter to Secret Committee, 1 March, 1820.
Also : Wheeler, Summary of Affairs p. 224.

26 *Ibid.*

27 *Ibid.*

28 "...I caused to be delivered to Scindia, in open durbar, his own letters, signed with his own private seal, addressed to a Foreign

Government and evincing the most hostile machinations already matured against us."

Lord Hastings speech at a dinner, Government of India Gazette, January-December, 1818.

29 *Ibid.*

30 Thornton : *The History of the British Empire in India*, Vol. IV, p. 452.

31 M.I.O.L.L. Hastings to Secret Committee, 1 March, 1820.

32 Summary of Operations, p. 99.

33 N.A.I. For. Sec. 1816 : O.C. No. 1, 15 June, 1816 : Governor-General's Minute, 1 December, 1815, para 19.

34 *Ibid.*

35 Governor-General's Minute, 3 April, 1814 : *op. cit.* D.C. Ganguly : *Select Documents of the British Period of Indian History* (in the collection of Victoria Memorial, Calcutta) Document No. 67, p. 197 Calcutta 1958.

36 M.I.O.L.L : Governor-General's Minute, 19 December, 1816.

37 N.A.I. For. Pol. 1813 : O.C. No. 17, 23 July, 1813 : G.R. Carnac, Resident at Baroda to Francis Warden, enclosing Extracts of a Report by C.T. Metcalfe, A.G.G. to the Rt. Hon'ble Lord Lake, Commander-in-Chief.

38 N.A.I. For. Sec. 1814 : O.C. No. 1, Edmonstone's Minute 21 June, 1814, para 29.

39 N.A.I. For. Pol. 1808 : O.C. No. 51, 16 May, 1808 : Seton to Edmonstone, Delhi, 26 April, 1808.

40 N.A.I. For. Pol. 1813 : O.C. No. 17, 23 July, 1813 : Carnac to Warden, 11 June, 1813, enclosing a Report from C.T. Metcalfe to Lord Lake.

41 N.A.I. For. Pol. 1812 : O.C. No. 18, 21 February, 1812, Metcalfe to Edmonstone, Delhi, 31 January, 1812, para 6.

42 Letter from Sir Charles Metcalfe, Resident for Rajputana, June, 1816 : *op. cit.* Lyall : Rise, p. 287.

43 Prinsep : *History, Political & Military Transactions* : Vol. II, p. 22.

44 For. Misc. 124 A : Pindary and Maratha Wars : Hastings to Secret Committee, 1 March, 1820, p. 386, para 13.

45 The extension of "our protection to the Rajpoot States who from their political circumstances are our natural allies and the natural enemies of the Marhattas... the establishment of our influence over those states would interpose a strong barrier, between the Seiks and those powers who might be expected to aid them in a war."

N.A.I. For. Sec. 1816 : O.C. No. 1, 15 June, 1816 :

Governor-General's Minute, 1 December, 1815, para 84.

Also : Making a reference to Jaipur, Lord Hastings very much regretted that had the British retained the alliance, concluded in the first instance with Jaipur "the predatory Patan force might not at this day have been in existence, and would at least, there is every reason to suppose, have been far inferior in number, power & consequence to what it is at present." N.A.I. For. Sec, 1816 : O.C. No. 1, 15 June, 1816, G.G's. Minute, 1 December, 1815, para 282.

46 Lord Hastings recorded "I had adopted a thorough conviction that the mere expulsion of the Pindaris from their actual haunts would in no degree, secure the future peace of India, or prevent the revival of the predatory system in perhaps a still more dangerous form. I felt it, therefore, to be an imperious duty to combine with the dispersion of those freebooters, the establishment of a system of political alliance, which should prevent the revival of the system under any form in any part of India."
For. Misc. 124 A : Hastings to the Secret Committee, 1 March, 1820, p. 386, para 15.
Also : N.A.I. For. Sec. 1817 : O.C. No. 26, 28 October, 1817 : Adam to Metcalfe, 8 October, 1817, paras 2 to 7.

47 For. Misc. 124 A ; Hastings to Secret Committee, 1 March, 1820, p. 390, para 34.
Also : N.A.I. For. Sec. 1817 : O.C. No. 26, 28 October, 1817, Adam to Metcalfe, 8 October, 1817.

48 N.A.I. For. Sec. 1811, O.C. No. 1-2, 16 August, 1811, Metcalfe to Edmonstone, Delhi, 23 July, 1811.

49 Prinsep : *Political and Military Transactions* Vol. II.

50 N.A.I. For. Sec. 1817 : O.C. No. 26, 28 October, 1817 :
Adam to Metcalfe, 8 October, 1817, para 6.

51 The Governor-General himself was keen to conclude an alliance with Jaipur for he believed that "the advantage of such a league with Jeypore as would enable us to station a force within that country appears to me of the first rate. Nothing would be more efficacious in restraining the growth of the predatory system besides "extending still further the sphere of our protection and control."
N.A.I. For. Sec. 1816 : O.C. No. 1, 20 April, 1816 : G.G's Minute 13 April, 1816. para 15.
Also : M.I.O.L.L. Edmonstone's Minute, 10 April, 1816.

52 Marshman : *History of India*, p.328.

53 For. Misc. 124 A : Letter from Hastings to the Court of Directors, 19 May, 1818, p. 281, para 3.

54 (a) As late as 21 November, 1817, Scindia was sending secret instructions to the Pindari chiefs to join him in fighting against the British
N.A.I. For. Sec. 1817 : O.C. No. 100-101, 19 December, 1817 : Metcalfe to Adam, Delhi, 21 November, 1817.

(b) Scindia "is said to keep up a constant correspondence with the Pindaree leaders exhorting them to unanimity and encouraging them with the hopes of effectual aid and support from himself."

N.A.I. For. Sec. 1817 : O.C. No. 9-10, 30 August, 1817 : Letter from Maddock, Acting Superintendent of Political Affairs, Banda, 10 August, 1817.

(c) Scindia "not only encouraged the efforts of the Pindaris, but he was really adverse to their expulsion." Blacker : *Memoir of the operations*, p. 12.

(d) Scindia in a letter to Karim Khan said that he, Chitu and Dost Mohammad and other Pindaris ought to unite in resisting the enemy.

55 N.A.I. For. Sec. 1817 : O.C. No. 10-11, 10 October, 1817 : Close to Adam, Gwalior, 15 September, 1817, The vakeels were Nathu Pant, Jumeeyut Roy, Esoba Pant, Hira Lal, Ramzan, Ratan Kumar and Bapoo Bhai.

56 N.A.I. For. Sec. 1817 : O.C. No. 34-35, 17 October, 1817 : Letter No. 17, R. Close to Lord Hastings, 27 September, 1817.

57 Parliamentary Papers : Letter from the Marquis of Hastings to the Secret Committee, 1 March, 1820, p. 387, para 18.

58 Article eighth of the Treaty of November, 1805 concluded between Daulat Rao Scindia and the East India Company was : "The Honourable Company engage to enter into no treaty with the Rajahs of Odeypur, and Jodhpur, and Kotah, or other chiefs, tributaries of Dowlat Rao Sindhia, situated in Malwa, Marwar, and is in no shape whatever to interfere with the settlement which Sindhia may make with them."

Aitchison : *A Collection of Treaties*, Vol. IV, p. 61, Calcutta. 1912.

59 N.A.I. For. Sec. 1817 : O.C. No. 24, 25 July, 1817 : Close to Hastings, Gwalior, 9 July, 1817, para 6.

60 For. Misc. 124 A : Hastings to Metcalfe, 5 October 1817, p. 459

61 N.A.I. For. Sec. 1817 : O.C. No. 4 & 5, 28 October, 1817 : Adam to Close, 29 September, 1817.

62 Hastings wrote "that it would be requisite that I should proceed to the Upper Provinces .. my being on the spot would be so ostensible a proof of the determination of the Government to carry the matter through and would be so well understood by Scindia and Holkar with regard to the facility & promptitude with which the whole of our strength could thence be launched upon them, that it would be the least devisable security against more extensive trouble than the simple dispersion of the Pindaris."

M.I.O.L.L. Governor-General's Minute, 19 December, 1816.

63 In order to prevent Scindia's forces collecting at one place and thereby endangering the British positions "two strong divisions were interposed between him and all his corps, stationed at Bahadurgarh, Ajmer, Jawud, Badnawar and Sahajahanpur."

Burton : *For the General Staff* : p. 21.

64 Lord Hastings' speech at a Dinner, Government of India Gazette, 1818—January-December.

65 Hastings' Summary of Operations, p. 99.

66 N.A.I. For. Sec. 1817 : O.C. No. 8, 28 October, 1817 : Hastings to Hislop, Kanpur, 30 September, 1817, para 6.

67 N.A.I. For. Sec. 1817 : O.C. No. 13-15, 26 December, 1817 : Private Letter from Adam to Close, 3 November, 1817.

68 "If on the one hand, we could not calculate on Scindia's troops affording active assistance, on the other, there was reason to apprehend that they might, through the laxity of their discipline, on the attachment of their leaders to the predatory cause, give support to the Pindaris, or at least obstruct our operations." For. Misc. 124 A : Hastings to Secret Committee, 1 March, 1820, p. 387, para 22.

69 N.A.I. For. Sec. 1817 : O.C. No. 16, 28 October, 1817 : Adam to Close, Kanpur, 5 October, 1817.

70 N.A.I. For. Sec. 1817 : O.C. No. 5-8, 12 December, 1817 : Adam to Close, camp at Eritch, 21 November, 1817, paras 1 to 3.

71 The Governor-General wanted four fortresses as security, Asirgarh and Hindia in the Deccan and Nurwar and Chanderi in Hindustan, but later decided to tone down to two, Hindia and Asirgarh.

72 Wheeler, *Summary*, p. 225.

73 For. Misc. 124 A : Letters from Hastings to Secret Committee, 1 March, 1820, p. 392, para 44.

74 N.A.I. For. Sec. 1817 : O.C. No. 53. 26 December, 1817 : Governor-General's Minute, 10 December, 1817.

75 N.A.I. For. Sec. 1817 : O.C. No. 13, 28 October, 1817 : Adam to Metcalfe, Kanpur, 1 October, 1817, para 15.

76 N.A.I. For. Sec. 1817 : O.C. No. 9-11, 2 January, 1818, Capt. Tod to Malcolm, Rowtah, 27 November, 1817.

77 B.G.R.D. No. 304 : Pol. Deptt. 1817 : Malcolm to Adam, Mahidpur, 24 December, 1817.

78 *Ibid.*

79 Government Gazette Extraordinary, 15 January, 1818, Extract Letter from Hislop to Hastings, camp near Seepra, Opposite Mahidpur, 23 December, 1817.

80 For. Misc. 124 A : Letter from Lt. Gen. Sir Hislop to Hastings, camp on Seepra, Opposite Mahidpur, 23 Deeember, 1817.

81 N.A.I. For. Sec. 1818 : O.C. No. 35-40, 23 January, 1818 : Adam to Lushington, Acting Secretary to the Government, Fort William, 13 January, 1818.

82 Col. J. Sutherland called the negotiations with Amir Khan of 'doubtful character'. Sutherland : *Sketches of the Relations subsisting between the British Government in India and the different Native States*, p. 69, Calcutta. 1837.

83 N.A,I. For. Sec. 1818 : O.C. No. 33, 6 February, 1818 : Donkin to George Swinton, Persian Secretary, Camp Gyata Ghat, 28 December, 1817.

84 Amir Khan had made overtures to the British for protection, but the conditions he proposed were too extravagant for the British to accept.

85 N.A.I. For. Sec. 1817 : O.C. No. 35, 26 September, 1817 : Metcalfe to Adam, 7 September, 1817.

86 Adam also left the conduct of relations with the Rajput Rajas to Ochterlony. He was appointed Resident in Rajputana and Commissioner General with the Rajput States with Headquarters at Rampurah (Tonk). He was accredited to Udaipur, Kota, Bundi, Jodhpur, Karauli and later Jaipur and Kishangarh. N.A.I. For. Pol. 1817 : O.C. No. 13, 24 April, 1817 : Adam to Ochterlony, Camp Pursah, 27 March, 1818.

87 For. Misc. 124 A : Hastings to Secret Committee, 1 March, 1820, p. 394, para 52.

88 J.W. Kaye : *The Life & Correspondence of Charles Metcalfe*, Vol. I, p. 457, London.

89 It was decided that "the expiration of this term without the arrival of the ratification, would necessarily place Meer Khan in the situation of an enemy."
N.A.I. For. Sec. 1817 : O.C. No. 113-115, 19 December, 1817 : Metcalfe to Donkin, Delhi, 25 November, 1817, para 5.

90 N.A.I. For. Sec. 1817 : O.C. No. 13, 28 October, 1817 : Adam to Metcalfe, Kanpur, 1 October, 1817, para 16.

91 N.A.I. For. Sec. 1817 : O.C. No. 32, 5 December, 1817 : Letter No. 669, Metcalfe to Adam, Delhi, 11 November, 1817.

92 N.A.I. For. Sec. 1817 : O.C. No. 13, 28 October, 1817 : Adam to Metcalfe, Kanpur, 1 October, 1817, para 25.

93 N.A.I. For. Sec. 1817 : O.C. No. 32, 5 December, 1817 : Letter No. 669, Metcalfe to Adam, Delhi, 11 November, 1817.

94 See appendix I.

95 The treaty "will withdraw him and his principal adherents from the cause of the predatory powers."
H.R.R. S. No. 236, Vol. No. 56, Adam to Bunce, of His Majesty's 24 Light Dragoon, 9 November, 1817, p. 433.

96 It was recorded that "circumstances have taken place in another quarter, which may dispose him to waver, and which render it necessary that we should ascertain his present intentions, and act in a manner suited to them."
N.A.I. For. Sec. 1817 : O.C. No. 113-115, 19 December, 1817 : Metcalfe to Maj. Gen. Donkin, Delhi, 25 November, 1817.

97 (a) Donkin believed "I have no hesitation in saying that I think that chief is sincere." N.A.I. For. Sec, 1817 : O.C. No. 40-42, 26 December, 1817 : Donkin to Metcalfe, camp Kushalgarh, 30 November, 1817.

(b) Sir David Ochterlony had such great faith in him that at one stage when Amir Khan was in financial difficulty during the course of negotiations, Sir David Ochterlony remarked, "If I had two lakhs of rupees of my own, I should not hesitate to give it to Mir Khan; so completely has he assured me of his sincerity."

(c) Further on a very ticklish question of should Amir Khan be allowed to keep the Pathan levies, Ochterlony "conceiving a higher opinion of the sincerity of that chief's than Metcalfe had ever entertained, he was anxious to keep the Pathan levies together, and was not without a hope that they might be advantageously employed against our enemies." Ochterlony also allowed him to retain 40 guns. N.A.I. For. Pol. 1818: O.C. No. 13 B, 24 April, 1818 : Ochterlony to Adam, Lucknow, 25 March, 1818.

98 N.A.I. For. Sec. 1817 : O.C. No. 113-115, 19 December, 1817 : Metcalfe to Donkin, Delhi, 25 November, 1817.

99 Amir Khan delayed ratification in order to be "at liberty to take advantage of any turn of events favourable for the pursuit of another line of policy."
N.A.I. For. Sec. 1818 : O.C. No. 41, 15 February, 1818 : Metcalfe to Adam, Delhi, 21 January, 1818.

100 N.A.I. For. Sec. 1817 : O.C. No. 40-42, 26 December, 1817 : Donkin to Metcalfe, camp at Dholpur, 30 November, 1817.

101 N.A.I. For. Sec. 1817 : O.C. No. 13, 28 October, 1817 : Adam to Metcalfe, Kanpur, 1 October, 1817, paras 21 to 35.

102 N.A.I. For. Sec. 1817 : O.C. No. 113-115, 19 December, 1817 : Metcalfe to Donkin, Delhi, 25 November, 1817.

103 N.A.I. For. Sec. 1817 : O.C. No. 113-115, 19 December, 1817 : Adam to Metcalfe, Camp at Eritch, 3 December, 1817.

104 Metcalfe in a letter to Adam explained the manner in which Article 4 was to be executed : "The son and heir of Meer Khan is to come to Dihlee and reside here as a hostage, for the due fulfilment of the stipulations............After his arrival, the sum of two laks of Roopees is to be paid, to enable Meer Khan to proceed in the work of disbanding his army & delivering up his guns & equipment..... (and the rest) by instalments to the extent of three laks more."
N.A.I. For. Sec. 1817 : O.C. No. 32, 5 December, 1817 : Metcalfe to Adam, Delhi, 11 November, 1817.

105 N.A.I. For. Sec. 1817 : O.C. No. 53, 26 December, 1817 : Governor-General's Minute, 10 December, 1817.

106 N.A.I. For. Sec. 1818 : O.C. No. 4-6, 30 January, 1818, Adam to Metcalfe, Camp Oochan, 8 January, 1818.

107 For. Misc. Vol. No. 136, Adam to Ochterlony, 23 December. 1817.

108 Murray : History, Vol. II, p. 198.

109 N.A.I. For. Sec. 1817 : O.C. No. 41, 10 May, 1817 : Substance of a private examination of the Gosain Kempooree on whose person a Maratha paper was found. It read "A large number of Gossayns entertained by order of the Peishwa, assembling about Poona."

110 The Peshwa wrote a number of letters to various Indian chiefs. One of the letters was written to Amir Khan, calling on him to join him against the British. N.A.I. For. Sec. 1817 : O.C. No. 43-45, 26 December, 1817: Donkin to Adam, Camp two Koss East of Onearah, 5 December, 1817, para 7.

111 For. Misc. 124 A : Hastings to the Secret Committee, 1 March, 1820, p. 395, para 58. Also : B.G.R. D. No. 303, Pol. Deptt. 1817 : Hislop to Officer Comdg. Gujrat Field Force, camp at Koolorda, 22 November, 1817, and a private letter to the Governor of Bombay, camp at Charwar, 26 November, 1817.

112 Hislop was told by Hastings that in spite of any difficulty, action against the Pindaris must continue. In regard to the Peshwa affair, he wrote to Hislop "the actual occurrence of hostilities between the Peshwa and the British government may not interfere with the active pursuit of the Pindaries by the columns destined for that service" and he was further told "notwithstanding the unsatifactory intelligence of the Peshwa's conduct Your Excellency will have lost no time in crossing the Nerbudda and attacking the Pindaris according to the arrangements formerly concerted."
N.A.I. For. Sec. 1817 : O.C. No. 72-74, 19 December, 1817 :
Hastings to Hislop, Camp at Talgaon, 14 November, 1817.

113 Hastings warned Hislop that "under any contingency until you shall receive advices of a contrary tenor either from me or from Capt. Close to shape your measures without any reference to apprehended hostilities on the part of Scindia or Ameer Khan."
N.A.I. For. Sec. 1817 : O.C. No. 1, 19 December, 1817 :
Hastings to Hislop, camp at Eritch, 21 November, 1817.

114 B.G.R. D. No. 303 : Extracts of a private letter from Hislop to Bombay Governor, 26 November, 1817.

115 Lt. Col. MacMorine, Commanding Detachment Nagpur Subsidiary Force, Nagpur reported to the Officer Commanding the Nagpur Subsidiary Force, Lt. Col. Adams that the Berar Government was raising obstacles at the slightest pretext.

116 N.A I. For. Sec. 1817 : O.C. No. 31-34, 26 December, 1817 :
James Nicol to Brig. Gen. Hardyman, HQ camp, Lakeria, 3 December, 1817.

117 N.A.I. For. Sec. 1817 : O.C. No. 10-12, 26 December, 1817 :
Adam to Jenkins, camp Eritch, 3 December, 1817.

118 N.A.I. For. Sec. 1817 : O.C. No. 10-12, 26 December, 1817 :
Adam to Nicol, camp Eritch, 3 December, 1817.

119 Jenkins at 12 midnight wrote to Major Pitman "The Raja's troops attacked us this evening."

B.G.R. D. No. 303, Pol. Deptt. 1817 : Jenkins to Pitman, 26-27, November, 1817.
Also : N.A.I. For. Sec. 1818 : O.C. No. 35-42, 6 February, 1818, Jenkins to Adams, 30 November, 1817.

120 For. Misc. 124 A : *Pindary and Maratha Wars* : Jenkins to Pitman, 26 November, 1817.

121 N.A.I. For. Sec. 1812 : O.C. No. 47, 30 October, 1817 :
G.H. Fagan, Adjutant General to Edmonstone, Chief Secretary to the Government, 18 October, 1812, para 5.

122 The letters were written to the Rajas of Bharatpur, Alwar, Fyz Mohemmed Khan, Ahmad Buksh and Begum Samru of Sardhana.
N.A.I. For. Sec. 1817 : O.C. No. 1-4, 17 October, 1817 :
Adam to Metcalfe, Kanpur, 26 September, 1817.

123 N.A.I. For. Sec. 1817 : O.C. No. 1-4, 17 October, 1817 :
Adam at Kanpur to Metcalfe, 26 September, 1817.

124 H.R.R. S. No. 236, Vol. No. 56, Adam to Wauchope, 6 October, 1817.

125 N.A.I. For. Sec. 1817 : O.C. No. 26, 28 October, 1817 :
Adam to Metcalfe, 8 October, 1817.

126 H.R.R. S. No. 236, Vol. No. 56, Adam to Metcalfe, 8 Oct. 1817.

127 N.A.I. For. Sec. 1817 : O.C. No. 26, 28 October, 1817 : Adam to Metcalfe, Kanpur, 8 October, 1817.

128 N.A.I. For. Sec. 1817 : O.C. No. 1-4. 17 October, 1817 : Adam to Metcalfe, Kanpur, 26 September, 1817, paras 2 to 4.

129 For. Misc. 124A : Malcolm to Governor-General, 21 April, 1818, p. 270.

130 N.A.I. For. Sec. 1817 : O.C. No. 26, 28 October, 1817 : Adam to Metcalfe, Kanpur, 8 October, 1817, p. 16, para 11.

131 N.A.I. For. Sec. 1817 : O.C. No. 2-6, 28 November, 1817 : Hastings to Raja Zalim Singh of Kota and Raja of Bundi, 6 November, 1817.

132 H.R.R. S. No. 236, Vol. No. 56 : Adam to Close, 7 November, 1817.

133 T.P.P.R. O.C. No. 304, 22 October, 1817 : Begum Samru wrote "in the destruction of that accursed race of the Pindaris...I had at the instance of Mr. Matcalfe sent my troops to the appointed place Gurgaon."

134 N.A.I. For. Sec. 1817 : O.C. No. 1-417, October, 1817 : Adam to Metcalfe, Kanpur, 26 September, 1817, paras 3 and 4.

135 *Ibid.*

136 H.R.R. S. No. 236 Vol. No. 56, Adam to Major Bunce of His Majesty's 24 Light Dragoon, 9 November, p. 378.

137 For. Misc. 124 : Tod : Memoir of Meywar or Oodipur.

138 B.G.R. D. No. 301 : Evan Nepean and the Bombay Council to Hastings, Bombay, 29 October, 1817.

139 B.G.R. D. No. 301 : Nepean maintained that the Bhils could even

obstruct the advance of the British forces if they wished. Such was the situation and strategic importance of their land.

140 B.G.R. D. No. 301 : Warden to Capt. Carnac, Resident at Baroda, 29 October, 1817, para 16.

141 H.R.R. S. No. 232, Vol. No. 338 : Lt. Gen. Sir John Hislop, Head Quarters at Burhanpur, 31 to the Marquis of Hastings, Burhanpur, October, 1817, para 22.

142 B.G.R. D. No. 303 : Pol. Deptt. 1817 : Resident at Baroda to Warden, Baroda, 21 November 1817.
Also : Carnac to William Moris, Commanding the Guicowar Subsidiary Force, Baroda, 18 November, 1817.

143 N.A.I. For. Sec. 1817 : O.C. No. 149-153, 19 December, 1817 : A Circular Letter to the Chiefs of Bundelkhand, 17 October, 1817.
Also : Please see Appendix No., II.

144 M.I.O.L.L. Extracts from Capt. Carnac's despatch to the Governor of Bombay, 9 September 1815.

145 B G.R. D. No. 303 : Malcolm to Hislop : 23 October, 1817.

146 B.G.R. D. No. 439, Maj. Gen. W.G. Keir to Carnac, 14 December, 1817.

147 N.A.I. For. Sec. 1817 : O.C. No. 13-14, 28 November, 1817 : Metcalfe to Adam, Delhi, 1 November, 1817.

148 N.A.I. For. Sec. 1817 : O.C. No. 304, 22 October, 1817 : Letter from Begum Samru Zeboor-Nissa Begum.

149 N.A.I. For. Sec. 1817 : O.C. No. 13-14, 28 November, 1817 : Metcalfe to Adam, 1 November, 1817.

150 N.A.I. For. Sec. 1818 : O.C. No. 23-25, 9 January: 1818, Letter from Fyz Mohammad Khan, received 21 November, 1817.

151 N.A.I. For. Sec. 1818 : O.C. No. 13-14, 28 November, 1817 : Metcalfe to Adam, Delhi, 1st November, 1817.

152 N.A.I. For. Sec. 1817 : O.C. No. 13-14, 28 November, 1817 : Metcalfe to Adam, Delhi, 1st November, 1817.

153 *Ibid.*
Also : N.A.I. For. Sec. 1818 : O.C. No. 23-35, 9 January 1818, Donkin to Raja of Bharatpur and a reply from him. Supplement to the Government of India Gazetteer, November 27, 1817 mentions the figure to be 120 Cavalry, which joined Gen. Donkin's Divisions on the 6th November.

154 N.A.I. For. Sec. 1817 : O.C. No. 13-14. 28 November, 1817, Metcalfe to Adam, Delhi, 1 November, 1817.

155 Blacker : *Memoir*, p. 13.

156 N.A,I. For. Sec. 1817 : O.C. No. 24-30, 28 November, 1817, A.H. Cole, Resident at Mysore to Brig. Gen. Sir J. Malcolm, Mysore, 10 October, 1817.

157 N.A.I. For. Sec. 1817 : O.C. No. 93-94, 26 December, 1817, Wauchope to Adam, Camp Talgaon, 14 November, 1817.

158 Sutherland : *Sketches of the Relations*, p. 80.

159 N.A.I. For. Sec. 1818 : O.C. No. 23-35, 9 January, 1818, Letter from Maharaja Ranjit Singh of Lahore, received on 28 November, 1817.

8

British Military Preparations

Plan of Lord Hastings

The problems that Hastings faced, whether of Nepal, the Marathas, the Pathans or the Pindaris, needed careful deliberation and preparation. Hastings, a soldier-statesman, was eminently qualified to deal with them.

Having decided to crush and exterminate the Pindari menace and to deal with all those who aided and abetted them, he proceeded vigorously with necessary preparations and deployed all the resources to execute them.[1] He collected the largest and strongest army that India had till then sent.[2] It numbered about 1,20,000 soldiers including the military resources of the Presidencies.[3] In these preparations, he took into account the possible forces that might combine with the Pindaris.[4] He made a rough calculation, on the basis of the approximate strength of the various Indian chiefs, that an army of about 2,50,000 men with about 600 guns might take the field against the British. His military acumen could not allow him to overlook this factor. No aspect of the campaign was, therefore, ignored. Grain sufficient for two months was collected, half of which was to accompany the army into the field. Grain and fodder were stored in Asirgarh and Hindia, the two forts ceded by Scindia.

It will not be out of place to mention here that the cost of putting the 'Grand Army' in the field and the consequent campaign was vast and on "the large and most expensive scale, still the ultimate saving of charge and increase of reputation from avoiding a warfare protracted indefinitely from year to year, were objects worth any sacrifice," and outweighed the expense.[5] Hastings determined to assume the direction of the operations.[6] This was necessary to contract all obstacles that might come in the way by open or secret maneuvres of the Pindaris or Indian chiefs.

Though the resolution for starting the Pindari operations was adopted as early as December, 1816 the army actually took the field only in October, 1817.[7] In the intervening period the Governor-General continued to make preparations quietly,[8] thereby avoiding public attention, so that "the troops might be enabled to take the field without any delay at the period appointed, before those against whom they were directed, and other powers who might be disposed to obstruct our views, should be prepared to meet us.[4]" This period was also most advantageously utilised in negotiations with Indian states.

Before commencing the war, he invited Sir John Malcolm to Calcutta for further consultations. Hastings laid bare all the state papers including the most confidential communications and secret instructions from the Board of Control and and Court of Directors and unfolded the plan for the extermination of the Pindaris, for further examination. Sir John Malcolm observed that during his eight days stay in Calcutta, he derived a greater insight into the politics and schemes of the whole of the Indian Powers than he had during the course of his former political career. On his return to Madras, he discussed the matter with Sir Thomas Hislop in the light of information he had gathered at Calcutta. He then studied the situation personally at Poona and Hyderabad. In the end, he finalised the plan with Hislop in the light of the experience he had gained at the two places. After this he visited

Nagpur also. He was, however, unable to fathom the duplicity either of the Peshwa or the Bhonsla. Meanwhile, Lord Hastings consulted Metcalfe, who submitted to him the famous 'Metcalfe Note' which advocated a policy of "war-with-a-vengeance"[10] which was accepted *in toto* by Lord Hastings.

Hastings' plan aimed at the encirclement of all the states of Rajputana and Central India by a cordon of British troops so deployed as to leave no route of escape unguarded. It was also his intention to confine all the operations within this limit. Having satisfied himself that every contingency had been amply provided for, he started on his second voyage up the Ganges on July 8, 1817 and arrived at Kanpur on September 13. On his way to Kanpur, he stopped for a few days at Patna "whither a complimentary deputation had come from Katmandoo, to which it was thought politic to show every possible attention."[11]

Theatre of Operations

The whole object of the extermination of the Pindaris may be considered limited in the sense that the Pindaris were concentrated on the banks of the Narbada, and in the dense jungles nearby. But it was no less imperative to have a close watch on the Maratha chiefs whose dominions extended far and wide.

It was, therefore, decided to close in upon them from all sides, which meant that the British forces had to be distributed all over the north in Rajputana and Central India, besides Orissa, Bombay Presidency and Hyderabad regions. A check over the Marathas required the posting of armies in the south also. Thus "it will be seen that the theatre of operations extended over the greater part of India, for the dominions of Peshwa extended far south to the Tunghbhadra, while those of Scindia reached Hindustan."[12]

It was in the table land of Malwa that the Pindari chiefs had their headquarters. Physical, climatic and vegetational growth of the area suited the Pindaris admirably and they made it their abode, maybe because of some premonitionl, design or accident.[13] In spite of their mountain strongholds, they were strategically not well placed.

Having a central situation, their headquarters were open to attack on all sides. On the south was the Narbada, on the west and the north were Scindia and Holkar, the Gujarat area of the Peshwa and the Baroda territory. The kingdoms of Bhopal and Bhonsl a surrounded their territory on the east. Except the Scindia, all the states allowed a free passage to the British armies and Scindia too, after some hesitation, agreed to give passage to them. Thus, the Pindaris were "exposed on every side except the north, to an attack from the contiguous frontiers of states through which a ready access was open to the British forces."[14]

Then, there was the Saugar land, a plain area, broken by hills and ridges covered with forests. This area was divided between Benaik Rao, Scindia and the Bhonsla.

Khandesh in the south, roughly covered the area of the Satpura mountains with very thick forests. The mountains were studded with strong forts, for which it was said that if properly defended they could have proved impregnable. The river Tapti divided the tableland of Khandesh into two parts. The area was mostly inhabited by Bhils.

Poona region, the seat of the Peshwa, was full of dense forests and very high mountains of the Western Ghats. On the extreme west of this region were the Sahyadri hills. The mountains having flat tops had a number of forts some of which were of the time of Shivaji.

Konkan, another very thickly forested and mountainous area situated between the sea and the Western Ghats, was often visited by the Pindaris. This area was once the appendage of the Peshwas.

In the north lay Rajputana, which was partly mountainous, partly desert and partly fertile plain area. The Aravali Hills and the Haraoti plateau formed the main hilly areas. They had a number of fortresses situated on their tops, like the Ranthombore, Chittore etc. It gives rise to Chambal and Luni, the two main rivers of Rajputana. Such was the wide region in which the British Army was to operate.

Governor-General's Instructions to Military and Political Staff

Lord Hastings was very particular about issuing detailed instructions to officers touching all aspects of the operations—military and political.

Instructions to Hislop

Hislop was instructed to treat all lands evacuated by the Pindaris, on political grounds, to belong to those Indian chiefs who were the rightful owners before their acquisition by the Pindaris.[15] He was specifically told that all forts, defended by garrisons and requiring prolonged seige or fight, were to be overlooked—a point of military strategy, and the main bodies of the Pindaris were to be pursued. Hastings further instructed Hislop to pursue the enemy as long as there was a prospect of overtaking them, even though it meant breaking the relay.[16]

A proclamation was also immediately issued assuring the villagers that "the Pindari will never be permitted to re-establish themselves, so that the villagers may be freed from the apprehension which might otherwise restrain them from discovering any Pindaris attempting to conceal themselves in the vicinity of their ancient stations."[17]

Instructions to Marshall

Marshall was advised not to bother about the heavy guns, equippage and superfluous stores, which he was told to leave immediately, at a safe place with a strong guard. He was further advised to pursue the Pindari parties "as long as any chance remained of overtaking and destroying them.'[18]

A rendezvous was also to be fixed, so that the light pursuing parties could reassemble there after the pursuit of the Pindaris. Hastings considered this as one that "holds out any reasonable prospect of success over an enemy as rapid and so irregular in their motions."[19]

Instructions to Tod

Tod was directed to assure Zalim Singh of Kota of absolute British protection, in consequence of his support to the British in their action against the Pindaris.[20]

Instructions to Sir David Ochterlony

Metcalfe's instructions to Sir David Ochterlony were not to proceed too far in Rajputana to prveent endangering his own position by placing Amir Khan and his army in the rear.[21]

Instructions to Jenkins

Jenkins was asked to be ready for any eventuality arising from Nagpur Raja's hostility to the British. He was allowed to requisition the services of Brig. Gen. Hardyman. At the same time instructions were issued to Nicol to post additional British troops in Nagpur Raja's territories.[22]

Wauchope appealed to Bundela chiefs to adopt such arrangements as their means permitted for the defence of the passes and fords in their territories.[23] Malcolm issued a general order warning the forces of good behaviour towards the people and not to destroy their crops.

Effect of War Preparations on Pindaris

The news of British preparations for operations had been slowly trickling to the Pindaris. The recent appeal of the British to the Indian states for help against them and the changing attitude of Scindia, who was once their god-father, excited considerable attention of the Pindaris. They realised that though the various Rajas and chiefs were secretly encouraging them in their activities and particularly urging them to resist the British, none was bold enough to give their families an asylum. They were, therefore, greatly depressed and consequently remained inactive for some time near Bhilsa in the hope that something would happen.[24]

The taking up of forward positions by the British Army brought great consternation among the Pindaris. They gave up all hopes of security as the barrier of the Narbada no more protected them. Their dismay was all the more increased by the ambiguous conduct of Scindia. While he was privately sending letters of assurance and encouragement, the public reports mentioned him as not only helping the British, but also taking active steps to prosecute the Pindaris.

In despair they wrote to Baptiste desiring positive information regarding the preparations going on against them. Baptiste in reply assured them that "such preparations were mere sound."[25] This reply did not satisfy them.

Concern for Families

Their first reaction was to find a safe place for their families. It may be observed that though the Pindaris were devoid of all sympathy, humanity and follow-feeling, they had great attachment to their families. "Even amidst their wandering life they were still susceptible of the strongest domestic attachment."[26] Chitu was particularly worried about the safety of his family. He wrote to Hindu Rao Ghatge: "until a place of refuge to the families of your slaves is in our hands we are helpless to take action against the British."[27] In another letter to Amir Khan, he made a fervent appeal to provide shelter to the Pindari families.[28] As late as November, 1817 Karim Khan and Wasil Mohammad were frantically searching for such a place for their families, who were constantly moving with them.[29]

Chitu wrote another letter to Raja Man Singh of Jodhpur to whom an appeal was made for allowing the Pindaris a shelter. He requested him for the same place which was assigned for the family of Jaswant Rao Holkar.[30] These appeals produced no results. Scindia made a frank reply regretting his inability to provide shelter to the Pindaris and their families. He wrote "At this time my friendship with the English is strong and undivided; to break it now is not advisable....to give a place for your families would be cause of immediate rupture with them."[31]

When the Pindaris realised that Scindia was not prepared to have an immediate rupture with the British, they approached his Commanders, Jaswant Rao Bhao and Baptiste. Of the two, Bhao extended an invitation to the Pindaris for shelter at Jawud.[32] Karim received a letter from Baptiste desiring him to send his family and baggage to Kumbhalmere and to prepare for a fight against the British.[33] Zalim Singh of Kota also gave a flat refusal when requested for help.

Attempt at Unity

Finding that none of the Indian princes was coming forward to their succour, the Pindaris made efforts to forge unity among themselves. Chitu tried to awaken his fellow Pindari chiefs to the grave danger in which they were placed and incited them to offer combined resistance to the British, by preparing a comman plan of action. He maintained that when the British armies crossed the Narbada, the Pindaris should separate themselves into numerous groups for cutting off British supplies and harassing their rear in all possible ways.[34] Their families were to be left in some inaccessible jungle with a strong posse of about one thousand horse and five hundred foot and some guns for their protection.

Hearing of the British advance, Chitu evacuated his cantonment at Nimawar and his fort of Satwas. He, along with all his property, guns, elephants, family baggage, left Satwas with the intention of going over to Jaswant Rao Bhao.[35] Ultimately he succeeded in finding a retreat for his family in Kumbhalmere in Rajputana. Karim Khan sent his wives and baggage to Kota.[36]

The Pindari leaders took immediate military steps. Chitu established 'chowkies' on the northern bank of the Narbada.[37] Karim Khan began raising Mewati and Arab troops.[37] Chitu, not to lag behind, also recruited infantry and cavalry, including two thousand Rohillas and Afghans,[39] paying each horseman six rupees per month.[40]

The Pindaris desperately tried to forge unity amongst themselves. With this end in view a consultation was held between Chitu, Karim Khan and Wasil Mohammad, when presents were exchanged and promises to maintain unity given.[41] It was resolved to preserve unity and unanimity.[42] The unity was, however, shortlived because of jealousy, differences and enmity between Chitu and Karim.[43] Even in the face of common danger, their unity was rancorous.

Attempts to forge unity were again made and this time they prepared a plan of operations to be adopted against the British. It was decided that the three chiefs, after organising their durras would cross the Narbada and then separate themselves. One of the divisions would cross the Narbada at Baglatir Ghat; the second was to go eastward and lay waste that region; while the third wouid follow the other two divisions in their rear.[44] This was a fine plan, but only if it could be put into execution. Nothing came out of it. Yet another attempt to forge unity was made but without success. According to this plan Baptiste, Roshan Beg, Jaswant Rao Bhao, Bappoo Scindia and all the Pindari chiefs would unite and try their fortune in one single battle against the English.[45] Like the previous one, this plan also came to naught. The unsuccessful bid for unity among the Pindaris and the unhelping attitude of Indian chiefs made the Pindari force a most disjointed and disunited lot ever to face an enemy.

Displacement of the British Army

The military preparations that were undertaken against the bands of marauders for their extermination were on such an unprecedented scale as looked almost out of all proportion to the object in view. But military strategy demanded such vast preparations. In order to strike a severe blow the army was deployed in an inward circle. The epi-centre of the circle, about seven hundred miles in radius was somewhere near Hindia.

Hislop's Appointment

Hastings was of the opinion that since operations were on a very large scale, needing co-ordination, it was necessary that the British forces be placed under one general authority, responsible for its control and regulation, thereby securing the utmost possible advantage. Such extensive authority and command required a person of great confidence, ability and personality who could win respect and obedience and exact discipline from the large forces under him.[46] Sir Thomas Hislop was such a person.[47]

Hislop was directed to "proceed with the least practicable delay to assume the command of all the troops in the Deccan" and also "to undertake the general direction and control of military operations and of the political arrangements and negotiations connected with them in that quarter." He was further vested with the entire political and military responsibility.[48] However, he was subject to the authority of the Commander-in-Chief.[49] When this appointment was made, a very great consideration was given to the fact that the Residents placed in various courts would not be interfered with in their normal duties.[50] It was, therefore, expressly declared that he was not supposed to wield any authority over the Residents. He was further directed to abstain from any "interference in the details of their official duties or in the affairs of the courts."[51] Such were the delicate tasks which Sir Thomas Hislop was to perform and he was well qualified for the job.

Malcolm's Appointment

Since it was thought that one individual may not be able to discharge such onerous work all by himself, it was deemed necessary that some other person of equal eminence should help him in the execution of his political duties.[52] Malcolm, on grounds of "his acknowledged abilities, judgement, experience and his extensive and accurate acquaintance with every branch of our British political interests,[53] was appointed as an Agent to the Governor-General "for the purpose of being a channel of communication between His Excellency and the several Residents and Political Agents....and to be employed in such negotiations with the native states and the chiefs as be empowered to prosecute."[54] While acknowledging his political acumen the Governor-General did not lose sight of his military abilities and, therefore, made a provision that Sir Thomas Hislop was empowered to avail himself of Malcolm's services on any distinct military command.[55]

Hastings also appointed the following officers as Brigadiers for the Bengal Army: Cols. Hardyman, Toone, Watson, Frith, Arnold, and D'Auvergue; Colonels Munro, Doveton, Malcolm, Floyer and Pritzler of Madras Army, and Colonel Smith of Bombay Presidency.[56]

The Grand Army was commanded by Lord Hastings himself. For convenience, the army was divided into two main divisions—the Northern and the Southern, the Armies of Hindustan and the Deccan respectively. While the Army of Hindustan was commanded by Hastings himself, that of the Deccan was commanded by Sir Thomas Hislop. The deployment of the Grand Army by Lord Hastings exhibited his thorough knowledge of the theatre of operations.

The Army of Hindustan

The Northern Army or the Army of Hindustan, commanded by Lord Hastings consisted of 29,000 infantry, 14,000 cavalry and 140 guns (both horse and foot artillery). It assembled at Sikandra and crossed the Jamna near Kalpi.[57]

Corps of Observation

The army was composed of four divisions with two Corps of Observation posted at Mirzapur and on the frontiers of South Bihar to protect the Southern frontier from any attempt at predatory incursion into British provinces.[58] The two detachments were formed for the purpose of defence, but posted to act on an offensive in case of necessity.

Under Brig. Gen. Toone

The force under Brig. Gen. Toone was posted near Oontari on the frontier of Bihar to protect the line of Upper Soane up to the South of Rohtasgur, keeping in touch with the Ramgur Battalion at Chota Nagpur.[59] Brig. Gen. Toone was directed to have a detachment always moving on the line from Ratanpur to Kairagur or Raipur, keeping a watch on the Ghats across this line.[60] He distributed his troops in such a manner as to occupy all the main passes, keep guard over them and maintain active communication with Hardyman's extreme post of Bardi. Toone arrived at Oontari on November 7, 1817.[61] One corps of Ramgur Battalion stationed at Hazaribagh was ordered to help him.

Under Brig. Gen. Hardyman

Another corps of observation was under Brig. Gen. Hardyman. It was to advance to Rewa for the purpose of securing the Bundlekhand passes, so that no Pindari could penetrate for plunder in that direction. Brig. Gen. Hardyman was joined in the beginning of November by a cavalry force of two hundred and fifty sent by the Raja of Rewa. It was not thought necessary to make any provision for defence of the Southern and Western frontiers of Bengal because it was thought that they were well-guarded by the troops already stationed at Midnapore and Cuttack. But when the Raja of Nagpur rose in revolt, a reinforcement was sent from the Bengal Presidency which included a squadron of Dragoons. Brig. Gen. Hardyman was directed to keep in touch with the Resident at Nagpur and to move at the first news of indications of hostility by the Nagpur Raja without waiting for a requisition for help from the Resident.[63]

Centre Division

The Centre Division, commanded by Maj. Gen. Brown, consisted of three Regiments of Cavalry, one of His Majesty's Foot and Light Battalions of Indian Infantry, with a number of detachments of artillery. It was assembled at Kanpur, where Hastings joined it on September 14, 1817. It crossed the Jumna on October, 26, and took up position on the Kali Sind river on November 6, though it was expected to be ready on the Kali Sind by November 1. He was instructed that in case of a war with Scindia, the Centre Division in co-operation with the Right Division under Donkin was to move down on Scindia. In case Scindia concluded an alliance with the British, it would keep a close watch upon him and prevent his going over to the enemy.

Right Division

Maj. Gen. Donkin's Right Division was formed at Agra. It consisted of two regiments of Cavalry, one regiment of Europeans and three battalions of Indian Infantry and Artillery. It reached Dholpur on the left bank of the Chambal to keep an eye on Scindia and Amir Khan. Donkin was particularly warned to be careful about the various fords on the Chambal, and to prevent the Pindaris from approaching either the Jumna or making escape through this region into Rajputana.[64] Donkin was ordered to co-operate with Hastings in holding Scindia in check. He was warned not to allow the Pindaris to pass through Scindia's territory to the British possessions south of Jumna, and if any such attempt was made, he was to inflict severest punishment upon them.[65] He was to co-operate with the force from the Deccan, if necessary,

Left Division

The Left Division was under Major General Marshall with Headquarters at Kalinjar in Bundelkhand. This Division consisted of one regiment of Indian Cavalry, two corps of Irregular Horses and five battalions of Infantry with guns. The Left Division in collaboration with the Nagpur Subsidiary Force was to look after the Western Frontier. Though this Division was expected to be in position by October, 10, it took position at Saugar by November 12, 1817 only.

Marshall was told that "the service expected from your Division is that it shall take its share in dislodging the Pindaris from their present haunts and in destroying (them) to the utmost of your power." [66] He was also ordered to respect the territories of Bhopal, a friend of the British. Marshall was warned against the possibility of Pindaris or their parties sneaking into and through the frontier of Bundelkhand absolutely unprotected, Major Cunning was deputed to look after this region with a detachment consisting of 2nd Rohilla Cavalry at Azamgarh and two troops and three Companies of 1st Battalion of the 14th Indian Infantry at Lohargaon. This was done to prevent the Pindaris harassing and disturbing the country in the absence of troops withdrawn for forward duty. Marshall was, therefore, advised to form a plan in collaboration with Wauchope for the defence of this frontier, for which he was empowered to make use of Indian forces under various chiefs. [67] The general object of this Division was to co-operate with the advanced Division of the Army of Deccan and prevent the escape of Pindaris towards Nagpur.

Reserve Division

The Reserve Division was placed under Sir David Ochterlony. It consisted of Artillery, one regiment of Indian Cavalry, two Corps of Skinner's Horse, one European and five Indian battalions and Sirmoor Battalions with some field pieces and a battering train. This Division was posted at Rewari with the intention to give strength to the negotiations carried with the Rajputs and to give cover to Delhi area. It was expected to be at Rewari by November 1, 1817.

It was realised that the services that would be required from Sir David Ochterlony very much depended upon the results of the negotiations going on with the Rajputs and Amir Khan and hence only general instructions were given to him. He was to advance to Rewari which was his headquarters. He was given three important duties to perform in case of need viz. (a) to control any forward disposition of Amir Khan; (b) to intercept any bodies of Pindaris who tried to fly west, towards Kota and Bundi; and (c) to afford support to the Rajput states in case they desired British protection.[68]

Ochterlony was reminded that any one of these undertakings or all at the same time might need his attention. He was to act in the best manner possible according to circumstances. The decision regarding the priority to these problems was left to Ochterlony's judgment and discretion. He was directed to keep in touch with Metcalfe, whose opinions and advice were to be respected by him in all political affairs.[69] He was to frame his military operations on the basis of these instructions.

He was also to keep himself in readiness for action in the event of Scindia rising in arms against the British, in which case he was to proceed against Scindia's troops in Ajmer and Marwar and interpose a force between Scindia's territories and the position of Amir Khan, thereby paralysing them both at the same time.[70] Again, in case Holkar joined Amir Khan in revolt, Ochterlony was to march against them. The Governor-General wanted Ochterlony to use the troops of various Indian chiefs near about Delhi, as auxiliaries, relieving the regular forces for field service.[71]

Army of the Deccan

The Army of the Deccan was under the general command of Sir Thomas Hislop. It amounted to 52,000 infantry, 18,000 cavalry and 62 guns. His force had five Divisions.

First Division

The First Division which was with the headquarters and commanded by Sir Thomas Hislop, consisted of a detachment of European Cavalry and two regiments of Indian Cavalry, a detachment of European Infantry, the Madras European Regiment and six battalions of Indian Infantry besides artillery. It was directed to cross the Narbada by the end of October and to occupy the position at Harda by about October 25; but was detained at Hyderabad on account of Sir Thomas Hislop's illness. It was to look after the fords of Narbada.

Before leaving Hyderabad to assume command of the Deccan Army, Sir Thomas was able to obtain a letter issued by the Nizam under his seal and signatures where by he invested him with full powers over the military and civil officers of the Hyderabad government. They were exhorted to extirpate the Pindaris and were promised rewards. He was also to make arrangements for forming depots of grain at Mulkapur, Amrawati, Nanded, Aurangabad, Ajanta, Akola, Badein and Jalna.

The First Division of Sir Thomas Hislop, because of its peculiar situation in the South, was to penetrate the Pindari haunts on the other side of the Narbada from the south, to occupy their territories, throw them out and finally to annihilate them. This Division was also assigned the task of keeping an eye on both Scindia and Holkar, and in case of a war against them, to swoop down upon their possessions in Malwa and on their capitals at Gwalior and Indore. In the end, Hislop was specially directed to pursue the enemy, as long as there was a prospect of overtaking him.

Second Division

The Second Division, also called Hyderabad Division, was placed under the command of Brig. Gen. Doveton, with headquarters at Hyderabad. It consisted of one regiment of Indian Cavalry, one of European Infantry and six Battalions of Indian Infantry along with horse and foot artillery. The Hyderabad and Berar Brigades were also with the Second Division. Doveton was assigned a position near Akola, with instruction to protect the British interest at Nagpur.[73] The Second Division was expected to assemble at Bassein by October 28.

Third Division

The Third Division, commanded by Sir John Malcolm, consisted of one regiment of Indian Cavalry, a detachment of Indian Infantry, the Russell and Elichpur Brigades and Mysore Auxiliary Horses. This Division was divided into three columns : Right Column commanded by Lt. Col. Adams, Centre Column by Sir John Malcolm, and Left Column by Lt. Col. Deacon.[74]

The Right Column was to advance on Raiseen, the Centre on Ashta and Left on Onchode. From these positions they were to advance with the greatest possible rapidity against any body of Pindaris in their vicinity and were to pursue them as long as there was any chance of success. After the pursuit of the Pindaris, the Columns were to reassemble—the Right at Bhilsa, the Centre at Ashta and the Left at Onchode.[75]

The Third Division was to move against the Pindaris across the Narbada in co-operation with the First Division.

Sir John Malcolm crossed the Narbada near Hindia on November 15, though he was expected to be at Hoshangabad by about October 25. The light corps of four battalions and 6,000 Silehedar Horses were to operate between the Second and Fourth Divisions of Doveton and Smith.[76]

Fourth Division

The Fourth or Poona Division under Brig. Gen. Lionel Smith consisted of one regiment of Indian Cavalry, a European regiment, six battalions of Indian Infantry and a body of Poona Horse under European officers. Poona was its headquarters.[77] It was intended to safeguard British interests in Poona by covering the Peshwa's territory and to operate in case of necessity against Holkar's possessions in the south. It was thought that Smith's force was likely to be confined to Khandesh to prevent the diversion of the Pindaris. The Fourth Division was expected to be in position at Biryapur by October 25. It was to march to Khandesh to cover the gap between Poona and Berar.[78]

Fifth Division

The Fifth Division consisted of the Nagpur Subsidiary Force under Lt. Col. Adam. It consisted of three corps of Horse, a contingent supplied by the Nawab of Bhopal and six battalions of Indian Infantry. Its headquarters was at Nagpur and it was to cross the Narbada at Hoshangabad.

Gen. Martindale, in Bundelkhand, was to advance towards Saugar to co-operate with Lt. Col. Adam's Division. The advance party of this Division was ready to cross the Narbada on November 10. This Division was expected to keep in touch with Brig. Gen. Marshall and to advance across the Narbada east of Bhopal.

Reserve Division

The Reserve Division under Brig. Gen. Pritzler was to be stationed on the bank of River Krishna, from where it could easily be moved to Hyderabad or Poona as the contingency arose and thus look after the area between the two rivers the Krishna and the Bhima.

One force was stationed in Cuttack to guard that frontier from the Pindaris who might attempt an entry from Nagpur side or against those who might slip through the gaps.[79]

Gujarat Force

Another force commanded by Maj. Gen. Sir W.G. Keir was kept at Baroda in Gujarat. It was to advance in such a way as to ultimately join the army of the Deccan. It was to be ready to move into Malwa to co-operate with Sir Thomas Hislop according to circumstances and to prevent the retreat of the Pindaris in Marwar and Mewar. Itwas, also, to prevent the flight of Amir Khan and Scindia in case of a showdown with them. A detachment was placed at Ratlam also. The Gujarat Force was to be ready to march from Baroda by November 1. This force was also instructed, in case of a war with Scindia and Holkar, to seize their territories in Gujarat. The Gujaratforce consisted of one contingent of 2,000 cavalry. It was also to keep an eye on the Pindaris attempting to cross the Narbada.

Brig. Gen. Munro, placed directly under the command of Sir Thomas Hislop, was directed to occupy the ceded districts of the Peshwa.

The Poona Auxiliary Horse, 5,000 Cavalry and 3,000 Infantry, were to defend the Poona territories, while one battalion of European Infantry and three battalions of Indians were posted at Poona.

Other Army Postings

Besides the general distribution of the troops as shown above, British forces continued to be maintained at the three important capitals of Hyderabad, Poona and Nagpur. Two battalions of the Madras Army were posted at Nagpur. This and a contingent of 3,000 horse and 2,000 Infantry from Nagpur Subsidiary Force were specially instructed to look after the British interests in Nagpur, besides safeguarding it from Pindari incursions.

At Hyderabad, four battalions of Nizam's own troops were placed under Major Pitman in addition to 4,000 Reformed Horse (irregular). The Second Division of Doveton was also ordered to look after the Nizam's interests.

One body of irregular Horse was to look after Guntoor. The Madras government also established a chain of defensive posts from one end of the British frontiers on the Tungbhadra, to its junction with the Krishna and thence to the Chilka Lake in Orissa. These posts were established at different distances. They were expected to keep guard over river fords and hill passes. The total troops consisted of six squadrons of dragoons, six squadrons of Indian Cavalry, nine battalions of Indian Infantry and 5,000 Mysore Horse and Foot. This force covered and guarded an area of about 850 miles in length.[80]

Proposed Plan of Campaign

Lord Hastings reached Kanpur in September. His idea was to have at least two divisions on the Narbada ready against the Pindaris in October. Besides, he wanted the two forces of the Grand Army viz., the Army of the Deccan and the Army of Hindustan to meet simultaneously at one place in Central India. But the original plan of crossing the Narbada and the two armies meeting simultaneously could not be adhered to because of two reasons.[81]

Delay in Operations

In the first place, unprecedented downpour resulted in the impracticability of the use of roads and the swelled rivers baulked down the movement of the army. The second and more important reason was the sudden illness of Hislop from 12th August to 1st October, 1817.[82] It was, therefore, thought inexpedient to advance the Bengal Army alone to the assigned position, thereby losing the great advantage of the impact of the arrival of the two armies simultaneously.[83]

After his sickness, Sir Thomas Hislop assumed command only by November 10, when the Ist and 3rd Divisions of the Deccan Army took position at Harda, near the south bank of Narbada. The 5th Division advanced to Hoshangabad by November 6. The 2nd Division was posted at Akola.[84] The 4th Division under Gen. Smith was directed to move towards Khandesh to defend the Peshwa's territories or be readily available in case of hostilities breaking out between the two. The manifestation of this hostility of the Peshwa[85] "took place sooner than was anticipated."[86] Thus the deployment of those Divisions resulted in a complete encirclement of the Pindaris.[87] Hastings should be given credit not only for his rare military acumen but also for his marvellous capacity for organisation.

Cholera in British Camp

While the British Army was in the vicinity of Gwalior, in August 1917, before the campaign opened, cholera in the most virulent form broke out in India. It soon spread with amazing rapidity. It made its appearance, for the first time, in the Eastern Districts of Bengal in Jessore near Calcutta in May and June 1817. It began to spread gradually along the Ganges and passed through Trihut, to Ghazipur and then to Rewa and Bundelkhand. It was at that time it hit the Centre Division of the Grand Army. Brig. Gen. Hardyman's force also was its victim,[88] both in Indian and European troops, but particularly in camp followers.

Hastings' Army suffered the most from that appalling epidemic, termed as 'cholera spasmodica' in the month of November. The army while passing through Bundelkhand was attacked by this disease. Lack of good, clean water, extreme heat of the season, unhygienic conditions in the tents and the unhealthy region of Bundelkhand, through which the army passed, when it was attacked by this disease, all contributed to the virulence of the epidemic. It began in a creeping manner among the camp-followers and subsequently developed into a sudden and serious affliction. For a period of about ten days the army suffered very severely. The whole camp looked like a hospital. Wilson has given a graphic account of the conditions in the British camps:

> "...a mournful silence succeeded to the animating notes of preparations which had hitherto resounded among the tents; in place of the brisk march of soldiers in the confidence of the vigour and in the pride of the discipline, were to be seen continuous and slowly moving trains of downcast mourners, carrying their comrades to the funeral pyre and expecting that their own turn would not be long delayed. Even this spectacle ceased. The mortality became so great, that hands were insufficient to carry away the bodies and they were tossed into the neighbouring ravines or hastily committed to a superficial grave on the spot where the sick had expired. The survivors then took alarm and deserted the encampments in crowds.[89] Many bore with them the seeds of the malady and the fields and the roads for many miles around were strewed with the dead."[90]

As many as two hundred persons died in a day.[91] The silence of the dead prevailed over the camp.[92] The army marched mutely not knowing who shall be the next victim. Since the army was on the march, and since not much provision had been made for the camp-followers, they were accommodated in their officers' tents. This resulted in the disease spreading to the European officers also.[93] It was at that stage that Lord Hastings, issued instructions to his staff that in case he were to die of this disease, his body was to be silently buried in the tent "lest his death should discourage the troops and embolden Scindia to attack the encampment in its prostrate condition. [94]

When the disease continued unabated,[95] and mortality was at the peak, it was decided that the whole camp be broken and set up in new and healthy surroundings. On November 10, the army changed the camp to higher, congenial and dry banks of the river Betwa at Eritch and the disease disappeared as if by magic.[96] Except for stray cases there was no instance of cholera after December 8.[97] Soon it disappeared from India, but it spread via Persia and Russia to Europe and America, and caused numerous deaths.

The loss sustained by this Division of Lord Hastings' army has been exaggerated in several accounts even to the extent of 8,000 out of the total strength of 10,000. According to Prinsep, heavy casualties occurred only among the camp followers, while the Europeans escaped with little loss. The approximate figure of dead was 764 soldiers and eight thousand camp followers.

Pindari Strength on the Eve of Operations

Various estimates were made of the strength of the Pindaris by contemporary writers and also by those who were witness to the events and who took part in their suppression. Lt. Col. Adam, Commander of the Nagpur Subsidiary Force estimated their strength at about 20,000 Cavalry and Infantry with twenty-two guns. Lt. Burton, however, gives the figure as 1,06,000 horse, 81,000 infantry and 589 guns belonging to all the Indian powers likely to fight against the British.[98] However, a correct reckoning of the strength of the Pindaris alone may be about 15,000 foot and 15,000 horse, with twenty guns. Making due allowance for exaggeration, this is a reasonable estimate of the Pindari strength on the eve of operations against them.

Inducement to Villagers

In order to impress upon the masses that the Pindari War was being fought for their good, Adam accepted Malcolm's suggestion to induce the villagers to attack and plunder the Pindaris. Arms and ammunitions were distributed among the Bhils and other villagers as a measure to help them fight the Pindaris.[99] They were also allowed to appropriate the properties seized by them from Pindaris.[100] As a result of this policy Chitu was repeatedly subjected to harassment by the villagers.[101]

The above account of British military preparations, threatening and formidable in character and appearance, shows that Lord Hastings forestalled every kind of emergency. The very flower of the three Presidencies spread themselves over a vast territory encompassing the Hindustan and the Deccan. Kaye writes that people in the country got the impression that "the Feringhees were putting forth all their immense military resources in one comprehensive effort to sweep the native principalities from the face of the earth.[102] The campaign directed by the Governor-General naturally aroused all the fear of Maratha States. They could not believe that it was directed merely againt the Pindaris.

FOOT-NOTES

[1] It took the Governor-General "more than a year to draw up an effective plan for the destruction of the Pindaris." Ganguly : *Select Documents*, p. 43.

[2] The military operations "on which Lord Hastings entered were upon a larger scale even than those of Lord Wellesley and embraced the whole extent of the country from the Kistna to the Ganges and from Cawnpore to Guzerat." Marshman: *History of India*, p. 328.

A combination "so extensive under the direction of one authority, has nothing exactly similar, or parallel to it, in European warfare. The armies which attacked the power of Bonaparte, after the failure of the Russian expedition were indeed drawn from points scarcely more distant than were the corps lately co-operating in India."
Blacker : *Memoir*, p. 8.

[3] Wilson gives the figure as 1,13,000 troops.

4 "The total strength of the native powers eventually arrayed against us was estimated as follows:—

	Horse	*Foot*	*Guns*
Scindia	15,000	16,000	140
Holkar	20,000	8,000	107
Peshwa	28,000	14,000	37
Bhonsla	16,000	18,000	85
Amir Khan	12,000	10,000	200
Pindaris	15,000	15,000	20
	1,06,000	81,000	589"

Lt. Burton: *Printed for the General Staff:* p. 11, Simla.

5 Prinsep: *Political and Military Transactions:* Vol. I, p.413.

6 Hastings explained the reasons for taking the Command personally. He wrote : "It would be requisite that I should proceed to Upper Province...... my being on the spot would be so ostensible a proof of the determination of the Government to carry the matter through and would be so well understood by Scindia and Holkar."

N.A.I. For. Sec. 1816: O. C. No. 17, 28. December, 1816, Governor-General's Minute, 19 December, 1816.

7 This was because "the hot winds would be at hand; and I dare not expose to such a season our troops...which have been singularly debilitated by the most servere and extensive epidemic fever ever known in India." *Private Journal,* Hastings, p. 270.

8 The preparations were made "with as much privacy as possible, in order to avoid giving alarm to those against whom they were directed." E. Thornton. *History of the British Empire in India,* Vol. IV, p. 425.

9 For. Misc. 124A: Hastings to Secret Committee, 1 March, 1820, p. 384.

10 *Calcutta Review:* Vol. XXIV-1855, pp. 142-143.

11 Prinsep: *History,* Vol. II, p.17, 1825.

12 Burton: *For the General Staff,* Simla, P. 15.

13 This was the one reason why the Pindaris never undertook excursions prior to or during the rains. It is surprising how Wellesley suggested the rainy season to be the best season for starting operations against the Marathas. Though of course it is to be noted that he had pontoon bridges and boats ready to cross the swollen river, for which Lord Hastings had made no provision in his operations.

14 The Pindaris "have for a long time past found security of their families whilst absent on their destructive excursions." Tod: *Origin*, p. 21.

15 Wilson : *History of the British Empire*, p. 162.

16 N.A.I. For. Sec. 1817: O.C. No. 1-2, 12 December, 1817: Hastings to Hislop, 20 November, 1817.

17 N.A.I. For. Sec. 1817: O.C. No. 77-79, 19 December, 1817: Letter No. 12, Hastings to Hislop, Camp Eritch, 25 November, 1817. Also: "Our troops instead of being kept in large bodies, at stationery positions, were divided into small detachments and spread through the country, with orders to be continually in easy motion, each within the limits of a certain range and to pursue closely every party that came near it, until it fell within the range of a fresh detachment, the enemy would always be distracted and harassed in their movements."
N.A.I. For. Pol. 1817: O.C. No. 95, 22 February, 1817: Russell to Adam, Hyderabad, 23 January, 1817.

18 N.A.I. For. Sec. 1817: O.C. No. 1-2, 12 December, 1817: Letter No. 10, Hastings to Hislop, 20 November, 1817, para 1.

19 N.A.I. For. Sec. 1817: O.C. No. 58-63, 19 December, 1817: Nicol to Marshall, 25 November, 1817, p. 34.

20 *Ibid.*, para 35.

21 N.A.I. For. Sec. 1817: O.C. No. 3-9, 26 December, 1817: Adam to Tod, Camp Eritch, 3 December, 1817.

22 N.A.I. For. Sec. 1817: O.C. No. 3-9. 26 December, 1817: Adam to Metcalfe, Camp Eritch, 3 December. 1817.

23 N.A.I. For. Sec. 1817: 10-12, 26 December, 1817: Adam to Lt. Col. James Nicol, Camp Eritch, 3 December, 1817.

24 N.A.I. For. Sec. 1817 : O.C No. 21-22, 26 December, 1817 : Adam to Wauchope, 3 December, 1817, para 2.

25 N.A.I. For. Sec. 1817 : O.C. No. 46-57, 19 December, 1817 : Marshall to Nicol, Camp Seemeerah, 23 October, 1817.

26 N.A.I. For. Sec. 1817 : O.C. No. 17-18. 21 June, 1817 : Close to Adam, Gwalior, 29 May, 1817.

27 Murray : *History*, Vol. II, p. 189.

28 N.A.I. For. Sec. 1817 : O.C. No. 1-3, 11 February, 1817 : Close to Adam, Gwalior, 23 January, 1817, enclosing substance of a letter No. 1 from Chitu to Hindoo Rao Ghatge, 25 December, 1816.

29 Chitu wrote to Amir Khan "that the place which was formerly assigned for the residence of Holkar should be appointed for us... and from it my heart may be set at ease and that I may face the English with confidence. Then for once ! by the helping of God, and the fortunes of the exalted, to the environs of Calcutta the tumult shall be spread. The whole country shall be consigned to

ashes and such distress shall they be reduced to that the accounts shall not fail to reach you."
N.A.I. For. Sec. 1817 : O.C. No. 1-3, 11 February, 1817 :
Close to Adam, enclosing letter No. 2. from Chitu to Amir Khan.

30 N.A.I. For. Sec. 1817 : O.C. No. 35-39, 26 December, 1817 :
Marshall to Nicol, Camp near Seronj, 30 November, 1817.

31 In this letter Chitu uttered the most prophetic and pregnant words, words with great future in their store and words which proved most true as time showed. Chitu wrote "But if this is not to be your pleasure, recollect this tribe (the English) are wise and full of penetration and by slow imperceptible degrees will root out every chief of Hindustan. Do not forget these words of your slave."
N.A.I. For. Sec. 1817 : O.C No. 1-3, 11 February, 1817 :
Letter No. 3 Chitu to Man Singh of Jodhpur.
In another letter from Chitu to Hindu Rao Ghatge, Chitu made another very significant remark : He wrote, "recollect, when we are extinguished, how long will you be spared."
N.A.I. For. Sec. 1817 : O.C. No. 44-45, 10 May, 1817 : Close to Adam, Gwalior, 20 April, 1817, enclosing substance of a letter from Chitu to the address of Hindu Rao Ghatge, dated 31 March, 1817.

32 N.A.I. For. Sec. 1817 : O.C. No. 1-3, 11 February, 1817 :
Close to Adam, enclosing Letter No. 2 from Chitu to Amir Khan.

33 N.A.I. For. Sec. 1817 : O.C. No. 3-4, 4 February , 1817 :
Close to Adam, Gwalior, 10 January, 1817.

34 N.A.I. For. Pol. 1817 : O.C. No. 35, 19 Sept. 1817 : Jenkins to Adam, Nagpur, 25 August, 1817. Enclosing a substance of a Paper of Intelligence for Karim's camp, 19 August, 1817.

35 N.A.I. For. Sec. 1817 : O.C. No. 3-4, 4 February, 1817 :
Close to Adam, 10 January, 1817 : Enclosing Akhbar dated the 20th of Mohurrum.

36 N.A.I For. Pol. 1817 : O.C. No. 102, 22 February, 1817 :
Jenkins to Adam, Nagpur, 3 February, 1817.

37 N.A.I. For. Sec. 1817 : O.C. No. 54, 19 December, 1817 :
Marshall to Nicol, 25 November, 1817.

38 N.A.I. For. Pol. 1817 : O.C. No. 46-47, 21 November, 1817 :
Jenkins to Adam. Enclosing intelligence from Chitu's camp, Nagpur, 22 October, 1817.

39 B.G.R. D. No. 302, Pol. Deptt : Malcolm to Hislop, Hoshangabad, 23 October, 1817. Enclosing substance of a letter from the Munshi of Poona Subsidiary Force, 17 Nov. 1817.
Also : N.A.I. For Pol. 1817 : O.C. No. 15-16, 15 August, 1817 : Jenkins to Adam, Nagpur, 14 July, 1817 : Translation of a substance of a Paper of Intelligence from the camp of Wasil Mohammad, 8 July, 1817.

40 N.A.I. For. Sec. 1817 : O.C. No. 9-10, 30 August, 1817 : T.H. Maddock, Acting Superintendent of Political Affairs, Banda, 10 August, 1817.

41 B.G.R.D. No. 438, Pol. Deptt. 1817 : Intelligence from Chitu's camp, 12 October, 1817.

42 B.G.R.D. No. 437, Pol. Deptt. 1817 : Translation of an intelligence from Karim's camp.

43 N.A.I. For. Pol. 1817 : O.C. No. 34, 7 November, 1817 : Jenkins to Adam, Nagpur, 28 September, 1817.

44 N.A.I. For. Pol. 1817 : O.C. No. 42-43, 7 November, 1817 : Close to Adam, Extracts and Translations from Akhbars, Gwalior, 5 October, 1817 : "Cheetoo from his numerous troops had become arrogant that he would agree to no terms of friendship with Kureem."

45 B.G.R.D. No. 438, Pol. Deptt. 1817 : Intelligence from Karim's camp.

46 N.A.I. For. Pol. 1817 : O.C. No. 9-10, 28 October, 1817 : Jenkins to Adam, Nagpur, 9 October, 1817 : Encolsing a Paper of Intelligence from the camp of Wasil Mohammad, dated 3 October, 1817.

47 N.A.I. For. Sec. 1817 : O.C. No. 1, 10 May, 1817 : Governor-General's Minute, 10 May, 1817.
Hastings wrote that so "extensive and important a command can be vested only in an officer of high rank and consideration, possessing the confidence of the Governor-General in Council, capable of being charged with large political as well as military powers."

48 N.A.I. For. Sec. 1817 : O.C. No. 2, 10 May, 1817 :
Moira, Edmonstone, Seton and Dowdeswell wrote, ".........assumption by his Excellency Lt. Gen. Sir. Thomas Hislop of personal command of all troops in the Deccan and of the general control, subject to the authority of the Governor-General in Council only, of the military operations and political negotiations and arrangements connected with the proposed service in that quarter of India."

49 B.G.R.D. No. 300, Pol. Deptt. 1817 : Moria, Edmonstone, Seton and Dowdeswell to Sir Thomas Hislop. Ft. William, 10 May, 1817.

50 N.A.I. For. Sec. 1817: O.C. No. 1, 10 May, 1817: Governor-General's Minute, 10 May, 1817.

51 At this time Close was Resident at Scindia's Court, Metcalfe with Holkar at Delhi, Jenkins at Nagpur, Russell at Hyderabad, and Elphinstone at Poona.

52 N.A.I. For. Sec. 1817 : O.C. No. 1, 10 May, 1817 : Governor-General's Minute, 10 May, 1817.

53 Sir John Malcolm "on whose zeal, talent and judgement I feel assured that I may rest with confidence as far as successful execution of this service as the intangible nature of the enemy will admit." N.A.I. For. Sec. 1817 : O.C. No. 77-79, 19 December, 1817 : Letter No. 12, Hastings to Hislop, Camp Eritch, 25 November, 1817.

54 N.A.I. For. Sec. 1817 : O.C. No. 1, 10 May, 1817 : Governor-General's Minute, 10 May, 1817.

55 *Ibid.*

56 *Ibid.*

57 Blacker : *Memoir*, p. 10.

58 For. Misc. 124 A : Hastings to the Secret Committee, 1 March, 1820. p, 384, para 4.

59 N.A.I. For. Sec. 1817 : O.C. No. 3-6, 26 September, 1817 : Adam on the Ganges to W.A. Brooks, A.G.G. at Benaras, 9 September, 1917.

60 For. Misc. 124 A: Hastings to the Secret Committee, 1 March, 1820. p. 384, para 5.

61 N,A,I. For. Sec. 1817 : O.C. No. 64-66, 19 December, 1817 : Jenkins to Brig. Gen. Toone, Dinapur, 23 October, 1817.

62 Burton mentions the date of arrival at Oontari as 6th November, 1817.

63 N.A.I. For. Sec. 1817 : O.C. No. 31-34, 26 December, 1817 :
James Nicol to Brig. Gen. Hardyman, HQ. Camp at Laherie, 3 December, 1817.

64 Brig. Gen. Frith Commanding Agra was directed to proceed to the various fords at Dholpur to prevent the passage of th e Pindaris in that direction.
N.A.I. For. Sec. 1817 : O.C. No. 31-34, 26 December, 1817 :
Nicol to Brig. Gen. Frith, 4 December, 1817.

65 Donkin was instructed to "advance to Dholpur on the Chambal to command the principal fords of the river, and to co-operate with the Division under Commander-in-Chief in holding Scindia in check at Gwalior." This plan would result in "preventing the Pindaris from approaching the Jumna." N.A.I. For. Sec. 1817 : O.C. No. 24-26, 7 November, 1817 : Nicol to Maj. Gen. Donkin, 9 October, 1817.

66 N.A.I. For. Sec. 1817 : O.C. No. 24, 28 October, 1817 : J. Nicol, Adjutant General of the Army to Maj. Gen. Marshall, 5 October, 1817, Headquarters, Kanpur.

67 N.A.I. For.Sec. 1817 : O.C. No. 13-14, 14 November, 1817 : Nicol to Marshall, Headquarter Camp at Bellarah Mow, 19 October, 1817.

68 N.A.I. For. Sec. 1817 : O.C. No. 17-18, 14 November 1817 : Nicol to Maj. Gen. Sir David Ochterlony, HQ. Camp Jooee, 16 October, 1817.

69 N.A.I. For. Sec. 1817 : O.C. No. 17-18, 14 November, 1817 : Nicol to Maj. Gen. Sir David Ochterlony, Headquarter camp Jooee, 16 October, 1817.

70 B.G.R. D. No. 301, Pol. Deptt. 1817 : Extract from Instructions to Sir Thomas Hislop under date, 6 October, 1817.

71 N.A.I. For. Sec. 1817 : O.C. No. 1-4, 17 October, 1817 : Adam at Kanpur to Metcalfe, Kanpur, 26 September, 1817.

72 20,000 camp followers also accompanied the army.
Burton : *The Mahratta and Pindari War:* p. 20.

73 This was necessary because the Raja of Nagpur "had become an object of suspicion."

74 N.A.I For. Sec. 1817 : O.C. No. 75-76, 19 December, 1817 : Hislop to Hastings, Headquarters of the Army of Deccan, Camp at Hurdah, 14 November, 1817.

75 *Ibid.*

76 M.I.O.L.L. For. Misc. Vol. No. 521 (6) Document No. 282.

77 N.A.I. For. Sec. 1817 : O.C. No. 1, 10 May, 1817 :
Lord Moira in his Minute wrote, "The Divisions under Col. Doveton and Col. Smith, are in fact armies and far exceed the largest amount of forces ever collected at any one time under either Lord Lake, or the Duke of Wellington in the wars of 1803 and 1804."

78 Burton : *For the General Staff* : p. 20.

79 For. Misc. 124 A : Hastings to the Secret Committee : 1 March, 1820, p. 384, para 5.

80 Burton : *For the General Staff* : p. 20.

81 "It happened that this year there had been an uncommon, draught in Hindustan, while in the Deccan, the monsoon, which should have gradually subsided in the month of September, augmented its violence in a manner unexampled." Blacker : *Memoir* p. 39.

82 "In consequence, however, the extra-ordinary severity of the monsoon and the illness of Sir Thomas Hislop who was detained on that account a considerable time at Hyderabad, the troops of the Deccan were unable to reach their destined position on the Nerbudda before the middle of November. This retardment necessarilly compelled me to delay the march of the Bengal division."
For. Misc. 124 A : *Pindari and Maratha Wars :* Letter from Hastings to Secret Committee : 1 March, 1820, para 4.

83 "It being inexpedient to place the latter in circumstances which would deprive it of those advantages of combined operation and support, which .... it had been a chief object of the Governor-General to secure."
Thornton : p. 442.

84 Blacker said that "Doveton was directed to move his Headquarter to a position immediately in the rear of Mulkapur, either above or

below the Berar Ghats, with the view and possible necessity of beseiging Asirgarh."

85 Infra pp. 288-292.

86 Wilson : *History of British India*, p. 166.

87 "The plan of Lord Hastings embraced the whole circle of Reserved possessions of Scindia and Holkar including like-wise a great part of Rajputana. Within these limits it was his intention wholly to confine the whole campaign by surrounding them."
Prinsep : Vol. II, p. 10.

88 N.A.I. For. Sec. 1817 : O.C. No. 46-57, 19 December, 1817, Hardyman to Nicol, 3 November, 1817.

89 "Desertions succeeded to the amount of several thousands."
Blacker : *Memoir*, p. 96.

90 Wilson : *History*, p. 179.

91 Blacker : *Memoir*, p. 96.

92 "The usual bustle and hum of a crowded camp was changed into an awful silence, broken only by the groans of the sick and lamentations over the dead."
Murray : *History*, p. 19.

93 "Wilson placed the figure of European casualty at five officers and 143 men of European force and according to an Official return : Within ten days six European officers and 200 soldiers, with 300 sepoys and several thousands of the followers of the army were buried. In the same period, from deaths or desertion caused by the dread of the epidemic, the camp diminished in number...."
Fitzclarence, p. 45.

94 Marshman : *Abridgement* : p. 329.
Also : Surgeon Corbyn of the Bengal Establishment in his Book '*The Treatises on Epidemic Cholera*' mentioned that His Lordship was himself apprehensive of dying of the disease and had given secret instructions to be buried in his tent, that his death might not add to the discouragement of the troops or tempt the enemy to attack the division in its crippled state."
Wilson : *History* : Footnote 1 on p. 178.

95 "Our troops, which, native as well as European, have been singularly debilitated by the most severe and extensive epidemic fever ever known in India. The 87th Regiment alone has buried above one hundred and twenty men..."
Private Journal : Hastings, p. 270.

96 Adverting to the sudden change in the abatement of the disease it was reported that "yesterday and today have produced such material alteration in the health of the camp, that we may look on the disease as extinguished. All is now cheerfulness among the people."
Letter of 23rd Nov. 1817, Supplement to the *Government of India Gazette*, December 4, 1817.

97 Mr. Jamieson was of the view that this sudden and almost complete disappearance of Cholera was due not because of change of the place, but because of the nature of the disease itself, which does not remain at one particular place for long. *Report on the Epidemic Cholera Morbus in the Bengal Provinces* in the years of 1817, 1818 & 1891. By Assistant Surgeon J. Jamieson, Secretary to the Medical Board, Calcutta, 1820.

98 Burton : *For the General Staff*, p. 11.

99 N.A.I. For. Sec. 1818 : O.C. No. 8-45, Delzell to Chief Secretary, St. George, Madras.

100 N.A.I. For. Sec. 1818 : O.C. No. 10-12, 1 May, 1818, Adam to Malcolm, Camp at Koolwall, 8 April, 1818.

101 N.A.I. For. Sec. 1818 : O.C. No. 49-52, 17 April, 1818, Hislop to Moira, Camp at the bottom of the Samrval Ghat, 9 February, 1818.

102 Kaye : *Life of Malcolm*, Vol. II, pp. 188-189.

9

Operations against the Pindaris

Opening of the Campaign

Lord Hastings, now an old man of sixty-five, took the field with tremendous enthusiasm. When the operations against the Pindaris began in November, they occupied positions between Gyaraspur in Bhilsa to Shujawalpur, a distance of about one hundred miles. On the left was Wasil Mohammad's durra in the centre was Karim Khan's and on the right Chitu's.[1] Each of the durras consisted of about 8,000 cavalry and infantry. They had twenty-two guns, Chitu having ten. Karim Khan and Wasil Mohammad had six each. Their intention was to concentrate their entire force near Bhopal. However, this position of the Pindaris did not remain static and was soon given up as the Army of the Deccan began its march towards the Narbada.

Sir Thomas Hislop had his own plan of attack, according to which, the Third Division was to cross at Baglateer Ghat and advance via Ashta. The Fifth Division after crossing at Oontari Ghat near Hoshangabad was to advance via Raiseen. The Left Division under Lt. General Marshall of the Army of Hindustan was to advance on Bhilsa from Raili, intercepting the fugitive Pindaris, trying to escape towards Bundelkhand or the upper part of the Narbada. Marshall crossed the Narbada on November 21, 1817. The First Division under the immediate command of Sir John Malcolm was to cross at Hindia and to advance for Vinchode and intercept the Pindaris should they flee westwards, or to act as a Reserve to the Third Division, as circumstances required.

The Fifth Division crossed the Narbada on the 14th, and on the 15th they were on the right bank. The Third Division crossed the Narbada on November 15, at Baglateer Ghat, while the Reserve crossed it at Hindia. It was thought necessary to leave some force at Hoshangabad to keep in readiness for action in Nagpur should it be necessary. Accordingly, orders were passed for a detachment from this force, consisting of three battalions of cavalry and one battalion of Infantry to be left there.

Hindia, according to the terms of the treaty with Scindia, was occupied by the British forces on November 21, by a party of Infantry which entered the town under the cover of darkness.[2]

Meanwhile, the reinforced Third Division of Brig. Gen. Sir John Malcolm crossed over and advanced on November 16, for Ashta,[3] Chitu's stronghold, via Sundelpur, Harringaon and Kirwani Ghat—one of the best passes into Malwa from the south, where he reached on November 21. Malcolm was able to capture a fort held by one of Chitu's chief officers. Chitu, of course, did not wait for the British to approach. He retreated with his whole force towards Indore so hastily that Malcolm had no chance, whatever, of overtaking him.[4]

When Malcolm arrived at Ashta, he learnt that the Pindaris, on receiving the news of the British forces crossing the Narbada, had moved in a northerly direction. Malcolm, therefore, made a speedy advance in the same direction in concert with Lt. Col. Adams, with whom he was in continual communication. Adam crossed the Narbada on November 14 and headed for Seronj, where Wasil Mohammad's durra had earlier moved. Marshall reported that 4,000 Pindaris belonging to Wasil Mohammad went towards Saugar, where they perpetrated enormous atrocities on its inhabitants.[5]

From Ashta, Malcolm marched to punish Karim's durra which had assembled in the vicinity of Shujawalpur. Chitu and Karim's Pindaris made for Kokra. About a thousand of them were near Nulkhera and Jeerapur, while their families moved towards the perganna of Omatwara.[6] Gen. Malcolm then moved to Shujawalpur. Chitu's Pindaris fled from Tullain towards Chapra, and Karim's from Bersia to Rahatgarh.[7]

Wasil Mohammad, hearing of the British crossing the Narbada, immediately moved to Imlani, on the way to Seronj. The Pindaris were encumbered with their families and moveable property,[8] and were on the retreat. Lt. Col. Adams and Malcolm crossed the Narbada, almost on the same day, and after providing for the defence of Narbada from Jabalpur to Hindia, advanced towards Raiseen and then upon Bersia, the stronghold of Karim Khan and almost simultaneously upon Ganj Basonda, the principal station of Wasil Mohammad. They arrived at both the places on November 27, 1817. They found them deserted. The durras of Karim and Wasil having withdrawn, the Pindaris—combined parties of Karim and Wasil—fled towards Kolarus and then to Bahadurgarh, the seat of Baptiste.[9] The Pindaris, during the course of their flight, continued to plunder.

Having got an inkling about the movement of the Pindaris towards Gwalior, Adjutant General Nicol issued immediate orders to Lt. Col. Philpot to march with all possible speed via Jhansi and Datia to the ford at Sonari Ghat, from where he was to prevent them from reaching Gwalior.[10] Marshall also proceeded towards Kolarus presuming that either he would be able to check the advance of the Pindaris, or his movement will have the effect of driving them in the direction of Gen. Donkin's division, or that of Lt. Col. Philpot, who was then at Barwa Sagar near Jhansi.[11] It is not easy to conjecture what would have happened had the

Pindaris succeeded in establishing contacts with Scindia. However, nothing untoward happened, as the Pindaris were checked in their progress towards Gwalior. On hearing that Wasil Mohammad and Karim Khan had moved to the south, Lt. Col. Adams, who was following the same route, sent Major Clarke to pursue them and himself marched to Raiseen on the 22nd, where he learnt of the movements of Maj. Gen. Marshall of the Left Wing. However, it was learnt that the Pindaris were not inclined to go towards the south as anticipated by the British. Accordingly, Lt. Col. Adams crossed the Narbada on November 14, and marched to Raiseen from where he moved to Railee, Saugar, Rahatgarh and Ganj Basonda. The Fifth Division after establishing a depot at Gulgaon, given by the Nawab of Bhopal, marched towards Bersia in pursuit of Karim Khan. But he had moved towards Agra and Wasil Mohammad was on the way to Shergarh via Gutwa Dawnga. Gen. Marshall reached Seronj on November 30. The Killedar, who had earlier refused to receive Pindari families, received him well.

Meanwhile Sir John Malcolm after establishing a post at Ashta, followed Chitu. He soon received information that some Pindaris of Chitu's party had occupied the fort of Talyne, about thirty-two miles from this camp. Malcolm immediately despatched Capt. James Grant with a body of 1,200 Mysore Horse in the night, in the expectation that the fort would be surrounded before day-break. Capt. Grant made a swift march of thirty two miles and surprised the garrison, and forced them to surrender. Wahid Kunwar, an adopted son of Chitu, and fifty infantry and a few horse were captured.[12] The Third Division moved to Shujawalpur and Talyne on November 26.

This movement of the Third Division under Malcolm and that of Maj.Gen. Marshall and Lt. Col. Adam drove out the Pindaris from their haunts and the entire territory upto the Narbada was combed clear of them except stray bands or the individual Pindaris who might have mingled themselves with the masses. The first task being over, new points and new targets were fixed and future operations planned out for Maj. Gen. Marshall, Lt. Col. Adams and Brig. Gen. Smith, viz., Raghogarh, Raigarh and Susner respectively.

Lt. Col. Adams left a sizable portion of his artillery at Bersia, under the care of five companies of Indian Infantry. Adam was at Rajgarh on December 4, and then at Manohar Thana, in the Kota territory, on the 8th, where he received his supplies. Meanwhile, the Pindaris moved towards Kolarus and Narwar.

Lord Hastings ordered Marshall to divest himself of all heavy guns, baggage and other superfluous stores so that he could move with rapidity. Accordingly Maj. Gen. Marshall divided the Third Division into two parts, one of which was left at Seronj with all heavy baggage and guns,[13] and the other, lightly equipped, was sent on for forward march. This was delayed from November 30 to December 7, due to several reasons. Marshall maintained that the distance between the Pindaris and his Division was considerable, while the Centre Division was nearer their positions. Secondly, he thought that if he pursued the Pindaris, they might take shelter in the Jumna ravines. Thirdly, he could not take for granted the loyalty of Amir Khan under whose care he had left his baggage and guns. However, the Commander-in-Chief disapproved of the delay at Seronj.[14]

Sir John Malcolm, placed as he was, attached the greatest importance to apprehending the Pindari leader Chitu, who had all along been the chief object of his exertions. Immediately after the crossing of the Narbada by the British, Chitu had taken a more westerly route than Karim Khan or Wasil Mohammad. The *akhbars* from Chitu's camp stated that the durra moved on October 27 and 29, 1817, from Pepertoun with 13,000 or 14,000 Horses and Foot to the village of Kokra on the Parvati river, 35 miles from Pepertoun.[15] It was feared by Malcolm that the three chiefs of Scindia, Jaswant Rao Bhao, Ambaji Pant, and Annah Bhao might give protection to Chitu and other Pindaris. Though Scindia was a British ally and his chiefs were supposed to be helping the British, Malcolm believed them "to be so averse to the destruction of the Pindaris as to forbid any well-founded reliance on their co-operation."[16] Malcolm, therefore, warned them of the consequences of such a step. What a contrast to Zalim Singh, whom Malcolm considered "the most important man on this scene !"[17]

Malcolm's Third Division was joined by the Russell Brigade, whereafter, leaving all encumbrances to follow under a Reserve, Malcolm with a light detachment including 3000 Mysore Horse and Four Horse Artillery guns marched towards Nalkhera. Meanwhile, Chitu received a check at Narod on the Kota frontier, from where he proceeded towards Mahidpur. On learning this Malcolm immediately marched towards Saugar, in close proximity to Holkar's army, where he reached on December 4.

Though Malcolm never lost sight of Chitu, he failed to check him in his flight. Chitu was able to escape the fury of the Third Division because of the favourable conditions in the territory under Holkar, and his diplomatic declaration that he was going to Poona to join the Peshwa via Indore and Mahisasur. Finding his force inadequate to launch an attack on the formidable combination of the two forces of Holkar and Chitu, then at Indore, Malcolm sought Hislop's guidance who was already moving towards him. Malcolm, however, continued his march and reached Shahjahanpur, where he was joined by his baggage, guns and reserve. At that stage, under instructions from Hislop, Malcolm detached 600 Mysore Horse to join the First Division. On December 11, Malcolm reached Ursoda near Tajpur in the expectation of instructions from Sir Thomas Hislop. Meanwhile, Satwas was captured.[18]

The First Division of the Army of the Deccan was at Nimawar, on the right bank of the Narbada. Hislop decided to march on the road to Ujjain, which was on the left bank of the river. The Third Division was directed to keep on the right bank. Maj. Lushington was posted at Unchode to prevent the escape of the Pindaris into the Deccan. This was necessitated by the sudden withdrawal of the Fourth Division to Poona.

On December 3, the First Division moved to Sandalpur and then to Soankeir, where it halted and on December 7, it was at Unchode. Brig. Gen. Frith, officer commanding at Agra, was directed by Nicol to detach half of the 2nd Battalion of 2nd Indian Infantry with two field pieces to the fords at Dholpur to prevent the passage of any party of Pindaris in that direction.[19] Hastings directed the Gujarat Division at Baroda to place itself under the orders of Sir Thomas Hislop and asked Sir W. G. Keir to proceed to Ujjain.

Meantime, Holkar's generals itching for action were staging rowdy demonstrations against the British. Hislop on learning the same, recalled Sir John Malcolm in order to reorganise the plan of operation. In the light of the prevailing circumstances at Indore and the fact that South Malwa was now rid of the Pindaris, Sir John Malcolm was directed to reach Tajpur near Ujjain and was to wait for further instructions.

Hislop then left Soankeir and reached Duttana-Muttana. On December 14, Malcolm met Hislop at Ursoda camp and returned the same night with orders to leave for Ujjain the following morning. On 12th December, both the First and the Third Divisions encamped on the left bank of the Seepra. The army was then arranged in such a manner as to command passages to Ujjain and the road to Mahidpur, where the combined forces of Holkar and Chitu were stationed.

The various divisions on march in the Southern Malwa were able to disperse and expel the Pindaris from that region. All this while, the Grand Army was also moving and converging upon them. As if from the frying-pan into fire, the fugitive Pindaris trying to escape the fury of the First and Third Divisions fell right into the arms of the Grand Army, then moving towards them. Caught between the two, the Pindaris were completely crushed.

Movements of the Grand Army

Though Lord Hastings was very well-placed and secure on the banks of the Kali Sind, he was forced to leave for Erich on the Betwa on account of the outbreak of Cholera.

At Erich the Bengal Army remained till the end of November. It was here that notwithstanding Scindia's repeated declarations of loyalty to the British, Hastings learned of his encouragement to the Pindaris to take shelter at Gwalior. Evidences were daily received by the British of Scindia's inimical behaviour. Scindia had also failed to fulfil his various promises. By article fourth of the Treaty of Gwalior (1817), he was to contribute a contingent of 5,000 horse. But Scindia showed no enthusiasm for raising that contingent. Besides, he had moved his army from Gwalior against the Treaty stipulations. Finding that Scindia could not be relied upon, Hastings immediately ordered the movement of the army to check his union with the Pindaris. Himself absolutely cut off from all his forces, and communications with the Pindaris and the Peshwa, Scindia tamely submitted.

Conclusion of a treaty with Scindia had resulted in the withdrawal of the Right Division from Dholpur, as it was no longer thought necessary to keep it there. Donkin withdrew. He was ordered to go to Kushalgarh; on the way he stopped at Hindon and then reached Kushalgarh awaiting instructions from the headquarters. Donkin established a depot there. He marched from Kushalgarh on December 2, leaving a detachment which consisted of Dholpur Cavalry, 12th Indian Infantry and two six pounder guns. Amir Khan offered to look after the rear. He continued his march, crossed the Banas at Bhagwantghar, on December 5, with a part of his force very lightly equipped for active pursuit of the nimble Pindaris. Donkin moved towards Bundi, halting at Keria on the 10th. On the 11th, taking supplies, the whole Division crossed the Chumbal eight miles below Kotah at Gamak Ghat on December 13. The Division separated. A light party after a forced march moved to Sultanpur, when it was learnt that the Pindaris had already been checked and repulsed by the Kota troops.

Marshall's Operations against the Pindaris

It has been mentioned that the Pindari leaders Wasil Mohammad and Karim Khan were moving towards Gwalior. It was therefore thought necessary to check such a move without giving any indication to Scindia that his sincerity to the British was suspected.

The pursuit of the Pindaris brought the troops from the south in contact with the Second Division. Maj. Gen. Marshall, who was at Seronj started on December 8 from there and arrived at Naya Sarai on the 12th when he divided his Division into two parts. He put the main party, most lightly equipped for active pursuit under his own command. Maj. Gen. Marshall then took the route to Kolarus. The Pindaris now found themselves pressed from all sides and cut off from Gwalior (by Lt. Col. Philpot's detachment). They, therefore, preferred to go towards the side which was under Kota troops, with a view either to seek shelter with Zalim Singh of Kota or with Amir Khan whose forces lay beyond. On December 25, 1817 Capt. Tod in command of the Rajah of Kota's troops fell in with about a thousand Pindaris. He dispersed them with considerable loss.[20] Thus hemmed in from all sides, the Pindaris were left in a most precarious position. The combined flight of Chitu, Rajun and Kadir Buksh to Mewar left them isolated from the other Pindari hordes in the north of Malwa. This enabled Malcolm to liquidate them easily. Chitu retired towards Udaipur.

The united durras of Karim Khan and Wasil Mohammad marched to Bitalgarh, reaching there on December 9, where they wanted to deposit their families. But they could not do so owing to the continued pressure of the British army. Therefore, they turned towards Neem Ghat on Kurah river in the Kota territory and succeeded in forcing a passage at Laddana near Sirsi on December 13, and waited at Beechee Tal for their baggage. It was then that Maj. Gen. Marshall, who had left Seronj on December 8, reached Bijrawa on December 13, heard of the Pindaris at Beechee Tal and left for the same place on the 13th night. Unfortunately his movement was slackened owing to the bad state of the roads. He could reach Beechee Tal only at two in the afternoon.

The Pindaris, on learning of the British troop-movement, immediately left Beechee Tal at twelve in the noon leaving a thousand horse to fight rear-guard action, to cover their retreat.[21] Col. Newsberry of Marshall's troops killed about fifty or sixty in the first instance. Having been dispersed the Pindaris were pursued for about ten miles. The British lost ten men, killed and wounded, and also sixty horses.[22] The division reassembled on the Parvati on the road to Barra on December 18.

Meanwhile, the Right Division under Donkin, was at Sultanpur on December 14, but on learning of Marshall's action against Karim Khan and Wasil Mohammad at Beechee Tal, he alerted his army. Donkin, having seen that the treaty with Amir Khan was safely concluded, and his presence was no longer needed, immediately returned to the left bank of the Chambal. They crossed the same at Gamak Ghat. He left his heavy equipment and baggage behind and with a light army moved on the 17th night. He had learnt of Karim's forced arrival in his vicinity. Donkin reported that he was able to foil Karim and Wasil's durras in their intention to go to Jaipur, where he had an understanding with Mehatab Khan, one of Amir Khan's *sardars* to make repeated inroads into the British provinces from Agra to Saharanpur, where there were a number of *ghurries* and forts belonging to Mehatab Khan.[23] The British nearly destroyed the Pindaris. Karim Khan and Wasil Mohammad "by deserting their families and the great proportion of their troops, have escaped for the present."[24]

The Pindaris in their haste to escape the advancing British forces, threw away much of the grain and baggage, and left behind many heads of cattle on their march.[25] The inhabitants of the villages collected all that the Pindaris abandoned. Karim Khan's wife, and several of her female attendants and relatives and his state elephants, 'howdah' and standards were captured.[26] They were all placed in Lt. Col. Gardner's hands.[27] Lt.Col. Gardner was also successful in surprising another party of Pindaris and captured about thirty-two camels fully laden.

A stage had been reached when the Pindaris began to be killed, captured or dispersed in such a thorough manner that they no longer existed as a formidable power, but instead were scattered without resources, plans and hopes. The Pindaris appeared, then, to have reached the crisis of their fate and later events proved that it was so. The capture of Karim's wife was the beginning of the end and the undoing of the Pindari menace.

The Pindaris were thus opposed on almost all sides. Finding that all the passes on the Chambal were closely guarded and hence shut against them, they turned towards Bamolea, Shergar and Gogul Chapra, abandoning everything that was likely to hinder their flight. By a slow process of elimination Karim's durra was reduced to just above 2,000, the pick of the whole body. Meanwhile, Col. Adams. who was at Manohar Thana, had reached Gogul Chapra, from where he detached Maj. Clarke in pursuit of the Pindaris. While in the Kota territory, Adams learned that some of the people there were either giving shelter to the Pindaris or withholding information from the British, regarding the Pindari movements.[28] However, after great hardship—lack of supplies and continuous movements—Clarke, after a march of about thirty miles, was able to disperse a body of Pindaris at Pipli, killing about fifteen or twenty of them. Though the material damage was little, the Pindaris were greatly dispirited and dispersed. The main body continued its advance and fled towards Rajghar-Patun, where they reached on the 21st. Meanwhile, the Pindaris in shelter at Tara Ghat near Kota were forced out by the Bhopal Horse. Adam deputed the 1st Rohilla Cavalry under Capt. Roberts to overtake these ousted Pindaris and after a march of fifty-five miles he was able to destroy most of them except a paltry sixty or seventy. It was these fugitives from Donkins' Division which Gardner had attacked, as detailed above.

After receiving the beating, the two durras continued their flight towards Saugar, where they learned of Holkar's defeat at Mahidpur and the consequent flight of his army, which they joined after crossing the Chambal. Adam in his march suffered greatly due to inclement weather, bad condition of the roads and insufficient supplies. Heavy rains during the winter hindered Adam's progress and he finally reached Gangraur on January 6, and halted there for supplies and instructions and also for giving the much-needed rest to his army. At that time, he had 1,250 regular and irregular cavalry, 1,490 regular Indian Infantry and six pieces of ordnance.

We had earlier noted the retreat of Chitu in the face of British advance, when ultimately he went over to the rear of Holkar's army. He remained there for some time in comparative security till he was forced to quit this area and cross the Chambal. He turned towards the north and stopped at Singaoli, 25 miles west of Kota between Kota and Bundi. From here, on invitation, Chitu proceeded, after sending his family and heavy baggage to Kumbhalmere, to Jaswant Rao Bhao at Jawud. The Pindaris suffered a lot and the back of the Pindari resistance was severely broken. Meanwile, Maj. Gen. Marshall was recalled to South Malwa by Lord Hastings' orders.

Now that the Pindaris had been expelled from Southern Malwa,[29] the scattered bodies of the Pindaris took shelter—forts being closed to them—in the jungles and hills on the left bank of the river Chambal. Again, they were compelled to change their plan of taking shelter with the Kota Raja. The Pindaris were constantly pursued and perpetually harassed. They were also repeatedly surprised and punished. Their losses were severe. So alarmed were the Pindaris, that when halting, they were said to be distributed into parties of four each of whom, "in case of an alarm, one held the horses, and another cooked the victuals, while the remaining two were sleeping." [30]

Expulsion of the Pindaris from the Left of Chambal

Hastings continued to remain near the Kali Sind river throughout December, except for the change of ground, resulting in the movement of a few miles only. He found a position, convenient for guiding operations in Malwa, keeping an eye on Scindia while simultaneously maintaining communications with the various army units and keeping in readiness the reinforcements when required by any of the Divisions.

It is now necessary to follow the movements of Sir David Ochterlony, who was all the time at his Head-quarters at Rewari, keeping in readiness to take action against Scindia, if necessary. Immediately after the conclusion of a treaty with Scindia, he moved on to Jaipur, where he had an interview with Amir Khan and conducted negotiations with him. The various Sardars of Amir Khan and the tumultuous army which he led, were not happy at the turn of events—particularly with Amir Khan's acquiescence with the British proposals. The events in Nagpur and Poona all the more encouraged them to adopt hostile attitude towards Amir Khan and the British. Those Sardars were, therefore, likely to create certain difficulties. Hence Ochterlony moved from Rewari on November 27, and reached Jaipur via Sahajahanpur and Narayanpur on December 10. He met Amir Khan there and also dealt with his insubordinate army. The two Divisions under Rajah Bahadur and Mehatab Khan were ready for action against the British. Ochterlony, on a pretext to seek forage for his army, moved it between the two Divisions and remained there till they both delivered their guns. The remaining Division of Amir Khan which was placed under Jamshed Khan continued to disobey his orders to submit to the British.

Soon, Ochterlony received orders from the Governor-General for reorganising his irregulars, which then included the newly added eight battalions of Amir Khan's infantry and a corps of *golundazs.*[31] and several Risalas of irregular horse.[32] This measure of the Governor-General served a double purpose. Firstly, they were able to employ discharged and disbanded soldiers, who would otherwise have added to the Pindari strength; secondly, the infantry and the *golundazs* one of the best in the country now served the British for suppressing their former comrades-in-arms.

A new force, under Maj. Gen. Brown, lightly equipped for purposes of very rapid movement, set out towards Chambal.[33] It marched through Lodakah Ghat, Beechee Tal, Nahargarh and was at Chippa Burrod on January 1, 1818. Without a halt, he moved on to Soneil, from where he kept himself in touch with Lt. Col. Adams on his left and Capt. Tod on his right, who was then at Rowtah. After halting for two days, January 6 and 7, and after two days' march, he reached Peeplia on the 9th where he learned that Roshan Beg, Roshan Khan and Pain Singh of Holkar's army were at Rampura, about twenty miles from Peeplia. Brown at once left at one in the morning and reached Rampura most unexpectedly, at day-break, and surrounded the enemy. Later, it was found that the major portion of them had already left for Ahmed.[34] Those present, took to the hills, but were pursued and more than two hundred of them were killed and about hundred horses captured. Pain Singh was taken prisoner and Roshan Beg fled towards Mewar. It was also reported that the Rao Raja had agreed to surrender the part of the enemy guns, which were at Ahmed. Accordingly, a small posse was sent to Ahmed, which found the carriages of the guns broken. Due to shortage of time, the guns were all spiked and rendered unserviceable. Brown halted at Rampura for the baggage to catch up.

Meanwhile, parts of the durras of Chitu and Karim joined at Narwar, where the Governor-General sent a detachment against them. The Pindaris fled to Dholpur which they plundered. Some of the British detachments from Jaipur immediately moved against them and dispersed the Pindaris, inflicting some punishment on them. The Pindaris then fled towards Gangraur and were defeated by a detachment sent by the Governor-General who took a part of their baggage and plundered the stragglers. The Pindaris then fled into the territories of Kota. The Kota troops likewise attacked them. Receiving this check, the Pindaris then moved towards Chittor and from there, Karim and Chitu went to Bari Sadree. In the meantime, a detachment of Sir William Grant Keir came upon the party of Chitu. which was attacked, and captured four of their guns and baggage. Karim fled towards Udaipur, and Chitu reached Tandla via Dungarpur and Banswara, with about four thousand horses.[35]

Movements of the Second Division

It may be recollected that the Second Division was on the Chambal, after the defeat of the Pindaris in their attempt to cross the river below Kota. Donkin then determined to pin down the Pindaris, who were at that time concentrated in the Malwa territory. The Pindaris had, by then, been driven from South Malwa and the left side of the Chambal, and were confined in Mewar. Gen. Donkin, in order to keep them confined to this area, immediately closed all the outlets by posting his forces. Maj. Gen. Brown and Lt. Col. Adams were already guarding the eastern avenues of escape. At the same time, the Gujarat and the Deccan Divisions were guarding the southern regions.

Accordingly, Donkin recrossed the Chambal, called his detachments from Gamak Ghat, Patan and Kekri. Having reassembled his force, he ascended the Bundi Ghats for Shahpura on January 1, 1818. Another detachment under Col. Vaurener went to Dublana. Donkin continued his march, and finally stopped at Sanganer, where he reached on January 8, to await news of the British army advancing from the south.

The Gujarat Division

The Gujarat Division left Mundsore on January 3, in pursuit of Chitu, who was supposed to be in Jawud. But Chitu fled to Bunduta, where Fazil Khan Pindari helped him in procuring the much-needed provisions for his followers and himself. However, on learning of the approach of the English, he fled towards Bari Sadree, where he presented two shawls and a gold bracelet to the local chief, Pratap Singh's son. Sir W. G. Keir, sent in pursuit, advanced via Bantwari towards Bari Sadree, in search of Chitu, having left the heavy baggage to follow under the escort of five hundred Indian Infantry. But, on arrival at Munjari, he received contradictory reports of Chitu's movements and therefore he halted there. But again, he received reports of Chitu's presence at Doraha, to which place he personally led a party, and after a forced march reached there at one in the morning, but found only five guns and some baggage, Chitu having precipitately fled in the direction of Udaipur.[36]

Simultaneously, another detachment, consisting of three troops of Indian cavalry, 1,500 Mysore Horse and one battalion of light infantry, was sent in pursuit of Karim Khan under Captain James Grant. He marched towards Parsodah in search of Karim Khan, where he learnt of Karim's presence at Jawud, but on reaching there, he found that Karim had already fled on receipt of an information from a 'harcarra' of Jaswant Rao Bhao, of the British approach. Capt. Grant also learnt that Karim had joined Chitu, but the whereabouts of both were unknown.

General Donkin's Movements

We have already noted above that Maj. Gen. Donkin had reached Sanganer on January 8, 1818. Meanwhile, Sir Thomas Hislop moved to Poor and then left the Indian battalions at Sanganer to prevent Pindari escape. The Battalion that was left at Lakheri Ghat was ordered to move to Bundi, to facilitate the supply. The supply depot at Dublana was moved to Sanganer. Col. Gardner was ordered to proceed to Chittor, where the Pindaris had assembled, but on January 13, he learnt at Nathdwara that the Pindaris had taken the southern route. Donkin was then near Gangapur, while it was ascertained that the Pindaris had fled in two parties, one towards Gujarat and the other towards Malwa. Donkin returned to Sanganer and recalled Gardner also. On December 30, the Division was at Shahapura. Sir Thomas Hislop, anticipating the Pindari movements towards the south, sent a party under Lt. Col. Russell to Partapgarh to intercept them, but he returned with no success.

At that stage, on January 8, 1818, the general position of the various divisions of the Grand Army was : Sir W. G. Keir with the Gujarat Division was at Munjuree and Doraha. Capt. James Grant was at Jawud. Maj. Gen. Donkin at Sanganer and Maj. Gen. Brown at Rampura.

Sir W. G. Keir's Movements

In the meantime, Sir W.G. Keir, who was at Mundsore, moved to Doraha. His camp-followers, during the course of their march, were attacked by the Bhils. Keir was unsuccessful in preventing the Pindaris from escaping. Keir in his pursuit of Chitu had reached his camp at Doraha on January 6.

Chitu was at Salumbar in Udaipur state.[37] He was in the most distressing circumstances and contemplated going towards Gujarat.

While at Salumbar, Sir William received a letter from the Rana of Udaipur[38] stating that Chitu, who was at Salumbar sometime back with 3,000 horsemen and 3,000 followers,[39] elephants, camels etc., had left for Banswara intending to move towards Gujarat. The Rana also mentioned the miserable condition of Chitu and his followers. He also informed that the Pindaris were so afraid of the British that they seldom unsaddled their horses.[40] Sir William also learnt that the Bhils had inflicted great losses on the Pindaris in several attacks made during their journey through the jungles. Acting on information, a contingent was sent to Sita Kund, to find out the whereabouts of the Pindaris and their families believed to be there, but nothing came out of it. Sir W. G. Keir left for Partapgarh. While still on the way on January 19, he learnt of the presence of Pindaris in the village Mandapi under Fazil Khan, an officer of Jaswant Rao Bhao, who, like his master, connived at their safety, security and shelter. But, he simulated complete ignorance of the Pindaris. The Pindaris were completely surrounded, and Keir personally led a successful attack upon them, when about one hundred of them were killed and several camels and horses captured. However, when the village was on the point of being completely destroyed, one of the nephews of Fazil Khan came out and produced a letter of protection issued by Capt. Caulfield. This saved the people from plunder and destruction. In the meantime, Capt. Grant after various unsuccessful excursions against the Pindaris at Chittor, Neemkhera and Jawud, returned to Mundsore on January 18, 1818.

Karim Khan and Wasil Mohammad had joined hands at Jawud when Capt. Grant led an expedition against them. The two fled. The Pindaris under Namdar Khan, nephew of Karim Khan, passed round Neemuch, crossed the Chambal and passed Gangraur towards Kotri on the Kali Sind river. They were later heard of at Ambi, where Maj. Clarke, who was with the 5th Regiment of Bengal Indian Cavalry, was detached against them by Lt. Col. Adams. He started at 11 p.m. on January 12, 1818, marched throughout the night and when within a short distance of Ambi, he halted till day-break, so as to inflict a more severe punishment. Unaware of the danger, the Pindaris continued to sleep. As the day broke on January 13, 1818, Maj. Clarke, divided his party into two; he stationed himself on the route of their escape and deputed Lt. Kennedy to make a direct attack. They took the Pindaris completely by surprise, who ran, but fell directly into the hands of Maj. Clarke. Lt. Kennedy and Maj. Clarke inflicted heavy casualties on the Pindaris. They pursued for about twenty miles.[41] Out of about 1,500 Pindaris, a thousand were killed. It was here that Namdar Khan was reported killed, but the news proved to be wrong.[42]

The defeat the Pindaris received at the hands of Maj. Clarke, and their sufferings in a number of smaller encounters, reduced them to bodies of no consequence and they were, in the end, completely dispersed. Many of them were slain in these engagements, while many others were killed at the hands of the villagers who rose against the Pindaris everywhere, in revenge for their former cruelties. They were mercilessly killed by them. Their horses were captured or slain. Maj. Clarke's daring attack upon the Pindaris prevented their escape towards the Bengal Presidency, where there would have been ample opportunity for the Pindaris to commit serious depredations.[43]

The Deccan Army's Movements

At that stage, the Governor-General, considering the presence of the Headquarters of the Deccan Army unnecessary, directed their return to the south leaving four guns of Horse Artillery, 3rd Madras Indian Cavalry, 14th Madras

Indian Infantry, the Russell Brigade and 2,000 Mysore Horse for Sir John Malcolm to settle the Holkar affairs. Sir John was also directed to keep himself in touch with Lt. Col. Adams at Gangraur, Maj. Gen. Donkin at Sanganer, and Sir W. G. Keir at Neemuch. Orders were also issued for Col. Deacon to march with his troops including the Ellichpur Contingent and Capt. Davie's Horse from Jafarabad to Poona.

The situation created in the south consequent upon Peshwa's continued hostility towards the British forced Hastings to take this step. Asirgarh, too, continued to be inimical. Subsequent to the defeat of Holkar on December 21, 1817[44] and the Treaty of Mundsore, a British Resident was posted at Holkar's *durbar* and order was restored with British help. Some of the *sardars* voluntarily removed themselves from Indore. Ramdeen accompanied by Bara Bhai went to the south. Roshan Beg, after his defeat at Rampura, also went to the south and joined Bara Bhai. The victory obtained over Malhar Rao Holkar at Mahidpur had very great effect upon the Pindaris. They were then driven from Indore to Jawud. The durras of Karim, Wasil Mohammad and Chitu were very much reduced because of the constant pursuit by the Divisions of Maj. Gen. Donkin and Lt. Col. Adams.

The British forces, at that stage, were placed as follows : Lt. Col. Adams was at Gangraur, awaiting supplies; Maj. Gen. Brown was preparing for action at Nahargarh; Sir W.G. Keir was at Neemuch arranging affairs for the safety of the Gujarat area. Donkin was at Sanganer. Col. Deacon was ordered to proceed to Ahmednagar and then to Poona.

Having made all these arrangements, the First Division of the Deccan Army and the Headquarters, marched from the vicinity of Mundsore to Peeplaoti and then to Ujjain. One detachment was sent to Gujaratfrontier in search of the remaining parties of the Pindaris. Maj. Lushington was sent along the road to Ratlam, which commanded Dawud Ghat, in search of the remaining Pindaris. Capt. Grant was ordered to march from Mundsore to Banswara, Ratlam, and then to return to Ujjain, to rejoin the Headquarters, where he reached on January 29. Sir W.G. Keir was to look after the passes leading into Gujarat, through Dungarpur.

The Jawud Affair

Meanwhile, after meeting Sir John Malcolm on January 19, Maj. Gen. Brown moved via Reechary, Naraingarh, Polsoda and Neeninoh and reached Jawud on the 25th. Jaswant Rao Bhao had continued conniving at the Pindaris, whom he sheltered and as subsequent events proved, the Pindari leader Karim Khan was also given protection there. It was learnt that Bhao Singh and Imam Buksh, the two Pindari chiefs, were given shelter by Jaswant Rao Bhao, who refused to deliver them to the British,[45] and wasted time in fruitless negotiations. Meanwhile, Maj. Gen. Brown sent word to Bhao that any movement of his armed forces without his permission would be treated as an act of hostility. In spite of this warning, Bhao Singh made a move for escape to Kumbhalmere. On receipt of this information Brown posted more pickets, who were fired upon by Bhao's men. Bhao was immediately asked to surrender unconditionally, failing which his fort was to be stormed. The man carrying the message was fired upon. Capt. Ridge, Capt. Newbery and Maj Gen. Brown himself stormed Jawud on January 28, 1818, and the British forces swept everything before them.[46] Maj. Gen. Brown caused the gates of the fort to be blown off. Bhao escaped by the back-gate towards Kumbhalmere; while the storming party entered by the Rampura gate. Bhao suffered a loss of about one thousand men killed, while the British lost thirty-six men. The action at Jawud "had been swift and decisive and exercised a most salutary effect throughout that part of India."[47]

Maj. Gen. Brown, after completing his work marched out of Jawud on February 3, 1818 for Rampura, leaving a small force behind. Sir John Malcolm went to Jawud to settle its political affairs. Malcolm then instructed Maj. Gen. Brown to move towards Kumbhalmere. Raipur (usurped by Bapoo Scindia), Dyalgarh and Rajnagar were surrendered by Bhao and handed over to the Rana of Udaipur, to whom they rightfully belonged. Meanwhile, letters for handing over

Kumbhalmere were given by Jaswant Rao Bhao, who had earlier surrendered himself to Sir John Malcolm. The fort was occupied by Lt. Col. Casement. Thus, the Pindaris were driven away from the region of the famous plateau of Harauti and Mewar.

Sir W. G. Keir, while at Neemuch was, as previously noted, asked to look after the Gujarat frontier. He left the place on January 24 for Ratlam, from where he directed one party under Lt. Col. Corsellis to move towards Banswara and another under Lt. Col. Stanhope towards Dhar. The idea was to protect the southern-most entrance to Gujarat through Chota Udaipur and Ali Mohan, and also to keep a check on Bhima Bai,[48] Holkar's sister and Roshan Beg who were moving with the remainder of Holkar's force. Sir W. G. Keir arrived at Badnawar on February 3, where he found Bhima Bai encamped nearby. Not knowing how to treat her, he asked her to leave the place, which she did. In the meantime, instructions reached him for the treatment to be meted out to her. Holkar approached the British to disperse Bhima Bai's forces and to send her to Rampura, the residence of her brother. Maj. Gen. Brown marched to Jhabua where Bhima Bai was encamped. Terms for submission were sent to her, which she accepted, and she waited on Sir W. G. Keir with two hundred followers.[49] She was given an allowance of Rupees two hundred a day for herself and her party. Her troops numbering 2,500 were dispersed. She accompanied Sir W. G. Keir to Rajgarh and was ultimately sent to Rampura under the escort of Lt. Col. Corselliss' brigade.

After the expulsion of the Pindaris from the left bank of the Chambal, they could not exist as a collective body in that region. They were harried from almost all sides and were placed in the most hapless situation. They lost everything: family—towards whom they had the greatest attachment, cash, property and the most precious of all—their peace. Such was the uncertain state of their life that they did not know whether they would be alive the next moment. This was because they were constantly pursued and hunted by the British army. Not having any cash and not being able to go to the villages—because the villagers would attack them, they did not know from where to acquire the means of subsistence. Starvation stared them in the face. In the words of Adam. "The Pindaris appear to have arrived at the crisis of their fate."[50]

Had the Pindaris been a regular army, having a definite means of defence or offence, then a different strategy would have been required to fight them. The experience, gained with the adoption of the non-intervention policy, and so also, the policy of defence, had made it evident that the most effective mode of checking the Pindaris was the simultaneous use of a number of very lightly equipped detachments, which would constantly be on the move and inflict as heavy a punishment as circumstances permitted. To check such an enemy by means of cordons was almost ineffectual and impossible. Hundreds of miles of frontier could not be cordoned off, since the Pindari horsemen could easily escape through the openings, which no amount of thoroughness could completely plug.

In the operations conducted against the Pindaris, the British, by their prompt and continuous action, drove them from one area to another. Thus, constant harassment, fatigue and continual alarm broke their back.[51] When the Pindaris had been eliminated as a body, and when they could no longer face the British, a letter was addressed to the Pindari chiefs—Karim Khan, Wasil Mohammad, Namdar Khan and others—that there was no possibility of the British entertaining them or their followers in British service. However, a promise was made that those who surrendered to the British and promised to abandon their mode of life will be received well and provided for. The Pindaris were asked to contact either the Nawab of Bhopal or Lt. Col. Adams. Those, who would not surrender were to be persecuted and attacked.[52]

Withdrawal of the Grand Army

Having attained the object of annihilating the Pindaris as a body, for which the Grand Army had been assembled,

Hastings chalked out a plan of withdrawal. On January 25 he was at Oochar. Then, passing through Launch, and Kunjaoli, he reached Kanpur on February 25. The Centre Division of the Grand Army having reached Kanpur, was further withdrawn to Lucknow. One brigade consisting of two battalions, 1st Bengal Indian Infantry, and 13th Bengal Indian Infantry were left behind under Lt. Col. Dewar, who was ordered to join Maj. Gen. Marshall. Other Corps were placed under Brig. Gen. Watson. However, in view of the fact that some of the Pindaris individually or with their leaders had continued to evade punishment, he decided to withdraw by stages and thus always keep a part of his force in the field.

Lt. Col. Adams was at Gangraur from January 6 to 10, awaiting arrival of provisions, which were soon received under Maj. Logie's command. Karim and Wasil Mohammad, who had been forced out of the fort of Jawud, withdrew towards Malwa, where they broke into three parties, hoping to avoid a direct collision with the British and to escape punishment. Besides the party which was engaged by Maj. Clarke, another party of Karim Khan and Wasil Mohammad passed south of Gangraur. A third party passed along the frontier of Gujarat and went towards the Ghats of South Malwa. The first having been almost routed, the remainder joined hands with the second party and consequently swelled in numbers, which fact attracted the notice of Adams. He, therefore, decided to pursue this party. Meanwhile, he had been instructed by Sir Thomas Hislop to follow the Pindaris in their south-easterly direction. Lt. Col. Adams first marched to Burrod on January 18, and then to Saugar, the next day, where he left the infantry and artillery under Maj. Popham, with instructions to follow by slow stages and himself continued his march of pursuit. The Pindaris were not allowed to gather strength. He passed through Durrajpur near Bhilsa where he reached on January 28. Without slackening he continued his non-stop march at an average rate of eighteen miles a day. This pursuit drove the Pindaris towards Bhopal.

This decisive pursuit made it clear to the Pindaris that there was no escape from it, unless they fought or tamely surrendered. To them, the latter course seemed to be the more expedient under the circumstances then prevailing. Besides, the British had announced very liberal terms of surrender for the Pindaris. Having arrived in Bhopal territory, after some negotiations with Adams at Durrajpur on January 28, and with the help of the Nawab of Bhopal and Capt. Stewart, the then political agent at Bhopal, the Pindaris surrendered through the agency of Meer Zaffar Ali Khan. Karim's eldest son and other followers surrendered through Zalim Singh of Kota. This put an end to the operations against the durras of Karim Khan and Wasil Mohammad.

With the foresight of an astute leader, Karim Khan realised that the end was approaching fast and they were all likely to be exterminated. He, therefore, made a secret offer to the British to use his utmost endeavours, in co-operation with the British forces, to effect the destruction of his former comrades-in-arms, on the condition of being pardoned for his previous acts of omission and commission.[53] Malcolm to whom this offer was made, rejected it completely. Finding no escape from the stark reality of destruction looking into his face, Karim Khan, in a state of utter misery and despair, went to the camp of Sir John Malcolm on the morning of February 15, 1818 and surrendered to the British on a general promise of pardon and future subsistence through the good offices of Meer Zaffar Ali Khan.[54] Earlier thirty-six Pindaris of Karim's durra surrendered to Adam. Most of them were reduced to abject destitution. At the same time some of the subordinate Pindari leaders surrendered to Raj Rana Zalim Singh.[55]

Karim had suffered immensely prior to his surrender. When Jaswant Rao Bhao had been defeated, his Bukshy told Caulfield that Karim Khan remained close to the town for three days before he was compelled to retreat. His followers, at that time, did not amount to more than six hundred.[56] Karim himself further described the miserable conditions through which he had to pass earlier. He stated that he was compelled to leave Holkar's camp, where, he hoped, he would find shelter, because of a British declaration that they would not carry negotiations with a prince who continued to harbour Pindaris in his camp.[57] After leaving Holkar's camp, he took shelter with Jaswant Rao Bhao at Jawud, where he was received by Krishna Bhow, who helped him in securing the grace of Jaswant Rao Bhao. He was in Jawud when it was attacked by Maj. Gen. Brown on January 28. Karim Khan fled in disguise,[58] and found asylum in the house of a poor inhabitant of Jawud,[59] where he remained till the 30th night, when in darkness, he escaped to the hills. He wandered from village to village, ever in fear of being seized. One of his feet had swollen due to excessive walking—an exertion to which he was not accustomed.[60] When he first reached the British camp, he was in rags, lame from blistered feet which bled and was much fatigued. In spirit too, he was absolutely depressed.[61] At the time of his surrender, Karim was very apprehensive of the British but on assurance of generous treatment, he regained composure.

Almost simultaneously, another Pindari chief of note, Namdar Khan, who had earlier been taken by surprise and defeated at Ketri submitted to Lt. Col. Adams. He surrendered along with his father-in-law Nizam-ul-Deen, his maternal uncles Morea and Lal Khan and one hundred followers and dependants[62] through Shahazad Masih, Commandant of the Contingent of the Nawab of Bhopal. Namdar Khan was promised that he would not be sent to Europe (Kala Pani).[63] Since he was one of the first to surrender voluntarily, he received kind and considerate treatment from the British,[64] and at the intercession of the Nawab, he was allowed to reside at Bhopal.

Wasil Mohammad had made an unsuccessful appeal to the British for shelter. He, therefore, ultimately decided to move secretly to Gwalior, where he lived for some time in the greatest secrecy.[65] When Scindia learnt of his presence in his camp, he became indignant. After some argument with Atma Ram Pandit, the Chief Counsellor of Scindia, Stewart, the Acting Resident in Scindia's camp, was able to persuade Atma Ram to deliver Wasil Mohammad to the British.[66] He was at last given up on the night of May 24-25 to Stewart. The surrender of Wasil Mohammad by Scindia was considered a material event of the time. Muzhar Buksh, another Pindari leader, and the nominal head of Wasil Mohammad's durra also submitted to the British, who allowed him to settle and reside in Malwa.

Kauder Buksh was attacked by the British troops on the frontier of Mangrol in the Kota territory, where he barely escaped with his life, while all his dependants and followers, numbering about one hundred and twenty were scattered far and wide.[67] Kauder Buksh, the principal Holkar Shahi Pindari chief, surrendered to Malcolm. He was the first Holkar Shahi Pindari to give up the struggle. When almost all the Pindari chiefs had surrendered, Rajun and Chitu continued to defy the British. At one stage, they went to the Nawab of Bhopal with the intention of delivering themselves up,[68] whereupon, Brig. Gen. Sir John Malcolm wrote to them, urging them to surrender on the promise of pardon and grant of land.[69] As a result of this appeal and a quarrel with Chitu, Rajun gave up Chitu's cause and surrendered to Malcolm through the son of the Raja of Bagli and Lt. Macdonald.[70]

Chitu alone remained to be accounted for. He had been driven from the Banswara, Ratlam and Taundala territories. He fled towards Onchod, the chief of which place plundered him and captured a number of Pindaris. Chitu then fled towards Kanode, with about 1,500 men only. Mohammad Puna, his son was also present with him. Major Heath, Commanding Hindia, learned of the presence of Pindaris at Kanode. The news was received at 1 p. m. and Heath immediately marched against the Pindaris with eight hundred and fifty men of Madras European Regiment, the 1st Battalion, 7th Madras Infantry and Silleder Horse. The British encountered the Pindaris at about eight in the night. Chitu immediately ran away. A few Pindaris were killed. One elephant, one hundred and ten camels and one hundred and thirty horses were captured. Chitu was pursued, but he took advantage of the darkness and escaped without much harm. The Bhils and Grassia Rajas, whose lands had been usurped and forcibly occupied by the Pindari chief Chitu, now attacked him and his followers with all their fury and spared none who fell in their hands.

After this blow Chitu fled towards Daulatpur and then to Keiree and Anwas where Kushal Singh, the Gond prince, once his comrade-in-arms, secretly helped him in his hour of distress. But when he found himself hard-pressed he had to leave soon. A detachment under Capt. Roberts was sent to pursue Chitu, which ultimately obliged him to leave that area also. He wandered about Malwa for some time, but found no relief from any quarter and in this desperate situation, Chitu was "everywhere and yet nowhere." This was because his durra as a united force was no more in existence. His durra had been broken in twos and threes, dispersed in the jungles and the ghats, and wandered about all over the countryside. The Pindaris were compelled to offer their horses in lieu of shelter and security.[71]

Here, a tribute may be paid to Chitu's continued defiance of the British. In spite of the most heavy odds against him, he carried on the struggle single-handed. A similar tribute may be paid to some of his followers. Throughout the march, his followers suffered the greatest privations, hardships and dangers, yet they showed the highest fidelity to their leader. This was the case not only with Chitu, but with almost all the Pindari leaders and their followers. It would have been most easy for any Pindari to have left his leader in the lurch and mix with the masses and escape punishment. But they did not do so.

Finding himself absolutely isolated and in a most desperate situation, Chitu suddenly decided to come to terms with the British and for this he went to the Nawab of Bhopal, whom he wanted as his intermediary to settle terms with the British. Finding that the British would not agree to his conditions of a *jagir*, personal immunity and employment of his Pindaris and himself in the British army, he again took to a wandering life.[72] He eluded the British and went towards Khandesh. He found an opportunity of joining hands with the defeated and dispersed bands of the Peshwa. Soon he was compelled to fly and ultimately joined Appa Saheb of Nagpur, himself a wanderer, among the Mahadeo Hills.[73] Chitu soon took the route to Asirgarh, where Yashwant Rao Lad, the *Killedar* gave him refuge early in 1818. In June 1818, he left Asirgarh to join the fugitive Bhonsla Raja of Nagpur. He was again checked by the British, when his followers were scattered almost to the last man. He again returned to Asirgarh in October, but was soon compelled to leave and took to his old haunts to the north of the Narbada.[74] Now he was left with his son Puna, and only five or six followers. They took the route of the Bagli pass, which he found closely guarded. The British did not give him a minute's respite. His durra was now completely dispersed and he was exposed to the attacks of villagers, who relieved the Pindaris of their horses and everything they could lay their hands on. Malcolm encouraged the villagers to plunder the Pindaris and retain the loot. This policy of Malcolm received the approbation of the Governor-General.[75]

The English, after their failure to capture the Pindari chief Chitu, issued instructions that should Chitu be captured, he was to be tried by Court Martial as an ordinary robber, and the punishment whatever it be, to be carried into immediate execution. Simultaneously, a proclamation was issued, announcing a reward of ten thousand rupees for any person who could help in the capture of Chitu, or give information leading to his capture. He was[76] hunted and tracked like a wild animal. He rode a horse with exceptionally large hoofs, whose imprints helped the British in tracking him through his flight. The vigorous pursuit did not give him a minute's respite and hunger stared him in his face. There was allround desperation. Under such conditions, he took leave of his son Puna and decided to cross the jungles of Kantapur, where he soon fell a prey to a tiger.[77] Chitu met a brave death—a fitting end to a brave man's defiant attitude to life. His son Puna was captured in the jungles of Kantapur by one of Holkar's officers.[78] Sir John Malcolm later released him out of charity and handed him over to Holkar's government, from whom he obtained land for cultivation, after giving him an advance of two hundred rupees for his expenses.[79]

It may be observed that the action against the Pindaris by the British forces was not an unqualified success. In spite of the presence of a great army in the field, and their being almost surrounded and pursued from all sides, the Pindaris escaped, defying the cordon drawn around them without much loss. They started withdrawing, without the least show of fightt, right from the beginning of the campaign.[80] Of the Pindari leaders, Chitu "always exhibited more marks of sagacity than any of the other Pindari chiefs."[81] Right from the beginning he adopted a north-westerly course which obviated all possibility of his being intercepted and hence could escape punishment.

The British had made thorough preparations, including those of sieges etc. Their baggage, therefore, was very heavy resulting in slow movement because of guns drawn by bullocks, condition of roads being extremely bad and unfit for carriage. The weather rendered inclement by heavy rains, slackened the British movement, as happened with Adam's Division. The halt of the Bengal Division at Seronj and the slow movement of the Fifth Deccan Division and Adam's Division, all contributed to facilitate the Pindari movement, and enabled Karim Khan and Wasil Mohammad's durras to escape from Narwar.

As far as the pursuit of the Pindaris was concerned, the heavy artillery of the British was also found to be a handicap. The British were compelled to encumber themselves with heavy guns, to fight a possible Maratha confederacy, or Amir Khan with a train of about two hundred guns and all the paraphernalia of a siege. Any war with them would have resulted in a disaster, had the British not been properly armed.[82]

Sir John Malcolm, who led the lightest of all the Divisions was relentless in his pursuit of Chitu, which he could not have done, had he been heavily armed. It was very fortunate for the British that ever since the Pindaris were attacked, "never was a gun brought to bear upon them." A few pieces of artillery, however great means of protection they might be, definitely hampered their rapid march. Major Lushington on December 26, 1816, admirably succeeded in inflicting heavy punishment on the Pindaris because he dropped his guns. He marched fifty-three miles in fourteen hours. Similarly, when Lt. Col. Adams sent his cavalry to pursue the Pindaris, they also succeeded in defeating them.

Whether it was Doveton or Donkin, time and again the British were obliged to halt for the arrival of their supplies, without which they could not go far, but the "wretched state of the cattle...were a continual clog on the rapid movements" of the British. This became all the more so during the rains. Under the circumstances then prevailing, it could be said that "an army is, in most situations, more or less controlled in its movements by a necessary attention to its provisions..." Whenever, the Second Division of the Hindustan Army moved rapidly, it had inevitably to halt for the coming up of the supplies.

Maj. Gen. Marshall and Lt. Col. Adams both complained of the non-cooperation of the inhabitants of Kota region, for fear of the Pindari raids, retaliation and future visitations. The Kota people were so afraid of the future Pindari raids that they would not open the gates of their houses or shops to sell provisions to the British, to say nothing of giving information about their whereabouts.

The Pindari horses were extremely handy.[82] and consequently their movements were very rapid and continuous. Besides, the Pindaris would rush to the central point of attack with such great rapidity that the first information of their attack were the persons who had suffered at their hands, and, their return was as rapid as their entry. The Pindaris and their horses were accustomed to travel the most rugged roads and mountainouns regions, which the best of the English cavalry was incapable of performing and there by "in the worst ground the Pindaris would have the greatest advantage over the pursuers."[83]

Another reason why the Pindaris could escape full retribution was that when the Pindaris were pressed, they fled, if possible collectively, otherwise, they broke into several parties, to unite again at another place. The apprehension of sudden attack by the British kept them usually in thick jungles. Sometimes, the Pindaris would take shelter in the hills and would remain there, exposed to the inclemencies of the weather, go without food and be vulnerable to the attack of wild animals till the danger of the British army had passed.

But it must be said in praise of the British officers whether civilian or military, from the lowest to the highest rank, including the commanders of the Divisions, and the Commander-in-Chief of the two armies, that they gracefully shared in the same trials and tribulations as their soldiers did. This endeared the British officers to their soldiers. Whether it was the hill, or the thick jungles, or the plains, the British officer was always on duty. Sir W. G. Keir was, for more than two months, in the thick of the jungles of Malwa, hunting the Pindaris and he admirably discharged his duties. When he ended the campaign, there was hardly any Pindari left in the area. The Governor-General, Lord Hastings, shared the cholera epidemic with the army. He did not abandon the army and seek shelter elsewhere. He remained steadfastly at the post. Again, the British officers, not finding a place for the camp followers to live in, continued to allow them a place in their own tents at the risk of contracting cholera. Again, in spite of the fact that the climate of India was enervating to the British officers, they continued to serve in all climes and regions. Theirs was the unflagging devotion to a public cause, and hence the ease with which they were able to score victory against very heavy odds.

FOOT-NOTES

1 N.A.I. For. Sec. 1817 : O.C. No. 46-57, 19 December, 1817, Lt. Col. J.W. Adam, Commanding Nagpur Subsidiary Force to Marshall, Hoshangabad, 23 October, 1817.

2 B.G.R. D. No. 304, Pol. Deptt. 1817 : Hislop to Warden, 23 November, 1817.

3 For. Misc. 124 A : Hislop to Hastings : 26 November, 1817. p. 131.

4 For. Misc. 124 A : Hastings to the Secret Committee, 1 March, 1820, pp. 395-96, para 58.

5 N.A.I. For. Sec. 1817 : O.C. No. 46-57, 19 December, 1817, Marshall to Nicol, Camp Hutteah, 31 October, 1817.

6 N.A.I. For. Sec. 1818 : O.C. No. 45, 9 January, 1818. Akhbars from Ujjain, 27 November, 1817.

7 N.A.I. For. Sec. 1818 : O.C. No. 47, 9 January, 1818 :
Akhbars from Ujjain and Jhatah, 30 November, and 1 December, 1817 respectively.

8 N.A.I. For. Sec. 1817 : O.C. No. 35-39, 26 December, 1817 :
Marshall to Nicol, Camp near Seronj, 30 November, 1817.

9 For. Misc. 124 A : Hastings to the Secret Committee, 1 March, 1820 p. 396, para 59.

10 N.A.I. For. Sec. 1817 : O.C. No. 31-34, 26 December, 1817 :
Express No. 993, Nicol to Lt. Col. Philpot, Commanding Detachment, HQ Camp Laherra, 4 December, 1817.

11 N.A.I. For. Sec. 1817 : O.C. No. 35-39, 26 December, 1817 :
Marshall to Nicol, Camp near Seronj, 2 December, 1817.

12 For. Misc. 124 A : A Private letter from Sir J. Malcolm addressed to a Colonel, without date and address, p. 141.
Also : N.A.I. For. Sec. 1818 : O.C. No. 49, 9 January, 1818, Malcolm from Talyne, 28 November, 1817.

13 N.A.I. For. Sec. 1817 : O.C. No. 35-39, 26 December, 1817 :
Letter No. 140, Marshall to Nicol : Camp Seronj, 1 December, 1817 and another letter of 2 December, 1817.

14 *Ibid* : Nicol to Marshall, Camp at Imleah, 9 December, 1817.

15 N.A.I. For. Sec, 1817 : O.C. No. 46-57, 19 December, 1817, Marshall to Nicol, Camp Kishanganj, 6 November, 1817.

16 Blacker : *Memoir*, p. 85.

17 Contrasting his zealous help, Tod said to him that, "it is a source great pleasure to observe in the midst of such deriliction of principle from those bound by solemn treaties, the different line of

conduct at once taken and uniformly pursued by the Raj Rana Zalim Singh."

N.A.I. For. Sec. 1818 : O.C. No. 43, 9 January, 1818, Tod to Adam, Camp Rowtah : 10 December, 1817.

18 N.A.I. For. Sec. 1817 : O.C. No. 66-68, 26 December, 1817. Malcolm to Adam, Camp at Mainah. 24 November, 1817.

19 N.A.I. For. Sec. 1817 : O.C. No. 31-34, 26 December, 1817, Nicol to Brig. Gen. Frith, Commanding Agra, HQ Camp Laheira, 4 December, 1817.

20 *Supplement to the Government of India Gazette* : 15 January, 1818.

21 *Government of India Gazette* : 15 January, 1818, mentions that the Pindaris left only 500 to 600 of their best cavalry to fight rear-guard action.

22 Pindaris were so discomfited that many individuals entreated the villagers to secrete and protect them from the vengeance the British arms.

N.A.I. For. Sec. 1818 : O.C. No. 14-16, 16 January, 1818, Marshall to Brig. J.W. Adams Comdg. Nagpur Subsidary Force, Camp Seronj, 6 December, 1817.

23 N.A.I. For. Sec. 1818 : O.C. No. 92, 16 January, 1818, Donkin to Adam. Camp on the Kali Sind, 2 coss north east of Burrode, 20 December, 1818.

24 For. Misc. 124 A : Extract Secret Letter from the Governor-General, dated Camp Oochar, near Sonari Ghat, 29 December, 1817, p. 131.

Also : N.A.I. For. Sec. 1818 : O.C. No. 14-16 January, 1818 : Marshall to J.W. Adam, Camp Seronj, 6 December, 1817.

25 N.A.I. For. Sec. 1818 : O.C. No. 17-19, 16 January, 1818 : &

N.A.I. For. Sec. 1818 : O.C. No. 48-51, 6 February, 1818, Tod to Adam, Rowtah, 2 January, 1818.

"Karim and Wasil Mohemmed are reported to have arrived without a particle of baggage, which has all been thrown away in the rapidity of their flight."

26 N.A.I. For. Sec. 1818 : O.C. No. 88, 16 January, 1818 : Extracts Division Orders by Maj, Gen. Donkin, HQ Camp Semree, 18 December, 1817 : "The State Palkee, elephants and velvet Howdah of Karim Khan brought into eamp and the two camels bearing the Nobuts and standards captured yesterday having been estimated at a fair valuation at 4,000 rupees to be purchased on the part of the government... these trophies being retained as public property to accompany the Division during the present operations."

27 N.A.I. For. Sec. 1818 : O.C. No. 20-22. 16 January, 1818 :
Donkin to Moira, 18 December, 1817.

28 Blacker : *Memoir*, pp. 102-103.

29 H.R.R.S. No. 239, Vol. No. 340, Hislop to Hastings : Camp Paun Bahar, 18 December 1817, para 4.

30 N.A.I. For. Pol. 1817 : O.C. No. 28, 11 February, 1817 : Russell to Adam, Camp Neemgaon. 4 January, 1817.

31 N.A.I. For. Sec. 1818 : O.C. No. 4-6, 30 January, 1818 : Adam to Metcalfe, Camp Oochar, 8 January, 1818. The Governor-General allowed Sir David Ochterlony "to entertain a body of these and of his best horse at the rate of pay established in his army."

32 In April, 1818 the remaining divisions of Amir Khan were recorganised under Lt. Col. Knox.

33 It consisted of 3rd and 4th Bengal Cavalry, 4 Risalas of Cunningham's Horse, Dromedary Corps, Galloper Guns, two 12 pounders, 18th Bengal Infantry and one Company of Pioneers.

34 Ahmed was once the seat of a powerful family, who held it as a fief from the Rana of Udaipur. The Rao Raja of Ahmed fought in the Deccan Wars of Aurangzeb.

Blacker : *Memoir*. p. 196.

35 For. Misc. 124 A : Deposition of two Cossids lately returned from the camp of the Rt. Hon'ble the Governor-General, p. 184.

36 N.A.I. For. Sec. 1818 : O.C. No. 51-54, 30 January, 1818 Adam to Close, 9 January, 1818.

37 For. Misc. 124 A : W.G. Keir to Hislop : 10 Jan. 1818, p. 182.

38 Burton : *The Maratha and the Pindari War*, p. 63

39 Burton mentions the figure as, 3,000 horsemen and 2,000 other followers.

40 *Ibid.*

41 Lt. Col. Adams however, mentions the distance of pursuit to be six or seven miles. N.A.I. For. Sec. 1818 : O.C. No. 16-17, 3 April, 1818, Lt. Col. Adams to Nicol, Camp Gangraur, 14 January, 1818.

42 For. Misc. 124 A : Major Clarke, Brig. Commanding Reserve, Camp Gangraur, 14 January, 1818, p. 303.

43 N.A.I. For. Sec. 1818 : O.C. No. 16-17, 3 April, 1818 : Lt. Col. Adams to Nicol, Camp Gangraur, 14 January, 1818.

44 For. Misc. 104 A : Letter from Sir T. Hislop to Hastings, 21 December, 1817, pp, 145-146.

45 *Government of India Gazette* : February 19, 1818.

46 *Government Gazette* of 19th February, 1818. Burton mentions the date of attack on the fort as 29th January, 1818. Also : N.A.I. For. Sec. 1818 : O.C. No. 88, 13 March, 1818, Malcolm to Lushington, Camp at Jawud, 17 February 1818.

47 Burton : *General Staff* p. 65.

48 Bhima Bai was daughter of Jaswant Rao Holkar (she was not born of Tulsi Bai, whose son Malhar Rao was the Holkar) she led her troops regularly. She was married to Kishan Rao, Governor of the country south of Dhar. But at the time her surrender she was a

widow, enjoying Jagir at Petalwad. She was then only twenty years of age.

49 N.A.I. For. Sec. 1818 : O.C. No. 58-62, 17 April, 1818, Hislop to Moira, Camp on the North Bank of Narbada, 23 February, 1818.

50 N.A.I. For.Sec. 1818 : O.C. No. 51-54, 30 January, 1818, Adam to Close, 9 January, 1818.

51 "In fine, being viewed, as public robbers, their extirpation was aimed at, and not their defeat as an enemy entitled to the rights of war."
Fitzclarence : Journal of a route across India, p. 42.

52 N.A.I. For. Sec. 1818 : O.C. No. 69-79, 13 March, 1818, Draft of a note addressed by Capt. Stewart, on a commission to Bhopal, first Assistant to Brig. Gen. Sir John Malcolm to Karim Khan, Wasil Mohammad, Namdar Khan and chiefs of the Pindaris : dated 25th January, 1818, Nawab of Bhopal also wrote a similar letter to Namdar Khan, Wasil Mohammad, Buksh Khan, Chiefs of Pindaris, dated 27th January, 1818.

53 B.G.R: D. No. 304 Pol. Deptt. 1817 : Malcolm to Hislop Camp at Mundsore, 1 January, 1818.

54 N.A.I. For. Sec. 1818 : O.C. No. 58-62, 17 April 1818, Malcolm to Hislop, Jawud, 17 February, 1818.

55 N.A.I. For.Sec. 1818 : O.C. No. 69-79, 13 March, 1818, J.W. Adams to J. Adams, HQ 5 Dn. Camp, Deorajpur, 5 February, 1818.
Also : N.A.I. For. Sec. 1818 : O.C. No. 69-79; 13 March, 1818 : Tod to Adam : Rowtah, 26 January, 1818.

56 N.A.I. For. Sec. 1818 : O.C. No. 45-50, 30 January, 1818: Caulfield to Malcolm, 6 January, 1818.

57 N.A.I. For. Sec. 1818 : O.C. No. 342, 24 July, 1818 : Memorandum.

58 Busawan Lal : *Memoir of Amir Khan*, p. 469.

59 N.A.I. For. Sec. 1818 : O.C. No. 88, 13 March, 1818, Malcolm to Lushington, Camp at Jawud. 17 February, 1818.

60 N.A.I. For. Sec. 1818 : O.C. No. 58-62, 17 April, 1818 : Malcolm to Hislop, 17 February, 1818.

61 N.A.I. For. Sec. 1818 : O.C. No. 342, 24 July 1818, Memorandum.

62 N.A.I. For. Sec. 1818 : O.C. No. 69-79, 13 March, 1818 : Lt. Col. J.W. Adams, Comdg. 5th Division, HQ 5th Division, Camp Deorajpur, to J. Adam, 3 February, 1818, para 23.

63 N.A.I. For. Sec. 1818 : O.C. No. 69-79, 13 March, 1818 Stewart to Malcolm, Raiseen, 1 February, 1818.
Also : It may be interesting to note that the Nawab of Bhopal, while on a visit to Stewart, mentioned that the Pindaris were greatly alarmed in regard to their being rent to Europe—which they termed as *Kala Pani*—so much so that Chitu during his wanderings used shout *Kala Pani* even in his sleep. Their conception of *Kala Pani* also included Calcutta. This fear of *Kala Pani* had held the Pindaris back from early surrender.

64 N.A.I. For. Sec. 1818 : O.C. No. 69-79, 13 March, 1818 : Stewart to Malcolm, Raiseen, 1 February, 1818.

65 P.R.R. Daulat Rao Scindia and north Indian Affairs, 1810-1818 : Vol. No. 14, Letter No. 344 : Stewart to Adam. Gwalior, 24 April, 1818.

66 N.A.I. For. Sec. 1818 : O.C. No. 19, 19 June, 1818 : Stewart to Chief Secretary, Gwalior, 28 May, 1818.

67 T.P.P.R. O.C. No. 193, Enclosure in a letter from Capt. Stoneham dated and received 15 June. 1818, Translation of an Arzee from Kauder Buksh.
Also : N.A.I. For. Sec. 1818 : O.C. No. 346, 24 July, 1818, Malcolm to Adam, Holkar's camp, 1 March, 1818.

68 C.I.A.R. File No. 4, Bhopal Letter Book, Vol. V of Special Papers and Correspondence : Translation of a letter addressed by Brig. Gen. Sir John Malcolm to Pindari Chief Seetoo and Rajun, p. 144.

69 N.A.I. For. Sec. 1818 : O.C. No. 390, 24 July, 1818 : Translation of a letter addressed by Brig. Gen. Sir John Malcolm to the Pindari Chiefs Chitu and Rajun.

70 N.A.I. For. Sec. 1818 : O.C. No. 386, 24 July, 1818 : Malcolm to Adam, 5 April 1818.
Also : For. Misc. 124 A : Malcolm to Hastings, 8 April, 1818, p. 169.

71 N.A.I. For. Sec. 1818 : O.C. No. 49-52, 17 April, 1818 : Extract from Capt. Grant to Lt. Col. Blacker, Camp at Bagli, 11 Februry, 1818.

72 N.A.I. For. Sec. 1818 : O.C. No. 24-27. 1 May, 1818 : Henley to Adam : Bhopal, 25 March, 1818.

73 For. Misc. 124 A : Hastings to the Secret Committee : 1 March, 1820, p. 397, para 67.

74 Central Provinces District Gazetteers : Nimar District, Vol. A, p. 40.

75 N.A.I. For, Sec. 1818 : O.C. No. 10-12, 1 May, 1818 : Adam to Malcolm, Camp Koolwaee, 8 April, 1818.

76 N.A.I. For. Sec. 1819 : O.C. No. 61, 13 March 1819 : Malcolm to Adam, Camp at Bikungaun, 17 February, 1819.

77 "Chitu and his son on quitting the Hursode jungles crossed the Nurbuddah at Poongaut. Here they separated: Cheetoo directing his course towards the village of Bhatiah in the Sutwas District and through these jungles to those of Kantapore, travelling both day and night, he took the road to Bagley, but the passes were all watched by the Kantapore troops. Passing by the village of Deyree, between Kantapore and Bagley, he turned off the hight road and entered a valley abounding with tigers, ten or fifteen people having lately been destroyed by them near the same spot,"
Also: "At day break on the 19th instant Cheetoo pursued his journey, when it is supposed a tiger sprung on him from behind and dismounting him away to a river not far off. On loosing its rider, the

horse returned to the high road it bad lately quitted when it was shortly after perceived and seized by a body of Holkar's Horse proceeding from Bagley to Kantapore. Near the spot they found Seetoo's sword and woollen coat, and in the saddle bag were three rings and 250 rupees. His Horse and other articles were brought into Kantapore ... the whole were recognised as Cheetoo's property by a Pindarry residing at that place."
N.A.I. For. Sec. 1918 : O.C. No. 14-15, 3 April, 1819 : Translation of a letter from Nanah dated Kantapore, 27 February, 1819.

78 N.A.I. For. Sec. 1818 : O.C. No. 14-15, 3 April, 1818 : Malcolm to Metcalfe, camp Boargaun, 2 March, 1819.

79 N.A.I. For. Sec. 1819 : O.C. No. 70-71, 8 April 1819 : Malcolm to Metcalfe, Camp near Assergarh, 12 March, 1819.

80 "Their early retreat saved them."
For. Misc. 124 A : Hastings to the Secret Committee : 1 March, 1820, p. 396, para 60.

81 Blacker : *Memoirs*, p. 105.

82 "In such a case, the absence of artillery might have exposed them to a serious check, which very few officers, after a long service, will voluntarily hazard."
Blacker, *Memoirs*, p. 105.

83 Supra, pp. 35-37.

84 Blacker : *Memoirs* pp. 107-108.

10

Resettlement of the Pindari Chiefs

Policy towards Pindaris after Surrender

Even before the general war against the Pindaris was declared, the Governor-General laid down certain principles on the basis of which, the problem of dispersed and defeated Pindaris was to be solved.

Hastings, a man of foresight as he was, not only planned for the annihilation of the Pindaris, but also took necessary steps to prevent their revival. To attain this objective, Pindari leaders and their followers were encouraged to surrender to the British, so that they could be settled under their protection. This arrangement, it was considered, would induce the Pindaris to take to peaceful occupation.[1] Hence a public announcement was made declaring that the Pindari chiefs could come under the protection of the British on the promise that they would never again resort to their old mode of life. Excepting the chiefs who were permitted to retain their horses and arms, all other Pindaris were required to surrender their accoutrement.

It was decided that the Pindari chiefs were to be re-settled in distant parts of the country, where, though subject to certain vigilance, they would be free to carry on their avocation of agriculture. This would remove them from their former haunts,[2] which would otherwise have constantly reminded them of their past and might have lured them at the slightest opportunity to reveal to the same mode of life. To develop attachment to their new habitations the Pindaris were granted lands, grains, agricultural implements, cattle, seeds etc.

The principle to which the British would not strictly adhere to was the concentration of various resettled Pindari chiefs at one place. Hence, as far as possible, they were to be settled apart from one another under the Superintendentship of Capt. Henley.[3]

The British intended to afford them the means of a comfortable and respectable subsistence for themselves, their families and immediate dependents. Their generosity attracted a huge number of the hapless Pindaris seeking British shelter, the number increased so enormously that the Governor-General, ordered their immediate release.[4] They were liberated and furnished with adequate means of living.[5] However, to prevent ill-use of such doles, a rule was made that no Pindari of any description, the chief excepted, would be allowed to receive subsistence until the expiry of fifteen days from the date of their surrender. In this manner the time factor helped in establishing the correct identity of one, who was to receive help. The British decided to allot subsistence at the following rate.[6]

	per day	
	Rs.	As.
(a) Horseman being of the Pindari Tribe by birth or long adherence	0	2
(b) Tokhdars of less than 100 horse	0	4
(c) Tokhdars of less than 200 horse	0	8
(d) Chief of durra, each	1	8

The Nawab of Bhopal was also allowed to rehabilitate some of the Pindaris in the arid desert and wastelands of Bhopal.[7] To encourage Pindaris to settle in his territory, the Nawab offered them any quantity of land that they could cultivate. However, when Capt. Henley went to inspect the

Pindaris resettled there, he laid a uniform standard which determined the proportionate allowances according to the class of the Pindari[8]:—

(a)	To each Pindari Horseman	25 Bighas and Rs. 50/-
(b)	To each Jemadar, Mohulladar or Thokdar	50 Bighas and Rs. 125/-
(c)	To each Jemadar, Mohulladar or Thokdar of Superior ranks	70 Bighas and Rs. 200/-
(d)	Such chiefs as it was particularly desirable to settle, from their activity and enterprising character and the influence they may possess among the Pindaris.	Rs. 300/-

Henley also drew the attention of the British Government to the state of starvation and misery among the Pindaris and suggested that the allowances be enhanced. He recommended that it may be increased to Rs. 4/- per Pindari Horseman, while each chief be given an extra allowance for maintaining slaves etc., for which he suggested Rs. 8/- per month for second rate chiefs and Rs. 16/- for the first rate. It was further suggested that Kunwars were to be given Rs. 6/- as an allowance for subsistence and Rs. 90/- for the purchase of cattle.[9] It was also decided that on the land allotted to the Pindaris, there was to be no revenue for the first two years, but from the third year progressive assessment was to begin.[10]

Karim Khan

Malcolm, to whom Karim Khan surrendered, after discussion, decided a plan for his resettlement, to which Karim Khan readily agreed. According to the general principle of removing the Pindaris from their former haunts to far-off lands, Karim was allotted land in the Gorakhpur region for the support of his family and immediate dependents.[11] For this purpose, orders were issued to Ricketts, Collector of Gorakhpur, to purchase a piece of land for allotment to Karim. Instructions were also issued to the Collector not to place any restrictions on him, except that police and revenue officers were to keep strict vigilence on his movements.[12] Consequently, Ricketts purchased the estate of Barriapur and Ganeshpur for the Pindari chiefs Karim Khan and Kauder Buksh.[13] Meanwhile, suitable houses in the city were procured for the accommodation of the Pindari chiefs.

Karim Khan's family consisted of his wife and two sons, Shahmat Khan and Shamsher Bahadur. He had about one hundred and fifty attendants, serving him and his wife Lalkee Begum. His son Shahmat Khan had two wives and about one hundred dependants. Another of his sons Shamsher Bahadur, had about fifty dependants. Sahdil Khan, one of Karim's nephews, had about ten. In addition to the above, the following *kunwars* and *jemadars* were also considered to be members of his family: Ratan, Khuda Buksh, Bhekan, Ramzan 1st and 2nd, Moti, Salabat, Parman, Bharta and Kushal Kunwars,[14] Kalloo, Saranjit, Imam Buksh, Goriyat, Puran and Bapu Jemadars. The Kunwars and Jemadars among themselves had about two hundred and fifty hangers-on. In all Karim Khan had about five hundred and ninety dependents.[15]

Karim was allowed land the value of which was Rs. 16,000/- per annum.[16] Till he was given the actual possession of the land, he was granted a monthly allowance of Rs. 1,000/-. Later, after due improvements, the land yielded a revenue of about Rs. 20,000/- annually.[17]

According to the general policy of the British to disallow any of the Pindari chiefs to settle in Malwa, Namdar, who was Karim's nephew, was allotted lands at Gorakhpur. While his family had covered half way to Gorakhpur, he made a petition to the Governor-General praying that he be allowed to settle in Bhopal, which surprisingly enough was accepted on humanitarian grounds.[18] The decision of the British greatly piqued Karim Khan who was thrown to a place far away from his home.

Karim Khan made a representation to the British Government for the grant of land to his sons Shahmat Khan, Shamsher Bahadur and Chelas Kushal Khan and Ratan Khan, who, Karim maintained, had to leave their 'jagirs' when they gave themselves up to the British.[19] The request was rejected as extravagant. He was reminded that the big allowance of Rs. 1,600/- was meant for himself and the family and hence no separate allowance could be granted to his sons.[20]

Namdar Khan

Namdar Khan was allowed by the Governor-General, on the recommendation of Lt. Col. Adams, to remain in Malwa under the Superintendentship of the Nawab of Bhopal, who had earlier stood guarantee to Namdar's good conduct. The Nawab was however soon relieved of this obligation by the Governor-General.[21] This was a special consideration shown to him because of his early surrender and past services to the Nawab. Even before permission to remain in Malwa was given, it was made clear that no lands would be granted to him in Bhopal and that his monetary allowances would be reduced.[22] His younger brother Shojat Khan was given help to the extent of Rs. 2,000/- per annum, which commenced right from the date of his arrival at Bhopal.[23]

Namdar's allowance was fixed at Rs. 8,125/- (Bhopal currency) payable in quarterly instalments.[24] The first instalment was to commence on February 1, 1818 when Namdar Khan surrendered.[25] Namdar was told that in case he continued to behave well, suitable provision would be made for his posterity.[26] His family and he fixed their abode in the district of Bersia, now under British possession. He was also allowed to farm a village which was assessed to yield a revenue of Rs. 601/- a year.

Wasil Mohammad

After Wasil Mohammad had been apprehended at Gwalior,[27] the Acting Resident to Scindia, Stewart, immediately sent him under a guard, commanded by Lt,

Mackennon, with a detachment of 1st Battalion of the 21st Regiment of Infantry. He reached Gazipur on July 7, 1818.[28] The Governor-General felt that it was not advisable to establish Wasil Mohammad near Karim and hence Gazipur was chosen.[29]

During the course of his journey, he was given an allowance of Rs. 5/- a day. He was also allowed a small sum for the purchase of the immediate necessities of life, as he was a destitute. A monthly stipend of two hundred rupees was also granted.[30]

In consequence of the manner in which he was captured, the facilities which had been given to Karim and Namdar Khan and to others were denied to Wasil Mohammad. Stewart warned the Government of Wasil Mohammad's future conduct, particularly the possibility of his escape.[31] Consequently, strict watch was kept on him and his residence,[32] fixed in the immediate vicinity of the principal *thana* of the town.[33] Police officers were specially instructed to see that his attempt to escape, if any, was foiled.

Wasil Mohammad was a man of action and therefore, he did not like the sedentary mode of existence at Gazipur. Though he was treated well, he was all the time restless.[34] The Magistrate was thinking in terms of making a permanent provision for him, but this restless spirit, however, could not brook his condition. He, therefore, made an attempt to escape, but his plan leaked out prematurely and he was caught in the act of escaping. He swallowed poison, which he had prepared for such a contingency, and died on the spot.

Kauder Buksh

Kauder Buksh surrendered on February 28, 1818 to Malcolm.[35] He expressed a desire to settle at Gorakhpur, where land was allotted to him. The family of Kauder Buksh consisted of his wife, five sons, three daughters, two nephews and one son-in-law. Three of his sons and one of his nephews were married. They all had chidlren. Kauder Buksh had a number of male and female servants. His family comprised of thirty-one persons. In addition to the above, Kauder Buksh had more than fifty slaves, of whom about twenty-five were married and had children. Thus his family and slaves numbered one hundred and twenty-one persons.[36]

When he surrendered he was given an advance of twelve hundred rupees for his immediate needs including his expense for the journey. He was also granted land which yielded between three to four thousand rupees per annum.[37] Kauder Buksh made a request that Raza Kunwar, who was then reported captured by Malcolm, be sent to Gorakhpur. The request was accepted.[38] He was finally allotted four thousand per annum which was to continue till he was to realise the produce of the land granted to him.[39]

Rajun

Rajun surrendered to Malcolm. He accompanied Lt. Macdonald and the son of the Raja of Baglee, when he gave himself up.[40] Malcolm allowed him to go to Baglee and subsequently to Kota for about five or six months to collect his family and followers.[41] He was paid in advance three months allowance at the rate of two hundred rupees per month. He was sent to Gorakhpur, where Stoneham, Superintendent of the Pindari camp, reported his arrival on March 5, 1819. He was given a temporary residence in the city and two chaprasis were placed at his disposal.[42] A personal allowance of three hundred rupees was also allowed. Rajun had only seven or eight followers at the time of his surrender. He was given the promise that on his family joining him, he would be given an additional allowance of one hundred rupees.

Immediately after his incarceration, Rajun or Raja Mohammad as he was also called, made an application to the Government soliciting permission for return to Bhopal, where the principal members of his family were living.[43] He also prayed for the grant of land in lieu of the allowance he was receiving or to continue to receive allowance and also to settle in Bhopal itself. This request was allowed by the Governor-General,[44] and he settled in the village Peeplianagar or Shujawalpur near Sehore[45] where a further request, of his family being allowed to hold the land in their possession after his death, was allowed.[46] Rajun continued to be loyal to the British, so much so that during the rise of an imposter at Nalkhera[47] he and his Pindari followers remained absolutely quiet.

Mirza Buksh

Mirza Buksh was allowed a pension of six hundred and seventy Bhopal rupees per month in addition to one hundred and fifty Bhopal rupees towards the maintenance of late Wazir Mohammad's family.[48]

Mazhur Buksh

Mazhur Buksh was allowed to settle down in Malwa, under the personal guarantee of the Nawab of Bhopal for peaceful conduct.

The underlying policy of the British in granting allowances, pensions and land was to convert the Pindaris from idle, dissipated pensioners into useful and contented members of the society. In spite of opportunities coming their way, most of the Pindari chiefs continued to behave faithfully.

Their General Progress after Re-settlement

The Pindari chiefs and their followers carried on their avocations peacefully. However, like ordinary agriculturists, they now had to face a number of difficulties. In his report,[49] Henley, after visiting the various villages in which the Pindaris had been settled in Gorakhpur, Gazipur and Bhopal,[50] brought to the notice of the Governor-General, the extreme difficulties that the Pindaris had to face. At the outset he reported that the season had been most unfavourable, resulting in the loss of their crops, thereby, causing great distress to them. The monsoon, in 1818, was unusually heavy, which not only rendered it impossible to plough the land, but also promoted the growth of grass and jungle in an unusual exuberance. The task of clearing this jungle was arduous. The Pindaris tried their best to cultivate as large a tract as possible. Yet, all that was not sufficient for their subsistence.

The monthly allowances were proposed to be discontinued in December, 1818. Henley, knowing the difficulties of the settlers, recommended its continuance until March, 1819, after which period, the spring harvest would afford an abundant supply.[51] Thus it will be seen that but for the normal day to day struggles of life the Pindaris were making rapid progress towards a contented and peaceful life. Since Bhopal was very thickly forested, a number of Pindaris were killed by tigers while clearing the land allotted to them.[52] However, their allowances were continued to be disbursed to their successors and other members of their families. A small allowance of Rupees six was granted to each village to meet the expenses incurred in the performance of religious ceremonies at the time of re-occupation of the villages which had been destroyed and deserted in consequence of the Pindari raids.

Within three decades of their final suppression, most of the Pindari leaders passed to the heavenly abode. Karim Khan died a peaceful death.[53] Namdar Khan died on May, 12, 1846.[54] Mirza Buksh enjoyed the British allowances till November 9, 1843 when he died.[55] Mazhur Buksh died in 1843.[56] His pension at that time amounted to Rs. 8,040/-per annum. Rajun died on October 26, 1831.[57]

Evasion of Arrest

Here, mention may be made of the Pindaris who evaded arrest. In spite of the best efforts, some petty leaders and ordinary Pindaris managed to escape. They spread themselves in Scindia's far-flung districts and remained active.[58] It was estimated that nearly three hundred and fifty Pindaris were employed in Scindia's forces alone.[59] Besides, some were given protection and shelter by different officers of Daulat Rao Scindia.[60]

A number of Pindaris attached themselves to the successors of Jai Singh, one of the rebel chiefs against Scindia. They were very well acquainted with the region and therefore carried on their depredations, though on a very small scale. The British were worried on that score. They realised that if the Pindaris were allowed to follow their former pursuits, they would have a very bad effect upon those who had already submitted and had started leading a peaceful life. There was another danger too. A number of Pindaris were wandering about unemployed and in a state of starvation, living on casual labour. Coming in contact with the Pindaris already settled, they influenced them also.

The only Pindari leaders of note who continued to evade arrest and who carried on depredations were Buksh Khan, Ghasita Jemadar and Rajan Chella, besides Sheikh Dulla. For years Sheikh Dulla carried on depredations in and around the region of Asirgarh and Burhanpur. He was a terror to the people and committed the most cruel barbarities upon them. He was supposed never to have "dismounted from his black mare even at night." The local people said of him:

> "*Niche Zamin aur upar Allah,*
> *Aur bichmen phire Sheikh Dullah.*"[61]

In 1824 he espoused the cause of one "imposter pretending to be Chimnaji Appa, the brother of ex-Peshwa." He also assisted the Bhils in their depredations. On being turned out by Maj. Seyer from the Asirgarh area, he fled to Nasik, but soon returned and took shelter in the jungles of Tapti in 1825. He continued his depredations, with occasional defeats at the hands of the British officers Lts. Harkness and Twiner. In 1828, he was killed by the treachery of one of his associates. Namdar Khan made fruitless attempts to wean him away from such activities.

Ghasita Jemadar and Rajun Chella were serving the followers of Jai Singh, while Lodi Jemadar was seen in the service of Ajit Singh. Mugal Ali, a minor Pindari was employed by Pattunkar, a Scindia's officer.

Daulat Rao Scindia was requested to order his officers not to employ Pindaris in their forces, but with no result.

Dhonkal Singh, pretender to the Jodhpur throne, also engaged Pindaris in his depredations. Ajit Singh and Dhonkal Singh were both approached by the British to dismiss the Pindaris from their services but the advice was disregarded. However, from time to time the Pindaris were liquidated. In Rajputana, Zalim Singh succeeded in curbing them.

Some of the Pindaris, although peacefully settled for long, joined the mutineers in the Mutiny of 1857. Shojat Khan, brother of Namdar Khan, participated in the mutiny and was responsible for the murder of the Superintendent of Bersia, Babu Soob Ram.[62] Of the four half-brothers of Namdar Khan, three were executed for rebellion.[63] A few more minor Pindaris were executed for their part in the rebellion. A minor chief Kamdar Khan was executed by hanging on the gateway of the fort of Rahatgarh.[64] His property was also confiscated by the Government.[65] This brings the story of the Pindaris to a close. In the end it has to be admitted that their suppression and rehabilitation was a notable achievement of the British Government.

FOOT-NOTES

1 N.A.I. For. Sec. 1818 : O.C. No. 8-10, 6 February, 1818 : Adam to Malcolm, Oochar, 7 January, 1818.

2 The British officers were told that "no single measure is so well calculated to aid in preventing the revival of the system of which they formed so conspicuous a part as their separation from the mass of their followers and their removal to a distance from their former connections and the scene of their past exploits."
N.A.I. For. Sec. 1818 : O.C. No. 2, 29 May, 1818 : Adam to Malcolm, Gorakhpur, 10 May, 1818, para 6.

3 N.A.I. For. Sec. 1818 : O.C. No. 69-79, 13 March, 1818 : Stewart on a Commission to Bhopal to Lt. Col. Adams, Raiseen, 25 February, 1818.

4 The release of the Pindaris was free, and assumed such proportions that Capt. Henley, Superintendent of the Pindari Camp, drew the attention of the Government, warning that the number of such people might create a situation of law and order. Henley suggested

that instead of releasing these people they should be despatched to the eastern frontier region where they would be utilised on public works.
N.A.I. For. Pol. 1818 : O.C. No. 113, 26 December, 1818 : Henley to Adam, Camp at Tullyn, 4 December, 1818. To this proposal the Governor-General agreed in his letter to Henley.
N.A.I. For. Pol. 1818 : O.C. No. 114, 26 December, 1818 : Adam to Henley, Fort William, 26 December, 1818.

5 N.A.I. For. Sec. 1818 : O.C. No. 27, 13 March, 1818 : Adam to Wauchope, Shankarpur Camp, 19 February, 1818.

6 N.A.I. For. Sec. 1818 : O.C. No. 80-81, 13 March, 1818 : J.W. Adams to J. Adams, HQ 5th Division, Camp near Bhilsa, 15 February, 1818.

7 However, when the question of actual allotment of land to the Pindaris arose, they were given the best of lands in Bhopal.
N.A.I. For. Sec. 1818 : O.C. No. 89, 29 August, 1818 : Capt. Henley on Duty at Bhopal to Adam, Sehore, 26 July, 1818.

8 N.A.I. For. Sec. 1818 : O.C. No. 19-23, 1 May, 1818 : Henley to Adam, Raiseen, 13 March, 1818.

9 It was estimated that the approximated figure of Rs. 53,149 was needed for subsistence among the Pindaris, including the chiefs, who surrendered. *Ibid* : Enclosure—statement.

10 N.A.I. For. Sec. 1818 : O.C. No. 19-23, 1 May, 1818 : Henley to Adam, Raiseen, 13 March, 1818.

11 For. Misc. 124 A : Extract letter from Sir J. Malcolm to Adam, Camp Ujjain, 23 March, 1818.

12 N.A.I. For. Pol. 1818 : O.C. No. 29, 1 May, 1818 : Adam to Mordaunt Ricketts, Collector of Gorakhpur, Camp Boojpur, 10 April, 1818.

13 N.A.I. For. Pol. 1818 : O.C. No. 65, 24 July, 1818 : Ricketts to Adam, Gorakhpur, 23 June, 1818.

14 N.A.I. For. Sec. 1818 : O.C. No. 368, 24 July, 1818 : Memorandum of the family and immediate dependents of Karim Khan.

15 *Ibid.*

16 B.G.R. D. No. 447 : Malcolm to Adam, Camp Ujjain, 23 March, 1818.
Also : N.A.I. For. Sec. 1818 : O.C. No. 967, 24 July, 1818: Stoneham to Adam, Gorakhpur, 13 June, 1818.

17 C.I.A.R. Bhopal Book B. 26 : Report by Cunningham, Political Agent in Bhopal to R.N.C. Hamilton, Resident at Indore, Camp Sehore, 13 January, 1847.

18 N.A.I. For. Sec. 1818 : O.C. No. 435, 24 July, 1818 : Malcolm to Adam, Camp at Mhow, 11 May, 1818.
Also : Letter of 3rd May, 1818.

19 T.P.P.R. O.C. No. 193, 15 June, 1818 : Enclosure in a letter from Capt. Stoneham dated and received 15 June, 1818.

Also : Translation of a copy of an Arjee from Karim Khan Pindari.

20 N.A.I. For. Pol. 1818 : O.C. No. 46, 10 July, 1818 : Adam to Stoneham, June, 1818.

21 N.A.I. For. Sec. 1818 : O.C. No. 3, 29 May, 1818 : Adam to Henley, 10 May, 1818.

22 "I could only state that Namdar Khan by remaining in Malwa forfeit many of the advantages which he would have received in Bengal and that he would have no land assigned to him in Bhopal." N.A.I. For.Sec. 1818 : O.C. No. 392, 24th July, 1818 : Malcolm to Adam, Camp at Tapah, 12 April, 1818.

23 N.A.I. For. Sec. 1818 : O.C. No. 89, 29 August, 1818 : Henley to Adam, Sehore, 26 July, 1818.

24 C.I.A.R. Letter Book No. 118 : Sunad granted to Namdar Khan under the seal and signature of Marquiss of Hastings Governor-General of India, 28 November, 1818.

25 N.A.I. For. Sec. 1818 : O.C. No. 61, 29 May, 1818, Henley to Adam, Ashta, 17 April, 1818.

26 *Ibid.*

27 "About 9 O'clock last night I received a communication from Atma Ram that if I would send a guard into the town of Gwalior, Wassell Mohemmed would be delivered up. A guard was accordingly sent and about midnight the Pindari chief was brought a prisoner to the Residency."
N.A.I. For. Sec. 1818 : O.C. No. 39, 12 June, 1818 : Stewart to Adam, Gwalior, 25 May, 1818 :
Also : N.A.I. For. Sec. 1818 : O.C. No. 19, 19 June, 1818, Stewart to Adam, Gwalior, 28 May, 1818.

28 N.A.I. For. Pol. 1818 : O.C. No. 147, 14 August, 1818 : R.M. Bird, Magistrate Gazipur to Adam at Murshidabad, Gazipur, 23 July, 1818.

29 N.A.I. For. Sec. 1818: O.C. No. 11. 26 June, 1818: Adam to Stewart, Gorakhpur , 1 June, 1818.

30 N.A.I. For. Pol. 1818 : O.C. No. 147, 14 August, 1818 : R.M. Bird, Magistrate Gazipur, to Adam at Murshidabad, Gazipur, 23 July, 1818.

31 How correct the forecast was !
N.A.I. For. Sec. 1818 : O.C. No. 19, 19 June, 1818 : Stewart to Adam, Gwalior, 28 May, 1818.

32 N.A.I. For. Sec. 1818 : O.C. No. 19, 26 June, 1818 : Adam to Stewart, Gorakhpur, 6 June, 1818.

32 *Ibid.*

34 Bird, Magistrate Gazipur, writing about Wasil Mohammad, said, "It is impossible that he can avoid contrasting the enterprize and activity and interest, and consquent comparative happiness of his former life, with his present sedentary mode of existence without occupation and without object." N.A.I. For. Pol. 1818 : O C. No.

147, 14 August, 1818, R.M, Bird, Magistrate Gazipur to Adam at Murshidabad, Gazipur, 23 July, 1818.

35 N.A.I. For. Sec. 1818 : O.C. No. 346, 24 July, 1818 : Malcolm to Adam, Holkar's camp, 1 March, 1818.

36 N.A.I. For. Sec. 1818 : O.C. N. 369, 24 July, 1818 : Memorandum of the family of Kauder Buksh.

37 N.A.I. For. Pol. 1818 : O.C. No. 28, 1 May, 1818 : Adam to Malcolm, Boojpur, 10 April, 1818.

38 N.A.I. For. Sec. 1818 : O.C. No. 10, 17 July, 1818 : Adam to Malcolm, Gorakhpur, 29 June, 1818.

39 N.A.I. For. Pol. 1818 : O.C. No. 34, 26 June, 1818 : Adam to Stoneham, Gorakhpur, 10 June, 1818.

40 N.A.I. For. Sec. 1818 : O.C. No. 386, 24 July, 1818 : Malcolm to Adam, 5 April. 1818.

41 N.A.I. For. Sec. 1818 : O.C. No. 391, 24 July, 1818 : Malcolm to Adam, Camp at Tapah, 11 April, 1818.

42 U.P.G.R, Revenue Commissioner's Office, Gorakhpur, File No. 10-14-1 : Vol. IX, Stoneham to Newnham, Secretary to the Board of Commissioners, Farrukhabad, Gorakhpur, 9 March, 1819, pp. 109-117.

43 N.A.I. For. Sec. 1818 : O.C. No. 391, 24 July, 1818 : Malcolm to Adam, 11 April, 1818.

44 C.I.A.R. Bhopal Letter Book. Vol. V : Swinton, Secretary to Government, to Stoneham, Fort William, 4 July, 1823.

45 C.I.A.R. Bhopal Book, B 10 : Letter No. 830, T.H. Maddock, Political Agent to Swinton, Sehore, 14 September. 1825.

46 C.I.A.R. Bhopal Letter Book A No. 6 : Swinton to Maddock, Fort William, 7 October, 1825.

47 C.I.A.R. Bhopal Letter Book B, No. 15 : L. Wilkinson, Acting Political Agent in Bhopal, to G. Wellesley, Resident at Indore, Sehore, 31 October, 1831.

48 C.I.A.R. Letter Book No. 58, Letters to Government of India from 1843-44. Letter No. 65, Hamilton, Resident at Indore to F. Currie Secretary to the Government of India, Indore 2 May, 1844 : Governor-General's Orders : 3 April, 1819.

49 N.A.I. For. Pol. 1818 : O.C. No. 105, 26 December, 1818 : Capt. Henley on Duty at Bhopal to Adam, Camp at Talleyn, 28 November, 1818.

50 The Pindaris in Bhopal were settled under Shahzad Masih, who was invested with unlimited power, who, however, treated the Pindaris with sympathy and consideration. N.A.I. For. Pol. O.C. No. 22-23, 17 December, 1818 : Henley to Adam, Camp Tulleyn, 26 November, 1818.

51 N.A.I. For. Pol. 1818 : O.C. No. 105, 26 December, 1818 : Henley to Adam, Camp at Tulleyn, 28 November, 1818.

52 N.A.I. For. Sec. 1818 : O.C. No. 89, 29 August, 1818 : Henley to Adam, Sehore, 26 July, 1818.

53 The date on which Karim Khan died is not traceable in the available records.

54 C.I.A.R. Bhopal Book, B 26 : Report by J.A. Cunningham, Political Agent in Bhopal to R.N.C. Hamilton, Resident at Indore, Sehore, 13 January, 1847, para 6.

55 C.I.A.R. Bhopal Letter Book No. 58 : R.N.C. Hamilton to F. Currie, Secretary to the Government of India : Indore Residency, 2 May, 1844.

56 C.I.A.R. Bhopal Book B 26 : J.A. Cunningham to R.N.C. Hamilton, Sehore, 13 January, 1847.

57 C.I.A.R. Bhopal Book B 15 : L. Wilkinson, Acting Political Agent in Bhopal to G. Wellesley, Resident at Indore, Sehore, 31 October, 1831.

58 N.A.I. For. Pol. 1818 : O.C. No. 22-23, 17 December, 1818 : Henley to Adam, Camp at Tulleyn, 26 November, 1818.

59 N.A.I. For. Pol. 1818 : O.C. No- 22-23, 17 December. 1818 : Memorandum of Pindaris who have evaded submitting to the British and who are in military employment within the territory of Scindia.

60 N.A.I. For. Pol. 1818 : O.C. No. 22-23, 17 December, 1818 : Henley to Stewart, Camp Bheelkhera, 4 November, 1818.

61 *Central Provinces District Gazetteer*, Nimar District, Vol. A, pp. 41-41.

62 C.I.A.R. Book No. 91 : H.M. Durrand, Officiating A.G.G. for Central India to G. F. Edmonstone, 5 August, 1857.

63 C.I.A.R. Bhopal Letter Book No. 118 : Letter No. 282, Sir R. Shakespeare, A.G.G. for Central India, to the Secretary to the Government of India, 6 June, 1859.

64 C.I.A.R, Bhopal Book No. 95 : Hamilton to Edmonstone, 30 January. 1857.

65 *Ibid.*

11

The Last Phase

Results of the Pindari War

The War against the Pindaris was not an attack upon a state, but upon a system, for the Pindaris represented an organised military system of spoliation. It was a conflict of two diametrically opposite forces — order contending against chaos, law prevailing against brute force and right against might.

The operation against the Pindaris ended in a significant triumph for the British in India, and their defeat and dispersion heralded the dawn of a new age. They were now completely routed and scattered. Those who survived the war mingled themselves with the population and melted away so much so that after a lapse of two years or so, not a trace of the Pindaris remained.

Surprisingly enough, this great organised system of banditti, which at one time numbered more than 60,000, was completely crushed within a short period of about four months. "Such a complete example of the extinction—of the corporate existence—of so large a body within so short a period is hardly to be found in history."[1] Not only militarily, but politically too, the operations against the Pindaris had been remarkably swift. Indeed, the military action suppressed the Pindari menace once for all and crippled the Marathas, while the political action re-drew the map of Central India and Rajputana in a such a thorough manner that it would be no exaggeration to say that it remained the same down the century.

The Pindaris, having been chased and dispersed, converted themselves into peaceful subjects. Most of them were now absorbed in the labouring classes. Some took to selling of wine; a few even learnt the art of making small household articles like utensils or thatching of roofs. Many of them engaged themselves in carrying building material, firewood and grass from one place to another. While, still others were absorbed in the recently-established military cantonment at Mhow, as water-carriers, coolies and in various other capacities. Hundreds of them were encouraged to settle near Indore by Tantia Jogh as grain carriers. Duff testifies to the Pindaris settling in the Deccan and taking to agriculture., They also settled in Malwa and Bhopal as farmers. Thus the freebooters, the one-time terror of India, were completely liquidated. There now remained hardly a spot in India which a Pindari could claim as his home and they were now a memory of the past.[2] To the contemporaries, the Pindaris appeared like an incurable malady which contaminated extensive areas. Rightly, Malcolm observes: "They were created and sustained by distempered times, and on return of order and strength, they disappeared like a morbid excresence when health is restored to the diseased body to which it had appertained."[3]

Effect on Central India

Henceforth, Central India, the main base of operations of the Pindaris, was free from incessant strife and continual alarm. The rehabilitation of the Pindaris not only secured peace and stability for the first time in the history of war-torn Central India, but also added to the prosperity and security of the people, as a result of the alliances with Scindia, Holkar, and Bhopal.

Effect on Maratha Politics

The annihilation of the Pindaris ironically synchronised with the extinction of the glory of their erstwhile masters, the Maratha chiefs, whose power was wholly and irretrievably broken. Sir John Malcolm, in a letter to Lord Hastings wrote that "we shall not have to encounter any combined opposition from these chiefs."[4] No wonder, therefore, that the British were supreme masters of all that they surveyed. Though some of the Maratha chiefs, like Scindia still maintained a qualified independence within their dominions, their foreign relations were controlled by the British, and all external disputes had to be submitted to British arbitration.

A direct consequence of the suppression of the Pindaris was the dissolution of the Maratha Confederacy, which had successfully defied the British for more than four decades. The Peshwa, the head of the confederacy, was now a fugitive, and the Raja of Satara replaced him. The Peshwa was removed from Poona and settled in the village of Bethur near Kanpur, with a liberal pension. He was reluctant to proceed to Benaras on accont of his aversion to the place, and the British would not allow him to remain at Mathura, as it was a frontier station. This brought to a close the career of the Peshwas as king-makers in this country. [5]

The Pindari War left Scindia as the only Indian Raja with some show of independence, but he stood "insulated and precluded from any extraneous assistance.[6] But all his rivals were reduced to such straits that they were now no more a danger to any one. With the termination of the Pindari War, the British were generous enough to restore all such lands to him which he had earlier granted to the Pindaris. He emerged out of the war more strengthened than any other prince. The only territorial loss he suffered was the retention of Asirgarh by the British, besides the cession of Ajmer. The tributes due from various Rajput states were now fixed and the payment henceforth was made to him through the British treasuries.

As far as the Holkar state is concerned, all mercenaries were detached. Amir Khan and Gaffoor Khan were settled as independent rulers of Tonk and Jaora respectively. Holkar's power was irretrievably broken. He was, hereafter, a puppet in the hands of the British Resident, who was stationed at his court.

To Bhonsla, the Pindari War proved very costly. Not only was he defeated, but he lost his kingdom too. Circumstances forced Appa Saheb to escape from Nagpur for personal safety. Frequent rumours were received of his unexpected appearance at different places, but he proved to be as elusive as the wind. He made an unsuccessful attempt for a settlement with the British through an appeal to the Nawab of Bhopal to plead his case.

Effect on the Rajput States

The Pindari War was the salvation of the Rajput states. An alliance with the Rajput states was the central pillar of Mughal policy. The British fully realised the importance of the Rajputs, long before they came into open conflict with the Marathas. It was Hastings who rightly assessed their immense strategic advantage for the Company's military and political position in Central India. It must be borne in mind that the resources of the Rajput states could be effectively used for defensive and offensive purposes. Besides, the Rajput States acted as a buffer between the Sikhs and the British. [7] During a short period of five years, 1818-1823 the Rajput states were completely confederated with the British.[8] To many of these states, the British protection was a blessing in disguise. Some of them regained the lost territory or acquired new lands. [9] Tributes claimed from these Rajput states by the Marathas were no longer exacted or forcibly acquired but were collected by the British Residents on their behalf. In the words of Lord Hastings, the Rajput states "have been delivered from an oppression more systematic, more unremitting, more brutal than perhaps ever before trampled on humanity." [10] Security was established, where nothing but terror and misery existed before. Hastings concluded "it is a proud phrase to use, but it is a true one that we have bestowed blessings upon millions." [11] Since then the Rajputs became staunch and loyal allies of the British and their steady support was a *sine qua non* of British success in 1857.

The post-Pindari period witnessed unprecedented improvement in the territories of Rajputana. With peace, prosperity and security returning, there was considerable increase in population; the enlarged areas brought under cultivation, yielded additional revenue to the coffers of these states.

Long after peace had been established, Sir David Ochterlony reported: "I have only to add that throughout my tour I have derived the most sincere gratification, from observing the prevalent tranquillity and increasing prosperity of the country. From the prince to the peasant I have found every tongue eloquent in the expression of gratitude to the British Government from the blessing they enjoy. Discontent or oppression appears equally unknown." [12]

Effect on the British

When the operations against the Pindaris came to an end, large slices of territories were added to the British possessions. It has been asserted that territorial expansion was never originally intended by the British. Lord Hastings had repeatedly repudiated any aggressive designs. [13] In 1820 when the passion of war had cooled down, he communicated his views to the Home Authorities in the following words: "But for the perfidy and unaccountable folly of the Peshwa and the Raja of Nagpore I might have congratulated myself and your Honourable Committee on the successful accomplishment of my original hope of affecting the suppression of the predatory system, without disturbing any of the established powers of India or adding a rood of land to the possessions of the British Government."[14] But the march of events which we have narrated above, resulted in the acquisition of extensive areas in Central India. It enhanced British power and prestige and paved the way for the consolidation of British rule in India. The liquidation of the Marathas and the protection of the Rajputs further transformed a commercial body into a growing political power only sixty years after Plassey.

Although Hastings appeared to be too modest to congratulate himself, the Home Government was conscious of his remarkable contribution to the cause of the British rule in India. The House of Commons expressed its deep sense of appreciation, on a vote of thanks moved by Mr. Canning, the President of the Board of Control, for the services rendered by Lord Hastings. But he qualified his appreciation with the remark that his actions were "questionable in point of justice" because they led to "systematic encroachement and ambition." [15] The Court of Directors, while giving due recognition to "the foresight, promptitude and vigour with which Lord Hastings had dispersed the gathering elements of a hostile conspiracy," recorded its deep regret for the extension of British territory. [16] Like Clive, Warren Hastings and Lord Wellesley, the Marquiss of Hastings had to face public censure for his actions. The censure was on two accounts. Firstly, Hastings had disregarded the Court's orders for the reduction of the Army, for any such redution, Hastings believed, would have proved fatal to the existence of the British Empire in India. Secondly, he reorganised the Quarter Master General's Department without the previous permisson of the Court.[17]

The Pindari War extended into the Maratha War, a contingency which the Home Authorities were very keen to avoid. Yet, they not only maintained a deliberate and discreet silence but also patted him on the back and passed a resolution whereby they fixed the entire blame and responsibility on the Marathas. The resolution said : "That the operations undertaken by the Governor-General-in-Council against the Pindaris were dictated by the strictest principles of self-defence and that in the extended hostilities, which followed upon those operations, the Maratha princes were in every instance the aggressors."[13]

The Court of Directors realised the exigencies of the situation and praised the work of Lord Hastings in a lengthy resolution which reads as follows :

"Resolved unanimously, that the thanks of this Court be presented to the Most Noble the Marquiss of Hastings K.G......for the wisdom, skill and energy, so eminently displayed by His Lordship, in planning and conducting the late military operations against the Pindaris of which the happy result has been the extinction of a predatory power, which had established itself in the heart of Hindostan, and whose existence experience has shown to be alike, incompatible with the security of the Company's possessions and the general tranquility of India.

" Also, that this Court, whilst it deeply regrets the occurrence of any circumstance leading to an extension of the Company's territories, duly appreciate the foresight, promptitude and vigour, with which the Marquiss of Hastings, by a combination of military with political talents, dispersed the gathering elements of a hostile confederacy amongst the Mahratta states against the British Power." [19]

A similar resolution was passed by the Court of Direc tors, on Tuesday the 20th April 1819 :

" Resolved by the ballot, that the Court (of Directors) recommend to the General Court of Proprietors that the sum of 60,000 be granted from the territorial revenues of India ..for the benefit of the Most Noble the Marquiss of Hastings, Governor-General of India or the Most Noble the Marchioness his present wife, and their issues, in such manner as the Court of Directors shall deem best adapted to their welfare and to perpetuate the sense entertained of His Lordship's high and meritorious services as Governor-General of the British possessions in India."[20]

General Effect

To Lord Hastings nothing appeared to be more gratifying than a permanent solution of the vexed problem of the Pindaris and the Marathas. Indeed, it was rather difficult, though not impossible, to evaluate the full impact of his astounding success. In February, 1818, he felt that he was "still too near it to comprehend it thoroughly."[21]

Following the Pindari and Maratha Wars, Lord Hastings took one of the most significant steps in the formal abolition of the fiction of the Mughal Government, which in fact had ceased to exist as a power much earlier. The Mughal Emperor Akbar II was forced to give up all ceremonial symbols which implied Mughal supremacy over the Company's dominion in India.

A band of able, efficient and zealous officers effected the work of reconstruction, setting up and consolidation of the administration of the Indian states which had come under the British protection. Elphinstone in Western Deccan, Munro in Madras, Malcolm in Central India and Metcalfe, Tod and Ochterlony in Rajputana, completed the task in record time.

The new order which was then established, though not perfect, provided sufficient safeguards against the possibility of future rise of the predatory system. Though minor abuses continued for some time, after about hundred years of misrule, the people saw a benevolent government which did not permit the military adventures in wandering bands to disturb the life of peace-loving people. "The dark age of trouble and violence which so long spread its malign influence over the fertile regions....has thus ceased from this time; and a new era has commenced, we trust, with brighter prospects, an era of peace, prosperity and wealth at least, if not of political liberty and high moral improvement."[22]

The people who had earlier sought shelter in hills and jungles, forts and fortresses came out and reoccupied their old deserted villages and resumed tilling. It was, therefore, not without reason that Lord Hastings and Sir John Malcolm boasted of conferring peace and good government upon the people who had earlier groaned under the Pindari, Afghan and Maratha tyranny. From Sutlej to Cape Comorin, India had not witnessed such tranquillity since the days of Akbar the Great. There was security from external violence and progressive improvement in internal administration. The supremacy of the British was accepted by the masses with a sign of relief, the common man now returned to his normal life, gathering the fruits of a blissful peace.

The rise and growth of the Pindaris during 1789-1816 in the Indian body politic was the direct result of the utter state of anarchy and confusion, consequent upon the downfall of the Mughal Empire. The disintegration of the states and the steady decline of the Marathas after 1805 accelerated the growth of the Pindaris. The non-intervention policy of the successive Governor-Generals saw them assuming alarming proportions. The Pindaris who had so far restricted themselves to the looting and plundering of the Indian states, also extended their depredations to the British territories. They were now a menace both to the British and the Indian rulers.

The Pindaris were nothing but an organised system of bandits. Theirs was a heterogeneous collection of people, a unique fraternity of diverse castes and creeds, religions and faiths. In fact, their artificial combination was the very factor which prevented their solidarity and hastened their downfall. They despoiled small principalities but they could never establish a kingdom of their own. They were always guided by considerations of plunder and pillage.

The sudden collapse of this well-organised military banditti during the two years (1816-1818) of warfare against the Pindaris may be attributed to a variety of causes.

The Pindaris were never able to unite. Discord and disunity were the order of the day, and hence the discordant assemblage could never put forth and execute a sustained and planned warfare. Internecine conflicts and dissensions in a growing community are always the potential factors of its dissolution. The Pindaris, who were initially successful against the British, ultimately succumbed to the superior skill and ability of the latter. The absence of unity of command and lack of leadership also contributed to their defeat. The inferior and obsolete arms and ammunition of the Pindaris handicapped them from the very outset. Here was a typical example of the Indians fighting against the Indians. The Indians under the command of the British and trained and equipped with the latest Western weapons and technique proved themselves immensely superior to the Pindaris who had almost become a rabble during the last phase of their struggle. Lack of whole-hearted sympathy and enthusiastic support from the Indian rulers and masses stood in the way of consolidating their conquests which were held together by sheer force. No wonder, therefore, that their military setbacks were a source of rejoicings to the innocent and helpless people of Malwa, Central India and Rajputana. The Pindari chieftains lacked integrated outlook or goal and refused to subordinate their individual interest to a common cause. The inherent incapacity of the Pindari leaders to devise a sound system of administration which could ensure peace and guarantee prosperity to the subjects, prevented their having popular support.

Realising the huge stature the Pindaris had attained, Lord Hastings decided to put end to their menace. He gave up the old and unsuccessful policy of no-intervention, and adopted a dual policy of force and conciliation. His was a liberal approach to the problem. He realised the military weakness of the Pindaris, who had no knowledge of the science of war. Though numerically superior, they were inferior in all aspects of war. This hastened their downfall. They were in fact no match for the British. Had they won over the sympathies and support of the Rajputs and concluded an alliance with them, they might have created a strong confederacy of Indian rulers in Northern India against the British. This would have altered the course of subsequent events. British diplomacy, statesmanship, constructive genius, tact and liberality, both in war and peace, checked all such threatening possibilities. It has, however, to be admitted that the Pindari system of plunder and loot on a large scale, across the heart of India, speaks highly of their military capabilities. Their meteoric rise and rapid expansion left their imprint on the pages of British Indian history.

It is indeed significant that some of the discontented lot of Pindari survivors participated in the 'Mutiny of 1857'. Had the British failed to liquidate the Pindaris in 1818, they would have certainly joined hands with the 'rebels of Mutiny' to overthrow the British rule in India. It should, therefore, be borne in mind that the British, under the able stewardship of the Marquiss of Hastings, crushed the Pindaris before it was too late. Delay would have sounded the death-knell of the British Empire in India.

FOOT-NOTES

1 Malcolm : *The Rise and Progress* :Preface.

2 "Several of the subordinate chiefs and some of their followers have been settled in agricultural pursuits in the territories of the Nawab of Bhopal, and converted into peaceful and profitable subjects. Those who survived the conflics, mingled with the population and melted away, in so much that a trace of the Pindaris does not remain." For. Misc. 124 A : Letter from Marquiss of Hastings to the Secret Committee. 1 March, 1820, p. 397, para 69.
Also : Malcolm : *Rise and Progress*, para 35.

3 Malcolm : *Report*, Preface.

4 M.I.O.L.L. Vol. No. 521, Item No. 9 : Abstract of a letter from Malcolm to Hastings, 1 July, 1817.

5 Peshwa's adopted son, Nana Saheb played a leading role in the First War of Indian Independence, 1857.

6 Dinner Speech of Lord Hastings : *Government of India Gazette*, 1818, January-December.

7 N.A.I. For. Sec. 1816 : O.C. No. 1, 15 June, 1816 : Governor-General's Minute, 1 December, 1815. para 84.

8 Treaties were concluded with the state of Kota on 26th December, 1817. Udaipur, 16 January, 1818, Bundi, 10 February, 1818; Kishangarh and Bikaner, March, 1818; Jaipur 2 April, 1818, the three kingdoms of Partapgarh, Banswara and Dungarpur branches of Udaipur House on 5 October, 5 December, and 11 December,; 1818, respectively; Jaisalmere on 12 December, 1818 and Sirohi in 1823.

9 The districts of Gungram, Digh, Putchpahar and Ahor were given to Kota by the Treaty of Mundsore.

10 *Summary of Maharatta and Pinbari Campaigns*, p. 273.

11 *Ibid.*

12 Summary of Hastings : p. 19.

13 In this "extensive plan, the addition of a rood to your territory had not been contemplated. Our projects were urged and guided strictly by consideration of self defence."
For. Misc. Vol. 124 A : Hastings to the Court of Directors, 19 May, 1818, p. 282, para 6.

[14] For. Misc. Vol. No. 124 A : Hastings to the Secret Committee, 1 March, 1820, p. 392, para 47.

[15] Marshman : *History of India*, p. 337.

[16] For. Misc. 124 A : Extract Political letter to Bengal, 24 February, 1819, p. 382.

[17] Marshman : *History of India*. p. 337.

[18] M.I.O.L.L. Drafts to India : Letter No. 131 : Secret Committee to the Governor-General, 30 January, 1819, para 19.

[19] For. Misc. 124 A : Extract Political Letter to Bengal, 24 February, 1819, p. 382,

[20] For. Misc, 124 A : Extract Political Letter to Bengal, 30 June, 1819, p. 383.

[21] *Private Journal*, Vol. II, p. 277.

[22] Prinsep : *History of the Political & Military Transactions* : Vol. II, p. 421.

TABLE No. 1
Genealogy Of Pindari Chiefs

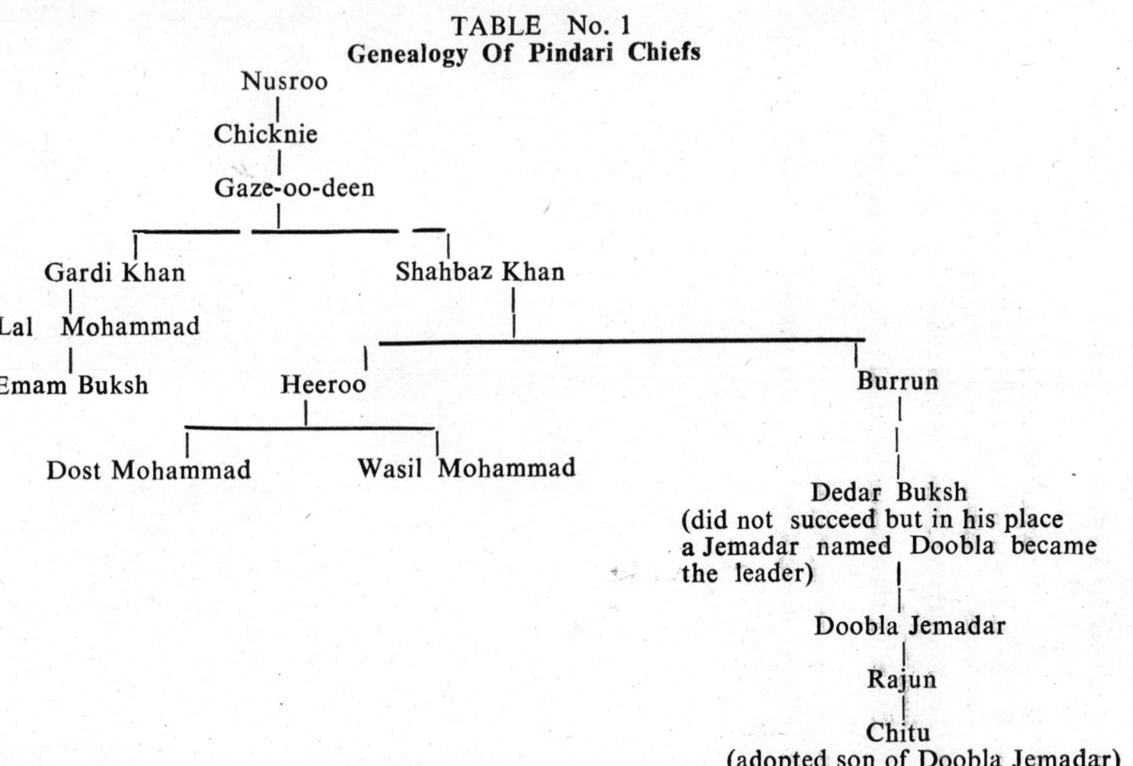

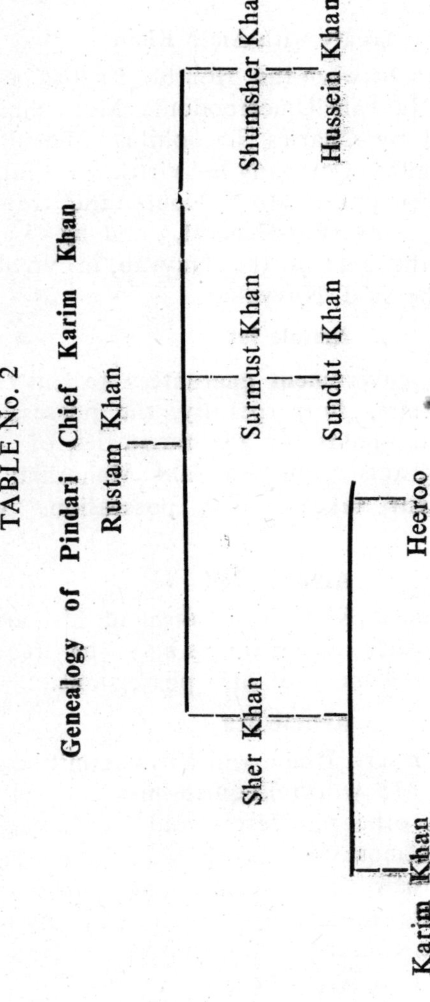
TABLE No. 2
Genealogy of Pindari Chief Karim Khan
Rustam Khan
Sher Khan
Surmust Khan
Shumsher Khan
Sundut Khan
Hussein Khan
Karim Khan
Heeroo

APPENDICES

Treaty with Amir Khan

Engagement between the Hon'ble English East India Company and Nuvvab Umeeroodoula Mohummed Umeer Khan concluded by Charles Theophilus Metcalfe on the part of the Hon'ble Company in virtue of full powers from His Excellency the Most Noble the Marquess of Hastings, K. G., Governor-General, and by Lalla Nur-unjun Lal, on the part of the Nuvvab, in virtue of full powers, from the said Nuvvab.

Article 1st

The British government guarantees to Nuvvab Umeer Khan and his Heirs, in perpetuity, the possession of the places which he holds in the territories of Maharaja Holkur, under grants from the said Maharaja; and the British government takes those possessions under its protection.

Article 2nd

Nuvvab Umeer Khan will disband his army, with the exception of such a portion as may be requisite for the internal arrangement of his possessions.

Article 3rd

Nuvvab Umeer Khan will not commit aggressions in any country. He will relinquish his connections with the Pindaris and other plunderers and will moreover co-operate to the utmost of his power with the British government for their chastisement and suppression. He will not enter into negotiations with any person whatever, without the consent of the British government.

Article 4th

Nuvvab Umeer Khan will deliver up to the British government all his guns and military equipments with the exception of such a portion as may be requisite for the internal management of his possessions and the defence of his forts and shall receive in exchange an equitable pecuniary compensation.

Article 5th

The force which Nuvvab Umeer Khan may retain shall attend at the requisition of the British Government.

Article 6th

This engagement of six articles having been concluded at Dihlee, and signed and sealed by Mr. Charles Theophilus Metcalfe and Lalla Nurunjun Lal, the ratification of the same by His Excellency the Most Noble the Governor General and Nuvvab Umeer Khan shall be delivered at Dihlee within a month from the present date.

November 9th, 1817.

Sd. C. T. Metcalfe. Sd. Lalla Nurunjun Lal.
(seal) (seal) (seal)

Sd. Hastings.

Ratified by His Excellency the Governor General in camp at Sulvah this fifteenth day of November, one thousand eight hundred and seventeen.

National Archives of India, Foreign Secret, 1817, O.C. No. 21-22, 5 December, 1817

APPENDIX II

A CIRCULAR LETTER TO THE CHIEFS OF BUNDELCUND

You are probably already apprized that the British Government is about to adopt measures for exterminating those vile freebooters the Pindaries, and as it is possible that when they are attacked by the British troops from the banks of the Nerbudda and other quarters they may divide into small gangs and endeavour to escape in this direction, I have been desired by the Most Noble the

Governor-General to require you to take every possible precaution within your *jageer*, first by blocking up the passes of the Ghauts leading into your *Jageer* and secondly by giving vigorous pursuit to any such detached bands as may appear in your vicinity, and destroying them. I have urgently to request that you will without any delay carry these instructions into effect, by employing all the horse and foot in your service and if necessary by entertaining more.........

That these measures are not less calculated for the security of your *jageer*......from predatory invasion.

National Archives of India, Foreign Secret, 1817 O.C. No. 149-153, 19th December, 1817.

APPENDIX III

TRANSLATION OF A PAPER OF INTELLIGENCE FROM SEETOO'S CANTONMENT, DATED 2ND JANUARY, 1816

29th December, 1816: The Labhur from the Deccan arrived. Seetoo Nawab was highly delighted. They have only brought gold, silver and clothes .....They were sitting under an awning weighing an idol of gold.

Bombay Government Records, Diary No. 424. Political Department, 1815.

APPENDIX IV

THE ARMY OF BENGAL

First or Centre Division

Major General Brown, commanding.

First Brigade of Cavalry

Lieutenant Colonel Philpot, 24th Light Dragoons, to command.

3rd Regiment Native Cavalry.

His Majesty's 24th Light Dragoons.

7th Regiment Native Cavalry.

First Brigade Infantry

Brigadier General d'Auvergne, to command.
2nd Battalion 25th Native Infantry.
H. 87th Regiment of Foot.
1st Battalion 29th Native Infantry.

Third Brigade of Infantry

Colonel Burrell, 13th Native Infantry, to command.
2nd Battalion 11th Native Infantry.
1st Battalion 24th Native Infantry.
2nd Battalion 13th Native Infantry.

Second Brigade of Infantry

Col. Dick, 9th Native Infantry, to command.
2nd Battalion 1st Native Infantry.
Flank Battalion.
1st Battalion 8th Native Infantry.

The Second or Right Division

Major General R.S. Donkin commanding.

Second Brigade of Cavalry

Lt. Col. Westenna, 8th Light Dragoons, commanding,
1st Regiment NC.
HM 8th Light Dragoons.
Col. Gardiner's Irregulars.

Fourth Brigade of Infantry

Lt. Col. Vamennon, 12 NI.
HM 14th Foot.
1st Battalion 27th NI.
1st Battalion 25th NI.

The Third or Left Division

Major General D. Marshall, commanding.

Third Brigade of Cavalry

Col. Newberry, 24th Light Dragoons, commanding.
4th Regiment NC.
2nd Rohilla Horse.
Four Russalahs 3rd Rohilla Horse.

Fifth Brigade of Infantry

Brigadier General Watson, to command.
1st Battalion 1st NI.
1st Battalion 26th NI.
1st Battalion 7th NI.

Sixth Brigade of Infantry

Lt. Col. Prince, 28th NI, commanding.
1st Battalion 14th NI.
2nd Battalion 28th NI.

The Reserve Division

Maj. Gen. Sir D. Ochterlony, Bart. G.C.B., commanding.

Fourth Brigade of Cavalry

Lt. Col. A. Knox, 2nd NC, commanding.
2nd Regiment NC.
Two corps of Colonel Skinner's Horse.

Seventh Brigade of Infantry

Colonel Huskisson, HM's 67th, to command.
2nd Regiment, 5th NI.
HM's 67th Regiment of Foot.
1st Battalion 6th NI.

Eighth Brigade of Infantry

Brigadier-General Arnold, commanding.
2nd Battalion 7th NI.
1st Battalion 28th NI.
Detachment Simroor Battalion.
2nd Battalion, 19th NI.

THE ARMY OF THE DECCAN

The First or Advanced Division

Under the personal command of His Excellency Lt. Gen. Sir Thomas Hislop, Bart., Commander-in-Chief.

Light Artillery Brigade

Captain-Lieutenant H, Rudyerd, commanding.
The Troop of Horse-Artillery, and the Cavalry Callopers incorporated with it. The Rocket Troop.

Cavalry Brigade

Major Lushington, commanding.
4th Regiment Light Cavalry.
Detachment of HM 22nd Light Dragoons.
8th Regiment Light Cavalry.

Light Brigade

Lieutenant Colonel Deacon, commanding.
The Rifle Corps.
1st Battalion 3rd or Palamcottah Light Infantry.
1st Battalion 16th or Trichinopoly Light Infantry.
2nd Battalion 16th or Chicacole Light Infantry.

First Infantry Brigade

Lieutenant Colonel Thompson, commanding.
Flank Companies HM's Royal Scots.
1st Battalion 7th Regiment NI.
Madras European Regiment.

Second Infantry Brigade

Lieutenant Colonel Robert Scott, commanding.
1st Battalion 14th Regiment NI.
2nd Battalion 6th Regiment NI.

The Second, or Hyderabad Division

Brigadier General J. Doveton, commanding.

Cavalry Brigade

Major H. Hunt, commanding.
Three Brigades Horse Artillery.
6th Regiment Light Cavalry.

First Brigade of Infantry

Lieutenant Colonel N. Macleod, commanding.
HM Royal Scots.
2nd Battalion 13th Regiment NI.
2nd Battalion 24th Regiment NI.

Second Brigade of Infantry

Lieutenant Colonel Mackellar, commanding.
1st Battalion 11th Regiment NI.
2nd Battalion 14th Regiment NI.
1st Battalion 12th or Wallajahbad Light Infantry.
1st Battalion 2nd Regiment NI.

Berar Brigade

Major Pitman, commanding.
Four Battalion NI.
Detail of Artillery, Eight guns.
Reformed Horse.

Hydrabad Brigade

Colonel Sir Augustus Floyer, KCB, commanding.
1st Battalion 22nd Regiment NI.
1st Battalion 21st Regiment NI.
Five companies Madras European Regiment.
Detail or Artillery.
1st Battalion 8th Regiment NI.

The Third Division

Brigadier General Sir J. Malcolm, KCB and KLS.
Colonel Patrick, Walker, Brigadier.
One Brigade Horse Artillery.
3rd Regiment Light Cavalry.
Five Companies 1st Battallion 3rd or Palamcottah Light Infantry.
Russell Brigade ....1st Regiment.
2nd Regiment.
Ellichapoor Contingent, two Battalions and four guns
4,000 Mysore Horse.

The Fourth or Poonah Division

Brigadier General Smith, CB, commanding.

Cavalry Brigade

Lt. Col. Colebrooke, commanding.
Three Brigades Horse artillery.
2nd Regiment Madras Light Cavalry.
Light Battalion.

First Infantry Brigade

Lt. Col. Milnes, commanding.
1st Battalion 2nd Regiment Bombay NI
HM 65th Regiment Foot.

Second Infantry Brigade

Lt. Col. Fitzsimons, commanding.
1st Battalion 3rd Regiment Bombay NI.
2nd Battalion 15th Regiment Madras NI.

Third Infantry Brigade

2nd Battalion 9th Regiment Bombay NI.
2nd Battalion 1st Regiment.

The Fifth or Nagpoor Division

Lieutenant Colonel J.W. Adams, CB, commanding.

First Infantry Brigade

Lt. Col. M. Morin, commanding.
1st Battalion 10th Regiment NI.
2nd Battalion 23rd Regiment NI.
1st Battalion 19th Regiment NI.

Second Infantry Brigade

Major Popham, commanding.
2nd Battalion 10th Regiment NI.
1st Battalion 23rd Regiment NI.
1st Battalion 19th Regiment NI.

Reserve Brigade

Lt. Col. Gahan, commanding.
Three troops Native Horse Artillery.
5th Regiment Native Cavalry.
6th Regiment Native Cavalry
1st Rohilah Cavalry.
Light Infantry Battalion.

The Reserve Division

Brigadier General Munro, commanding.
Brigadier General Pritzler, second in command.

Artillery

Lieutenant Colonel Dalrymple, commanding.
Detachment Madras Artillery.

Cavalry Brigade

Major Doveton, 7th Light Cavalry, commanding.
HM 22nd Light Dragoons.
7th Regiment Madras Cavalry.

Infantry Brigade

Colonel Hewitt, CB commanding.
European Flank Battalion.
Four Companies Madras Rifle Corps.
2nd Battalion 4th Regiment NI.
2nd Battalion 12th Regiment NI.

The Goozerat Division

Major General Sir William Grant Keir, KMT.

Cavalry Brigade

Lt. Col. the Honourable L. Stanhope, commanding.
HM 17th Dragoons.
Flank Battalion.

First Infantry Brigade

Lt. Col Erlington, commanding.
HM 47th Regiment.
2nd Battalion 7th Regiment.

Second Infantry Brigade

Lt. Col. Corsellis, commanding.
Grenadier Battalion.
1st Battalion 8th Regiment.

GLOSSARY

APPENDIX I

Aftabgir — A kind of umbrella
Bargeer — A rank in Maratha Artillery
Bazar — Market accompanying the Army on march
Beldars — Diggers
Bhagwa — A mixture of yellow and red colours
Bheeneewalla — Quarter Master General
Bumedar — Quarter Master
Bunga — Baggage of an army
Chabutra — An elevated stone platform
Chana — Gram
Chapati — Bread
Chauth — One-fourth part of the total revenue
Chela — Adopted son of a Pindari leader; ordinarily it means a disciple
Chowki — Outpost
Danka — Drum
Durra — An organised group of Pindari freebooters.
Dashera — A Hindu festival to celebrate the victory of Lord Rama over Ravan, the demon-king, usually celebrated in the month of October
Devi — Goddess
Dhobi — Washerman
Fadnis — A letter writer
Fakeer — A beggar
Gharry — A fortress
Ghat — Mountain pass
Gurgees — A garment worn by Pindaris
Golandaz — Gunner
Gosain — A religious mendicant

Harkara	—	A messenger or a spy
Howdah	—	A seat placed on an elephant's back to seat two or more persons
Inam	—	Gift
Jageer	—	Land or territory given to an individual for his private use or for the maintenance of some organisation of public utility
Jemadar	—	A rank in army; a minor Pindari rank
Joari	—	Grain
Johar	—	An act of self-immolation by Rajput women
Jowar	—	Grain
Kaul	—	An assurance in writing
Khasge	—	Private troops
Khilat	—	Dress of honour conferred by a king on his subject or by a paramount power on his vassal
Killedar	—	Commandant of a fort
Koss	—	Two miles
Lubhur	—	Main body of Pindaris
Lubheareah	—	The leader who used to be entrusted with the conduct of Pindari excursion
Luggee	—	A small flag
Mahadev	—	A Hindu god
Masnad	—	A long round pillow on which a man reclines while sitting on the ground
Math	—	A temple where the priest also lives
Mhorladar	—	A Mhorladar was the commander of one hundred to five hundred Pindaris

Mohar	—	A golden coin
Nalla	—	A rivulet
Namda	—	Coarse woollen cloth
Naubat	—	An Indian drum
Nawab	—	A Muslim Governor or official or the Mulim ruler of a state
Nazar	—	Gift or presentation
Nishan	—	Letter written by a prince under his seal
Ogura	—	Strangers i. e. persons other than the Muslims who joined the Pindari ranks
Palki	—	Palanquin
Palki Nashin	—	One who sits in the Palanquin, an honour bestowed in reward for some meritorious service
Palpati	—	A tax paid by Pindaris for permission to loot under Maratha protection
Pardesi	—	An outsider
Pargana	—	A division of land for administrative purposes
Penchwa	—	A way of tying turbans with twists
Rassaldar	—	A rank in Pindari hierarchy
Sanad	—	Documents of a grant of land or other properties
Sardars	—	Chief Officers in a state; Military Commanders
Sardeshmukhi	—	A kind of revenue ownership
Sati	—	The practice of the woman burning herself alive with the dead body of her husband
Seebundee	—	Soldiers meant for the collection of revenue

Singha	—	Blowing horn
Talisman	—	A charm engraved on metal or stone worn to ward off danger
Tatoo	—	A very handy but inferior horse
Thok	—	A body of Pindaris
Thokdar	—	A commander of 500 to 1000 Pindaris
Tobra	—	A horse nose bag
Toll	—	The united body of Pindaris
Toranadar	—	A Pindari chief of minor rank
Tull	—	Each of the halts which the Pindaris made during an excursion
Vakil	—	An agent in a court or an agent from an Indian court to the British Residencies
Zeree	—	A golden flag

A British officer of the Indian Army on Camel back, with, Indian Soldiers as guards

Soldiers on horseback

The Pindaris

BIBLIOGRAPHY

I. Unpublished Records in the National Archives of India, New Delhi :

(i) Manuscript

(a) Indices and proceedings of the Secret Department of the East India Company, from 1764 to 1858.

(b) Indices and proceedings of the Political Department of the East India Company, from 1764 to 1858.

(c) Indices and proceedings of the Military Department of the East India Company, from 1800 to 1823.

(d) Translation of Persian Papers Received by Governor-General from 1800 to 1820.

(e) Translation of Persian Papers issued by Governor-General from 1800 to 1820.

(f) Central India Agency Records, 1815 to 1859.

(g) Hydrabad Residency Records, 1810-1818.

(h) Letters to and from the Court of Directors. 1803-1858.

(i) Letters to Europe : 1820 : Military Department (Secret and Separate Branch) 1761-1811.

(j) Home Miscellaneous Series Vol. No. 124 : Lt. Tod : Origin, Progress and Present State of the Pindarras.

(ii) Printed ·

(a) Home Miscellaneous Series Vol. No. 124 A.

(b) Parliamentary Papers, 1831-1832.

II. Unpublished Records In State Archives

(a) Political Diaries in the Maharashtra Government Archives, Bombay, 1800 to 1823,

(b) Secret Diaries in the Maharashtra Government Archives, Bombay, 1800 to 1823.
(c) Judicial and Revenue Records in the West Bengal State Archives, Calcutta.
(d) Pre-Mutiny Records in the Uttar Pradesh State Archives, Allahabad.
(e) Records preserved in the Settlement Commissioner and Director of Land Records, Land Alienation Office, Poona, 1812-1815.

III. Unpublished Records Preserved in Foreign Countries

(a) Microfilm copies of Records including various Home Miscellaneous Series obtained from India Office Library, London.
(b) Extract of Information from the Italian Embassy, New Delhi

IV. Published Records

(a) Charles Ross : Correspondence of Lord Cornwallis, 3 Vols. 1859.
(b) Marquiss of Hastings : Private Journal, Vol. I and II, Edited by his daughter, Marchioness of Buts, Allahabad, 1907.
(c) A Collection of Treaties, Engagements and Sunuds relating to India : Sir C. Aitchison, Vol. III, Calcutta, Office of the Superintendent of Government Printing, 1892.
(d) Dehradun Survey Records, Vol. II, 1800-1815 : Collected and compiled by Col. R. H. Phillimore, Dehradun, 1950,
(e) Dehradun Survey Records : Vol. III, 1815-1830.
(f) Selections from Peshwa Daftar, Vol, I to 46 : Peep into the Mahrahtta History on the eve of Last Days of the Mahrahtta Raj, Edited by G. S. Sardesai, Bombay, 1934.
(g) Residency Records, Vol. VII, Poona Affairs (1801-1810) Edited by G.S. Sardesai, Bombay, 1940 : Vol. XIII, Poona Affairs (1815-1818) Edited by G. S. Sardesai, Bombay. 1956.

(h) Vad, Ganesh Chimnaji : Selections from Satara Rajas' and the Peshwa's Diaries; Vol. V—Baji Rao II, India Press, Poona, 1908.

(i) Residency Records, Vol. IX, Daulat Rao Scindia's North Indian Affairs (1800-1803). Edited by Dr. Raghubir Singh, Bombay, 1943.
Vol. IV, Daulat Rao Scindia's North Indian Affairs (1810-1818), Edited by Sir J. N. Sarkar, Bombay, 1951.

(j) English Records of Maratha History, Vol. XII, Poona Affairs Part I (1811-1815), Edited by G.S. Sardesai.
Vol. XI Daulat Rao Scindia's Affairs (1804-1809), Edited by N.B. Roy, Bombay, 1943.
Vol. XIV, Daulat Rao Scindia's Affairs (1810-1818), Edited by Sir J. N. Sarkar,
Vol. V, Nagpur Affairs, (1781-1820), Edited by Y. M. Kale, Bombay, 1938.

(k) Select Documents of the British Period of Indian History, (in the collection of the Victoria Memorial, Calcutta, Edited by D.C. Ganguly. Calcutta, 1958.

(l) The Last Phase, Selections from the Deccan Commissioner's Files (Peshwa Daftar) 1815-1818, R.D. Choksy, Phoenix Publications, Bombay, 1948.

V. Published Works of Government of India

(a) *Imperial Gazetteer of India*, the Indian Empire, Oxford, 1909.

(b) *Imperial Gazetteer of India*, Provincial Series, Rajputana, Calcutta, 1908.

(c) *Imperial Gazetteer of India*, Provincial Series, Central India, Calcutta, 1908.

(d) *Imperial Gazetteer of India*, Provincial Series, Central Provinces, Calcutta, 1908.

(e) *Government of India Gazette* 1816, 1817, 1818 (including Gazette Extra-ordinary and Supplement to Gazettes.)

(f) *Central India State* Gazeteer *Series*, Bhopal State Gazetteer, Vol. II, Calcutta, 1908.

(g) *Central India State Gazetteer Series*, Indore State Gazetteer, Vol. II, Calcutta, 1908.

(h) *Central Provinces District Gazetteer*, Nimar District, Vol. A, Edited by R. V. Russell, Allahabad, 1908.

(i) *Central Provinces District Gazetteer*, Hoshangabad District, Calcutta, 1908.

(j) *Central Provinces District Gazetteer*, Nagpur District, Vol. A, Edited by R.V. Russell, Bombay, 1908.

(k) *Gazetteer of Sirohi State compiled in 1910*, Scottish Mission Industries Ltd., Ajmer, p. 255.

(l) *Calcutta Gazette*, 1816-1820.

(m) *Selections from Calcutta Gazette* of the years 1816 to 1823, Vol. V, by H.D. Sandeman, Central Press, Calcutta, 1869.

VI. PUBLISHED BOOKS

(i) Contemporary

(a) An Officer of the East India Company : *Origin of the Pindaris*, Allahabad Reprint, Painani Publications, Allahabad, 1928.

(b) Blacker, Lt. Col Valentine. *Memoir of the Operations of the British Army in India during the Maharatta Wars of 1817, 1818 and 1819*, Black Kingsbury Parbury and Allen, Leadenhall Street, London, 1821.

(c) Broughton, T.D. *Constables's Oriental Miscellany of Original and Selected Publications*, Vol.IV, Letters written in a Maharatta Camp, during the year 1809.

(d) Burton, Lt.Col. R.G. *The Maharatta and the Pindari War compiled for General Staff, Simla.*

(e) Busawan Lal Memoir of Ameer Khan, Translation by H.T. Prinsep, Calcutta, 1832.

(f) Duff, J. G. *A History of the Marathas*, 4th Edition, Vol. II, Published at the Times of India Office, Bombay 1878.
Vol. III, London: Longman, Rees, Orme, Brown, and Green, 1826.

(g) Fitzclarence, Lt. Col. *Journal of a Route Across India*, from Egypt to England in the latter end of the year 1817, and the beginning of 1818, London, John Murray, 1819.

(h) Hamilton, W. *Geographical, Statistical and Historical Description of Hindustan*, 2 Vols. London, 1820.

(i) Manucci, N. Irvine, W. *Storia Do Mogor*, Vol. II, London, 1907.

(j) Malcolm, Sir J. *Rise, Progress and Annihilation of the Pindaries* : A Memoir of Central India, including Malwa and Adjoining Provinces, II Vol. I.

(k) Malcolm, Sir J. *A Memoir of Central India including Malwa and Adjoining Provinces*, Vol. II, Thacker, Spink and Co., London, 1880.

(l) McNaghten, R.A. *A Memoir of the Military Operations of the Nagpur Subsidiary Force, from its first Formation in 1816 to the Termination of the Campaign against the Goands, etc.*, in 1819, Calcutta, 1824.

(m) Prinsep, H.T. *History of the Political and Military Transactions in India during the Administration of Marquiss of Hastings —1813-1823*, London, Kingsbury, Parbury and Allen, 1825.

(n) Tod, Lt. Col., J. *Annals and Antiquities of Rajasthan*, Vol. I, Humphrey Milford, London, Oxford University Press, 1829.

(o) By His Great Niece, The Countess of Minto. *Lord Minto in India*, London: Longman, Green & Co., 1880.

(p) *An Essay on the Origin, Rise and Consolidation of the Indian States*, 1929. (For Private Circulation)

(q) *Operations in India, with their results, from the 30th April, 1814 to the 1st January, 1823. The Marquiss of Hastings, Summary of the Operations in India.*

(r) *Summary of the Maharatta and Pindarree Campaign, during 1817, 1818 and 1819, under the direction of the Marquiss of Hastings:* Chiefly embracing the operations of the Army of the Deccan under the command of His Excellency Lt. Gen. Sir Thomas Hislop. London, E. Williams 1820.

(s) *The Annual Biography and Obituary for the year 1817*, Vol. I, London, Longman, Husset, Rees, Orme and Brown 1817.

Modern

1. Auber. P. *Rise and Progress of the British Power in India*. Vol. II, London, Wm. H. Allen & Co., 1837.
2. Basu, Maj. B.D. *Rise of the Christian Power in India*. Published by R. Chaterjee, Calcutta, 1931.
3. Beale, T.W. *The Oriental Biographical Dictionary*, Edited by the Asiatic Society of Bengal under the Superintendence of H. G. Keene, Calcutta, J. W. Thomas, Baptist Mission Press.
4. Burgers, J. W.H. *The Chronology of Modern India*, 1494-1894, Edinburgh, John Grant, 1913.
5. Davenport Adams, *The Makers of British India*, London, John Hogg.
6. Forsyth' Capt.J. *The Highlands of Central India*, London, Chapman & Hall Ltd., 1889.

7. Gleig, G.R. *History of the British Empire in India*, London, John Murray, 1835.

8. Hough, Maj.Wm. *Political and Military Events in British India* from the years 1756-1849, London, W.H. Allen & Co., 1853.

9. Kaye, J.W. *The Life and Correspondence of Charles, Lord Metcalfe*, late Governor-General of India, Vol. I, London, Richard Bentley.

10. Kaye. J.W. *Life of Malcolm*, Vol. II.

11. Keene, H.G. *Hindustan under free lances*, 1770-1820, London, Brown Langham & Co., 1907.

12. Keene, H.G. *History of India*, Vol. II, Edinburgh, John Grant, 1915.

13. Lyall, Sir A. *The Rise and Expansion of the British Dominion in India*, London, John Murray.

14. Marshman, J.C. *History of India from the Earliest Period to the Present Time*, London, William Blackwood and Sons.

15. Martineau, H. *British Rule in India:* A Historical Sketch Bombay, Smith Elder & Co., 1857.

16. Mehta, M.S. *Lord Hastings and the Indian States*, Bombay, D.B. Taraporewala & Sons, 1930.

17. Muir, R. *The Making of British India*, 1756-1858, Manchester: At the University Press, 1923.

18. Murray, H. *History of British India*, London, T. Nelson & Sons, 1855.

19. Murray, H. etc. *Historical and Descriptive Account of British India*, Vol. II, London, Oliver & Boyd.

20. Nolan, Dr. E.H. *The History of the British Empire in India and the East from the Earliest Times to the Suppression of the Sepoy Mutiny in 1859*, London, James S. Virtue.

21. Ros — *Rulers of India*—The Marquiss of Hastings K.G. and the Final Overthrow of the Maratha Power, Oxford, Clarendon Press, 1900.

22. Sardesai, G.S. — *New History of the Marathas*, Vol. III, Sunset Over Maharashtra, 1772-1848, Bombay, Phoenix Publications, 1948.

23. Sardesai, G.S. — *The Main Currents of Maratha History*, Bombay, Keshav Bhikaji Dhavle, 1933.

24. Sarkar, J.N. — *Military History of India*, Calcutta, M.C. Sarkar & Sons, 1960.

25. Sen, S.N. — *The Administrative System of the Marathas*, Calcutta, 1925.

26. Sen, S.N. — *The Military System of the Marathas*, Bombay, Orient Longmans, 1958.

27. Singh, Dr. Raghubir — *Malwa in Transition*, Bombay, D.B. Taraporewalla, 1936.

28. Stocqueler, J.H. — *The Oriental Interpreter and Treasury of East India Knowledge*, A companion to *The Handbook of British India*, London, James Madden.

29. Sutherland. J. — *Sketches of the Relations Subsisting between the British Government in India and the Different Native States*, Calcutta, 1837.

30. Thornton, E. — *The History of British Empire in India*, Vol. IV, London, Wm. H. Allen & Co., 1843.

31. Wheeler, J.T. — *Summary of Affairs of the Mahratta States, 1627-1856*, Calcutta, Office of the Government Printing, 1878.

32. Wilson, H.H. — *The History of British India* from 1805-1835.

33. Yule & Burnell — Hobson Jobson, being a Glossary of Anglo-Indian Colloquial Words and Phrases, 1886.

VII. Published Articles in Journals

(a) *Annual Asiatic Register*: 1806-Pt. II, p. 352.

(b) *Asiiatic Annual Register*, 1810-1811, Vol. XII, London, 1812, pp. 34-35.

(c) *Asiatic Annual Register*, pp. 208-210, 1813.

(d) *Asiatic Annual Register* : 1816, London, 1817, pp. 169-170.

(e) *Asiatic Annual Register*: 1817, London, Chapter XV.

(f) *Asiatic Annual Register*: Vol. XII for the year 1810-1811, E. Samnel, London. 1812, p. 38.

(g) *Calcutta Review*, Vol. XXIV, 1855, pp. 142-143.

(h) *Navneet*, Bombay, Sept. 1961, "Pindari Gangs which caused untold harassment to the Marathas and the English in the 19th Century" by V.S. Kamat, Superintendent, Maharashtra State Archives, Bombay.

(i) *Indian Historical Records Commission*, Proceedings of Meetings, Vol. XVI, Calcutta, December, 1939. "Defence of the Frontier of Bihar and Orissa against Maratha and Pindary incursions (1800-1819), pp. 6-7, by K.P. Mitra.

INDEX